M. CHERIF BASSIOUNI, EDITOR

The Islamic Criminal Justice System

OCEANA PUBLICATIONS, INC.
LONDON ROME NEW YORK

Library of Congress Cataloging in Publication Data

The Islamic criminal justice system.

Primarily selected papers from the 1st International Conference on the Protection of Human Rights in the Islamic Criminal Justice System held May 1979 at the International Institute of Higher Studies in Criminal Sciences, Syracuse, Sicily, and sponsored by the International Association of Penal Law and the Arab Organization for Social Defense against Crime.

Bibliography: p.

Appendices (p.): A. Summary report of the first International Conference on the Protection of Human Rights in the Islamic Criminal Justice System, May 1979, International Institute of Higher Studies in Criminal Sciences, Siracusa, Italy—B. List of conference participants—C. Final resolution adopted by conference.

1. Criminal procedure (Islamic law)—Congresses.
2. Criminal law (Islamic law)—Congresses.

I. Bassiouni, M. Cherif, 1937- . II. International Conference on the Protection of Human Rights in the Islamic Criminal Justice System (1st : 1979 : International Institute of Higher Studies in Criminal Sciences) III. International Association of Penal Law. IV. Munazzamah al-Dawliyah al-'Arabiyan lil-Difa 'al-Ijtima'i.

Law 340.5'9 81-22370
ISBN 0-379-20745-1 AACR2

Manufactured in the United States of America.

بِسْمِ ٱللَّهِ ٱلرَّحْمَٰنِ ٱلرَّحِيمِ

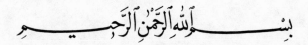

In the Name of the Lord
The Most Gracious, the Most Merciful

CONTENTS

Preface **ix**
Introduction **xiii**
Acknowledgements **xxi**

PART ONE

The Criminal Process and the Protection of Individual Rights

Sources of Islamic Law, and the Protection of Human Rights in the Islamic Criminal Justice System **3**

Dr. M. Cherif Bassiouni
Professor of Law, De Paul University;
Secretary-General, International Association of Penal Law;
Dean, International Institute of Higher Studies in Criminal Sciences

The Right of the Individual to Personal Security in Islam **55**

Dr. Osman Abd-el-Malek al-Saleh
Associate Professor of Public Law
University of Kuwait

The Rights of the Accused Under Islamic Criminal Procedure **91**

Dr. Awad M. Awad
Professor of Criminal Law
University of Alexandria

General Principles of Criminal Evidence in Islamic Jurisprudence **109**

Dr. Ma'amoun M. Salama
Professor of Criminal Law
University of Cairo

PART TWO

Criminal Responsibility, Crimes and Punishment

The Basis of Islamic Penal Legislation **127**

Dr. Muhammad Salim al-'Awwa
Professor of Criminal Jurisprudence
University of Riyadh

The Principle of Legality and its Application in Islamic Criminal Justice **149**

Dr. Taymour Kamel
Judge (Conseiller), Council of State (Conseil d 'Etat)

Criminal Responsibility in Islamic Law **171**

Dr. Ahmad Fathi Bahnassi
Attorney, Senior Researcher, The Supreme Council of Islamic Research

Hudud *Crimes* **195**

Dr. Aly Aly Mansour
Justice, Supreme Court of Egypt
President, Commission of Revision of Laws of the United Arab Emirates

Quesas *Crimes* **203**

Dr. M. Cherif Bassiouni

Ta'azir *Crimes* **211**

Dr. Ghaouti Benmelha
Attorney, Adjunct Professor of Law
University of Algiers

Punishment in Islamic Criminal Law **227**

Dr. Ahmad Abd al-Aziz al-Alfi
Professor of Criminal Law, and Dean of the Faculty of Law
University of Zagazig

Appendices

A. Summary Report of the First International Conference on the Protection of Human Rights in the Islamic Criminal Justice System, May, 1979, International Institute of Higher Studies in Criminal Sciences, Siracusa, Italy **237**

B. List of Conference Participants **243**

C. Final Resolution adopted by Conference **249**

Glossary of Terms **251**
Bibliography **253**

Preface

This is the first comprehensive book on the Islamic criminal justice system to be published in the English language. It includes contributions by distinguished Muslim scholars who covered the most important aspects of Islamic jurisprudence, criminal law, criminal procedure, evidence, sanctions, corrections, criminal justice policy and the protection of human rights. In that respect its content and coverage gives the non-Muslim reader a comprehensive perspective of the subject.

As my Acknowledgements indicate, this book is an outgrowth of a Conference held at the International Institute of Higher Studies in Criminal Sciences—ISISC—(Siracusa, Italy, 1979) which was under the co-sponsorship of the International Association of Penal Law—AIDP—and the Arab Organization for Social Defense Against Crime.

The contributions published in this book were, (with the exception of those of Professor Abdel-Malek, Judge Kamel, and one of my two articles and my Introduction) all presented at the Conference. Several other valuable papers were also presented at the Conference but, due to space limitation in this book, they regrettably could not be included herein.

Since the Introduction explains the purpose and scope of the book, and the Acknowledgements express my appreciation to those who contributed to its realization, this Preface is intended to explain some of the particularities of this work.

Any student of Arabic will readily admit to the difficulty of translating from that language into English. But that difficulty is compounded here by the fact that the material in question is of a complex legal nature. After translation, each contribution had to be edited three times in order to make the text more meaningful to an audience which may be unfamiliar with the different aspects of the topics presented. It was also necessary because the Islamic legal system differs from others with respect to its religious basis, philosophical conceptions, sources of law, unarticulated legal premises, specific legal proscriptions, intellectual approach, cultural and historical framework, framework of analysis, methodological approach and terminology. All of this would make an unedited translation of little relevance and interest to the uninitiated. As Editor I perceived the need to meaningfully relate the presentation of the Islamic criminal justice system, as described by the various authors, to the legal systems of the intended readership. This is why I took some liberties in editing the English translation of the original Arabic texts, including the condensation of certain contributions—I hope that the authors will approve of the final product. In the event I may have strayed from their intended meaning, which is possible considering the richness of the Arabic vocabulary and the complexity of the topics covered, I extend to them my apologies.

Several problems were encountered in editing the manuscripts. The authors did not always refer to their sources, and whenever possible I supplied the citation, but to find such resources outside major Muslim captials and some western cities is very difficult. Thus in some cases citations were left incomplete and I apologize to the reader for these instances. The choice was either to remove the reference altogether or to leave it, albeit incomplete as to date of publication or page number. The latter was more often the choice because of the intrinsic importance of the reference. In many instances, however, Arabic language books do not bear a date of publication (which is particularly true of older texts).

Some of the authors refer to certain *Hadith* and to the writing of one or more of the founders of the four major *Sunni* schools of jurisprudence without citing a source. This is a somewhat common practice in Islamic legal literature because of the assumption that the reference is so well known that it does not necessarily require a citation. Whenever possible I supplied it, but in addition I included a short BIBLIOGRAPHY to assist the researcher who wishes to be referred to principal sources.

There is finally the problem of maintaining consistency in spelling and transliteration. For ease in production and reading the appropriate accents were not placed on the transliterated words, which were written phonetically for the convenience of the reader.

The content of the contributions presented many challenges. For instance many authors covered the same or similar material, but because their topics relied on such material it was not possible to edit them beyond what was done, without distorting the meaning of the respective contributions. I hope I was able to avoid too much repetition without detrimentally affecting the substance of each author's contribution.

The material has been organized in two parts:

Part I deals with the sources of Islamic law, the nature of the criminal process, the rights of the accused and its balance in the social-religious context of Islamic criminal justice policy, and the evidentiary requirements. This later topic could equally have been included in Part II, because it can be considered part of the procedural context as well as the substantive one.

Part II deals with the basis of criminal responsibility, the principle of legality, the three categories of crimes under Islamic law, and covers broadly and specifically the various penalties and their application. The division is thus *latu senso* between the procedural and substantive matters, though the topics of sources of law and jurisprudence, and their application, are covered in contributions appearing in both categories (*i.e.* procedure and substance).

As a first attempt* to explain to a non-Muslim audience in a language other than Arabic the richness, complexity and intricacy of Islamic criminal justice, the

---

**N.B.* The Institute of Crime Prevention, Ministry of Interior, Kingdom os Saudi-Arabia published in Arabic, and then in an English translation, under the auspices of the U.N. Social Defense Research Institute in Rome, the Proceedings of an International Conference held in Riyadh in 1976, on certain aspects of the Islamic criminal justice system as applied in Saudi-Arabia. The Arabic text was published in 1978 and the English translation in 1981.

book may have its shortcomings. It is my wish, however, that it will accomplish its informational if not scholarly purposes and stimulate others to publish more detailed works in the future on the same subject and on the topics covered herein.

Chicago October 8, 1981
10 Dhul-Hejja 1401

Introduction

Islam is the last of the Divine Revelations. As the *Qu'ran* states, Islam is not a new religion but the culmination of God's spiritual and temporal commands made known to mankind through Moses and Jesus and the prophets, and Muhammad the last prophet. Islam, therefore continues as the successor and final expression of the Judeo-Christian revelations.

The *Qu'ran*, which is the principal source of Islamic law (*Shari'a*), contains the rules by which the Muslim world is governed (or should govern itself) and forms the basis for relations between man and God, between all persons whether Muslim or non-Muslim, as well as between man and all aspects of the creation. The *Shari'a* also contains the rules by which Muslim society (or societies) is organized, and it provides the means to resolve conflicts between individuals and between the individual and the state. As such one of the acknowledged goals of the *Shari'a* is to combat crime through faith and religious observance, and through the various proscriptions and modalities for the establishment of a just criminal justice system.

There is no dispute among Muslims that the *Qu'ran* is the basis of the *Shari'a* and that its specific provisions are to be rigorously and scrupulously observed.

The *Sunna* is a complementary source to the *Qu'ran* and consists of both the sayings (*Hadith*) of the Prophet and accounts of his deeds. The *Sunna* explains and amplifies the *Qu'ran*, and it cannot be interpreted in any way which alters the *Qu'ran* or is inconsistent with the meaning of any of its specific provisions. The *Qu'ran* and *Sunna* thus constitute the very substance of the *Shari'a*.

Though there are other sources of law, a principle of gradation and priority of sources exists which makes the *Qu'ran* the first source, followed by the *Sunna*, and this in turn followed by other sources of law and rules of interpretation of the *Qu'ran* and the *Sunna*.

The *Qu'ran* contains a variety of law-making provisions and legal proscriptions interspersed throughout its chapters (*Surat*) and verses (*Ayat*). A number of rules exist for interpreting these provisions such as the position of a given *Ayat* within the context of the *Surat*, which in turn is interpreted in accordance with its place in the sequence of revelations, its reference to other revelations, and its historical context in relation to particular conditions which existed at the time of the given revelation. These and other rules are known as the science of interpretation (*Ilm usul al-fiqh*).[1] According to these rules one initially is to refer to a

---

[1]*See e.g. Bibliography,* at 253, for the four *Sunni* schools and for the *Shi'a* sources. For a contemporary summary, *see* A. HASSAHALLAH, OUSOUL AL-TASHRI'I AL-ISLAMI [THE PRINCIPLES OF ISLAMIC LEGISLATION] (1976).

specific provision and then to a general provision dealing with a particular situation. No general provision can be interpreted so as to contradict a specific provision, and a specific rule will be controlling over a general proposition. A general provision, however, is always interpreted in the broadest manner, while a specific provision is interpreted in the narrowest manner. Reasoning by analogy is permitted as are applications by analogy.

Besides the *Qu'ran* and *Sunna*, other sources of law make possible the application of Islam to contemporary situations. Muslim scholars do not consider Islam to be an adaptable religion or system of law, in the sense that it is evolutionary, but rather that it is a religion and legal system which applies to all times. It is therefore the application that is susceptible to evolution. Indeed, the provisions of the *Qu'ran* are such that by their disciplined interpretation, with the aid of the *Sunna*, and in reliance on other sources of interpretation and sources of law, Islam can provide the solution to contemporary social problems through the rule of law.[2]

Fourteen centuries ago, Islam was a spiritual, social and legal revolution; its potential for the same remains unchanged.

In the context of this book it is particularly important to appreciate the purposes of Islam and its principles. Islam can produce a system of criminal justice capable of meeting the needs of modern societies in accordance with the *Shari'a* and its policy, *Siysat al-Shari'a*, whose wisdom through the ages demonstrates its capabilities for the future, although that task remains to be accomplished.

The western reader will doubtless encounter some difficulty in grasping the manner in which the *Qu'ran* elaborates the blueprint for a legal system and the methodology by which provisions of the *Qu'ran* are interpreted and applied. This problem will be apparent throughout this book as references are made to specific verses of the *Qu'ran* or statements of the *Sunna*, which to an Arabic-speaking Muslim might be more readily understood, than to the non-Muslim non-Arabic speaking person. The problem is essentially cultural (and linguistic), but also conceptual and methodological. Even for the Muslim world the matter is arduous.[3]

Islamic jurisprudence developed over fourteen centuries from the first Islamic revelation in 622 A.D. to contemporary times. During that history various schools of jurisprudence emerged, each giving its own view of the meaning and application of the *Shari'a*. Many schools even spawned sub-schools with different interpretative approaches and applications.

Islamic jurisprudence has also been influenced in its evolution by the various cultures and social systems which it has encompassed. Furthermore, the spread of Islam in time was also across much of the earth's surface, extending at its height from southern France to Central Asia, assimilating races and transforming

---

[2]*See* Bassiouni, *Sources of Islamic Law, and the Protection of Human Rights in the Islamic Criminal Justice System,* at 3.

[3]*See e.g.* IBN KHALDOUN, AL MUQQADIMA [THE INTRODUCTION OR PROLEGOMENON].

cultures without destroying them.

Islam took root and spread among so many peoples enduring for so long, notwithstanding human cultural differences, because one of its basic premises is equality in diversity.

The *Qu'ran* expressly states in *Surat al-Hujurat*:

> O people, we have created you male and female and we have made you peoples and tribes so that you may come to know one another, but the best of you in the face of God is the most pious among you.[4]

Adding to this is the Prophet's *Hadith* which states:

> The people are equal as are the teeth of a comb. There is no one better than another, whether he be Arab or non-Arab. The best among you is the most pious.

In another *Hadith*, the Prophet said:

> God brought about Islam in order to eliminate the ignorance of the past and those people who had pride in their ancestors because people are all descendants of Adam, and Adam was made of dust. The best among you before God is the most pious.

Because Islam is eternal and attuned to cultural diversity and provides for equality for and among all people, Islamic jurisprudence must be understood both in its temporal and spatial contexts. It is significant in this regard that the *Sunni* tradition (which today comprises approximately 90% of all Muslims) as opposed to the *Shi'a* tradition (approximately 10% of all Muslims)[5] has always believed, based on a specific *Qu'ranic* provision, that matters and decisions among the people of Islam are to be governed by consensus among Muslims.[6] The interpretation of this provision led the *Shi'a* to believe that the *Imam* or *Khalifa* must be a descendant of the Prophet. The concept of descendancy of the Prophet thereby establishes a hereditary class hierarchy in the *Shi'a* tradition, which, for the *Sunni* is contrary to the principles of equality and consensus and has been for this reason rejected by them since the seventh century.[7]

The political rift between followers of the principle of election and those favoring appointment by descendancy from the Prophet has created distinctions between *Sunni* and *Shi'a* approaches to law and jurisprudence which evolved in time. As a consequence, the *Shi'a* view the sayings of the daughter of the Prophet and of his nephew Ali ibn Abu-Talib, who was the third *Khalifa* of Islam, as equally authoritative as the *Sunna* among the sources of Islamic law.

---

[4] XLIX:13

[5] A. MASSIGNON, ANNUAIRE DE MONDE, MUSULMAN 24, 38 (1929).

[6] *Surat al-Shoura* XLII:38

> And those who answer the call of their Lord and attend to their prayers (establish worship) and whose affairs are decided by consensus (a matter of consultation)...

and *Surat al-Omran (al-Imran)* III:159

> ...and consult with them upon the conduct of affairs.

[7] For *Shi'a* positions, *see Bibliography*, at 253, *also* ABDEL HUSAYN ALI, AL-MUHUTASSAN AL-NAFEH and SHARA'II AL-ISLAM (n.d.).

Furthermore, they consider the *Sunna* as authoritative only if a particular *Hadith* is recounted by a member of the Prophet's family, and only secondarily so if recounted by any other follower of the Prophet who witnessed the deed or heard the *Hadith* even though confirmed by other persons. The *Sunni* make no such differences, though they have exacting rules to confirm a deed or saying of the Prophet, and thus distinguish between a *Sunna moakada* (confirmed) also referred to as *sahih* (true), and a *Sunna* which is not confirmed.[8] Even as to that there are gradations of forms of confirmation indicating the degree of sophistication of early Islamic jurisprudence. The danger in such sophistication is that unless it is controlled it can lapse into sophistry (as has been the case at times). Because the *Sunni* tradition represents, as it has throughout, the overwhelming majority of Mulsims (90%), it is the basis of this book.

One of the major sources of law is *Ijma'* (consensus), which is also a subsidiary source of interpretation of the *Shari'a*. Indeed, in a saying, *Hadith*, the Prophet is quoted as saying: "My people would not all agree to something which is wrong," meaning that when the consensus of the people develops it is that which is correct and makes it a reliable source of law. Combined with the democratic notion of political consensus, *Ijma'* is the most authoritative basis for the legislative development of Islamic criminal justice.

There are four major schools of jurisprudence which have been followed throughout the *Sunni* Islamic world in the past fourteen centuries. They are those of *Malek*, *Abu-hanifa*, *ibn-Hanbal*, and *al-Shafei*,[9] and they are periodically referred to throughout this book. Although there are differences among these authorities, all are within the general framework of the *Shari'a* and are considered acceptable interpretations. Frequently in this book, the contributing authors discuss differences among these schools of jurisprudence in an effort to demonstrate their diversity and compatibility with Islam. The existence of these schools and the variety of viewpoints expressed within each one further attests to the flexibility and adaptability of the *Shari'a*.

In Islam's most glorious period, from the seventh to the ninth century, Islam produced a legal system nurtured by faith which has endured the test of time. But during that period it was *Ijtihad* which produced the most far-reaching developments. Since then, *Ijtihad* was arbitrarily foreclosed and Islamic jurisprudence became stagnant and largely sterile.

Contemporary jurisprudential developments can continue the work begun ages past and still remain compatible with Islam while meeting present day demands in the field of criminal justice.

The development of the policies of the Islamic criminal justice system, already evident at an earlier time in the writings of the followers of the four major

---

[8] SAHIH AL-BUKHARI and SAHIH MUSLIM, multi-volume works by IMAM AL-BUKHARI and IMAM MUSLIM. Each of these works has been reprinted many times throughout the Muslim world. SAHIH MUSLIM was edited with annotations by Imam al-Nawawi in a six-volume work consisting of 18 parts (Cairo, 1924).

[9] *See Bibliography*, at 253.

schools of jurisprudence, is best exemplified in the work of a famous judge named Abu-Youssef who is credited, among other things, with founding a sub-school within the *Hanafi* school. His writings in Islamic Jurisprudence are what contemporary writers would refer to as criminal justice policy. Abu-youssef (frequently referred to by authors in this book) pioneered the protection of human rights long before the subject was ever broached by writers in other legal systems.[10] Indeed what he advocated then is today compatible with many of the rights enunciated in the Universal Declaration of Human Rights and other international human rights instruments. Also worthy of particular attention is the work of the late Abdel Kader Odeh, who in the 1950s produced two volumes comparing the system of Islamic criminal justice to contemporary positive systems.[11] Both jurists (at a distance of twelve centuries) underscored the fact that the *Shari'a* can and must be interpreted in light of an enlightened and humane criminal justice policy, that the *Shari'a* must be understood as such—and not as many see it, exclusively through the eyes of writers many centuries departed. Nothing inherent to Islam precludes the embodiment of the *Shari'a* in contemporary codes whether they concern substantive criminal law, criminal procedure or the law of corrections.

Regrettably, the understanding of Islamic criminal justice policy is not sufficiently widespread in the world of Islam. Consequently, those who now claim Islamic resurgence frequently refer and relate only to certain periods of Islamic history without understanding the policies adopted at that time, which by their very application then, mandate change now.[12] Thus the manner in which the *Shari'a* was applied in the past may be totally irrelevant to the contemporary framework. For example, in the days of the Prophet there were no prisons. Should none exist today? But in the case of a person detained in someone's house during that time the Prophet had ordered that the detainer feed the detainee and treat him humanely and with dignity. In the days of Umar ibn al-Khattab, the second *Khalifa* of Islam, the principle was even established that the detainer pay the wife or the family of the detainee a stipend during the detention period so that they can adequately survive.[13] What better inspiration could these examples be for a modern Code of Corrections. Can one say that such examples in early Islam are not appropriate in their application with all due regard to contemporary exigencies? Conversely the fact that evidence during the seventh century was almost entirely based on the oral testimony of eyewitnesses does not in any way preclude the use of the most modern technical and scientific means of securing evidence. No serious scholar would argue that because only eyewitness testimony

---

[10] Abu-Youssef is quoted and cited in Abd-el-Malek, *The Right of the Individual to Personal Security in Islam,* at 55, and Salama, *General Principles of Criminal Evidence in Islamic Jurisprudence,* at 109.

[11] A. ODEH (also spelled *Awdah*), AL-TASHRII AL-JINAI AL-ISLAMI (2d ed. 1969). Another enlightened contemporary author is the late Sheikh Mohammad Abu-Zahra, who was a professor of *Shari'a* and Chairman of that department at the University of Cairo, Faculty of Law, *infra* note 13.

[12] *See e.g.* Bassiouni, *Protection of Diplomats Under Islamic Law* 74 A.J.I.L. 609 (1980).

[13] *See* al-Alfi, *Punishment in Islamic Criminal Law,* at 227, and M. ABU-ZAHRA, AL JARIMA WAL-OUQUBA FIL ISLAM (n.d. *circa* 1950).

was relied upon in the days of the Prophet that all other evidentiary means are today prohibited. *Siyasat al-Shari'a*, the policy of the *Shari'a*, I contend, mandates the resort to such advances. In fact the Prophet in two *Hadith* urged the search for science and knowledge.[14] To claim otherwise would be to negate the scientific orientation of Islam, which is best expressed by the *Qu'ran's* approach to problems of the creation and the universe—essentially a scientific approach demonstrating in fact that which others have been asked to accept only on faith. But any scientific approach takes into account new discoveries and findings. Similarly the administration of criminal justice must respond to contemporary scientific developments whether it be in the computerization of court dockets or in the examination of reliable scientific evidence. There are also matters dealing with the rights of accused and the quality of justice. It is utopian, for example, to believe that nowadays the thousands of judges needed to staff the courts of all Muslim states will be like the ideal judge described in the famous letter of Umar ibn al-Khattab to Judge Abu-Mussa al-Ashali.[15] Thus the rules of procedure in contemporary criminal justice must rely on something other than the complete faith in the equanimity, fairness and competence of all judges. Other mechanisms can and must be found to achieve the just result which the policy of the *Shari'a* aims at. In that respect the rights of the accused are well protected in rules of procedure[16] and evidence.[17] Considering how, for example, confessions could not be coerced, and could be withdrawn at any time as early as the seventh century, what better inspiration could one find for the protection of human rights and human dignity in criminal processes in modern times.[18]

Other practices which existed then and are not specifically mandated by *Qu'ran*, must be changed to reflect the humanism of Islam, and the needs of modern society.

All of this makes it appear to be a very incoherent system. In reality it is one which has not benefited since the early *Sunni* Jurisconsults (*Malek*, *Shafe'i*, *Hanafi*, *Hanbal*) from comprehensive compilations, let alone codifications. There are, however, many worthy authors whose words are reliable summations deserving careful study. It is therefore not the fact that things were done in a certain way at one time that is part of the *Shari'a* when there is nothing more that compels its preservation if it no longer serves the intended purpose of Islamic justice.

The western world has all too often seen the wrong side of Islam. Some of it is due to the distorted perceptions of orientalists,[19] but the blame also rests on

---

[14] The two *Hadith* are: "Search for knowledge from the cradle, to the death-bed", and "Search for knowledge even if it is in China" (indicating distance and difficulty in reaching it).

[15] *See* Bassiouni, *supra* note 2, at xiv.

[16] *See* Abd-el-Malek, *supra* note 10, and Awad, *The Rights of the Accused Under Islamic Criminal Procedure*, at 91.

[17] *See* Salama, *supra* note 10.

[18] *See* Resolution of the First International Conference on The Protection of Human Rights in the Islamic Criminal Justice System, at 249.

[19] E. SAID, ORIENTALISM (1978). *See also* E. SAID, COVERING ISLAM (1981).

Muslim scholars, who did not rise to the true challenge of Islam: the challenge of developing a fair and adequate, a just and effective system of criminal justice, as the philosophy and policy of Islam requires.[20] It is to this end that this writer has undertaken the difficult task of producing this book, in the hope that it contributes something to a better understanding of Islam and its criminal justice system among Muslim as well as non-Muslim jurists, policy-makers, and persons interested in this field.

M. Cherif Bassiouni

October 8, 1981
10 Dhul-Hejja 1401

---

[20] *Surat al-Nahl* XVI:90:

> Lo! Allah Enjoineth (orders) justice (or injustice) and kindness (or unkindness) and to give to (one's) kinsfolk...

and in the same *Surat, Ayat* (verse) 125:

> call (others) onto the way of thy Lord with wisdom and fair (gracious or kind) with them in best way.

Surat al-Baqara II:86:

> Allah asketh (or burdeneth) not a soul (also meaning a person) beyond what it can bear. It has (receives) what it has earned and owes only what it has deserved. Lord do not condemn us for what we have forgotten or for what we have mistaken. Lord do not impose upon us the burdens you have imposed on those before us. Lord do not impose upon us that which we cannot bear.

Surat al Nissaa IV:58:

> Lo! Allah commandeth you to restore (or return) that which you have been entrusted with to their owners and, if you judge between the people judge justly...

in *Ayat* 135:

> O ye who believe! Be staunch in justice, in witness for Allah (meaning saying the truth) though it be against yourself or (yours) parents of (yours) kindred, whether (a case be of) a rich man or a poor man, for Allah is nearer (then ye are) (meaning He is the One most apt to judge among people). So follow not passion lest you stray from the truth, and if you lapse or deviate Allah is ever knowing and informed.

ACKNOWLEDGEMENTS

Most of the contributions contained in this book were papers presented at the First International Conference on the Protection of Human Rights held at the International Institute for Higher Studies in Criminal Sciences—ISISC—(Siracusa, Italy) in May 1979. The Conference was under the joint co-sponsorship of the International Association of Penal Law (AIDP) and the Arab Organization For Social Defense Against Crime. (The names of the distinguished participants appear in Appendix B.)

My appreciation is therefore first extended to the Institute which hosted the Conference, to the AIDP and the Organization for co-sponsoring it and to the speakers and participants in the Conference. In particular to Ahmad Fathi Sorour, Professor of Criminal Law, the University of Cairo, who helped me organize the Conference and co-chaired it, and to Geroge Abi-Saab, Professor of International Law, Institut des Hautes Etudes Internationales (Geneve) who was the Conference Rapporteur (and whose final Report appears in Appendix A).

The Conference produced a rather unique document which appears in Appendix C. Since it was adopted unanimously (save for one abstention) it is truly a credit to all the participants.

All the contributions presented to the Conference could regrettably not be included in this book because of the size that it would have comported. But I wish to extend my appreciation to those who contributed and whose work was ultimately published in Arabic in the MAJALLAT AL-DIFA'A AL IJTIMAI DID AL-JARIMA (THE ARAB REVIEW OF SOCIAL DEFENSE AGAINST CRIME, 1979).

In addition to conference contributions appearing herein, there are contributions by Professor Osman Abdel-Malek al-Saleh, Judge Taymour Kamel, and myself. Almost all of the contributions were in Arabic and were translated by Khalil Jahshan (M.A., Ph.D. Cand. Chicago) to whom I extend my appreciation for his laborious work. Upon translation, the manuscripts were edited three times by myself and my assistant John Evrard (B.A.; M.A.; J.D. DePaul, Member, Illinois Bar) to whom I extend my appreciation for his hard work and also for his assistance and support in many aspects of completing this project. Also to Rhiman Rotz (Ph.D., J.D. Cand. De Paul) who edited the first draft of Judge Kamel's contribution.

The typesetting was expertly done by Communica Inc. of Chicago, and I acknowledge the effective technical assistance of Didge Donovan.

The funding for the Conference was from the ISISC and the Muslim League, and for the translation, and other costs incurred in the realization of the book, funding came from the Institute of Crime Prevention, Ministry of Justice, Kingdom of Saudi Arabia. I therefore extend my appreciation to the Kingdom, the

Ministry, to His Excellency Ibrahim El-Awagi, Under Secretary, and Dr. Farouka Mourad, Director of the Institute. In addition I appreciatively acknowledge the financial assistance of the U.S. Arab Chamber of Commerce (N.Y.) and its Executive Director, Mohammad Baghal, and the Mid-America Arab Chamber of Commerce (Chicago), and thank its officers for their financial support which along with that of the Kingdom of Saudi-Arabia made it possible to make this book available to the members of the International Association of Penal Law in 68 countries of the world.

Part One

The Criminal Process and the Protection of Individual Rights

SOURCES OF ISLAMIC LAW, AND THE PROTECTION OF HUMAN RIGHTS IN THE ISLAMIC CRIMINAL JUSTICE SYSTEM

M. Cherif Bassiouni

INTRODUCTION

Over seven hundred and fifty million Muslims inhabit the earth.[1] Sixty-nine countries have a significant fixed population, which in 37 countries constitute more than 50% and in 28 countries more than 85% of the population. Seventeen states formally adhere to Islam by so declaring in their constitution.[2] The re-emergence of Muslim and Islamic states in the world community of nations and the adherence of some to Islamic law as a basis of their legal system emphasizes the importance of understanding the values and attributes of Islam and Islamic law.[3]

The purpose of this article is to demonstrate (in an Islamic state) the potential of Islam in theory and practice to protect fundamental human rights as they are enunciated in international conventions in an Islamic criminal justice system. (*See* Appendix III.)

The difficulty inherent in such a task arises primarily from conceptual and cultural differences between Islamic philosophy and social values and those of Western Civilization. This is what probably caused the heretofore limited public

---

*Portions of this article are based on an article by this author entitled *Islam: Concept, Law and World Habeas Corpus* 1 RUTGERS-CAMDEN LAW JOURNAL, 163 (1969), and are reprinted with permission. The author also relies in part on his article, *The Protection of Diplomats under Islamic Law* 74 AJIL 609 (1980).

[1] 113 No. 16 TIME 40 (April 16, 1979). *See also* Appendix I, at 45, 46.

[2] *See* A. BLAUSTEIN and G. FLANZ, CONSTITUTIONS OF THE WORLD (1976-1977). *See* Appendix II). These constitutional provisions are only illustrative and their application under the prevailing laws on criminal procedure may offset their impact.

[3] Throughout this Article, *Muslim State* means a state in which there is a Muslim majority or a government representing a Muslim majority. *Islamic State* refers to a form of government wherein the conduct of all aspects of human endeavor and law is subject to Islamic law, *i.e. Shari'a*. Countries which purport to apply Islamic law in their criminal justice systems are: Saudi-Arabia, Libya, Iran, Pakistan, Kuwait, United Arab Emirates, Quattar. On the penetration and influence of Islam on the criminal law of Arab states, *see* M. MOSTAFA, PRINCIPES DE DROIT PENAL DES PAYS ARABES (1973).

interest in the study of Islam and its criminal justice system.

Mr. Justice Jackson eloquently stated in these terms:

> Greater barriers have discouraged any general interest in Islamic Law. Though our debt to (Islamic) culture is exhibited in the customary enumeration to our astonishing output of law reports, we long held the impression that the Muslim world had nothing to contribute to what was inside the covers. Islamic Law was regarded as of speculative rather than of practical interest and received attention from a relatively few specialists and scholars. But a review of the reasons we have deemed such knowledge too alien but useful to us show the reasons why we should abandon the smug belief that the Muslim experience has nothing to teach us.[4]

It cannot be emphasized enough that to understand Islam and the manner in which its criminal justice system could function in contemporary times requires a vast and deep knowledge of the history and evolution of Islamic thought and practice over almost fourteen hundred years and throughout different cultures in Africa, North Africa, the Arabian Peninsula, the southern Mediterannean, Asia-Minor, the Indian Sub-Continent, Pacific Asian states, China and the U.S.S.R. (*See* Appendix I.)

The reader should be conscious of the fact that Islamic thought and practice originally emanated from an Arab cultural context and though it was absorbed by other cultures, the Arab influence remained, though of course in different ways and in varying degrees of influence.

The historical development of Islam from 622 onward was necessarily predicated on the experiences of the times viewed in evolutionary context of cross current of cultural perceptions. One must also consider that Islam is essentially a theocratic system of government as is discussed below and as such throughout its history politically motivated leaders have sought and used the flexibility of Islamic thought to suit their self-serving purposes. Thus historical precedents must be viewed not in isolated instances, but in a totality of circumstances context in order to avoid the narrow specifics of a given precedent which may be distinguishable or outrightly contrary to the mainstream of Islamic consensus. Such consensus is difficult to ascertain because of the vast amount of written records, writings of commentators, scholarly opinions and recorded practice. That material has to be examined in the aggregate, and in accordance with one of the four recognized authoritative schools or *Fiqh* (Hanafi, Hanbali, Malki, Shafei).[5]

Even so, overall approaches which have their basis in political ideological conceptions such as the Shiite and Sunnite approaches, bring to bear a certain influence on Islamic thought, its interpretation and application. It is perhaps because of the vastness of material which in the periods following the *Khoulafaa Al-Rashidin* (the four Khalifas after the death of the Prophet Muhammad: Abu-Bakr, Umar, Aly and Othman) gave rise to confusion and contradictions and thus lead to a movement of return to fundamental orthodox Islam of that early

---

[4] Mr. Justice Jackson, *Foreward*, to LAW IN THE MIDDLE EAST, M. Khadduri, ed. (1955).

[5] On the application of these four schools of thought in criminal law, *see* A.F. BAHNASI, NAZARIYAT FIL-FIQH AL-JINAII AL-ISLAMI (1969).

period. Such was the Wahabi movement to which Saudi-Arabia still adheres.

The premise of this study is also a return to such fundamental basics. The basic values of Islam and the type of orthodox interpretation given to the sources of Islamic law in the days of the Prophet and the *Khoulafaa Al-Rashidin* though not ignoring subsequent developments which relied on the same historical period and the methodology of analysis employed then. In essence, it is a return to the origins which gives the inquiry a more pristine quality. It is on the basis of this approach that I have concluded that the Islamic criminal justice system as it could be construed and applied in contemporary times would be perfectly compatible with what has come to be regarded by the world community as fundamental human rights which are embodied in international conventions on the subject.

A final introductory observation should be kept in mind by the reader, and that is that Islamic criminal justice is essentially what in contemporary terms would be called a policy-oriented system.[6] It is not as has been represented, or for that matter even practiced by some states which purport to apply Islamic law, a rigid and repressive system. If any, it is the opposite. In fact, many of the most forward looking concepts in today's criminal justice have been the mainstay of the Islamic approach for centuries. Consider for example the ideas of victim compensation, restitution and diversions, work release, periodic imprisonment, conditional release and others which have been part of the Islamic criminal justice practice. Even penalties are misunderstood and misapplied. A good example is the penalty for theft which is the cutting of the hand; but a thief is one who steals in a "just society," thus a society which eliminates need, and therefore the punishment may be appropriately deterring but not necessarily applied if the society in question does not have the characteristics of being "just" in the sense of Islamic social justice.[7] In addition the penalty is not applicable to him who repents, and consequently it reflects a rehabilitative rather than a repressive policy of punishment while reflecting a strong general deterrent aspect. Similarly, the penalty for adultery is misunderstood. Its purpose is deterring because of its harshness since it is lapidation. But its application depends on its proof which requires that four eyewitnesses could testify that if a hypothetical thread were to be passed between the two bodies, its passage would be impeded (*i.e.*, sexual penetration).

---

[6] A. ODEH, AL-TASHRII AL-JINAII AL-ISLAMI (Vol. I, 3d ed. 1977; Vol. II, 2d ed. 1977). The author discusses Islamic criminal law in comparison with positive criminal law as enacted in modern criminal codes and reveals the strong social policy-oriented approach of Islamic criminal law. *See also* the Proceedings of the conference to study the application of Islamic criminal law and its effect on the prevention of crime in the Arab Kingdom of Saudi-Arabia, held in Riyadh, *al nadwa al-ilmiya li derasat tatbik al-tashrii al-Jinaii al-islami wa atharaho fi mokafahat al-garima fil-mamlaka al-arabia al saoudia* (1977). *See also* A. HASSABALLAH, OUSOUL AL-TASHRII AL-ISLAMI (1977), wherein the author discusses the principles of Islamic legislation.

[7] It was reported to Omar (the third Caliph) that some boys in the service of Hatib Ibn Abi Balta'a had stolen the she-camel of a man from the tribe of Muznah. When Omar questioned the boys they admitted the theft so he ordered their hands to be cut. But on second thoughts he said, "By God I would cut their hands if I did not know that you employ these boys and starve them so that they would be permitted to eat that which is prohibited unto them." Then he addressed their employer saying: "By God, since I have not cut their hands I am going to penalise you with a fine that shall pain you" and he ordered him to pay double the price of the (female)-camel.

The requirement of proof and its exigencies lead to the conclusion that the policy of the harsh penalty is to deter public aspects of this form of sexual practice.

SOME BASIC CONSIDERATIONS OF THE CONCEPT OF ISLAM

A prefatory remark is that unlike any other legal-political-social system, Islam is an integrated concept of life in this world and in the hereafter. It regulates the conduct of the state and of the individual in all aspects of human concerns linking the wordly and past-life aspects in an unseparable whole in which the Will of the Creator is part of the interrelationship of men, and of man and his Creator. It is not fatalistic with respect to individual responsibility, but presupposes the knowledge of the omnipotent Creator. Thus the pre-established knowledge of the Creator is in no way a factor bearing on the individual's freedom of choice and decision, though it is in the scheme of the creation pre-ordained. The degree of social responsibility of the individual remains objective, while his accountability to the Creator is subjective. Islam as a monotheistic, universal and eternal concept and faith underscores two fundamental aspects: the universality and humanism of the creation of which man is the essential part. It is these characteristics of epistemological and social considerations that give Islam its universal and perpetual significance. Failing to understand the above consideration will inevitably lead to misapprehension and misinterpretation of Islam and more specifically of its criminal justice system and the protection of fundamental human rights.

The word *Islam* in Arabic means *submission* or *surrender* to God.[8] Its derivation is from the word *Selm* or *peace*; wherefore the traditional Islamic greeting of *As Salam Aleikum*—"May peace be on you." The full import of the meaning of Islam departs from any identifying label generally given to a belief. The idea of submission to God through the recognition of Him as Creator with all its logical consequences, is a global concept of acceptance and surrender to His divine sovereignty. Therefore, when Orientalists speak of Islamic morality to indicate a similarity to Christian morality, the parallel may be misleading, because the *entire* fabric of Islam is *moral* and not merely an aspect thereof. Such Islamic morality is not a narrow concept connected exclusively to what is referred to as "Islamic revelations,"[9] but rather what Islam considers as the terminal and all-encompassing divine revelations of the *Qu'ran*. This broader, all-encompassing, universal belief is based on the three fundamentals of Islam: the Unity of God, the Unity of Mankind, and the Unity of Religion.[10]

1. The Unity of God: There is but one God, referred to as *Allah*. This belief in a central deity of exclusive prerogatives, qualities and attributes, the beginning and the end of everything, is, hence, undefinable. This one and

---

[8] *Mohammadanism* is often used as a misnomer; *see* H.A.R. GIBB, MOHAMMADANISM (2d ed. 1962).

[9] G.E. VON GRUNEBAUM, ISLAM: ESSAYS IN THE NATURE AND GROWTH OF A CULTURAL TRADITION (1955).

[10] E. BETHMANN, BRIDGE TO ISLAM (1950); A. MAUDUDI, TOWARDS UNDERSTANDING ISLAM (5th ed. A. Ghandi, transl. 1954).

only Creator, who is not born and who does not give birth, is the Creator of Mankind and the universe and, hence, the true "sovereign."[11]

2. The Unity of Mankind: Allah, the Creator, has created a single mankind through a process of development, which followed the creation of Adam and Eve. This common source of origin represents the Unity of Mankind. "Oh Mankind! Lo! we have created you male and female, and have made you nations and tribes that you may know one another. Lo! the noblest of you in the sight of Allah is the best in conduct."[12] The ethnological universality of mankind is the essence of international law, for it reflects the ideal of human harmony and the unity of those who emanate from the same source and will revert to the same end.
3. The Unity of Religion: There is but one religion under the Islamic concept because Islam is not a new religion.

> Say, Oh Muslims, we believe in Allah and that which is revealed unto Abraham and Ishmael and Isaac and Jacob and the tribes and that which Moses and Jesus received and that which the prophet received from the Lord. We make no distinction between any of them and unto them we have surrendered. (We are Muslims.)[13]

Successive revelations were delivered by the prophets of God sent to mankind bearing different messages at different times to accomplish different, specific or general objectives. Based upon the realization of those objectives, and as the need arose, new messages and revelations came to men. So came the law of Moses, supplemented by that of Jesus. Islam is only the last of the divine revelations. Muhammad, who is only a prophet and not in any way to be confused or likened to God or Allah, has merely brought to men the final concluding words of God's eternal messages.[14] Hence, the *Qu'ran* is the (last) concluding message which embodies the previous revelations.[15] Such incorporation of universal and eternal truth is designed to bring about a unified concept of morality in interpersonal and international relations, thereby barring the search for any different concept of morality and religion.

Because there is but one religion, which has been concluded by the *Qu'ranic* revelations and which embodies all previous revelations satisfying the needs and demands of all times for this one and only mankind, that is answerable before the one and only God, the *Qu'ran* is universal in application and eternal in scope. When referring to "Islamic morality," reference is made to that morality which applies to mankind as a whole, and the religion is that which God revealed through a succession of prophets to His created mankind. The morality that is derived therefrom is also universal and applicable to all mankind, and is based

---

[11] THE ENCYCLOPEDIA OF ISLAM (1960); W.H.T. GAIRDNER, THE MUSLIM IDEA OF GOD (1909); L.M. ZWEMBER, THE MUSLIM DOCTRINE OF GOD (1905).

[12] QU'RAN XLIX:13 [hereinafter cited as Q.].

[13] Q. II:136.

[14] P.W. PICKTHALL, THE MEANING OF THE GLORIOUS KORAN (2d ed. 1958).

[15] A. AZZAM, THE ETERNAL MESSAGE OF MOHAMMED (1964).

upon the same principles of all revelations made by God.[16] This concept of morality, based upon the belief in *Allah*, is the basis of individual responsibility and accountability[17] and is at the root of all subjective and objective human values and relations, irrespective of their extent. The belief in this concept of morality, as emanating from divine origin and sanctioned in the hereafter, eliminates the need for a distinction between practical and theoretical morality and transcends distinguishing theories of absolutism and relationism of moral judgment. It is applicable to an integrated human personality whose existence derives its meaning from a life created in furtherance of divine purposes.

The very first unifying thread between internationally protected human rights[18] and Islam is the universal humanism that underlines both. To recognize this common value in the context or the rule of law which derives its source from a higher moral and ethical plane makes internationally protected human rights a fertile ground for interrelation with Islam.

THE ISLAMIC CONCEPT OF THE STATE: SOURCE OF LAW AND SOVEREIGNTY

THE CONCEPT OF THE STATE

Allah, or God, is the principal unifying factor, if not the *raison d'être*, of the Islamic state. Von Grunebaum speaks of it in terms of the *staats-gedanke*, the ruler and governor of the world, including the state. The state, as well as the hereafter, is His creation and man and things respond to Him, the Creator.[19] This, according to Von Grunebaum, justifies and upholds the continuance of the Islamic commonwealth: a theocracy with the Lord generating the political-legal-religious power and constituting the sole source of authority, with the Caliph, or leader, acting as his deputy on earth. While the essential concept of God the "creator-center-and-source" of all authority is correct, the conclusion that the Islamic state is a theocracy regulated and controlled by its sole owner is not in accord with pure Islamic doctrine, unless, of course, it refers to a theory derived from practices during the Middle Ages that, by reason of the imperatives of the time, may justify such a conclusion. A noted Islamic author, Ramadan, distinguished Islam from theocracy, or rules vaguely governed by divine command, or devised by a sacerdotal class.[20] Theocracy is still man-made law in interpretation and application and leads to the struggle and division of church and state. Islam does not authorize a human institutional source of lawmaking, which results in the

---

[16] N.J. COULSON, A HISTORY OF ISLAMIC LAW 6 (1964), in which the author likens the concept to *ius naturae*, but recognizes that Islam is an "interesting amalgam" of *ius naturae* and Dean Pound's "social engineering."

[17] For individual criminal accountability, *see* ODEH, *supra* note 6.

[18] Internationally protected human rights means essentially the International Bill of Human Rights which consists of the Universal Declaration of Human Rights, The International Convention on Civil and Political Rights and the International Covenant on Social and Economic rights. It does not, however, exclude many other international conventions whose list and schedule of signatories is in Appendix I.

[19] G.E. VON GRUNEBAUM, MEDIEVAL ISLAM 142-54 (5th ed. 1962).

[20] S. RAMADAN, ISLAMIC LAW, ITS SCOPE AND EQUITY 42 (1961).

Islamic negation of the anthropomorphic implications of theocracy in the realm of faith. This can easily be verified from a close examination of a classification of Islamic sources of law.

A SUMMARY CLASSIFICATION OF ISLAMIC SOURCES OF LAW[21]

1. Chief Sources:
   a. The *Qu'ran*, or the Holy Book of Islam.
   b. The *Sunna*, or the authentic traditions of Muhammad.
   c. The *Ijma'*, or the consensus of opinion.
   d. The *Qiyas*, or judgment upon juristic analogy which could also include *al Ijtihad.*[22]
2. Supplementary Sources:
   a. *Al-Istishsan*, or the deviation from certain rules based on precedents derived from other rules based on relevant legal reasoning.
   b. *Al-Istislah*, which is an unprecedented judgment explicitly covered by the *Qu'ran* or the *Sunna* and necessitated by public interest.
   c. *Al-Urf*, or the custom and usage.
3. According to Hamidullah, the roots and sources of Islamic law, or the *Usoul*, are as follows:[23]
   a. The *Qu'ran*.
   b. The *Sunna*, or Tradition of the Prophet.
   c. The orthodox practice of the early Caliphs.
   d. The practice of other Muslim rulers not repudiated by the jurisconsults.
   e. The opinions of celebrated Muslim jurists:
      1. consensus of opinion, or *Igmah;* or
      2. individual opinions, or *Qiyas*.
   f. The arbitral awards.
   g. The treaties, pacts and other conventions.
   h. The official instructions to commanders, admirals, ambassadors and other state officials.
   i. The internal legislation for conduct regarding foreign relations and foreigners.
   j. The customs and usage.
4. The characteristics of Islamic philosophy of legislation can be summarized as follows:
   a. An inclination toward establishing general rules, indulging in great detail.

---

[21] *Id.* at 23.

[22] SAYF-AL-DIN AL-AMIDI, AL-ISTIHSAN FI USUL AL-AHKAM (1914), a multi-volume series of a scholar (d. 1233 A.D.). *See also* Weiss, *Interpretation in Islamic Law: The Theory of Ijtihad* 26 A.J. COMP. L. 199 (1978).

[23] M. HAMIDULLAH, MUSLIM CONDUCT OF STATE 18 (4th ed. 1961); and HASSABALLAH, *supra* note 6.

b. Precepts based on actual events and not hypothetical suppositions, thus strengthening case law as an expression of human behavior and judicial experience, which result in a deliberate and not coincidental determination.
c. The permissiveness of all that which is not prohibited, thus illustrating the flexibility which is needed to prevent human paralysis and intellectual stagnation.
d. The wording of specific prohibitions in such terms as to allow implementations by reason of necessity, social and public.
e. The use of language allowing the tempering of specific prohibitions by legal excuse or justification arising from necessity in its broadest form and granting judicial power to adapt as the requirements of society and circumstances justify.
f. The permissiveness and liberality in adapting useful and necessary guidelines not incompatible with the *Qu'ran* or *Sunna*.

Thus it is obvious that nothing in the characteristics of Islamic legislation, its interpretation, application and administration in a criminal justice system would in any way be contrary to the protection of individual guarantees of human rights which are consistent with the *Shari'a*—which can be interpreted and applied in a way that permits the applicability of those fundamental human rights guaranteed by international human rights conventions (as discussed below and illustrated in Appendix I).

SOVEREIGNTY

Submission to God in Islam is the acceptance of Him as the source of authority and the sole sovereign and lawgiver, while man, his trustee or vicegerent on earth, may be the lawmaker.

> The command is for none but God. He hath commanded that ye obey none but him: that is the right path.[24]
>
> And grant me from thy presence a ruling authority to aid me.[25]
>
> He unto whom belongeth the *sovereignty* of the heavens and the earth he hath taken unto himself no son nor hath he any father in the *sovereignty*.[26]
>
> Verily, his is the creation and his is the law.[27]

The sovereignty of God as the source of law and legality leaves to man the prerogative of earthly application, development and exercise of His commands, mandates, and the fulfillment of mankind's purposeful creation. The trusteeship or vicegerency of man is stated in these terms: "Allah has promised such of you as have become believers and done good deeds that he will most surely make them his *vicegerents* in the earth."[28] Thus, a divine rather than social contract is offered

---

[24] Q. XII:40.

[25] Q. XVII:80.

[26] Q. XXV:2 (emphasis added).

[27] Q. VII:54.

[28] Q. XXIV:55 (emphasis added). Also, note the similarity of God's sovereignty in Christianity. *Matthew* 6:10, 11:2-30, 15:3-9; *Luke* 19:38-46; *Mark* 7:5-13.

by the Creator-sovereign to man, its beneficiary, for the enjoyment and use of all other creations in consideration of man's submission to God, man's Islam.[29] The vicegerency of man should not be thought of as a de facto sovereignty versus God's de jure sovereignty, nor should it be likened to the "divine rights of kings" or papal authority. It is a concordat between free man, choosing to believe, accept and submit for the privilege of trusteeship or vicegerency. During the course of man's exercise of his derived powers over other created matters, he will be judged according to the law, laid down by the Sovereign in His revelations. Thus, free will, which is indispensable to the attainment of this delicate and precise balance, is not man-made but divinely endowed. Its operation is manifested by the obvious need to choose, but the criterion of choice lies in the purpose for the choice and not its empirical existence. Islamic polity is a "theo-democracy."[30] It is, therefore, distinguishable from the democracy in which constitutional principles place sovereignty in the people. Western political thought imparts the precept that sovereignty is in the "people" and is absolute.[31] The conduct of the affairs of state by its own people is original, unbridled, absolute, underived, independent, permanent and exclusive,[32] even when self-imposed limitations are included in certain constitutions to indicate the need for a higher order of legality.[33] The limitations imposed on the absolute powers of the ruler by internationally protected human rights for the maintenance of the inalienable rights of man as endowed by his Creator are, to that extent, wholly consonant with Islam.[34]

God is the lawgiver, his trustees or vicegerents compose the *Ummah* (Nation) and are empowered to make complementary laws, but their validity will depend upon their compliance with the *Shari'a; i.e.* Islamic law. The *Ummah* enjoys a derivative rule-making power and not an absolute law-creating prerogative.[35]

The interrelationship of the *Shari'a*, the source of law and legality for, and with, the rule-making power of the *Ummah*, and the *Imam* or Caliph are a trilogy of unequal value and standing. Because they are intertwined, they constitute a trinity of legislative authority.[36] They fulfill humanity's needs for legislation based

[29] A frequent error among Orientalists is to fail to comprehend God's sovereignty and man's vicegerency. Even the great Islamic scholar Coulson states: "While Mohammed's position gradually developed into one of political and *legal sovereignty*, the will of God was transmitted to the community by him in the *Qu'ranic* revelations." Muhammad is not the legal sovereign. N.J. COULSON, *supra* note 16, at 11 (emphasis added).

[30] A. MAUDUDI, ISLAMIC LAW AND CONSTITUTION 198 (3d ed. 1967).

[31] H. LASKI, THE PROBLEM OF SOVEREIGNTY (1917); E. MCCHESNEY, MASTERS OF POLITICAL THOUGHT (1949); Miliukov, *Religious Institutions, Christian-Russian*, 13 ENCYCLOPEDIA OF SOC. SCI. 265 (1934).

[32] *See, e.g.*, A. BRYCE, THE NATURE OF SOVEREIGNTY, STUDIES IN JURISPRUDENCE AND HISTORY (1901); I. MARTIN, THE CONCEPT OF SOVEREIGNTY: MAN AND STATE (1957).

[33] *See* U.S. CONST. amend. XIV, § 1 (the "due process clause").

[34] This is evidenced by the number of states who have signed and ratified human rights conventions, *see* Appendix III; and for those whose constitutions embody those rights, *see* Appendix II.

[35] D.B. MACDONALD, DEVELOPMENT OF MUSLIM THEOLOGY, JURISPRUDENCE AND CONSTITUTIONAL THEORY (1903); and for a western constitutional conception, *see* W. ROSTOW, THE SOVEREIGN PREROGATIVE: THE SUPREME COURT AND THE QUEST FOR LAW (1962).

[36] K. FARUKI, ISLAMIC CONSTITUTION (1953); L. GARDER & M.M. ANAWATI, INTRODUCTION A LA THEOLOGIE MUSULMANE (1948).

upon spiritual values giving man an appreciation of his position in the universal context of a "spiritual democracy which is the ultimate aim of Islam."[37] The logical continuity in Islamic thought rejects a doctrine of separation of temporal and spiritual—church and state—just as it must reject presently understood secularistic forms of state.[38]

CONCLUSION

Law in Islam is that which answers the following query: What should the conduct of man be in his individual and collective life,[39] in his relationship to God, to others and to himself in a universal community of mankind for the fulfillment of man's dual purpose: life on earth and life in the hereafter?

Law may be said to be the expression of controlled limitations over the liberty of creatures endowed with the characteristics of absolutism. Regulated by divine and human prescriptions, the knowledge of ultimate accountability to the Lord subordinates all man-made laws to the revered laws of God in letter and spirit. To balance the interrelationship of individual accountability and the limitation of freedom of conduct by law necessitates the following presuppositions.

Freedom of will and conduct is susceptible of absolutism but is so intended because absolute freedom negates social responsibility and results in self-destruction.[40] Limitations on such freedom are not, per se, arbitrary though the word *limitation* may imply it, because they are dictated by a rule of law conforming to "morality." Morality in this respect is meant in the sense of the entire divine purpose and human objectives, having divine judgment as its finality. Therefore, this morality is the foundation of social and religious order, which constitutes part of the human purpose of creation.[41] Those limitations on freedom are then laws which emanate from the "knowledge," in the broadest sense, which, when combined with the revealed source of law, destroys the dichotomy of man-made and divine-made law to become finally *ilm-ul fiqh*. This science of knowledge can be likened to the science of epistemology or the knowledge of things human and divine.

Man is simultaneously ruler and ruled. The Prophet stated: "Every one of you is a ruler and every one of you is answerable to his subjects." Von Grunebaum likens this to the Roman theory of *Jurisprudencia* or "*Rerum divinarum atque humanarum notitia*, or the knowledge of truth human and divine."[42] This knowledge is intended to cover all civil and religious functions of man to man, man to state, man to God and vice versa. While certain western scholars consider it as

---

[37] M. EQBAL, RECONSTRUCTION OF RELIGIOUS THOUGHT IN ISLAM 179-80 (1954); for the counterpart in western Christian thought, *see e.g.*, B. BROWN, THE NATURAL LAW READER (1964).

[38] C. SMITH, ISLAM IN MODERN HISTORY (1957); on the artificiality of secularism, *see* A. TOYNBEE, CHRISTIANITY AMONG THE RELIGIONS OF THE WORLD (1957).

[39] A. MAUDUDI, *supra* note 30, at 46.

[40] *See, e.g.*, A.S. TRITTON, MUSLIM THEOLOGY (1947); W.M. WATT, ISLAMIC PHILOSOPHY AND THEOLOGY (1962).

[41] *See, e.g.*, D.B. MACDONALD, *supra* note 35.

[42] G.E. VON GRUNEBAUM, *supra* note 19 at 144. *See also* Ion, *Roman Law and Mohammedan Jurisprudence*, 6 MICH. L. REV. 44 (1908). *See also* Badr, *Islamic Law: Its Relation to Other Legal Systems* 26 A.J. COMP. L. 187 (1978).

deriving essentially from Stoicism, the source is really to be examined in the context of the classification of Islamic law, which is more likely to reflect a different philosophical characterization.[43] Unfortunately, studies of Islamic law, its source and origin other than in Arabic have been undertaken mainly by western scholars who have always tried to view Islam from the western point of view and understanding. Islam is a radically different concept from that of the secular West and cannot be seen through the eyes and translations of other westerners. Thus, the search in western literature has always been for the use of terminology that would easily convey to the reader that which he is likely to equate with his own concepts and philosophies.

Islamic law is said to be moral and ethical in spirit, and the expression of this conclusion is found in the *Qu'ranic* principle of "*Hudud-Allah*," the divine limits. Those limits constitute the checks and balances placed upon man in his human endeavors to afford maximum personal freedom and to tolerate only those limited restrictions which distinguish anarchism from organized society. *Hudud-Allah* are the limitations placed on freedom to secure "a scheme of ordered liberty" and to prevent arbitrary and despotic limitations on human freedom.[44]

The limitations of personal rights operate as limitations against personal abuse of the rights of others. The object of International Protection of Human Rights is the protection of the individual through the due process of law. Islam affords this protection and guarantees due process and individual justice. To the end that the personal rights of individuals to life, liberty and property shall not be abridged without due process of law and that the rulers shall be subjected to the rule of law which shall prevent their tyranny, Islamic principles are in full accord with internationally protected human rights.[45]

THE INDIVIDUAL AND THE STATE IN ISLAM: RELATIONSHIP AND GROWTH OF THE LAW

THE STATE AND THE INDIVIDUAL

Islam introduced a social revolution. Its cornerstone was individual and collective morality. These principles of morality, which provide the basis for a society's spiritual values, are enunciated (among others) in terms of equality, justice, freedom, brotherhood, mercy and compassion. Unlike other sources of law, the *Qu'ran* emphasizes duties rather than rights. It insists upon the fulfillment of individual obligations before the individual can claim his privileges. The individual is neither apart nor separate from society, and his rights are neither different from nor conflicting with those of the community. He is part and parcel of society, and the fulfillment of his obligations and those of the other members of the society constitutes the reservoir of social rights which are then

---

[43] *Cf.*, *e.g.*, S. RAMADAN, *supra* note 20; G.E. VON GRUNEBAUM, *supra* note 19.

[44] *See* A. MAUDUDI, *supra* note 30, at 151; sources cited note 28 *supra*. *See also*, *e.g.*, W.M. WATT, FREE WILL AND PREDESTINATION IN EARLY ISLAM (1948).

[45] *Supra* note 34.

shared by all.[46] The individual enjoys as many privileges as society can afford, and society affords just as much as it receives from the individual.[47]

Brotherhood is solidarity, hence the magnitude of the role of the individual in the Muslim society. Community life is highlighted by the performance of community prayers. The two-way social responsibility—wherein the individual is the shepherd of society and in turn society takes care of its shepherd—represents a dual concept: 1) society is not a separate conflicting entity with the individual, it is not a system, but the highest form of integral and integrated collectivity; and 2) each individual is both a member and a leader. There can be no social classes, and any member of the community who is asked to be a leader or to be ready for leadership must also act at all times with the same degree of social responsibility as if he were in fact the leader rather than the follower.

The Prophet stated:

> Everyone of you is a shepherd, and everyone of you will be questioned about those under his rule: the Amir is a shepherd and he will be questioned about his subjects, the man is a ruler in his family and he will be questioned about those under his care; and the woman is a ruler in the house of her husband and she will be questioned about those under her care.

To fully realize the depth of this relationship, we must bear in mind that man is God's trustee on earth and that he represents God as His creation. Hence, he owes a duty of maintenance, prudence, and judicious use of himself and in the exercise of his endowed faculties. In addition, he owes a duty of care to all other creations of God. Man must preserve life and material objects subject to the judicious utilization of what is created for use and consumption. Most of all, he must preserve those subjective values which are at the base of mankind's creation. The preservation of life includes the protection of freedom, and the ability to exercise the functions of life requires justice. Thus, the protection of life, liberty, and property and human pursuit is secured by law and can only be abridged by due process of law.

To ask this solidarity and brotherhood of man because he is the trustee of God presupposes that all men are equal in the eyes of God. Consequently, equality under the law of God includes equality under the law of the trustees of God. Men of equal rank constitute a classless society and are simultaneously leader and follower. Therefore, no person can be denied the equal protection and enforcement of the law.

Freedom, justice and equality are inherent in the Islamic belief. Azzam, in *The Eternal Message of Mohammed*, states:

> Freedom in Islam is one of the most sacred rights; political freedom, freedom of thought, religious freedom and civil freedom are all guaranteed by Islam and carried forward to a point in the distance that has left modern civilization behind.[48]

---

[46] T.W. Arnold, The Preaching of Islam (2d ed. 1913); R. Roberts, The Social Laws of the Quran (1925).

[47] A. Azzam, Al Risalah al Khalidah (2d ed. 1954).

[48] A. Azzam, The Eternal Message of Mohammed 102 (1964).

But unlike justice for the Romans, equality for the Spartans, and freedom for the Greeks, Islamic freedom, justice and equality are as universal as the faith of which they are a part.[49] They lie at the very foundation of world order. Thus, Islam bears the seeds of universally accepted standards of due process of law.

A fundamental tenet of due process is a fair trial. Can it be phrased more eloquently than by the few and direct words of the *Qu'ran*: "Lo! Allah enjoineth justice and kindness . . ."[50] Elevating justice to the level of a duty-obligation incumbent upon all, it continues: "Deal justly, that is nearer to your duty. . . ."[51] To the query: "Is man his brother's keeper?" Islam replied, thirteen centuries ago:

> O Mankind: Be careful of your duty to your Lord who created you from a single soul and from it created its mate and from them twain hath spread abroad a multitude of men and women. Be careful of your duty toward Allah in whom ye claim [your rights] of one another.[52]

How else can it be when equality of mankind was so clearly enunciated:

> O Mankind! Lo! We have created you male and female and have made you nations and tribes that ye may know one another. Lo! The noblest of you in the sight of Allah is the best in conduct.[53]

The relationship of the state and the individual has always been troublesome and confusing to the western thinker. While certain authors deplore the lack of specific individual guarantees in Islamic law, and impute the weakness to the *Shari'a* itself, they fail to realize that the basis of the *Shari'a* is the principle of *original freedom*, for only free men can be free to choose Islam. The inalienability of life, liberty and property is indispensable to the general order and well-being of the community and needs no specific statement.

THE GROWTH OF THE LAW

In a system where the *basis of accountability is strictly personal and primarily subjective*, it is inconceivable to believe that there is a conflict between that which is the discretionary power of the leader and the individual rights of the followers.[54] While, as Gibb says, "The law precedes the state, both logically and in terms of time; and the state exists for the sole purpose of maintaining and enforcing the law,"[55] Coulson believes that individual rights and freedom and the power

---

[49] Azzam refers to an instance when Umar (the second Caliph after the Prophet) rebuked Amr, his governor and ruler of Egypt, when the latter sought to enslave a Christian Copt: "O Amr would you enslave a human being born to be free?" *Id.* at 99. M. RAHBAR, GOD OF JUSTICE, ETHICAL DOCTRINE OF THE QURAN (1960). *But see* I. AL-HAKIM, MAZE OF JUSTICE (1947).

[50] Q. XVI:90.

[51] Q. V:8.

[52] Q. IV:1.

[53] Q. XLIX:13. The limitations now existing and inherited from medieval doctrine are in the political inequality of Muslims and non-Muslims, but no reservations exist as to the equal application of law and justice to the citizens and subjects of the Islamic state.

[54] *See, e.g.*, Coulson, *The State and the Individual in Islamic Law*, 6 INT'L & COMP. L.Q. 49, 51 (1957) *citing* I. FARHUN, TAFSIRAT AL-HUKKAM II 133 (1937).

[55] H.A.R. GIBB, THE LAW IN THE MIDDLE EAST 3 (1955).

of the leader and discretion are mutually exclusive.[56] He characterizes what is known as *siyasat-al-Shari'a* as in fact the power of the leader in matters of law to determine whether or not there is a policy of the *Shari'a,* so that the *policy making is a process of the leader who more or less divines it.* This author justifies it by establishing that this is not contrary to *Shari'a,* because *the leader has to satisfy basically two requirements under it:* 1) *"Adala,"* which is *justice and probity;* and 2) *"Ijtihid,"* which is the ability to develop *legal reasoning.* Therefore, according to this writer, the development of the policy of the *Shari'a* is left to the leader, or Imam, who, by reason of having satisfied the prerequisite of being such a leader, needs nothing else except the general limitations of *Shari'a* imposed upon his policy decisions.

The concept of *siyasat-al-Shari'a,* which is the development of the policy of *Shari'a,* is indeed left to *Ijtihad,* or the legal reasoning and development of legal theories and philosophies. The imposed limitation is that *those legal theories must not be incompatible with the Shari'a.* However, while the administrative and executive power is left to the Ruler it is nonetheless true that he only rules with the consent of the people who, by reason of an electoral system, have placed him in such a position. Furthermore, he is to take counsel from the people. *The process of* Ijtihad *is not solely that of the leader, but it is the sum total of the jurisconsults of the nation.*[57] Therefore, *siyasat-al-Shari'a* is not made exclusively by the Iman, or leader, but made collectively by the jurisconsults, operating by *Ijtihad* and developing those legal theories. The failure to understand the real meaning of the process of *Ijtihad* is the result of attaching exclusive significance to medieval practices and historical facts.[58] Such reasoning stymies the understanding of Islamic law and prevents its development, because it demonstrates its futility by examining and comparing medieval Islam to modern legal development. To consider the experiment a valid one, the least expected would be to examine medieval law by medieval standards and not to compare it with modern law. The question still remains: If Islamic law had developed to such an extent in medieval times and was thereafter frustrated in its development, does it not then have something to contribute if it is presently allowed theoretical development and doctrinal progress?

To understand the concept, scope and spirit of Islam is a *conditio sine qua non* to build its future without breaking faith with its past. The divine *Qu'ranic* revelations are no impediment to the development of legal theories and structures able to cope with the changing times. It is not necessary, though true, that:

> Master architects were followed by builders who implemented the plans; successive generations of craftsmen made their own particular contribution to the fixtures, fittings and interior decor until, the task completed, *future jurists were simply passive caretakers of the eternal edifice.*[59]

---

[56] Coulson, *supra* note 54.

[57] *See, e.g.,* A.A.A. FYZEE, OUTLINES OF MOHAMMEDAN LAW (1949); J. SCHACHT, THE ORIGINS OF MOHAMMEDAN JURISPRUDENCE (1950). and *supra* note 22.

[58] *See e.g.,* D.S. MARGOLIOUTII, THE EARLY DEVELOPMENT OF MOHAMMEDANISM (1914); G.E. VON GRUNEBAUM, *supra* note 19.

[59] N.J. COULSON, *supra* note 16, at 2 (emphasis added).

The task of building an "eternal edifice" is never completed. Change is of the essence of mankind, and the refurbishing of a permanent edifice always goes on so long as mankind exists.

Islam does not change in concept and spirit, but the power of the *Ummah* (Nation) to develop and change its laws, customs and practices is inherent. The resolution of the Sixth International Congress of Comparative Law states it very aptly and succintly: "The Congress concludes that *Islamic Law has the power to adapt itself and by itself to the needs of modern life.*"[60] (Emphasis added.)

As a further indication of the elasticity and flexibility of Islamic legal thinking, the vast body of Islamic learning consists entirely of jurists' work and not of government codes and statutes. While their work has been covered by the dust of centuries and has come to be considered as both archaic and inflexible, it still remains that a system which allowed the development of the law in such a manner would certainly allow it to progress if the limitations imposed upon the Islamic states, whether by outside influence or self-imposed, were removed.[61] If, therefore, a Muslim state, or even the ideal Islamic state, wishes to adhere to all existing human rights conventions, it may do so without any legal or philosophical impediment.

The maxim that the king can do no wrong is rejected by Islamic law. What is adopted is the principle of the "just judge." Justice in Islam is not subjective but rests on the *Shari'a*, from which comes the guarantee that individual rights shall not be subjected to the whims of any intemperate judge, but to the due process of law.

Schacht considers, and justly so, the untidy relationship between ideal theory of Islamic law and actual practice by Muslims and their leaders.[62] The conflict is not what the ideal law is, but rather in its application, and this is transferred to the distinction between purely legal versus theological and metaphysical differences. Thus, Schacht considers Islamic law in its purest form a metaphysical and theological concept, while purely legal and constitutional norms and laws are in fact that which he and the modernists claim are in need of detachment, if not separation, from the former. This merely represents another form of expressing the concept of separation of church and state, or that which distinguishes religious and temporal law. The leaders of the Muslim states are still viewed by the Orientalists as precluded from adapting any modern or modernistic development to their legal theories and as devoid of the power to legislate. Strangely enough, this brings about an anachronistic conflict between Orientalists who claim the all-mighty power of the ruler under the doctrine of *siyasat ul fiqh* and those who claim that the religious concept of Islam binds the ruler and

---

[60] VI[E] CONGRES INTERNATIONAL DE DROIT COMPARE, RAPPORTS GENERAUX AU VI[E] CONGRES INTERNATIONAL DE DROIT COMPARE 1962, at 53 (1962). *See also* SEMAINE INTERNATIONALE DE DROIT MUSULMAN, TRAVAUX DE LA SEMAINE INTERNATIONALE DE DROIT MUSULMAN (1953).

[61] *See, e.g.*, M. MOUSSA, MUSLIM JURISPRUDENCE (1958).

[62] Schacht, *Islamic Law in Contemporary States*, 8 AM. J. COMP. L. 133 (1959). For the principle of legality in criminal legislation *see* A. F. SOUROUR, AL-SHARIIA WAL-IJRAAT AL-JINAII (1977), and A. Gamal-El-Din *al-Shariia fil-Shariia al-Jinaiia* 16 No. 2 MEJALAT AL-OULOUM AL-QANOUNIA WAL-IQTISADIA 359-517 (July 1974); *see also* 1 ODEH, *supra* note 6, at 41-46, 202-307.

prevents him from developing adequate modern legislation.[63] In reality, modern legislation in many Muslim states has demonstrated that there is no inherent immobility in contemporary Islamic legislation.

The need for a moral and ethical basis, which emanates from the *Shari'a*, is not to be confused with the freedom of the legislator who enacts laws befitting and necessary for the maintenance of a modern society.[64] Schacht states, however, that:

> Whatever may be the case of other features of traditional Islamic law, its fundamental concepts concerning the sanctity of contracts, the respect for private property, and the relationship of individual and state, are well in line with the trends of contemporary Western legal thought. Thanks to its lofty standards, Islamic Law still has an important part to play in providing legal stability and security in the Arab countries of the Near East, in the states of traditionalist orientation to the law of the land, and in the states of modernist orientation as an ideal inspiring their secular legislation.[65]

The significance of Islamic law in the world today is retraced, by J.N.D. Anderson, to the Ottoman reforms of 1850 and several other legislations in the Ottoman Empire and Egypt in 1879. Unlike other authors, Anderson explains the development of the reform movement by what he terms as mere "expedience."[66] The reform movement wrought procedural devices by means of which the court's jurisdiction was either enlarged or the previous decisions, which so far had paralyzed the development of the law, were circumvented by a re-interpretation of the *Qu'ranic* precepts.[67]

Recent developments in contemporary Muslim states, even though frequently departing from strict *Shari'a*, are clear indications that it is within the power of the *Ummah* and the ruler to interpret the *Shari'a* and to lead legislative reform movements within Islamic law. While it is still advocated by western Orientalists that Islamic law must modernize in the sense of becoming secular,[68] it is further

---

[63] *Id.* at 136.

[64] *See* the Tunesian Code of Family Law of 1956, Egyptian Civil Code of 1948, Syrian Civil Code of 1949, Iraqi Civil Code of 1951. See also the SYRIAN CONSTITUTION of 1950, which declares that Islamic law shall be the main source of legislation. Also, the Egyptian Civil Code, wherein any matter not specifically covered by the Code is referred to the *Shari'a* or religious tradition. *See also* D.H. ADAMS, ISLAM AND MODERNISM IN EGYPT (1933); J.N.D. ANDERSON, ISLAMIC LAW IN THE MODERN WORLD (1959); Nolte, *The Rule of Law in the Arab Middle East*, 48 MUSLIM WORLD 295 (1958), wherein he states that Islamic law has been the main guaranty of the rule of law in the Arab-Islamic countries of the Near East.

[65] *See* Schacht, *supra* note 62, at 147.

[66] Anderson, *Islamic Law in the World of Today*, 9 AM. J. COMP. L. 187, 191 (1960).

[67] For an examination of the development of civil law, carefully studied by authors such as Anderson, *see* the following works by that author, J.N.D. ANDERSON, ISLAMIC LAW IN AFRICA FROM HER MAJESTY'S STATIONERY OFFICE 16-18 (1954); Anderson, *The Problem of Divorce in the Sharia Law of Islam*, J. ROYAL CENTRAL ASIAN SOC'Y 169 (1950); *Recent Developments in Sharia Law* 8, 42 MUSLIM WORLD 190, 192-96 (1952); *Recent Developments in the Sharia Law in the Sudan*, 31 SUDAN NOTES & RECORDS 82 (1950); *A Reform in Family Law in Morocco* 2 J. AFRICAN L. 146 (1958); *The Syrian Law of Personal Status*, BULLETIN OF THE SCHOOL OF ORIENTAL AND AFRICAN STUDIES, pt. 1, at 34-49 (1955); *The Tunisian Law of Personal Status*, 7 INT'L & COMP. L.Q. 262 (1958).

[68] J.N.D. ANDERSON, ISLAMIC LAW IN THE MODERN WORLD (1959); H.A.R. GIBB, MODERN TRENDS IN ISLAM (1947).

advocated by Muslim modernizers that Islam should modernize in the Islamic sense; that is, without secularism and under the higher precepts of the *Shari'a.*[69] It is always a revelation for the student of Islamic law to realize how flexible Islamic law and the *Shari'a* precepts are and how fast and progressively they have developed for a millenium, and then how static they have remained ever since. Yet, when advocates of Islamic law resurgence call for modernization, they express their understanding of Islamic law in terms of stagnant, fixed and unimaginative body of medieval law. As many Islamic modernizers have advocated, not the least of whom is the Egyptian Sheik Mohammed Abdu, the return to the original sources will undoubtedly give a greater flexibility and strength, rather than weakness, to the development of Islamic law.[70]

Emphasizing the need for Muslim states to abandon their adherence to Islam as the official state religion and source of legality, Orientalists invariably fail to stress the same requirement of the Christian western world. If then Christianity is not offensive to non-Christian minorities living in Christian countries, why should Islam continue to be assailed?[71]

THE INDIVIDUAL AND INTERNATIONAL PROTECTION OF HUMAN RIGHTS IN ISLAM

THE INDIVIDUAL

In Islam the dignity of man is foremost for he is the prize creation of Allah; equality and justice are therefore a natural corollary. Nowhere is it better stated than in the following *Qu'ranic* verses: "Surely we have accorded dignity to the sons of Adam."[72] This alone explains why the "dignity" of mankind occupies a high position in Islam. The *Qu'ran* abounds with references to its attributes and "Justice," which is deemed a social obligation and a moral duty, is mentioned twenty times. Admonishments and warnings against "persecution" are referred to two hundred and ninety-nine times. Denunciations of "aggression" and its aims are stated eight times. Warnings against such "violation" are made twenty times.[73] The purpose of upholding "dignity" is that each man is not only the creature of God, but is the only creature susceptible of the choice of Islam (surrender to Him), *Ilhad* (the negation of God), *Shirk* (multiplicity), and *Kufr* (dejection of the faith or God). Furthermore, the glorification of man is not for what he is, but because of who created him and the role devolved to him on earth. This role he may assume (or reject) at any time from birth until death, and if and when that moment of choice comes, it must be received by a man endowed with human

---

[69] *See* A. MAUDUDI, *supra* note 30; S. RAMADAN, *supra* note 20.

[70] Sheikh Mohammed Abdu was a disciple of the great Muslim scholar Ghazali; *see* A.J. WENISINCK, LA PENSEE DE GHAZALI (1946).

[71] S. RAMADAN *supra* note 20, at 110-12, in which the author cites ten different modern constitutions that establish Christianity as the official religion of the state.

[72] Q. XVII:7. Such dignity is inherent in man and of equal magnitude.

[73] M. MOUSSA, ISLAM AND HUMANITY'S NEED OF IT 236 (1966).

dignity.[74] From that we derive the *raison d'être* of human rights, which are designed to insure man's dignity.

The individual is viewed by Islam both as a single and unique unit and also as part and parcel of a composite unit; *i.e.* mankind. The individualistic feature of Islamic law rests in part in "the fact that Islamic law generally aims at the public good [which] does not detract from its fundamental and individualistic character."[75] The assertion is made, however, that:

> Because [the state is the] properly constituted political authority representing the rule of divine wisdom, [and the state has] guarantee[d] the welfare of the subject in this world and in the world to come, it follows that the interests of the State and not those of the individual will constitute the supreme criteria for law.[76]

Such an approach, unfortunately, "fails to appreciate the [unique] relationship between strict legal doctrine and the practice of *siyâsa Shari'a* which has always prevailed in that field."[77] Another author confirms this latter point in the following terms:

> Islamic Law is purely individualistic in so far as the right of every single member of the community to share public responsibility with the Calif is recognized. Any individual has the right to correct the Calif and to attack his decisions if he commits an error. Moreover, positive Islamic Law on the whole is a system of subjective rights and personal privileges for all individuals as demonstrated by the text dealing with the principle of "original freedom" and the inviolability of life, liberty, property and honor.[78]

The individual is regarded in Islam as the most important unit of the Cosmos. Born free with a right to choose, he is offered Islam: The Right Path. The maintenance of freedom, therefore, cannot be temporary, or for that matter discriminatory, for anyone outside of Islam must be given the prerogative of free choice to become a Muslim and embrace the faith.

HUMAN RIGHTS

Classic Islamic law distinguishes between *Zimmi*, non-Muslims residing under the protective covenant of the Islamic state, because they are the people of the Book and recipient of divine revelations, and *non-Zimmi*, who are not people of the Book and have no protective covenant with the state, but who also live in the Islamic state. The relationship of Muslim, *Zimmi* and *non-Zimmi* falls within the purview of internal law, while relations and human rights with people who are not living within the Islamic territory are covered by the *Siyyar*, or external laws or Law of Nations.

The intrastate human rights are said to be unequal as between Muslims and non-Muslims, because of the political structure of the state. The state is under the

---

[74] *Id.* at 265.
[75] Salah-Eldin Abdel-Wahab, *Meaning and Structure of Law in Islam*, 16 VAND. L. REV. 115 (1962).
[76] Coulson, *supra* note 54, at 51.
[77] Schacht, *supra* note 62, at 138 n.12.
[78] Abdel-Wahab, *supra* note 75, at 130.

sovereignty of God; its laws depend for their validity on the *Shari'a;* and the Book is the primary source of law. Muslim citizens as a whole constitute the *Ummah,* or Islamic nation. Therefore, non-Muslims are not politically a part of that nation. In no way does this affect equality before the law or equal justice. All who live under the protective covenant of the *Shari'a* are entitled to all privileges and immunities without distinction of race, religion or national origin. The only real difference is one of authority, administration and jurisdiction. This concept of separate political administration, yet with equal justice for all, is likened to the Roman concept of jurisdiction in the *jus civile.* The analogy is misleading, because the distinction in Islam is not one concerning the rights of the people, but one concerning the administration of the political and legislative process of the state. Non-Muslims are not outside the "jurisdiction" as understood by the *jus civile, orbis Romanus* simply because Muslims are not *princeps orbis terrarum* (lords of the population of the globe).[79] Neither, for that matter, are the protective covenants between Muslims and non-Muslims a *pax Romana,* because the *Zimmi* is equal before the law in every aspect.[80] The distinction remains one of administration and not of human rights.[81] Translated in terms of the modern socio-political context, the Muslims constituting the majority govern and legislate but cannot affect matters specifically left to the minorities by the *Qu'ranic* mandate or by covenant. Islam foresaw the possibility of the majority repressing the minority and specified certain rights for the non-Muslim minorities which cannot be tampered with even by the ruling majority.[82]

Freedom of religious practice, personal-status matters, citizenship and protection of life, liberty and property are only some examples of specific guarantees that have to be afforded to the minorities who live under the protective covenant of the Islamic state. One author points out that:

> Whereas the Muslims are endowed with full legal capacity non-Muslims are considered not to possess the same capacity: the levy of *Jizya* is a case in point. In other words, Islamic law in at least its traditional interpretation considers certain human beings as more equal than others.[83]

Islamic traditional practice indicates a definite preferential treatment and higher status for the Muslim religion in the Muslim state governed by the Islamic majority. This does not, however, allow the imposition of any undue restriction on non-Muslims or interference with their religious freedom and practices. In that respect, Islamic law is not the most notorious of all national systems.[84] On the contrary, it considers itself, in comparison to other legal systems, as most be-

---

[79] *See* Ion, *supra* note 42, and Bassiouni, *A Survey of the Major Criminal Justice Systems in the World,* HANDBOOK OF CRIMINOLOGY, D. Glaser, ed. 527-592 (1974).

[80] M. HAMIDULLAH, MUSLIM CONDUCT OF STATE 150 (4th ed. 1961).

[81] For example, CONST. OF PAKISTAN art. 10a requires that the President be a Muslim.

[82] Ahmad, *Islamic Civilization and Human Rights,* 12 REVUE EGYPTIENNE DE DROIT INTERNATIONAL 1 (1956).

[83] Nawaz, *The Concept of Human Rights in Islamic Law,* 11 HOW. L.J. 325 (1965).

[84] S. RAMADAN, *supra* note 20, at 110-12, in which the author discusses preferential treatment to Christianity in some Constitutions.

nevolent and clairvoyant in that it guarantees the rights of the minorities, even if they conflict with the rights of the majority.[85]

The concept of *Jizya*, which is a tax levied on non-Muslims, has often been cited as the main discriminatory feature in Islamic human rights. It is unfortunate that the nature of this tax is not well understood, since the tax is not discriminatory, but different from similar taxes levied upon Muslims—unless the mere fact that the tax is different constitutes inherent discrimination. Traditionally, the *Jizya* constituted a ten percent tax on income to non-Muslims, while other taxes including the duty of the *Zakat* were only imposed upon Muslims. Furthermore, non-Muslims were not required to serve in the military or any public service duty as Muslims were.[86]

It is often said that while the enjoyment of life, liberty and property is an absolute right for Muslims, subject only to the limitations of the rights of the community as a whole for the maintenance of a scheme of ordered liberty which, by its very nature, requires certain self-imposed restrictions, the same right to life, liberty and property is qualified for non-Muslims. While the statement correctly reflects medieval practices in the context of the relationship of Islam and Christendom, it is theoretically incorrect insofar as the ideal Islamic state is concerned in its relationship with other treaty states or minorities living under its protection.[87]

In modern times, the emphasis in Muslim states has been on equality, and this is demonstrated by the constitutions of Islamic states and Muslim states (see Appendix II), to cite some examples: The Egyptian Constitution of 1958, the provisional Constitution of the United Arab Republic, Art. 7: "All citizens are equal before the law. They are equal in their rights and obligations, without distinction of race, origin, language, religion or creed." Also, Principle 2 of the law-making principles of the Constitution of Pakistan of 1962 declares that "all citizens should be equal before the law, be entitled to equal protection of the law and be treated alike in all respects." Under that Constitution only a Muslim can be a President (see Article 9 of the Constitution). Also Article 8, Paragraph 1, of the Malayan Constitution of 1957 states: "All persons are equal before the law and entitled to equal protection of the law." Paragraph 2 provides:

> Except as expressly authorized by this constitution, there shall be no discrimination against citizens on the grounds of only religion, race, descent or the place of birth in any law or in the appointment to any office or any employment under a public authority or in the administration of any law relating to the acquisition, holding or disposition of property or the establishing or carrying on of any trade, business or profession, vocation or employment.[88]

---

[85] M. HAMIDULLAH, *supra* note 80, at 132, in which the author states: "The ethical basis of Islam repudiates any distinction as to justice between Muslims and non-Muslims."

[86] K. CRAGG, THE CALL OF THE MINARET 339 (1964).

[87] *See* Ahmad, *supra* note 82, at 16-21.

[88] *See also* Groves, *Fundamental Liberties of Malaya—A Comparative Study*, 5 HOW. L.J. 190 1957).

The fundamental rights of a citizen, regardless of his faith, in the Islamic state, says Maududi, must be as follows:

a. Protection of life, honour and property;
b. Freedom of thought, expression, belief and worship;
c. Freedom of movement throughout the country;
d. Freedom of assembly and association;
e. Freedom of engaging in any profession or occupation and the right to own, acquire and dispose of property; and
f. Equality of opportunity in all walks of life, and equal right of benefiting from all public institutions.[89]

The discussion above on the Muslim and non-Muslim is necessitated by the frequently misunderstood application of that distinction. It is not discriminatory in nature, but a separate parallel equal application of justice based on different *criteria* in response to divergent purposes and goals.

It must be noted that whatever differences exist in the Islamic legal system in general as between Muslim and non-Muslim, these have no bearing on the fundamentals of the integrity of the criminal process in its pursuit of truth, the determination of individual responsibility, and the remedy of the victim irrespective of whether the accused or victim is Muslim or non-Muslim. Nevertheless, there are some differences. These are: (1) the social remedy, which is that portion of the punishment predicated on social obligation, to which a Muslim is held in different ways than a non-Muslim because of the very concept of Islam as a social order; and, (2) the method of proof, which in the Islamic criminal justice system relies heavily on oath-taking by the accused, the victim and the witness, which for the Muslim is an oath on the *Qu'ran* to which a non-Muslim is not eligible and that creates an imbalance in evidentiary symmetry.[90]

In the context of the broad question of Islamic criminal justice and international protection of human rights, the narrower question of the place of the individual, and implicitly his rights, is derivative of the conceptual relationship between the individual and the state. Unlike western philosophical and political perceptions on the separability of the individual and the state, Islamic social concepts do not make such a distinction. The individual does not stand in an adversary position vis à vis the state but is an integral part thereof. The consequences of this relationship which flows from the concept of Islam as discussed above, is that there is no apparent need to delineate individual rights in contraposition to the state. Thus the question more appropriately asked about the individual in the Islamic criminal justice is: What qualitative standards of administration of justice are required? That inquiry focuses on the integrity of the process and not on the allocation of rights or attribution of prerogatives to the

---

[89] A proposed constitution by Maududi for the establishment of an ideal Islamic state in Pakistan. A. MAUDUDI, *supra* note 30, at 339.

[90] *See* 2 ODEH, *supra* note 6, at 334 *et seq.*; and El-Berri, *La prestation de serment comme Processus d'Instruction des crimes d'Homicide das la legislation islalyique* 46 REVUE INTERNATIONALE DE DROIT PENAL, 373 (1975). *See also* Baroody, *Shariah, The Law of Islam* 72 CASE & COM. 2 (1967).

individual and to the state acting through its public agencies and agents. But the question of what standards of criminal justice administration are required by Islam is in its turn dependent on the purposes and goals of that system which are: (1) the ascertainment of the truth; (2) the determination of the responsibility of the accused; (3) the remedy to the victim; (4) the social remedy.

It seems clear that these purposes are not process-oriented but goal-oriented. It is that essential distinction with non-Islamic criminal justice systems which make it difficult to translate the role and rights of the individual in the Islamic system in terms that offer a comparable parallel to other systems.

Notwithstanding these difficulties it can be concluded that the nature of the Islamic criminal justice process is justice-fairness oriented. Such a system has in the past and is still capable of producing the same quality of justice rendered in non-Islamic systems in terms of general "due process" and specific guarantees of "fair trial" as embodied in the provisions of conventions on the International Protection of Human Rights (see Appendix III).

CRIMES AND THE CRIMINAL PROCESS

There are three categories of crimes in Islam: *Hudud*, *Quesas*, and *Ta'azir*.[91] *Hudud* crimes are punishable by a *Had*, which means that the penalty for them is established in accordance with "God's rights" and is prescribed by the *Qu'ran*. Prosecution and punishment for such crimes are mandatory, as opposed to *Ta'azir* offenses for which they are discretionary. The seven *Hudud* crimes are (1) adultery, (2) defamation (also referred to as slander), (3) alcoholism (which also refers to drinking alcoholic beverages), (4) theft, (5) brigandage (also referred to as highway robbery), (6) apostasy, and (7) rebellion and corruption of Islam (also referred to as transgression of Islam).

Quesas, the second category, are not always given a specific and mandatory criminal definition or penalty in the *Qu'ran*. What constitutes such crimes has evolved instead through academic, judicial, and even political supervision. These crimes are, however, specifically listed within the *Qu'ran*. They are: (1) murder, (2) voluntary homicide (manslaughter), (3) involuntary homicide (manslaughter), (4) intentional crimes against the person, and (5) unintentional crimes against the person. The latter two categories are equivalent to the crimes of assault, battery, mayhem, and other infringements of the person and bodily integrity of an individual that do not result in death.

Ta'azir offenses are those that are not encompassed by either of the above two categories but that result in tangible individual or social harm and for which the penalty is to be rehabilitative (the meaning of *Ta'azir*). Such a penalty could be imprisonment, the infliction of physical punishment, or the imposition of compensation in accordance with the principle of rehabilitation. The penal action and penalty for those crimes are discretionary and are based on the social

---

[91] *See* A. ODEH, *supra* note 6; and M. ABU-ZAHRA, AL-GARIMA WAL-UQUBA FIL ISLAM [CRIMES AND PUNISHMENT IN ISLAM] (n.d.). The following discussion of the three categories paraphrases one of the author's previous articles. *See* Bassiouni, *Protection of Diplomats Under Islamic Law*, 74 AM. J. INT. L. 609, at 623-25 (1980).

opportunities, meaning the social interest in prosecuting the case, rehabilitating the offender, and meeting the claims of the aggrieved party (*i.e.*, victim compensation).[92] Unlike *Hudud* and *Quesas* crimes, retribution is not a guiding principle.

Regardless of which category of crime is involved, the right to life, liberty and property; the right to petition for redress of wrongs and grievances; the requirement of a fair and impartial trial without distinction of color, creed, or origin are fundamental to them. Protection against unreasonable deprivation of any such right is subject to judicial scrutiny, and prompt legal determination is commanded. This is deemed essential not only as a human right, but as a political right that is indispensable for the maintenance of a scheme of ordered liberty and fundamental freedom.[93]

One primary requisite of such rights is nonretroactivity, and, in Islam, the principle that criminal laws and punishment shall not be applied retroactively is considered a "basic principle" or *Quaeda Usulia*, and finds express support in the *Qu'ran*.[94]

In *Surat al-Israa* (XVII:15) it is stated:

> And nor shall we be punishing until we had sent them an Apostle.

This statement means that the accused must first be given the opportunity to know the law, and thus that no punishment shall be imposed without prior law. Similarly, in *Surat al-Quesas* (XXVIII:59) it is stated:

> Nor was your Lord the one to destroy a population until we had sent to it an Apostle who shall divulge upon them our signs [commands].

In *Surat al-Nissaa* (IV:165) one finds:

> We have sent them . . . Apostles who gave good news as well as warnings, so that mankind after the coming of the Apostles should have no plea against God.

And in *Surat al-Maeda* (V:98):

> God forgives what is past.

Seldom does one find more unequivocal texts in the *Qu'ran* confirming the same principle so emphatically. There can be no retroactive application of penal laws in Islam.[95]

No Islamic tribunal may apply Islamic law to persons who by that very law are not subject to it because at the time of the alleged offense Islamic law was not declared applicable. There is specific application of this principle in the *Qu'ran* in connection with marriage. Men are prohibited from marrying certain women such

---

[92] *See generally* A. ODEH, *supra* note 6; and M. ABU-ZAHRA, *supra* note 91.

[93] See H.A.R. GIBB, *supra* note 8, at 163, in which the author refers to the creation of special tribunals called *Mazalim*, or courts, for the redress of wrongs.

[94] The following discussion on nonretroactivity is a paraphrase of one of the author's previous articles, *supra* note 91, at 621-22.

[95] For the view of a contemporary author, see A. MAHDI, SHARH AL-QUAWAED AL-AMA LI-QUANUN AL-UQUBAT [EXPLANATION OF THE GENERAL PRINCIPLES OF CRIMINAL LAW] 37-40 (1979).

as their mothers and sisters, and also from marrying two sisters (unrelated to them) at the same time. But since in the pagan pre-Islamic days marrying two sisters was permitted, the *Qu'ran* held that this prohibition would not be retroactive. This, it is stated in *Surat al-Nissaa* (IV:22):

> *except for what was done in the past;* for your Lord is forgiving and merciful [emphasis added].

Nonretroactivity was also the subject of the Prophet's "Final Pilgrimage" *Hadith* (A.H. 9), in which he said:

> [T]here is prescription for blood crimes spilled [committed] in the days of ignorance [before Islam was revealed]. . . .

Again the nonretroactivity of laws applicable to crimes and punishment before the promulgation of Islamic law is affirmed.

Another principle, basic to those fundamental rights, is the "presumption of innocence."[96] The Prophet said, "avoid using circumstantial evidence in *Hudud*,"[97] which are the most serious of all crimes since they are specified in the *Qu'ran*. Aicha, the wife of the Prophet, referring to the *Hadith* just quoted, reported that he also stated:

> Avoid condemning the Muslim to *Hudud* whenever you can, and when you can find a way out for the Muslim then release him for it. If the Imam errs it is better that he errs in favor of innocence [pardon] than in favor of guilt [punishment].

These words speak for themselves. It is also a well-established principle in *Quesas* crimes[98] that circumstantial evidence favorable to the accused is to be relied upon, while if unfavorable to him it is to be disregarded (though considered only for purposes of *Diyya* or victim compensation, subject, however, to other conditions of *Diyya*.

The presumption of innocence applies to the lesser *Ta'azir* offenses (discussed below) as well. In his "Final Pilgramage" *Hadith*, the Prophet said:

> Your lives, your property, and your honor are a burden upon you until you meet your Lord on the Day of Resurrection.

This passage is interpreted to mean that the duty to protect life, property and honor cannot be abridged without positive proof of a crime.[99]

But, the search for individual justice presupposes equality before the law, while the goal of a trial is to reveal the truth. Individual justice in Islam is sought to be accomplished on an individual basis and not through a series of general edicts which would result in justice by form. Justice notwithstanding the form is the goal.

---

[96] The following discussion on the presumption of innocence is a paraphrase of one of the author's previous articles, *supra* note 91, at 622.

[97] For *Hudud* crimes, *see supra* 24.

[98] For *Quesas* crimes, *see supra* 24.

[99] *See, e.g.*, IMAM ALAA EL-DIN ABU-BABKR MAS'UD AL-KASANI, 7 BADAEE AL-SANAEE FI TARTIB AL-SHARIA [THE BRILLIANT WORKINGS OF THE SHARI'A'S STRUCTURE] 67 (1st ed. A.H. 1327-1328). *See also* A.F. SOROUR, AL-WASIT FI QANUN AL-IGRAAT AL-GINAIA [A MANUAL OF CRIMINAL PROCEDURE] 71-73 (1980).

> The Quran and Sunna are full of words that oblige people to be just and to practise justice. The Quran forbids persecution, and threatens to punish any one who contemplates using it. If we read the Quran we find that the word "justice" and all its derivatives in that sense are mentioned more than twenty times. The word "persecution" and its derivatives are mentioned about 299 times. the word "aggression" is mentioned 8 times while the words "attack" or "violate" are mentioned twenty times.[100]

An illustration of the adherence of Muslim states (those who declare themselves to be Islamic) to these principles can be found in their constitutional provisions: they uphold the concept of the rule of law, require "due process" in criminal proceedings, and prohibit "arbitrary arrest and detention."[101] The concept of due process in criminal proceedings is found in early and recent writings of Muslim scholars and they are all in agreement on it.[102]

The rights of individuals in a Muslim state to the protection of life, liberty, honor, and property is embodied in the Prophet's "Final Pilgrimage" *Hadith*:

> Your lives, your property, and your honor are a burden upon you until you meet your Lord on the Day of Resurrection.

The Prophet in this *Hadith* emphasized the need to uphold due process of law whenever the life, freedom, honor, and property of individuals are at stake.[103] The *Sunna* is replete with examples in which personal freedom is upheld against the abuse of those who retain power.[104]

---

[100] M. MOUSSA, ISLAM AND HUMANITY'S NEED OF IT 236-37 (2d rev. ed. 1960). *See generally*, M. HAMIDULLAH, MUSLIM CONDUCT OF STATE 139 (4th ed. 1961); Nawaz, *The Concept of Human Rights in Islamic Law*, 11 HOW L. REV. 325 (1965); Ahmad, *Islamic Civilization and Human Rights*, 12 REV EGYPTIENNE DROIT INT'L 1 (1956).

[101] For the constitutional texts, *see* CONSTITUTIONS OF THE COUNTRIES OF THE WORLD (Blaustein & Flanz, eds., 1971–); for a specific analysis of constitutional principles of "due process," see A. MAUDUDI, ISLAMIC LAW AND CONSTITUTION (3rd ed. 1967); K. FARUKI, ISLAMIC CONSTITUTIONS (1953); and Hussain, *Due Process in Modern Constitutions and the Process of Sharia*, 7 KARACHI L.J. 57 (1971).

[102] *See, e.g.*, A. ODEH, *supra* note 6; SHEIKH AL-TAYEFEH AL-TUSI, 1 AN-NIHAYA [THE ENDING or THE CONCLUSION] 30 (A.H. 1342). SHEIKH AL-TAYEFEH AL-TUSL 2 AL-MABSUT 14-15 (1967); A. F. SOROUR AL-WASIT FI QANUN AL-IGRAAT AL-GINAIA [A MANUAL OF CRIMINAL PROCEDURE] 71-73 (1980); A. MAHDI, SHARH AL-QUAWAED AL-AMA LI-QUANUN AL-UQUBAT [EXPLANATION OF THE GENERAL PRINCIPLES OF CRIMINAL LAW] 37-40 (1979). M. HAMIDULLAH, USUL AL-TASHRI AL-ISLAMI [THE PRINCIPLES OF ISLAMIC JURISPRUDENCE] (1977); A. Gamal el-Din, *Al Shari'a a wal-Ijraat al-Jinaii [The Shari'a and Criminal Procedure.]* 16 MEJALLAT AL-ULUM AL-QUANOUNIA WAL IQTISADIA [REVIEW OF LEGAL AND ECONOMIC STUDIES] 359 (1974); S. RAMADAN, ISLAMIC LAW, ITS SCOPE AND EQUITY (1961); and the consensus of Muslim scholars in the 1976 Conference on Islamic Criminal Justice in Riyadh, in AL-NADWA AL-ILMIYA LI DERASAT TATBIK AL-TASHRII AL-JINAII AL-ISLAMI WA ATHAROHA FI MOKAFAHAT AL-GARIMA FIL-MAMLAKA AL-ARABIA AL-SAUDIA [THE SCIENTIFIC CONFERENCE ON THE STUDY OF THE APPLICATION OF ISLAMIC CRIMINAL JUSTICE AND ITS INFLUENCE ON COMBATING CRIME IN THE KINGDOM OF SAUDI ARABIA] (2 vols. 1977). It was also the consensus of the participants in the First International Conference on the Protection of Human Rights in the Islamic Criminal Justice System held at the International Institute for Higher Studies in Criminal Sciences in Siracusa, Sicily, in May 1979. For its final resolution, *see* Appendix C *infra*. The resolution also appeared in Bassiouni, *Iran's Revolutionary Justice Is Not Islamic*, CHRISTIAN SCIENCE MONITOR, 26 (Oct. 16, 1979). Some of the papers presented were published in Arabic in AL-MEJALLA AL-ARABIA LIL-DIFAA AL-IJTIMII [THE ARAB REVIEW OF SOCIAL DEFENSE].

[103] *See* A. MAUDUDI, *supra* note 101, at 339.

[104] *See* A. QUTB, ISLAM: THE MISUNDERSTOOD RELIGION 249 (6th ed. 1964), who quotes Imam Khattabi on the fact that there can be no detention without an order of a court of law, a position that is uniformly accepted among Muslim scholars as being in keeping with the *Shari'a*; and Bassiouni, *Islam, supra* note 102, at 36.

A. Maududi explains the Islamic concept of the right to justice as follows:

> This is a very important and valuable right which Islam has given to man as a human being. The Holy *Quran* has laid down: "Do not let your hatred of a people incite you to aggression" (5:3). "And do not let ill-will towards any folk incite you so that you swerve from dealing justly. Be just; that is nearest to heedfulness" (5:8). Stressing this point the *Quran* again says: "You who believe stand steadfast before God as witness for [truth and] fairplay" (4:135). This makes the point clear the Muslims have to be just not only with ordinary human beings but even with their enemies. In other words, the justice to which Islam invites her followers is not limited only to the citizens of their own country, or the people of their tribe, nation or race, or the Muslim community as a whole, but it is meant for all the human beings of the world. Muslims, therefore, cannot be unjust to anyone. Their permanent habit and character should be such that no man should ever fear injustice at their hands, and they should treat every human being everywhere with justice and fairness.[105]

As to the security of personal freedom, Maududi states:

> Islam has also laid down the principle that no citizen can be imprisoned unless his guilt has been proved in an open court. To arrest a man only on the basis of suspicion and to throw him into a prison without proper court proceedings and without providing him a reasonable opportunity to produce his defense is not permissible in Islam. It is related in the *Hadith* that once the Prophet was delivering a lecture in the Mosque, when a man rose during the lecture and said: "O Prophet of God, for what crime have my neighbours been arrested?" The Prophet heard the question and continued his speech. The man rose once again and repeated the same question. The Prophet again did not answer and continued his speech. The man rose for a third time and repeated the same question. Then the Prophet ordered that the man's neighbours be released. The reason why the Prophet had kept quiet when the question was repeated twice earlier was that the police officer was present in the Mosque and if there were proper reasons for the arrest of the neighbours of this man, he would have got up to explain his position. Since the police officer gave no reasons for these arrests the Prophet ordered that the arrested persons should be released. The police officer was aware of the Islamic law and therefore he did not get up to say: "the administration is aware of the charges against the arrested men, but they cannot be disclosed in public. If the Prophet would inquire about their guilt *in camera* I would enlighten him." If the police officer had made such a statement, he would have been dismissed then and there. The fact that the police officer did not give any reasons for the arrests in the open court was sufficient reason for the Prophet to give immediate orders for the release of the arrested men. The injunction of the Holy *Quran* is very clear on this point. "Whenever you judge between people, you should judge with (a sense of) justice" (4:58). And the Prophet has also been asked by God: "I have been ordered to dispense justice between you." This was the reason why the Caliph Umar said: "In Islam no one can be imprisoned except in pursuance of justice." The words used here clearly indicate that justice means due process of law. What has been prohibited and condemned is that a man be arrested and imprisoned without proof of his guilt in an open

---

[105] A. Maududi, Human Rights in Islam 19 (1977).

> court and without providing him an opportunity to defend himself against those charges. If the Government suspects that a particular individual has committed a crime or he is likely to commit an offense in the near future then they should give reasons of their suspicion before a court of law and the culprit or the suspect should be allowed to produce his defense in an open court so that the court may decide whether the suspicion against him is based on sound grounds or not and if there is good reason for suspicion, then he should be informed of how long he will be in preventive detention. This decision should be taken under all circumstances in an open court, so that the public may hear the charges brought by the Government, as well as the defense made by the accused and see that the due process of law is being applied to him and he is not being victimized.[106]

The *Sunna* is replete with examples where personal freedom has been upheld and its violations by the police powers of the state condemned. This is so, not because of the belief that the state seeks to suppress the individual, but because, in the face of the power of the state, the individual needs guarantees to protect himself against the abuse of power by other individuals.[107] The criminal process, through which oppression is most likely to occur, requires a valid accusation to be made in the face of the defendant who will confront his accusors, having a right to interrogate them, cross-examine them, and ask them to take the oath.[108]

Imam Ḳhattabbi explained that there are only two kinds of detention under law: 1) detention under the order of the court, and that is mainly when a person has been sentenced by a court; and 2) a detention prior to sentencing during the court's investigation of a criminal violation. He concludes that there can be no other ground for deprivation of a person's freedom.[109] It must be noted here that this in no way contemplates deprivation of freedom for what may be loosely termed political crimes, but only for specific common crimes validly prohibited by law.[110] Statutory criminal violations which are not part of the *Qu'ranic* precepts, but which are validly legislated will depend for their constitutionality on their adherence to the *Qu'ranic* precepts and their guarantee of the individual rights stated therein. The practice of the Prophet and tradition require that mere accusation, in the absence of tangible proof, is insufficient and that an accuser who is an interested party cannot be the sole evidence sufficient to sustain a criminal conviction. The moving plaintiff must appear personally and be accompanied by two witnesses who shall testify to the commission of the crime.[111] Omar, the Third Caliph after the death of the Prophet, is reported in a famous case to have decided: *"In Islam no one can be imprisoned without due course of justice."*[112] The presence of such a guarantee is indispensable for the maintenance of freedom of opinion and belief and to uphold the rights of the individuals com-

---

[106] *Id.*, 25-26.
[107] *Id.*, *see also* 1 ODEH, *supra* note 6, at 41-45.
[108] *See supra* note 90.
[109] A. MAUDUDI, *supra* note 30 at 267, in which the author cites M'Alim Al Sunnah.
[110] *See, e.g.*, A. ODEH, *supra* note 6.
[111] *See, e.g.*, J.N.D. ANDERSON, THE MALKI LAW OF HOMICIDE (n.d.).
[112] IMAM AHMAD IBN MALIK, KITAB AHKAM AL KHILAFAT (c. 1500) (emphasis added).

posing the Islamic nation as a whole and maintaining its political integrity. At an early stage of the Islamic nation, in the days of Aly the Fourth Caliph, a certain group known as the *Kharijite* revolted against his regime. This group was often labeled as anarchists since they denied the state openly and denied the need for its existence. It is reported that Aly sent them the following message: "You may live wherever you like, the only condition between us being that you will not indulge in bloodshed and you will not practice cruel methods."[113] On a different occasion he addressed them as follows: "As long as you do not indulge in any actual disruption and disorder, we will not wage war against you."[114] Maududi draws from these instances the logical conclusion that even an organized group, opposed to the form of government, may entertain its political opposition provided it is not done in a disorderly fashion and does not call for the destruction of the state by forceful means or violence.[115] The result of this philosophy is to secure the right to dissent and to be free from governmental compulsion or duress.

In addition to providing these individual and procedural rights, an Islamic state should provide substantive judicial means of protecting rights. For instance; the judge must be able to inspect the prison and release prisoners he discovers to be held arbitrarily. One author stated:

> The judge is advised to take an interest in the problems of prisoners and to know their numbers. He should also inform himself of the grounds for their imprisonment and its duration. Indeed, if imprisonment is a punishment, the prisons may contain unjustly held prisoners.
>
> If a prisoner claims he has been unjustly imprisoned, and if in addition he has not been formally accused, the judge must make enquiries to see if there is a possible accuser. Then, if none appears, the prisoner will be released, after designating a guarantor in order to safeguard the interest of a possible absent adversary.[116]

It follows that such an Islamic state will guarantee also that:

> No citizen of the state shall be deprived of the fundamental rights without his guilt being judicially established in an open court of law according to the common law of the land.
>
> Without this guarantee, nobody can feel secure against the high-handedness of the executive, and the feeling of constant insecurity cannot but breed discontent and even hatred against the Government itself. This, in its turn, will be most dangerous and harmful for the larger interest of national solidarity and sincere co-operation between the Government and the people.[117]

To further insure the individual against the abuses of the executive branch, Maududi maintains that the most effective remedy is *habeas corpus*.

---

[113] M. SHAWKANI, 8 NAIL AL-AWTAR 139 (1952).

[114] *Id.*

[115] A. MAUDUDI, *supra* note 30, at 268.

[116] S. E. el Nahi, Human Rights in Islam, Judicial Safeguards 20 (n.d.) 9-14 (An unpublished paper presented at the Conference on the Protection of Human Rights in Islam, held at the University of Kuwait, December, 1980).

[117] A. MAUDUDI, *supra* note 30, at 338-40.

> The Executive should in no circumstances be allowed to possess the power of suspending either the fundamental rights or the writ of *Habeas Corpus*. The maximum allowance that can be made in this respect is that in case of actual war, rebellious persons who are charged with high treason, conspiracy against the State or armed revolt may be tried *in camera*. But the power of detention without judicial trial or of suspension of fundamental rights or of the writ of *Habeas Corpus*, should in no case be granted to the Executive. And let it be known at this very moment that if any such attempt is made in our Constitution we are determined to resist it with all the force at our command.[118]

Maududi, a great Muslim scholar, was not alone in professing those thoughts. Between January 11 and 18, 1953, a special convention of Ulemas, representing all schools of Islamic thought, gathered to discuss the 1952 proposed Constitution of Pakistan.

The convention submitted a unanimous report on the Constitutional Commission's report submitted in 1952. It called for an immediate amendment of the following provision of Section 3 of the Constitution: "Except in the case of an external or internal threat to the security of the state or other grave emergency," the right to *habeas corpus* cannot be suspended by executive decree. The committee reports that Islamic *Shari'a* does not, in any circumstances, permit any Muslim or non-Muslim citizen to be deprived of his right to move the highest court for redress against unwarranted detention.

While restrictions imposed on individual freedom must be conceded to the state, they must be at all times "reasonable restrictions" and must always be subject to the right of the individual to petition a court of justice for redress in case of abuse or unreasonableness.[119] These contemporary Islamic scholars were quick to respond and assert the principles of the *Shari'a* to protect against potential threats to individual rights by abuse of the criminal process. The remedy of *habeas corpus* was singled out as the most important safeguard and became the counterpart of the tenth century *Mazalim* tribunal, which also allowed for an extraordinary remedy by which to petition for immediate redress of wrongs.[120]

The best guarantee for an accused is ultimately to have a fair trial and a fair judge and the best summary of the right to a fair and impartial trial before a fair and impartial judge is found in the message of the third Caliph, Umar ibn-El Khattab, to Abu-Musa el-Ashary on his appointment as judge:

> Henceforth, the right to adjudication is an absolute duty and a followed *Sunna* (before Islam disputes between persons of different tribes were the basis of war, revenge, or settled by negotiations and payment of compensation irrespective of right and wrong. As between members of the same tribe the Chief decided and revenge or compensation was the rule. There was arbitration and mediation but no adjudication and no same law for all. Islam established a unified system of law which required adjudication).
>
> Investigate any case you suspect (to bring about Right), for Right without execution (remedy) is futile.

---

[118] *Id.*, 341.
[119] *Id.*, at 385.
[120] H.A.R. GIBB, *supra* note 8, at 165.

Equalize (be equal) between the parties before you (and let equality be manifest) in your expression (demeanor) and in your judgement.

Your judgement (meaning also your attitude and disposition) should not be the basis for the noble (meaning powerful) to hope for your favor, and for the poor (meaning the weak) to despair from your justice. The burden of proof is on the accuser, and he who negates should be asked to take the oath. Reconciliation is desirable (meaning that is a preferred alternative to litigation) among Muslims except where there is agreement on something which legitimizes that which is prohibited or prohibits that which is legitimate. He who claims even a doubtful right and proves it, accord him the right (meaning that even if you doubt the merits of the claim which has been proven), but if he cannot prove it then rule against him (meaning the possibility of punishing false claimants), for (in both cases) it is the best that you can do (meaning that a judge must rule in favor of a proven claim no matter what his personal doubts are, but must scrutinize false claims to protect innocents from abuse and to insure the integrity of the judicial process, but in any event and whatever the outcome, the judge's best efforts is the best he can do, and he should seek no more of himself).

If you render a judgement and after a period of time you find it to be unjust, do not hesitate to revise it, unless it is so old that no one can change it (meaning that there is a finality in revision of judgements specially after new conditions become so established that they cannot be changed, and by implication that their revision would cause greater harm to others, which is a basic principle of equity justice). The revision of (wrong) judgements is better than preserving injustice.

Muslims are witnesses unto one another (meaning that any Muslim is a competent witness) except those who are well known for being liars and those who have been condemned for a *Had* (one of seven crimes prescribed by the *Qu'ran*), or those who are close to authority (meaning the excludability of those in authority). Only Almighty God knows the intention of each one of us, and we therefore can only judge (and condemn) on the basis of proof.

If a case is presented to you and you cannot find an applicable rule clearly stated in the Holy *Qu'ran* or the *Sunna*, you can reason the solution, contemplate (deliberate judiciously), try to find an analogy (to a rule in the *Qu'ran* or *Sunna*), and study the work of the wise and then render your judgement accordingly. Beware of anger, anxiety, monotony, disgust, and do not be biased against or for anyone even if he be your ally (friend).

Just judgement is rewarded by God, and rendering good judgement is appreciated by the people. If one is devoted (pious) to God and adheres to the Right, even when it is against one's own interest than God will save him (meaning save him from hell and thus reward him with heaven). He who pretends, God will punish him (meaning an admonition against hypocrisy and pretending to fulfill the duties enunciated above). God accepts from the believers only the Good (meaning that the Good is what counts, and the Good cannot be pretended, but done, though the doing is in the best efforts and not necessarily in the result).

Remember God rewards in riches (meaning both material and spiritual) and compassion (meaning also forgiveness).

Peace and blessings be on you.

e above text was translated with some explanation by the author.)

ISLAMIC INTERNATIONAL LAW AND INTERNATIONALLY PROTECTED HUMAN RIGHTS

The fundamentalism of mankind in Islam as expressed above is further highlighted by the following *Qu'ranic* verses: "O men revere your lord who created you from a single soul and made out of it a peer and therefore brought multitudes of men and women."[121] The importance of this *Qu'ranic* passage is to impress upon Muslims a consciousness of their belonging to a broader, larger and all-encompassing universe, rather than to consider themselves a parochial subdivision of a greater part with which no intercourse is invited. Muslim law is the fair regulation of the conduct of the faithful in this world and in the world hereafter. *Mutantis Mutandis*, Muslim international law aims at the fair regulation of the Muslim state in its foreign relations. It is directed also to the individual Muslim in his relations with the non-Muslim citizen of another non-Muslim state and any non-Muslim state.[122] That which sanctions the individual's private conduct also sanctions the individual's public conduct, and by reason of a unified source of moral precepts it prevents a duality of moral standards in national *versus* international affairs.

In Europe, political clericalism and religious wars resulted in the Europeans' distrust for the clergy's brand of morality. Morality and religion were gradually eased out of the *jus gentium* and replaced by more pragmatic materialistic rules of state conduct. The purpose of this development was to preserve this field of law from the reach and influence of the papacy, even though Christian concepts were still prevalent.[123] The basis of international law remained Christian and western-European until almost as late as the nineteenth century and was primarily designed for the benefit and use of Christian nations and was, therefore, limited in scope.[124]

The law of nations was largely based on natural law. The Treaty of Westphalia of 1648, however, was based upon the concept of *cuius regio, eius religio*, which sealed the separation between the religious moral concepts of intranational relations and the nonreligious or non-sectarian aspects of international relations.[125] This development, of course, remained totally alien to the Islamic law of nations, which preserved the ethical basis and moral source of its laws and individual relations including international relations.[126]

From the Middle Ages, the Islamic nation was ideologically stagnant and

[121] Q. IV:1.

[122] Note that Islam was first to recognize the individual as a subject of international law, *see* A. AZZAM, *supra* note 15.

[123] Scott, *Preface* to H. GROTIUS, DE JURE BELLI (1925).

[124] S.D. WOOLSEY, INTERNATIONAL LAW 1-20 (4th ed. 1889).

[125] THE STATE AND THE INTERNATIONAL COMMUNITY (D. Scott ed. 1939); Gentili, *De Jure Belli*, 1 CLASSICS OF INT'L L. 249 (1933); Korff, *An Introduction to the History of International Law*, 18 AM. J. INT'L L. 246 (1924); Suarez, *De legibus ac Deo legislatore*, 1 CLASSICS OF INT'L. L. 244 (1933).

[126] M. KHADDURI, THE ISLAMIC LAW OF NATIONS (1966).

gradually receded in importance, while the European countries and Christendom acquired a stronger position in Europe and in the world. The European resurgence as a world power bent on expansionism resulted in the rejection of Islam and the Islamic state as part of those nations engaging in the development of a law of nations concept.[127] In the development of the western-Christian states, religious and moral elements were separated from government and law. In sharp contrast, the Islamic Nation while gradually receding in its development and importance, clung to religion, and became insular.[128] The European club was a closed one, and Islam was at best deemed barbaric. Gradually, the monolithic Islamic state disintegrated, and its fragmented parts became colonies of the new imperial forces of Europe. Islam was no longer a contributing source to world civilization and its past influence was erased by the dominant West.

But the contributions of Islam to international law though significant have never received much recognition. One author notes:

> Almost unrecognizedly, through its contacts with the Western world, Islamic Law has preserved Greco-Roman legal concepts, and has made substantial contributions to international law and theory. Western scholars, such as Vitoria Ayala, and Gentili came from parts of Spain and Italy where the influence of Islamic law was great; great jurists, and theologians, like Martin Luther, studied Arabic; Western libraries carried the Arabic treaties on law; and even Grotius in his writing on the law of war recognized the humanitarian laws of what he called the "barbarians." The first codification of international law as a collection of cases and practices was made by the Muslim scholar Al-Shaybani in his *Siyyars* in the eighth century, preceding similar Western works by centuries.[129]

It must be emphasized that Islam had little if any influence that would be directly perceivable on the development of international law which was staged by the western-Christian world. This had nothing to do with the inability of Islam to make such a contribution or because of its inability to develop and adapt,[130] but rather because of the imbalance and power relations between Muslim states and the western-Christian ones. The greater development of international law took place during and after the 19th century and even though that discipline purported to be universal, it remains nonetheless narrow and power-oriented.[131] That was

---

[127] L. GUGGENHEIM, ITRAITE DE DROIT INTERNATIONAL PUBLIC (1953); Pollack, *The Sources of International Law*, 2 COLUM. L. REV. 511 (1902).

[128] *See, e.g.*, S. SINHA, NEW NATIONS AND THE LAW OF NATIONS (1967).

[129] C. RHYNE, INTERNATIONAL LAW 23 (1975); and al-Shaybani, 749-805, whose *Siyyars* or cases were first written in Haiderahad in 1335-36 even though he taught them during his lifetime. They were translated by M. Khadduri under the title THE ISLAMIC LAW OF NATIONS (1966). *See also* on the question of the Islamic contribution to the humanitarian law of war, Bassiouni, *An Appraisal of the Growth and Developing Trends of International Criminal Law*, 46 REVUE INTERNATIONALE DE DROIT PENAL, 3 (1975) and M. KHADDURI, WAR AND PEACE IN THE LAW OF ISLAM (1955); Rechid, *L'Islam et le Droit des Gens*, 60 RECUEIL DES COURS 375-505 (1937). *See also e.g.*, T. AL-GHUNAIMI, THE MUSLIM CONCEPTION OF INTERNATIONAL LAW AND THE WESTERN APPROACH (1968).

[130] VI[E] CONGRES INTERNATIONAL DE DROIT COMPARE, RAPPORTS GENERAUX AU VI[E] CONGRES INTERNATIONAL DE DROIT COMPARE 1962, at 53 (1962).

[131] Wilk, *International Law and Global Ideological Conflict: Reflections on the Universality of International Law*, 45 AM. J. INT'L. L. 648 (1959); Wright, *International Law and Ideologies*, 48 AM. J. INT'L. L. 616 (1954). *See* however Khadduri, *Islam and the Modern Law of Nations*, 50 AM. J. INT'L. L. 358 (1956).

true even after the Turkish-Ottoman empire entered into treaties with western countries and also admitted to the Concert of Europe in 1856. Some jurists even implying that the Law of Nations could not be applicable to that country because of its religious Islamic beliefs.[132]

The weakness of the modern Muslim and Islamic states and their alienation from the world community (since most were not independent and, therefore, not proper subject of international law) caused them to abandon rather than to strengthen, their international law concepts since they had no application or use. Foreign occupation reduced the Muslim states to accept the western concepts in its totality without bringing to it much of Islam's needed moralizing and ethical concepts.

In contrast to this narrow approach, Islamic international law, as early as 150 H., regulated the conduct and behavior of the Muslim state in war, peace and neutrality.[133] Unlike general concepts of international law, which restricted its jurisdictional application to nations, early Islamic international law regulated not only the conduct of the Muslim state with other states, but also the relationship of non-Muslim states and individuals in the Muslim state. Individuals in Islam acting as representatives of the state become subjects of international law. The object was never to limit Islamic international law to nations. The object was to enlarge it to encompass all public functions conducted by the state or its citizens in any intercourse not necessarily subject to private regulations in the performance of public needs or functions.[134] Early Islamic international law was not concerned with intra-Islamic relations as was early western Christian international law, because intra-Islamic relations were subject to internal private laws and did not need the regulation of an international body of law. All laws which derive from the *Shari'a* apply to all Muslims, even though they live in other political subdivisions. Islamic international law applies primarily whenever there is a non-Muslim foreign counterpart.[135] The concern for the development of a compendia of laws different, yet part of general Islamic *corpus juris*, is intended to subject state

---

[132] *See* Judge Weiss' dissenting opinion in the case of the S.S. "Lotus" (1927) P.C.I.J., ser. A, Judgment No. 9, wherein he considered Turkey not a subject of the Law of Nations. This was the position until Turkey entered the Treaty of Lausanne of 1923. *See also*, Wood, *The Treaty of Paris and Turkey's Status in International Law*, 37 AM. J. INT'L. L. 262 (1943).

[133] *See supra* note 129.

[134] M. HAMIDULLAH, *supra* note 23, at 20, in which the author cites the lectures of Abu Hanifa, in the years 130 to 150 Hejira, on War and Peace, using the case method of *Siyyar*.

[135] M. HAMIDULLAH, *supra* note 23, at 39, in which the author classifies the non-Muslim foreign counterpart as:

a. independent states and their relationship with other states;
b. semi-sovereign or semi-independent states possessing a limited but existing de jure or de facto foreign relations;
c. a belligerent state not yet recognized, or belligerent rebels having acquired an element of resisting and lasting power and territory over which they can exercise the ordinary function of state, however limited and restricted;
d. pirates, highwaymen and bandits operating not within a state but within more than one state or using the high seas;
e. resident aliens in Islamic territory;
f. resident Muslims in alien territory or foreign territory;
g. privileged non-Muslims or Dhimmis or non-Muslim subjects of a Muslim state to be distinguished from resident aliens.

rulers in their conduct to the *Shari'a* and to avoid unbridled discretion. The wisdom of such a measure is to prevent absolute discretion in the hands of the rulers for the conduct of foreign affairs, thus not only eliminating the dangers of absolute power, but recognizing the potential danger to others in matters of foreign affairs. The purpose of Islam was not the creation and protection of a parochial state limited in time and geography, but rather the achievement of a universal purpose. There can be no other choice for Muslim international law except to turn its eyes to the broadest possible concept of world relations and encompass the universe and mankind in its entirety and ad infinitium. This is reflected vividly as early as 100 H., by the inclusion of the subject of international relations as part of the *corpus juris* in the manuals of Muslim law.

International law, as a body of law, has changed rapidly with the increased needs of mankind to strengthen its ties in search of objectives highlighting commonality of purpose.[136] Significantly, the label has changed: *Jus Gentium, Droit des Gens, Völk errecht,* Transnational Law, World Law, and Common Law of Mankind,[137] but the goals remain the same.

The Islamic nation developed its foreign relations gradually while testing its legality by *Shari'a* standards.[138] The ad hoc case method *stare decisis* approach to the Islamic Law of Nations caused it to be named *Siyyar*, or the course of action and conduct of the state in its relations with the states outside the Islamic state. The *Siyyar* are, therefore, part of the *corpus juris* of Islamic Law and are just as binding as any other chapter of law.[139]

Up to the Middle Ages, the growth of the Islamic Law of Nations was accomplished primarily by rules derived from the traditional concept of the division of the world in two segments: *Dar al Harb* and *Dar al Selm*, meaning respectively "the land of war" and "the land of peace." The distinction rested upon the fact that the land of peace was the land of Islam and the land of war was that of those who were opposed to Islam and with whom Islam had no treaty. Not all non-Muslim territories were lands of war, but only those with which no treaty existed.[140] The moving factor in the foreign relations of the Islamic state was the concept of *Jihad*, which was primarily, at that time, a concept of Holy War. The objective of unifying the world under a single *Ummah* was a logical sequel to the belief in the fundamental unities of Islam,[141] which rationalize the need for the development of a unified world. Since the message of God was universal and eternal, directed to all mankind, without any distinction as to territory or people, the idea of a single nation under God was the logical conclusion. From the earlier days of the Islamic nations, treaties were entered into not only with minorities

---

[136] *See, e.g.*, A. NUSSBAUM, A CONCISE HISTORY OF THE LAW OF NATIONS (1947).

[137] C. JENCKS, THE COMMON LAW OF MANKIND (1958); P. JESSUP, TRANSNATIONAL LAW (1956).

[138] Reshid, *L'Islam et le Droit des Gens*, RECEUIL DES COURS DE L'ACADEMIE DE DROIT INTERNATIONAL DE LAHAYE 4-30 (1937). *See also* Draz, *Le Droit International Public de l'Islam,* 5 REVUE EGYPTIENNE DE DROIT INTERNATIONAL 17 (1949).

[139] M. KHADDURI, *supra* note 108; Majid, *The Moslem International Law*, 28 L.Q. REV. 89 (1912).

[140] For a compilation and commentary of those treaties, *see* M. HAMIDULLAH, CORPUS DES TRAITES ET LETTRES DIPLOMATIQUES D'ISLAM A L'EPOQUE DU PROPHETE ET DES CALIFES ORTHODOXES (1935).

[141] *See* text accompanying notes 6-15 *supra*.

living within the Islamic state but also with tribes and nations outside the purview of the Islamic nation.[142] Their purpose was to insure peaceful coexistence and, consequently, there are no grounds for the belief that the maintenance of friendly relations with non-Muslim states is incompatible with the goals of an Islamic state.[143] The principle of peaceful coexistence was enunciated by the Prophet in the seventh century when peace treaties were entered into with non-Muslim states and non-Muslim minorities.[144]

There is no question concerning the existence of human rights within the Islamic states, nor is there any conflict with the application of human rights in the Islamic states. The question, however, arises as to the protection of minorities within the Muslim states and the relationship of the Muslim states and other states with respect to questions of enforcement of human rights.

The protection of minorities in the Muslim states, as indicated above is regarded as a matter of internal law. Modern international law, however, seeks to cover human rights within a state itself. The United Nations Commission on Human Rights in a report outlined in the international criteria for equality as:

> The principle of equality or non-discrimination implies the following two consequences. In the first place, the members of the minority have the right to the nationality of the state which exercises sovereignty over the territory in which they reside. In a modern state, the possession of nationality implies equal rights for all those possessing it. Secondly, discrimination *de facto* or *de jure* against minority elements is forbidden.[145]

The report further attempts to identify what is meant by equality: "equality of all persons before the law, equal treatment *de facto* and *de jure*."[146] While the United Nations seeks to establish the guarantee of those rights by international obligation, one author commented:

> The general protection of fundamental human rights which Oppenheim hoped to have enacted as part of municipal laws conceivably "through the indisputably binding obligations under the aegis of the UN" after the generally admitted ineffectiveness of the League of Nations were more than 13 centuries ago both introduced and sanctioned as part of the fundamental laws of Islam.[147]

Notwithstanding the truth of that statement, an Islamic state can enter into an international treaty to sanction human rights.[148]

The revelance of Islamic concepts of international law is more imperative

---

[142] A. Azzam, *supra* note 47, at 92-97; M. Hamidullah, *supra* note 140.

[143] N. Armanazi, L'Islam et le Droit International (1929).

[144] M. Hamidullah, *supra* note 140.

[145] United Nations Commission on Human Rights, Sub-Commission on Prevention of Discrimination and Protection of Minorities, Document prepared for the First Session (Nov. 24 to Dec. 6, 1947) U.N. Doc. E/CN.4/Sub.2/SR.16, at 14 (1947).

[146] *Id.* at 16.

[147] S. Ramadan, *supra* note 20, at 159, in which the author cites L.F.L. Oppenheim, International Law 713-16 (1955).

[148] An examination of the following human rights treaties signed or ratified by the Muslim states shows that, if the need for securing human rights by international obligation arises, those states can and do take part in it. *See* Appendix III *infra*.

today than it used to be, especially in the light of the existence of the United Nations and the International Court of Justice.[149]

The Statute of the International Court of Justice states that one of the sources of international law is "the general principles of law recognized by civilized nations."[150] It is important therefore to understand the Islamic concepts of human rights since they will be part of those "general principles" that the Court will apply.[151] Greater significance must be attributed to the fact that all Muslim and Islamic states are signatories of the Charter of the United Nations; which, in its Preamble, states: "We, the peoples of the United Nations, determine to . . . reaffirm faith in the fundamental human rights, in the dignity and worth of the human person, and in the equal rights of men and women." Article 55 of the Charter provides:

> With a view to the creation of conditions of stability and well-being which are necessary for peaceful and friendly relations among nations based on respect for the principle of equal rights and self-determination of peoples, the United Nations shall promote: (a) higher standards of living, full employment, and conditions of economic and social progress and development; (b) solutions of international economic, social, health, and related problems; and international cultural and educational cooperation; and (c) universal respect for, and observance of, human rights and fundamental freedoms for all without distinction as to race, sex, language, or religion.

In Article 56 it states:

> All Members pledge themselves to take joint and separate action in cooperation with the Organization for the achievement of the purposes set forth in Article 55.

To recognize that man has certain inalienable and fundamental rights, which must be secured and protected against the overbearing power of a government overstepping its boundaries, is in conformity with Islamic principles.[152] The concept of the inherent dignity of man as enunciated in the United Nations Charter, the Universal Declaration of Human Rights, the Nuremberg principles, the Genocide Convention and other human rights conventions are indeed acceptable to the ideal Islamic state and to most Muslim states.[153]

But as discussed above with respect to the individual and human rights, they are subject to the purposes and objectives of a given society, subject to the due process of law.[154] Reference to absolutism is incompatible with Islamic relativism in individual rights; with the exception of the primacy of certain rights enunciated

[149] Rabbath, *Pour Une Theorie du Droit International Musulman*, 6 REVUE EGYPTIENNE DE DROIT INTERNATIONAL 1 (1950).

[150] I.C.J. STAT. 38

[151] *See, e.g.*, Friedman, *The Uses of "General Principles" in the Development of International Law* 57 AM. J. INT'L. L. 279 (1963); Lord McNair, *The General Principles Recognized by Civilized Nations*, 33 BRIT. Y. B. INT'L. L. 1 (1957).

[152] *See supra* note 62.

[153] *See* text accompanying notes 72-120 *supra* and Appendix III. For international criminal law conventions protecting human rights *see* M. C. Bassiouni, *International Criminal Law: A Draft International Criminal Code* (1980).

[154] *Supra* text accompanying notes 88, 89 and 90.

in the *Qu'ran*, with which no authority can tamper. Islamic tradition agrees with Chief Justice Marshall that when in doubt of the construction of a consititution, the courts will favor personal liberty.[155]

The rights enunciated above are protected by Islam if their objective is to insure a fair trial.[156] The specific standards of application will have to be adjusted, however, to a system of justice different from the Common Law or Romanist Civilist tradition, but the Islamic legal system is not the only one which differs from that tradition.[157] The specific guarantees stated above are intended to protect the freedom of an individual from injustice from his accusers or from his judge, and insure equality before the law, and fairness of trial.

Providing the shield of due process of law to individuals is also established by Islamic law. Its exercise and application, however, must be by an Islamic court which would take into account the specifics of Islamic *Shari'a*.

The Key to Islamic justice is the judge. His is the highest duty for he is answerable to Allah in the most rigorous way for the duties of his office. On the duty of Judges to deal equally with all persons rich and poor, mighty and weak the *Qu'ran* says: "Oh David! Lo! We have set thee as a vicerory in the earth, therefore, judge aright between mankind and follow not desire that it beguile thee away from the way of Allah."[158]

A common saying in Islamic tradition is "you can give the unjust law to the just judge, but you cannot give the just law to the unjust judge."[159]

It must be noted that the writings on Islamic criminal justice are essentially on substantive criminal law and little can be found in the specialized legal literature on criminal procedure. Interestingly, rules of evidence are part of substantive criminal law because of a linkage between crimes and their specific proof (which differs depending on the crime).[160]

To the extent that international conventions protect the same rights protected by *Shari'a*, nothing impairs an Islamic or Muslim state from becoming a signatory to any international convention on the protection of fundamental human rights.

The doctrine that an individual may also be a subject of the law of nations and

---

[155] *Ex parte* Burford, 7 U.S. (3 Cranch) 448 (1806) and 2 OUDA, *supra* note 6, at 307-341 and *supra* note 90. *See* M. QUTB, ISLAM: THE MISUNDERSTOOD RELIGION 249 (Arabic 6th ed., trans. 1976).

[156] On the administration of justice *see* A. A. ali-Mawardi, *Ahkam al-Sultaniyya* (b. 1058 A.D.) translated by E. Fagnan, LES STATUS GOVERNEMUTAUX ET REGLES DE DROIT PUBLIC ET ADMINISTRATIF (1915).

[157] *See e.g.*, M.C. BASSIOUNI and V. SAVITSKI, THE CRIMINAL JUSTICE SYSTEM OF THE U.S.S.R. (1979); and STRAFVERFAHRENSRECHT (1977).

[158] IBN KHALDOUN, THE MUQADIMAH: AN INTRODUCTION TO HISTORY 452-454 (trans. F. Rosenthal, 2d ed. 1967), quoting a letter from Omar the Third Caliph (but the first to appoint judges) to Abu-Musa-al-Ashari appointed judge of al-Kufah in which he admonishes and instructs the judge to perform his functions in a manner which is totally consonant with contemporary standards of fairness and impartiality, rectitude and temperance.

[159] No source can be found for this common saying of which Islamic tradition is replete because it is more an oral than a written tradition.

[160] *See e.g. Manar al-Sabil* an explanation of the text al-Dalil in accordance with the school of Imam Ahmad ibn Hanbal by Sheikh Ibralim ibn Muhammad ibn Salin ibn Duyan, a text required by the *Qadis* (judge) of the *Shari'a* courts of Saudi-Arabia; for an abbreviated translation with commentary *see* G. BAROODY, CRIME AND PUNISHMENT UNDER ISLAMIC LAW (1961).

may be endowed directly with rights and burdened with obligations under international law is not incompatible with Islam, if those rights and obligations emanating from the international law are not in conflict with Islamic law. However, under Islamic law, principles of Islamic international law are part of general law and, therefore, obligations arising under international law are as equally enforceable and applicable as those of national law.[161] The question does not, however, arise with respect to substantive rights of due process and fair trial but with respect to the sanction for their violation. The Islamic criminal justice system is as stated above, goal-oriented and not process-oriented. To establish a system by which a "procedural defect" can be the basis for the release of a person who otherwise would not be released is to substitute the rule of form for the rule of substance and would ultimately detract from the search for truth and individualized justice. Pursuant to the Islamic criminal justice concept, the search for justice is the search for the truth and veracity of the facts and matters stated and not for that portion of truth which certain rules of form may allow or disallow. Errors of form and defects of form rather than being permitted to constitute an absolute bar to admissibility, are best left to the judges who will determine the extent of their effect on the truth, the veracity of the matter and the credibility of the evidence presented. In this respect, both the Islamic and the civil law concept differ from the United States approach[162] and is closer to the English legal system in which procedural defects of form are not treated as an absolute bar to the admissibility of such evidence, but are left for the determination of the judge guided by the *Judge's Handbook on Evidence.*

CONCLUSION

International conventions on the protection of human rights, and in particular the Universal Declaration on Human Rights and the International Covenant on Civil and Political Rights, establish minimum standards which reflect contemporary values. Their purposes are unquestionably within the scope of Islamic law, though the general frame of references of all human rights convention is the western Judeo-Christian tradition. Other cultures, particularly third world ones have no visible effect in these prescriptions. As in the legal frame of reference, it is a combination of the Romanist and Common Law traditions with greater emphasis of the later and more particular on the United States model of constitutional prescriptive approach. In that respect also, no other third world system has had any visible impact. This may have been due to the fact that the Islamic legal system has since the Middle Ages produced no impact on international and comparative law, and consequently, its impact on the shaping of international human rights law has been nil. Probably for the same reasons that Islamic law had no significance in the shaping of past medieval international law, it has had no meaningful growth in Muslim and Islamic states. Surely the subjugation of Muslim and Islamic states to colonialism has been a prime factor in produc-

---

[161] *See* RAMADAN, *supra* note 20.

[162] M. C. BASSIOUNI, CRIMINAL LAW AND ITS PROCESSES, 370-375 (1969).

ing that result but another reason has been the closing of *Ijtihad* (reasoning by analogy and progressive interpretation of precedents) as of the Middle Ages which brought jurisprudential and doctrinal developments to a virtual standstill. The combination of these factors resulted in that Muslim states moved in the direction of codification of their laws and the enactement of penal codes in accordance with western models.[163]

The Administration of Justice in some Islamic states such as Saudi-Arabia remained based on traditional Islamic law,[164] with that country's Higher *Shari'a* Court engaging in jurisprudential development.

In the procedural area, Muslim states have adopted the western model with different variations in which judicial administration is not much different from the system and practice of most countries who follow that model whether they now be western European or socialist European, [165] or Asian states.[166]

With the admission of all Muslim and Islamic States to the U.N. and their adherence to its Charter, these states have accepted the obligations of the Charter among which are those relating to the protection of human rights. Such human rights have subsequently been embodied in various international conventions which have been signed and/or ratified by a substantial number of Muslim and Islamic states (see Appendix III). These internationally protected human rights arising out of these conventions and the United Nations Charter are binding obligations upon Muslim and Islamic states. Nothing in Islamic international law precludes the applicability of these international obligations to the domestic legal system of an Islamic state provided these obligations are not contrary to *Shari'a*.[167] The thesis of this article is that nothing in the spirit of *Shari'a* precludes the recognition of these rights. It is in their application that *Shari'a* law would differ from other legal systems. Chief among these differences are the automatic application of sanctions for violation of procedural defects,[168] limits on the discretionary powers of the judge,[169] and the evidentiary question such as oath-taking,[170] and the interpretation of "cruel and unusual punishment"[171] with

---

[163] *See* MOSTAFA, *supra* note 3; H. LIEBESNEY, THE LAW OF THE NEAR AND MIDDLE EAST (1975). In the case of Egypt, which has been the second Muslim state, Turkey being the first, to have secularized its criminal law and procedure, *see* Law No. 58 of 1937 (with subsequent amendments), and M. N. Hosni, *Sharh Qanun al-Qubat* (General Part, 4th ed. 1977 and Special Part, 1978).

[164] *See supra* note 160.

[165] *See e.g., supra* BASSIOUNI and SAVISKI note 157, and Bassiouni, *supra* note 79.

[166] *E.g.*, CRIMINAL STATUTES OF JAPAN (transl., The Supreme Court of Japan, 1968); OUTLINE OF CRIMINAL JUSTICE IN JAPAN (transl. Supreme Court of Japan, 1975); Dando, *System of Discretionary Prosecution in Japan* 18 AM. J. COMP.L. 518 (1970). THE ADMINISTRATION OF JUSTICE IN THAILAND (Thai Bar Association, 1969); COUNTRY LAW STUDY FOR THAILAND (U.S./D.O.D. 1971). COUNTRY LAW STUDY—KOREA (U.S./D.O.D. 1971).

[167] *See* RAMADAN *supra* note 20; HAMIDULLAH, *supra* note 23; AL-GHUNAIMI, *supra* note 129; and ARMANAZI, *supra* note 143.

[168] *See supra* note 162 and accompanying text.

[169] *See supra* notes 156-160 and accompanying text.

[170] *See supra* note 90.

[171] For a study of "Cruel and Unusual Punishment" in International and comparative law, *see* Bassiouni, *An Appraisal of Torture in International Law and Practice: The Need for an International Convention for the Prevention and Suppression of Torture* 48 REVUE INTERNATIONALE DE DROIT PENAL 23-114 (1977); and for a U.S. appraisal, see M. C. BASSIOUNI, SUBSTANTIVE CRIMINAL LAW 41-45 and 117-120 (1978).

respect to sanctions such as stoning for adultery, cutting of the hand for theft, and corporal punishment such as whipping and flogging for other crimes.

Certainly none of the fundamentals of "due process" and "fairness" as is understood in the liberal tradition of the Common Law and Romanist systems would be incompatible with the *Shari'a*. What is, however, significantly lacking in Muslim and Islamic states is an effort at progressive codification of Islamic criminal justice (procedure and administration) which could sift through and distill the law and practices of Islam and adapt it to a contemporary framework which would keep faith with the past while setting the foundations for the future. The irony about that vacuum is that the flexibility of Islam has been ignored by its proponents, who have instead relied on the rigidity of past traditions as necessarily binding on the future, and that is simply contrary to the spirit of Islam.

There is a commonplace belief among contemporary Muslim thinkers who seek to restore a system of orthodox Islamic justice, that Islamic criminal justice is less process and more substantively oriented, and as a consequence that judges have almost unbridled power. Surely if such judges can be found to fulfill the requirements of Umar as did Abu-Musa (*see supra* 31, 32) then they are correct. That expectation is embodied in an old popular Arabic proverb which states "you can give the unjust law (to apply) to the just judge, but you cannot give the just law (to apply) to the unjust judge." The "just judge" being Umar's model. But the exigencies of modern life make that pristine model an unattainable ideal. Not because such judges cannot be found, but because all the inarticulate premises of uncomplicated societies are inexistent in today's urban industrial society and the clock of time cannot be turned back no matter how nostalgic one may get about these simpler and presumably better and happier times. The volume of legal matters, the nature of administrative structures needed to support a system of justice with its personnel and costs, distances and problems of communication and movement, the human and economic burdens and costs of litigation, the erosion of commonly shared values, the demands of complex societies on its members, and certainly the type of impersonal society which has developed in the cities, are all among the reasons why the best of judges with the best of intentions have to rely more on rules and processes than on ad hoc approaches and on their personal wisdom. But also worthy of mention is the fact that the large number of judges that any judicial system in a modern society must employ is such that one can hardly expect to find so many paragons of virtue, knowledge, temperament, disposition and wisdom as in Umar's model who are desirous of being judges. That is why Islam has provided for process principles and rules. These principles and rules are applicable to contemporary needs. Islam sets the models, as Umar's ideal judge, it establishes the principles and guidelines in the *Shari'a*, and sets down many specific rules on evidence and procedure; and it also lays down the basis for historical evolutionary application through the sources of interpretation of the *Shari'a* (discussed above). To believe that Islam is static is to deny it, timeless and universality. Thus to believe that true Islam is only how it was applied in medieval times is heretical. As much so as the belief by reformist that the *Shari'a* is somewhat irrelevant, or that it should be reinterpreted. It is not

Islam that needs reinterpretation, it is its application that needs to be reconsidered. And the principles of Islamic justice, as well as the *Shari'a's* specific rules on the processes of justice offer ample support for its evolutionary application to the needs of contemporary times with all due regard for the rights of the accused and the guilty, for the rights the victim, and for those of society.

APPENDIX I

MUSLIM AND ISLAMIC STATES AND MUSLIM POPULATION OF THE WORLD*

Country	Pop. in Millions	Percentage of Total Pop.
Afghanistan	14.4	99
Albania	1.8	76
Algeria	17.3	97
Bahrain	0.3	91
Bangladesh	70.8	85
Benin	0.5	16
Brunei	0.1	60
Bulgaria	0.9	11
Burma	1.3	4
Cameroon	1.0	15
Cen. Afric. Emp.	0.1	5
Chad	2.1	50
China	17.9	2
Comoro	0.3	80
Cyprus	0.1	18
Djibouti	0.1	94
Egypt	35.4	91
Ethiopia	11.8	40
Gambia	0.5	90
Ghana	2.0	19
Guinea	3.1	65
Guinea-Bissau	0.2	30
India	80.0	13
Indonesia	123.2	90
Iran	34.1	98
Iraq	11.2	95
Israel	0.4	8
Ivory Coast	1.8	25
Jordan	2.7	93
Kenya	1.3	9
Kuwait	1.1	90
Lebanon	1.4	51
Liberia	0.3	15
Libya	2.3	98

*Muslim Peoples, *A World Ethnographic Survey*, ed. R. Weekes; Time Magazine, Vol. 113, No. 16, April 16, 1979, p. 43; Time Magazine, April 16, 1965. Some additional changes were made by the author based on other secondary sources. *See also*, H.S. Haddad and B. K. Nijim, *The Arab World: A Handbook* (1978).

Country	Pop. in Millions	Percentage of Total Pop.
Madagascar	0.6	7
Malawi	0.8	15
Malaysia	6.5	50
Maldives	0.1	100
Mali	3.5	60
Mauritania	1.4	96
Mauritius	0.2	17
Mongolia	0.1	10
Morocco	18.3	99
Mozambique	1.0	10
Niger	4.2	85
North Yemen	5.5	99
Oman	0.8	100
Pakistan	72.3	93
Philippines	2.3	5
Qatar	0.1	100
Saudi Arabia	7.2	95
Senegal	4.3	82
Sierra Leone	1.0	30
Singapore	0.4	15
Somalia	3.4	99
South Yemen	1.6	90
Sri Lanka	1.0	7
Sudan	11.7	72
Syria	6.8	87
Tanzania	3.8	24
Thailand	2.0	4
Togo	0.2	7
Tunisia	6.1	99
Turkey	41.1	98
Uganda	0.7	6
United Arab Emirates	0.2	92
U.S.S.R.	50.0	19
U.S.A.	6.4	3
Upper Volta	1.4	22
West Bank and Gaza	1.1	84
Yugoslavia	4.1	19

N.B. An estimated 10.0—12.0 million Muslims inhabit western Europe, in particular: The U.K., France, the Federal Republic of Germany, Italy and Belgium. An estimated 10.0—12.0 are distributed throughout other countries.

APPENDIX II

STATES IN WHOSE CONSTITUTION IT IS DECLARED TO BE *MUSLIM* OR *ISLAMIC*

Algeria	The Constitution of July, 1977 Table I, Chapter I, Article 2.
Bahrain	The Constitution of December, 1974 Part I, Article I.
Egypt	The Constitution of May, 1972 Part I, Article 2.
Iran	The Constitution of December, 1971 Article 2.
Iraq	The Constitution of February, 1974 Chapter I, Article 4.
Jordan	The Constitution of May, 1972 Chapter I, Article 2.
Kuwait	The Constitution of December, 1971 Part I, Article 2.
Libya	The Constitution of February, 1974 Chapter I, Article 2.
Malaysia	The Constitution of July, 1977 Part I, Article 3.
Maldives	The Constitution of October, 1976 Article 2.
Mauritania	The Constitution of October, 1973 Title I, Article 1.
Morocco	The Constitution of December, 1971 Preamble.
Oman	(No written constitution) Stated in 1st paragraph, p. 1, Law of December, 1974
Pakistan	The Constitution of July, 1973 Part I, Article I.
Qatar	The Constitution of July, 1973 Part I, Article 1.
Saudi Arabia	No Constitution Declares itself an Islamic State.
Singapore	The Constitution of March, 1976 Article 6.
Somalia	The Constitution of September, 1971 Article I.
Sudan	The Constitution of February, 1974 Part I, Article 9.
Syria	The Constitution of June, 1974 Chapter I, Part 1, Article 3.
Tunisia	The Constitution of July, 1977 Preamble.
United Arab Emirates	The Constitution of July, 1973 Chapter I, Article 7.
Yemen Arab Republic	The Constitution of December, 1971 Chapter I, Article I.

Afghanistan, Bangladesh and Turkey consider themselves Muslim states. Lebanon has a confessional system in which Islam is partially recognized as a state religion.

APPENDIX III

International Human Rights Conventions and signatory states with Muslim populations, and Islamic and Muslim States as identified in Appendix I and II.

STATES	(1) International Covenant on Economic, Social and Cultural Rights	(2) International Covenant on Civil and Political Rights	(3) Optional Protocol to the International Covenant on Civil and Political Rights	(4) Covention on the Prevention and Punishment of the Crime of Genocide	(5) Convention on the Non-Applicability of Statutory Limitations to War Crimes and Crimes against Humanity	(6) International Convention on the Elimination of All Forms of Racial Discrimination	(7) Convention relating to the Status of Refugees	(8) Protocol relating to the Status of Refugees	(9) Convention relating to the Status of Stateless Persons	(10) Convention on the Reduction of Statelessness	(11) Convention on the Political Rights of Women	(12) Convention on the Nationality of Married Women	(13) Convention on Consent to Marriage, Minimum Age for Marriage and Registration of Marriages	(14) Convention on the International Right of Correction	Slavery Convention of 25 September 1926: (15) Protocol amending Slavery Convention	Slavery Convention of 25 September 1926: (16) Slavery Convention as amended	(17) Supplementary Convention on the Abolition of Slavery, the Slave Trade, and Institutions and Practices Similar to Slavery	(18) Convention for the Suppression of the Traffic in Persons and of the Exploitation of the Prostitution of Others	(19) International Convention on the Suppression and Punishment of the Crime of Apartheid
Entry into force	*3 January 1976*	*23 March 1976*	*23 March 1976*	*12 January 1951*	*11 November 1970*	*4 January 1969*	*22 April 1954*	*4 October 1967*	*6 June 1960*	*13 December 1975*	*7 July 1954*	*11 August 1958*	*9 December 1964*	*24 August 1962*	*7 December 1953*	*7 July 1955*	*30 April 1957*	*25 July 1951*	*18 July 1976*
Afghanistan				X							X				X	X	X		
Albania				X	X						X	X				X	X	X	
Algeria	S	S		X		X	X	X	X							X	X	X	S
Bahrain																			

Bangladesh							S	X	X					X						X
Benin												S				X	X		S	
Burma					X															
Cen. Afr. Emp.							X	X	X			X						X		
Chad							X													X
China[a]																				
Comoro																				
Cyprus		X	X	S			X	X	X			X	X		X			X		
Democratic Yemen							X													S
Djibouti								X	X											
Egypt		S	S		X		X								X	X	X	X	X	X
Ethiopia					X		X	X	X			X			X		X	X		
Gambia								X	X											
Ghana					X		X	X	X			X	X					X		
Guinea		S	S	S		X	X	X	X	X		S	S	S	S	X	X	X	X	X
Guinea-Bissau								X	X											
India					X	X	X					X	S			X	X	X	X	X
Indonesia												X								
Iran		X	X		X		X	X	X									X	S	
Iraq		X	X		X		X									X	X	X	X	X
Israel		S	S		X		S	X	X	X	S	X	X	S		X	X	X	X	
Ivory Coast							X	X	X											
Jordan		X	X		X		X										X	X	X	S
Kenya		X	X			X		X												S
Kuwait							X										X	X	X	X
Lebanon		X	X		X		X					X								
Liberia		S	S		X		X	X		X		S				X	X	S	S	X

Continued

Appendix III (continued)

STATES	(1) International Covenant on Economic, Social and Cultural Rights	(2) International Covenant on Civil and Political Rights	(3) Optional Protocol to the International Covenant on Civil and Political Rights	(4) Covention on the Prevention and Punishment of the Crime of Genocide	(5) Convention on the Non-Applicability of Statutory Limitations to War Crimes and Crimes against Humanity	(6) International Convention on the Elimination of All Forms of Racial Discrimination	(7) Convention relating to the Status of Refugees	(8) Protocol relating to the Status of Refugees	(9) Convention relating to the Status of Stateless Persons	(10) Convention on the Reduction of Statelessness	(11) Convention on the Political Rights of Women	(12) Convention on the Nationality of Married Women	(13) Convention on Consent to Marriage, Minimum Age for Marriage and Registration of Marriages	(14) Convention on the International Right of Correction	Slavery Convention of 25 September 1926: (15) Protocol amending Slavery Convention	Slavery Convention of 25 September 1926: (16) Slavery Convention as amended	(17) Supplementary Convention on the Abolition of Slavery, the Slave Trade, and Institutions and Practices Similar to Slavery	(18) Convention for the Suppression of the Traffic in Persons and of the Exploitation of the Prostitution of Others	(19) International Convention on the Suppression and Punishment of the Crime of Apartheid
Entry into force	*3 January 1976*	*23 March 1976*	*23 March 1976*	*12 January 1951*	*11 November 1970*	*4 January 1969*	*22 April 1954*	*4 October 1967*	*6 June 1960*	*13 December 1975*	*7 July 1954*	*11 August 1958*	*9 December 1964*	*24 August 1962*	*7 December 1953*	*7 July 1955*	*30 April 1957*	*25 July 1951*	*18 July 1976*
Libyan Arab Jamahiriya	S	S				S										X		X	X
Madagascar	X	X	X			X	X				X					X	X		X
Malawi											X	X				X	X	X	
Malaysia												X					X		

Maldives																				
Mali		X	X		X		X	X	X			X	X	X		X	X	X	X	X
Mauritania							S					X								
Mauritius		X	X	X			X					X	X				X	X		
Mongolia		X	X		X	X	X					X					X	X		X
Morocco		*S*	*S*		X		X	X	X			X				X	X	X	X	
Mozambique																				
Nepal					X		X					X					X	X		X
Niger							X	X	X			X		X		X	X	X	X	
Nigeria						X	X	X	X								X	X		X
Oman																				S
Pakistan					X		X					X	S				X	X	X	
Qatar							X													X
Saudi Arabia					X												X	X		
Senegal		S	S	S			X	X	X			X								X
Singapore													X					X	X	
Somalia							X													X
Sri Lanka					X								X	S			X	X	X	
Sudan							*X*	X	X								X	X		X
Syrian Arab Republic		X	X		X		X									X	X	X	X	X
Thailand												X								
Togo							X	X	X											
Tunisia		X	X		X	X	X	X	X	X		X	X	X			X	X		X
Turkey					X		S	X	X			X				X	X	X		
Uganda								X	X	X			X				X	X		S

Continued

Appendix III (continued)

STATES	(1) International Covenant on Economic, Social and Cultural Rights	(2) International Covenant on Civil and Political Rights	(3) Optional Protocol to the International Covenant on Civil and Political Rights	(4) Covention on the Prevention and Punishment of the Crime of Genocide	(5) Convention on the Non-Applicability of Statutory Limitations to War Crimes and Crimes against Humanity	(6) International Convention on the Elimination of All Forms of Racial Discrimination	(7) Convention relating to the Status of Refugees	(8) Protocol relating to the Status of Refugees	(9) Convention relating to the Status of Stateless Persons	(10) Convention on the Reduction of Statelessness	(11) Convention on the Political Rights of Women	(12) Convention on the Nationality of Married Women	(13) Convention on Consent to Marriage, Minimum Age for Marriage and Registration of Marriages	(14) Convention on the International Right of Correction	Slavery Convention of 25 September 1926: (15) Protocol amending Slavery Convention	Slavery Convention of 25 September 1926: (16) Slavery Convention as amended	(17) Supplementary Convention on the Abolition of Slavery, the Slave Trade, and Institutions and Practices Similar to Slavery	(18) Convention for the Suppression of the Traffic in Persons and of the Exploitation of the Prostitution of Others	(19) International Convention on the Suppression and Punishment of the Crime of Apartheid
Entry into force	*3 January 1976*	*23 March 1976*	*23 March 1976*	*12 January 1951*	*11 November 1970*	*4 January 1969*	*22 April 1954*	*4 October 1967*	*6 June 1960*	*13 December 1975*	*7 July 1954*	*11 August 1958*	*9 December 1964*	*24 August 1962*	*7 December 1953*	*7 July 1955*	*30 April 1957*	*25 July 1951*	*18 July 1976*
U.S.S.R.	X	X		X	X	X					X	X				X	X	X	X
U.A.E.						X													X
United Republic of Cameroon				X	X	X	X												X
United Republic of Tanzania	X	X				X	X	X			X	X				X	X		X

U.S.A.		*S*	*S*		S		S		X			X		S		X	X	X		
Upper Volta					X		X							X					X	S
Yemen																				
Yugoslavia		X	X		X	X	X	X	X	X		X	X	X	X	X	X	X	X	X
Zambia							X	X	X	X		X	X				X	X		

X Ratification, accession, notification of succession, acceptance or definitive signature.

S Signature not yet followed by ratification.

S X Action taken in 1977.

D Declaration recognizing the competence of the Human Rights Committee under Article 41 of the International Covenant on Civil and Political Rights.

See, U.N. Doc. ST/HR/4, *Human Rights International Instruments*, Signatores, Ratifications, Accessions, etc. 1 January, 1978.

THE RIGHT OF THE INDIVIDUAL TO PERSONAL SECURITY IN ISLAM

Osman Abd-el-Malek al-Saleh

INTRODUCTION

The individual right to personal security in any state should include those guarantees which enable a person to live his daily life and plan his future without the threat of arrest and imprisonment, or the fear of severe and unjust punishment.

The individual right to personal security means legal security for the individual in relation to state authorities. It is the protective shield for all forms of personal freedoms. Without such rights personal freedoms could not exist especially in an era in which modern technology is largely state controlled and has been used to explore and, to varying degrees, control human existence.

The state has also assumed a greater role in the area of criminal justice by enlarging the list of criminal acts to include newly-defined political, economic, and social crimes. As a result many more citizens may face criminal prosecution. Thus, the individual is increasingly vulnerable to the power of the state.[1]

In spite of the magnitude of this phenomenon, it is difficult to find a systematic study in any of the positive law states (including common-law, civilist and socialist) which deals with the right of the individual to personal security.[2] Likewise, the treatises on the jurisprudence of the *Shari'a* do not offer an adequate study of this subject. Although it is possible to make a thorough study with respect to the right of individual security under positive law, this task is more difficult under Islam because the specifics of this subject are scattered throughout the textbooks on Islamic jurisprudence and are usually treated in a fragmented manner.

Accordingly, the present study has three principal purposes:

---

[1] SAMI SADIQ AL-MULLA, I'TIRAF AL-MUTTAHAM [THE DEFENDANT'S CONFESSION] 400-499 (2d ed., Cairo: al-Matba'ah al-Alamiyah, 1975), [hereinafter referred to as AL-MULLA].

[2] With the exception of Professor Burdeau's writing on the right to individual safety in the French system. *See* GEORGES BURDEAU, LES LIBERTES PUBLIQUES [PUBLIC LIBERTIES] 199 *et seq.* 3ème ed. (Paris: Librairie Générale de Droit et de Jurisprudence, 1966), [hereinafter referred to as BURDEAU].

1. to define the contours of the right of the individual to personal security in light of the theories of incrimination and penology under Islamic law;

2. to outline the right of personal security in Islamic criminal procedure;

3. to examine the principle of legality as the foundation of the right to personal security in Islam.

PERSONAL SECURITY UNDER ISLAMIC THEORIES OF INCRIMINATION AND PENOLOGY

INTRODUCTION

Islamic jurisprudence is unique in guaranteeing the right of individual security. Without the benefit of security and discipline, social order and individual development would be impossible. Islam guarantees five essential things to all persons and prevents unwarranted infringement of them by the state. These include: (1) religion, (2) life, (3) mind, (4) posterity, and (5) property.[3]

Islamic law provides the organizational framework for society and thereby appoints and maintains the legal relationship between individuals and protects the interests of one person from being attacked by another. It also guarantees personal security when the individual is accused of a crime by defining the relationship between the individual and the state. Islamic law embodies basic principles of justice aimed at balancing the interests of the state in enforcing the criminal laws and the interests of the individual by protecting his fundamental rights to peace and security. Positive legal systems did not arrive at this balancing of interests until many centuries later. In this respect, the *Shari'a* precedes all other legal formulations. In this contrast, the most important principles laid down in the *Shari'a* are:

1) The principle of criminal responsibility (according to certain basic rules);

2) The principle of the relationship of crime and punishment; and,

3) The principle of the non-retroactivity of criminal laws.

---

[3] In his explanation of the grounds of incrimination and punishment in Islamic law, AL-GHAZZALI writes:

> Obtaining benefit and preventing injury are human aims, concerned with human welfare only in human terms, whereas what we mean by interest (*maslahah*) is conservation of the aims of the *Shari'a*. The aim of the *Shari'a* in regard to men is fivefold: to conserve his religion, life, reason, offspring, and material wealth. All, then, that secures conservation of these five elements is an interest (*maslahah*), and all that jeopardizes them is corruption (*mafsadah*), prevention of which is an interest. The preservation of these five interests falls within the category of necessities—the utmost in interests... It is unfeasible for any creed or law designed for the betterment of mankind not to outlaw all attempts at denying or frustrating these five elements.

1 AL-GHAZZALI, AL-MUSTASFA MIN'ILM AL-'USUL, 286-287 (Cairo: al-Matba'ah al-Amiriyah, 1894), [hereinafter referred to as AL-GHAZZALI]. *See also* 2 MUHAMMAD ABU ZAHRAH, AL-JARIMAH WA-AL-'UQUBAH FI AL-FIQH AL-ISLAMI [CRIME AND PUNISHMENT IN ISLAMIC JURISPRUDENCE], (Cairo: Dar al-Fikr al-'Arabi, 1974); 2 FI-AL-'UQUBAH [PUNISHMENT], 38 *et seq.* [hereinafter referred to as ABU ZAHRAH].

THE PRINCIPLE OF INDIVIDUAL CRIMINAL RESPONSIBILITY

1. *The Meaning of the Principle*

The individual cannot be secure if he must answer for crimes he did not commit. Thus, the principle of individual criminal responsibility can be adjudged as one of the foundations of individual security. This principle means that the actor himself is the only person who can be accused of a particular crime and no one else, and no one shall escape responsibility irrespective of blood ties or friendship to the victim (or to the judge or ruler). A person who has taken part in a prohibited act whether he is the principal or an accomplice must be incriminated according to the rules of accountability.[4]

The *Qu'ran* repeatedly sets forth the principle of individual responsibility in the following verses:

1) And that man hath only that for which he maketh effort.[5]
2) Whoso doth right, it is for his soul and whoso doth wrong, it is against it.[6]
3) Each soul earneth on its own account.[7]
4) No burdened soul can bear another's burden.[8]
5) He who doth wrong will have the recompense thereof.[9]

The *Sunna* also confirms this principle. The Prophet said to Abi-Ramhah and his son, "He does not commit a crime against him." The Prophet also proclaimed, "A soul is not held responsible for acts committed by his father or by his brother."

2. *The Perspectives of Islamic Law and Positive Law Compared*

Islam developed and applied the principle of individual responsibility fourteen centuries ago, while its inception in positive law took place after the

---

[4] Evidently many jurists do not distinguish between the principle of individual criminal responsibility and the rule of unaccountability for acts committed by others (*le principe de l'irresponsabilité pénale du fait d'autrui*), on the one hand, and the principle of the individualization of penalties (*le principe de la personalité des peines*), on the other. They offer examples which are considered to be exceptions to the principle of the individualization of punishment, but in fact they are exceptions to the principle of individual criminal responsibility and that of unaccountability for the acts of others.

The two cases should however be differentiated. The principle of the individualization of punishment indicates that the person who committed the crime is the only one who should suffer punishment. Any departure from this rule means that punishment may extend further to reach persons other than the culprit without recourse to the law. Such an application nullifies the culprit's personal responsibility for the committed act which is not added to his criminal record. In contrast with that, the principle of individual criminal responsibility means that a person is not personally responsible for acts committed by others. Departure from this principle means holding a person accountable for a criminal act committed by another. However, this responsibility is presumed, for it is not determined nor does it serve as a basis for punishment, until the person is found guilty in court. And contrary to the previous case, the crime is recorded among his previous convictions (*son casier judiciaire*). It is evident therefore, that any departure from the principle of individual criminal responsibility is much more dangerous than departing from the principle of the individualization of penalties. On this question *see* ROGER MERLE AND ANDRE VITU, TRAITE DE DROIT CRIMINEL [TREATISE ON CRIMINAL LAW] 407, 507 (Paris: Cujas, 1974), [hereinafter referred to as MERLE AND VITU].

[5] *Surat al-Najm* LIII:39.

[6] *Surat Fusilat* XLI:46.

[7] *Surat al-An'am* VI:165.

[8] *Surat al-Fatir* XXXV:18 (or VI:165).

[9] *Surat al-Nisaa* IV:123.

French revolution.[10] Before that, a person was held responsible not only for acts he had committed, but also for acts committed by others, even though he had not taken part in them and had no control over the offender. Thus, a whole family could be held responsible for a crime committed by one of its members.[11]

THE PRINCIPLE OF LEGALITY OF CRIMES AND PUNISHMENT[12]

1. *The Meaning of the Principle of Legality and Its Importance to Individual Security*

In general the principle of legality of crimes and punishment (*nullum crimen nulla poena sine lege*) means that no person can be accused of a crime or suffer punishment except as specified by law. This principle also implies that crimes and punishments can only be defined by an arm of government having legislative powers.

The legality principle protects individual security by ensuring basic individual liberties against the arbitrary and unwarranted intrusion of the state. It also limits the power of the judge since he can impose no penalty except as provided by law, regardless of the degree to which the crime offends public morality. Law is, therefore, the dividing line between what is permitted and what is forbidden, and it alone in the temporal world is sovereign. No person can be subjected to punishment for an act or omission not expressly declared to be criminal and punishable prior to its occurrence. This principle is regarded as so basic to Islamic law that most constitutions of Moslem states provide for it in specifying individual rights and freedoms.[13]

2. *The Primacy of Islam in Establishing the Principle of Legality*

By contrast to positive legal systems which did not embody the principle of legality until the end of the eighteenth century,[14] Islam established this principle some fourteen centuries ago. Its existence under Islamic law is shown by the following passages from the *Qu'ran*:

---

[10] The principle of individual responsibility was legislated in France by the French Revolution in the Act of January 21, 1790, and the Constitution of 1791. *See* AL'SA'ID MUSTAFA AL-SA'ID, AL-AHKAM AL-'AMMAH FI QANUN AL-UQUBAT [THE GENERAL RULES IN THE PENAL CODE] 17 (4th ed. Egypt: Dar al-Ma'arif, 1962), [hereinafter referred to as AL-SA'ID].

[11] Compare for example, the old French Penal Code which considered uttering offensive words against Royalty as crimes punishable by death in addition to confiscating the property of the offender's family. *See* MERLE AND VITU, *supra* note 4, at 406.

[12] For further discussion of this principle under positive law, *see* AL-SA'ID, *supra* note 10, at 88 *et seq.*; and MERLE AND VITU *supra* note 4, at 103 *et seq. See also* 1 'ABD AL-QADIR 'AWDAH, AL-TASHRI' AL-JINA'I AL-ISLAMI [ISLAMIC CRIMINAL LEGISLATION] 117 *et seq.* (Cairo: Maktabat Dar al-'Urubah, 1960-63); and 1 ABU ZAHRAH, *supra* note 3, at 182 *et seq.*; and KHALID 'ABD AL-HAMID FARRAJ, DIRASAT MUQARANAH BAYNA AL-SHARI'AH AL-ISLAMIYAH WA-AL-QANUN AL-JINA'I: SHAR'IYAT AL-JARA'IM WA-AL-'UQUBAT [COMPARATIVE STUDIES BETWEEN ISLAMIC AND CRIMINAL LAW: THE LEGALITY OF CRIMES AND PENALTIES] (Alexandria, Egypt: Dar al-Ma'arif, 1976).

[13] *See, e.g.*, Article 32 of the CONSTITUTION OF KUWAIT; Article 20 of the CONSTITUTION OF BAHRAIN; and Article 27 of the CONSTITUTION OF THE UNITED ARAB EMIRATES.

[14] Some writers like Luis Jimenez de Asua trace the origin of this principle to the Magna Charta issued by King John of England in 1215. Actually, the Magna Charta does not include the principle of *nullum crimen nulla peona sine lege*. It does however contain other principles related to the legality of criminal procedure. In this regard, *see* MERLE AND VITU, *supra* note 4, at 103 (n. 3).

1) We never punish until we have sent a messenger.[15]

2) Messengers of good cheer and warning [were sent] in order that mankind might have no argument against Allah after the messengers. Allah is ever mighty and wise.[16]

3) And never did thy Lord destroy the towns until he had raised up in their mothertown a messenger reciting unto them.[17]

4) That I may warn you therewith, you and whomsoever it may reach.[18]

5) Every nation had its messenger raised up to warn them.[19]

Thus, the *Qu'ran*, the principle source of Islamic law, establishes the principle that no one accused of a crime can be punished unless he has been forewarned of the criminal nature of his conduct. That basic right to notice by means of a clear definition of the crime and its consequences is the essence of the principle of legality.[20]

3. *Application of the Principle of Legality in Islamic Law*

<u>The Effect of the Principle on *Hudud* and *Quesas* Crimes and *Diyya* (Compensation)</u>

There are seven *Hudud* crimes under Islamic law which carry fixed penalties: adultery, defamation, drinking wines, theft, *alhiraba* (rebellion), apostasy and oppression. The crimes which are subject to retaliation include murder, deliberate maiming, and deliberate wounding. The crimes punished with *Diyya* (compensation, also called "blood money") include crimes which are subject to retaliation but have been pardoned or vacated for a legal cause. These include quasi-murder, killing by mistake, unintentional maiming and unintentional wounding. Islamic law applies the principle of legality to each of these categories of crimes.

All of these crimes are expressly prohibited and the offenders are subject to punishment according to Islamic rules. Islamic law defines the penalties for each of these crimes and permits the judge no discretion once the offense is proved. Factors in aggravation or mitigation, such as the circumstances of the crime or the age and economic status of the offender, cannot be taken into account.[21]

<u>The Effect of the Legality Principle on the Crimes of *Ta'azir*[22]</u>

Concerning crimes of *Ta'azir*, the approach of Islamic law is to apply the

---

[15] *Surat Bani Isra'il* XVII:15.

[16] *Surat al-Nisaa* IV:165.

[17] *Surat al-Qasas* XXVIII:59.

[18] *Surat al-An'am* VI:19.

[19] *Surat al-Fatir* XXXV:25.

[20] The principle of "No legal consequence to the acts of the sane in mind prior to the advent of text" and the rule stating that "All things and acts are presumed permissible" are among the most fundamental rules of Islamic Law.

[21] *See* 1 ABU ZAHRAH, *supra* note 3, at 178 *et seq.*; and 1 'AWDAH, *supra* note 12, at 118 *et seq.*

[22] *See* 'ABD AL-'AZIZ 'AMIR, AL-TA'ZIR FI AL-SHARI'AH AL-ISLAMIYAH [REPROOF IN ISLAMIC LAW] (4th ed. Cairo: Dar al-Fikr al-'Arabi, 1969), [hereinafter referred to as 'AMIR].

principle of legality in a somewhat more limited manner. The application of the principle in this fashion can rarely result in a false incrimination and in that event it bars the imposition of penalty.[23]

Incrimination In general, *Ta'azir* cannot be imposed except in cases of disobedience, namely where an action is prohibited *per se* according to Islamic law. Nevertheless Islamic jurisprudence recognizes an exception to this general rule such that *Ta'azir* may be imposed for actions which are not prohibited *per se* if the general good so requires.

The principle of legality also has been applied to acts of disobedience to Islamic law. Such offenses are defined in the *Qu'ran* and in the tradition of the Prophet.[24] The only significant exception to the principle of legality is that of the offenses against the public welfare or public order. Such offenses are not explicitly designated in the sources of Islamic law but are determined on the basis of their presumed negative impact on the general welfare. If, in the discretion of the Muslim ruler or judge, no such adverse effect can be attributed to a given act, then it is not prohibited. The exercise of discretion is subject to several limitations. First, the action must in fact threaten the public welfare or public order. Harmless conduct cannot be deemed a crime. The ruler or judge must not be motivated by prejudice, and his decision must be consistent with the objectives of the law,[25] without undue infringement on the rights or freedoms guaranteed by Islamic law. Finally, the decision must contribute to the preservation of the five essential guarantees of Islam, namely: the practice of religion, the development of the mind, the right to have offspring and the right to possess wealth.[26]

Punishment The principle of legality is liberally construed and applied in Islamic law by assigning to all crimes a set of penalties, from which the judge can select the proper penalty according to the circumstances of each case, the background and personality of the accused and his inclination toward criminal conduct. In assessing those factors, the judge may rely on his own knowledge, perceptions and experiences, and he may consult any experts he deems necessary to better understand the technical problems involved or the psychology of the offender so that the proper penalty will be imposed and the ends of justice served.[27] The penalty must thereby be suited to the crime, the personality of the offender, his degree of social adaptation, and the protection of society.

The discretion of the ruler or judge with respect to the penalty imposed also is limited by several considerations. He must be aware, first of all, that the purposes of punishment in Islamic law are to deter criminal conduct and to reform and rehabilitate the offender. Islamic law prohibits all judicial conduct which is contrary to those ends, such as inflicting torture or humiliating the accused. It

---

[23] 1 'AWDAH, *supra* note 12, at 126.

[24] *Id.*

[25] On the subject of interest (*maslahah*), *see* 2 IBRAHIM IBN MUSA AL-SHATIBI, AL-I'TISAM 307 *et seq.* (Egypt: Matba'at al-Manar, 1913), [hereinafter referred to as AL-SHATIBI].

[26] 1 AL-GHAZZALI, *supra* note 3, at 286 *et seq.*

[27] *See* 'AMIR, *supra* note 22, at 531.

also excludes all punishment which may cause unnecessary harm.[28] The penalty should aim at the protection of lawful interests and must not be imposed to vindicate personal whims. Lastly, the penalty should be proportionate to the offense but without minimizing its gravity and at the same time ensuring that the punishment will not be more destructive to society than the crime itself.

Most jurists maintain that the *Hudud* penalties are considered the maximum and that *Ta'azir* should as a general rule not reach the limit of that penalty. This principle was first expressed by the Prophet: "He who imposes a *Had* penalty to a non-*Had* prescription is numbered among the oppressors." Thus, for example, theft is punished by severing the hand, but no *Ta'azir* penalty, particularly in money matters, goes to this extreme. Defamation is punished with eighty lashes, but abuse cannot reach this limit. Fornication is punished with one hundred lashes, but no other penalty of *Ta'azir* can reach this limit.[29] The judge must be certain that when a penalty is imposed, the offender is not punished in excess of the punishment legally imposed on his equals. It is better as a restraint on judicial discretion to attenuate the penalty than to intensify it. Thus Abu Hanifa's approach was to apply the most lenient penalties to the crimes of *Ta'azir*,[30] and this practice developed into a tradition which is exemplified by the maxim that "It is better that the Imam be wrong in his forgiving than to err in imposing the penalty."[31] The maxim rests as a *Hadith*.

An important restriction exists, however, which prohibits the ruler from imposing *Ta'azir* punishment without first consulting his advisors with respect to the punishment he may impose.[32] This is intended to reduce any potential abuse.

Thus, it is established in Islamic law that the ruler or judge is authorized to impose certain discretionary penalties within the limitations on his discretion and that the penalty imposed be the one best suited to each case. The ruler or judge has no inherent authority to punish but only such power as is expressly granted in the sources of Islamic law and that which is clearly implied as essential, indispensable or reasonably necessary to carry out his express functions.

The Legality of *Ta'azir* as Essential for the Welfare of the Nation

The traditional power of the ruler or judge to impose *Ta'azir* penalties as necessitated by the need to protect the public welfare should be substantially curtailed in present day Muslim societies, and *Ta'azir* must be the subject of specific legal prescriptions. The prescribed penalty for each crime should be binding on the judge, but he must at the same time have some flexibility in the performance of his judicial function.

---

[28] 3 'UTHMAN IBN 'ALI AL-ZAYLA'I, TABYIN AL-HAQA'IQ: SHARH KANZ AL-DAQA'IQ, 211 (Cairo: al-Matba'ah al-Amiriyah al-Kubra, 1893-96), [hereinafter referred to as AL-ZAYLA'I].

[29] TAQIY AL-DIN IBN TAYMIYAH, AL-SIYASAH AL-SHAR'IYAH FI ISLAH AL-RA'I WA-AL-RA'IYAH 134 (M.I. al-Banna and M.A. 'Ashur eds. Cairo: Matabi' al-Sha'b, 1970).

[30] IBN FARHUN AL-YA'MURI, TABSIRAT AL-HUKKAM FI USUL AL-AQDIYAH WA-MANAHIJ AL-AHKAM 369 (Cairo: Maktabat Mustafa al-Babi al-Halabi, 1958), [hereinafter referred to as IBN FARHUN].

[31] ABU ZAHRAH, *supra* note 3, at 312.

[32] 'AMIR, *supra* note 22, at 530-31.

The first argument in favor of reducing the judge's power is that Islamic law in fact permits the *Ta'azir* to be subject to legislative enactments which can provide for a minimum and a maximum penalty that can be imposed for each crime. In addition the actual application of certain penalties can remain a matter of judicial discretion.[33] The second argument is that the Islamic system protects against the abuse of power through the criteria set for the appointment of judges such as: academic excellence, integrity and stability of character. (These are among the factors to determine the fitness of potential judges.)[34] That is why the judge is given broad discretion in the application of *Ta'azir* penalties throughout the Islamic world. In contemporary societies, however, judges with such unimpeachable qualities are rare, and thus it is necessary to restrict the scope of the judge's discretion in penal matters.

The third argument arises as a result of the growing complexity of modern Islamic societies. The secular interests and expectations of Muslim peoples have changed, and their needs reflect the ever-widening scope of the problems confronting Islamic jurisprudence. Therefore, defining *Ta'azir* crimes within the framework of the principle of legality by bringing greater consistency to the law concerning the rights and duties of all persons and the resolution of disputes will aid the judiciary. Ultimately Islamic law will come to maintain an orderly society by establishing rules that lead to predictable results but not at the expense of needed flexibility. In this manner, the Islamic criminal justice system seeks to protect the welfare of society while preserving individual security. Both are nurtured in an atmosphere of traditional Islamic faith.[35]

THE PRINCIPLE OF NON-RETROACTIVITY OF PENAL LAWS[36]

1. *The Principle of Non-Retroactivity in Islamic Law and Its Importance to Individual Security*

Individuals can never be sufficiently secure to enjoy their rights and liberties if they can be accused of crimes for acts which were allowed when they were committed. Thus, Islamic law has long recognized the principle of non-retroactivity of criminal laws as part of the foundation of its criminal justice system. This principle means in essence that criminal laws have only prospective and not retroactive effect. The significance of this principle is that it protects individual security and prevents abuse of power.[37]

In view of the significance Islamic law attaches to the non-retroactivity principle, it is embodied in the constitutions of several Muslim states, and it is

---

[33] 'AWDAH, *supra* note 12, at 249; and 'AMIR, *supra* note 29, at 483.

[34] 'ALI IBN MUHAMMAD AL-MAWARDI, AL-AHKAM AL-SULTANIYAH 65 *et seq.* (2d ed. Egypt: Mustafa al-Babi al-Halabi, 1966).

[35] *See* 'AMIR, *supra* note 22, at 484.

[36] Concerning the application of this principle in positive criminal law, *see* MERLE AND VITU, *supra* note 4, at 167 *et seq.* And for its application in Islamic law, *see* 'AWDAH, *supra* note 12, at 261 *et seq.*; and 1 ABU ZAHRAH, *supra* note 3, at 321 *et. seq.*

[37] *See* BURDEAU, *supra* note 2, at 123-24.

deemed a constitutional principle applicable to all the authorities of the state.[38] This universal recognition of the principle of non-retroactivity in Islamic law is in large measure due to the emphasis placed on the principle of legality, which by its very nature precludes the retroactive application of the criminal law.[39]

2. The Precedence of the Non-Retroactivity Principle in Islamic Law

While the principle of non-retroactivity had its origin in positive legal systems with Article 8 of the French Declaration of the Rights of Man in 1789,[40] it has been an integral part of Islamic law for fourteen centuries. The only exception to this principle in Islamic jurisprudence is that the criminal law has retroactive effect if it favors the accused.

The *Qu'ran* cites many instances in which this principle was applied. For example, God prohibited the practice of usury, but he did not punish those who engaged in such acts prior to his decree.[41] God also forbids the marriage of one man to two sisters at the same time, but he did not punish such marriages which took place before the coming of Islam.[42] He also prohibits a man from marrying his father's wives, and condemns such practice as obscene, but he did not condemn such acts prior to Islam:

> And marry not those women whom your fathers married, except what hath already happened in the past (of that nature). Lo! It was ever lewdness and abomination, and an evil way.[43]

Similarly, the prohibitions of adultery, theft, drinking alcoholic beverages and other crimes did not apply in pre-Islamic times.

The underlying purpose of the non-retroactivity principle is to give reasonable notice to individuals of God's displeasure and to allow them time to put aside the old ways and conduct themselves according to God's command.

Most Muslim jurists believe there is only one exception to the principle of non-retroactivity,[44] and that is if the new law provides for a lesser penalty than the existing law at the time the crime was committed; in that case the less severe punishment is applicable. For example, the crime of *aldhahar* was punishable by mandatory and permanent divorce in pre-Islamic times. This penalty was believed to be too harsh, as it meant that the offending couple was forever deprived of their conjugal rights. Thus, the penalty was reduced to liberation of the offender's slaves, fasting for two successive months or feeding sixty needy men.

---

[38] *See, e.g.*, the CONSTITUTION OF KUWAIT, Articles 32 and 179; Article 20 of the CONSTITUTION OF BAHRAIN; and Article 27 of the CONSTITUTION OF THE UNITED ARAB EMIRATES.

[39] AL-SA'ID, *supra* note 10, at 106.

[40] *See* MERLE AND VITU, *supra* note 4, at 169.

[41] *Surat al-Baqarah* II:275.

[42] *Surat al-Nisaa* IV:23.

[43] *Surat al-Nisaa* IV:22.

[44] Some list another exception allowing retroactivity in case of high crimes which affect public security. As an example, they present the retroactive application of criminal law to crimes of rebellion and armed robbery (*hirabah*)... *See* 'AWDAH, *supra* note 12, at 266. However, this opinion is considered baseless by others, *see* 1 ABU ZAHRAH, *supra* note 3, at 326 *et seq.*

The Prophet applied this lesser sanction in the case of Aws ibn el-Samit's wife, even though the conduct took place prior to the revelation of Islam on that subject. Another application of this exception was in the crime of *al-la'n*, (falsely accusing one's wife of adultery). Before Islam declared this act to be a crime, it was subject to the same penalty prescribed for defamation, on the grounds that there is no difference between the defamation of one's wife and that of any other woman. But as the penalty for defamation was more severe than that imposed for *al-la'n*, the rule of *al-la'n* was retroactively applied.[45]

3. The Scope of the Non-Retroactivity Principle

There is disagreement as to the scope of the non-retroactivity principle. Some jurists question whether there is any need to establish it, as long as the penalties prescribed by the *Qu'ran* and the *Sunna* have been applied since their revelation from God and their communication by the Prophet. They maintain that there is no excuse for anyone to be ignorant of these rules, particularly after the spread of Islam, and that when the revelations ceased and the Prophet died, there was no room for further elaboration of the Laws. Thus, the application of the non-retroactivity principle and the related exception in favor of the accused are not required.

That argument lacks merit, however, when one considers the advantages that obtain through application of the non-retroactivity principle. In the first place, most Muslim jurists point out that the dissemination of Islam did not entail knowledge of Islamic law except for adherents to the faith. But those who are ignorant of God's revelations through the Prophet are excused if intellectual and physical barriers prevent them from knowing what God commands. Such ignorance thereby becomes an excuse which prevents punishment for violation of the law. Moreover, any new adherent to Islam cannot be questioned for criminal acts committed before embracing the faith. The *Qu'ran* states: "Tell those who disbelieve that if they cease from the persecution of believers that which is past will be forgiven them."[46] And the Prophet said to Amr ibn al-A'as when the latter embraced Islam: "The religion of Islam cuts off what [any conduct that] preceded it." The Prophet also did not question Abu Sufian and his wife for their previous conduct, nor did he question the man who had killed his uncle Hamza even though his death caused him deep sorrow.[47]

Muslim jurists further point out that because of the non-retroactivity principle, Islamic law does not apply to acts or omissions permitted under the positive laws which Islam supplanted.[48] The principle also applies to crimes of reproof for which discretionary punishment can be imposed.[49]

Finally, the principle applies when the ruler determines that restrictions

---

[45] 1 ABU ZAHRAH, *supra* note 3, at 327-28.

[46] *Surat al-Anfal* VIII:38.

[47] 1 ABU ZAHRAH, *supra* note 3, at 323.

[48] Dr. Muhammad Na'im Yasin, Memoranda on Islamic Criminal Jurisprudence 32 (1980-81) (The College of Law and Islamic Legislation, the University of Kuwait).

[49] *Id.* at 31.

must be placed on what is permissible for the public interest to prevent social and moral corruption. For example, the ruler may order the placing of road barriers to aid the flow of traffic, but in all such situations no penalty can be imposed unless the ruler first gives notice. The jurist Abu Ya'li applies the non-retroactivity principle in defining the duties of the *Mohtasib*, who was charged with enforcement of certain regulations called the *Hisba*. Abu Ya'li states: "He who is authorized to keep the people away from suspicious situations and to enforce his orders, should not discipline anyone before first cautioning him."[50] El Mawardi further points out that the Ruler may prohibit men and women from meeting in the *Kaaba*, but not without giving them notice, he states:

> Omar Ibn al Khattab prohibited men and women from mixing around the *Kaaba*. Having seen a man wandering with women he struck him with a rod. The man addressed him: "By God, if I have done wrong, you have not educated me." Omar said, "Are you not aware of my decree against men and women walking together around the *Kaaba*?" The man said, "I have not seen such a decree." Omar handed him the rod and said, "Retaliate." But the man said, "I am not going to retaliate today." Omar then asked his forgiveness, but the man said that he would not. Then the two men separated. When they met on the next day, Omar's face grew pale. The man said to him, "O Prince of the Faithful, it seems to me that you feel as I felt before." Omar said he did. The man said, "God is my witness that I have forgiven you."[51]

These examples demonstrate that the penalties which the Ruler may impose to eliminate corruption can never govern previously completed acts and that they are not binding on the people prior to the day of proclamation.

By establishing the principle of non-retroactivity in various forms, Islamic law from the beginning has recognized that it is essential to the protection of individual security.

THE RIGHT TO INDIVIDUAL SECURITY IN ISLAMIC CRIMINAL PROCEDURE

INTRODUCTION

Among the most important guarantees of personal security are those provided by criminal procedure. This set of rules seeks to balance the right of the state to enforce its criminal laws by apprehending criminals and to collect and present evidence to secure convictions. The state can perform that function only in a manner consistent with the interest of the individual in maintaining his basic rights and enabling him to defend his innocence and present a defense. The proper balance between these interests achieves a secure and stable society with a minimum infringement on individual freedom.

Under Islamic jurisprudence, men are equal like the teeth of a comb. They

---

[50] ABU YA'LA AL-FARRA, AL-AHKAM AL-SULTANIYAH 277 (Cairo: Mustafa al-Babi al-Halabi, 1938), [hereinafter referred to as ABU YA'LA].

[51] 'ALI IBN MUHAMMAD AL-MAWARDI, AL-AHKAM AL-SULTANIYAH 249 (Egypt: Matba'at al-Watan, 1880-81), [hereinafter referred to as AL-MAWARDI].

are presumed innocent until proved guilty. Thus, Islamic law has adopted rules of criminal procedure based on the principle that justice not only requires the offender to be punished for his guilt but also protects the innocent from punishment for crimes committed by another. Islamic criminal procedure further requires that in seeking evidence to support a charge, no threats or attacks against innocent and peaceful individuals in violation of their liberties and right to privacy are permitted.

For purposes of discussion, Islamic criminal procedure may be divided into four topics: (1) the presumption of innocence; (2) the investigation and primary questioning stage; (3) the rights of the accused during trial; and (4) the rights of the prisoner.

THE PRESUMPTION OF INNOCENCE

1. *Justification for the Principle*

From its inception Islamic law has recognized the presumption of innocence as a right inherent to all people.[52] The Prophet stated that: "Every infant is born primitive; it is his parents who subsequently convert him to a Jew, a Christian or a Magus."[53] He also said: "Prevent punishment in case of doubt."[54]

Islamic jurists interpret this principle by saying that the status of the accused is that of one who is in fact innocent, or that his condition is that of collateral innocence.[55] It is also fundamental that the rule be strictly discharged, since the law recognizes that without the presumption of innocence the accused faces the onerous if not impossible burden of proving he did not commit the crime. It is also significant that post-conviction legislation prescribes the means for attacking sentences and gaining a new trial in certain types of cases. Thus, an individual who is provisionally incarcerated but whose confinement is prolonged may secure release by proving his innocence. Newly discovered evidence proving innocence after conviction results in vacating a conviction. Often, however, the damage resulting from an erroneous sentence is irreversible, particularly if the punishment is not loss of liberty. Thus, it is far preferable as a safeguard to presume the accused to be innocent from the time he is accused of the crime until he is convicted.[56]

---

[52] The universal recognition of this principle is evident from the French Declaration of the Rights of Man of 1789 (Article 19); the International Declaration of Human Rights (Article 11); and the International Covenant of Civil and Political Rights of 1966 (Article 14). The principle is also included in many national constitutions: *e.g.*, the CONSTITUTION OF SYRIA of 1950 and 1973 (Article 28-1); the CONSTITUTION OF SOMALIA, 1960 (Article 42); the CONSTITUTION OF THE ARAB REPUBLIC OF EGYPT, 1971 (Article 67); the CONSTITUTION OF KUWAIT, 1962 (Article 34); and the CONSTITUTION OF YUGOSLAVIA, 1963 (Article 50). In addition, a number of countries have embodied the principle in their criminal procedural law. *See, e.g.*, the Russian Code of 1960 (Article 20) and Article 2 of the Czechoslovakian Code of Criminal Procedure. *See also* M.C. BASSIOUNI AND V. SAVITSKI, THE CRIMINAL JUSTICE SYSTEM OF THE U.S.S.R. 47-50 ((1979).

[53] Cited by AL-BUKHARI.

[54] For further discussion of repealing punishment in case of doubt, *see* 2 ABU ZAHRAH, *supra* note 3, at 218 *et seq.*

[55] *Id.* at 247-49.

[56] MAHMUD MUSTAFA, AL-ITHBAT FI AL-MAWAD AL-JINA'IYAH FI AL-QANUN AL-MUQARIN [EVIDENCE IN CRIMINAL ARTICLES OF COMPARATIVE LAW] 56 (Cairo: Cairo University Press, 1977), [hereinafter referred to as MUSTAFA].

2. Consequences of the Principle

Numerous effects on the rights of the accused and on the state flow from the presumption of innocence. One of the most important of these is that the burden of proof rests with the accuser. In Islamic law the burden of proving innocence is not imposed on the accused, for the application of the presumption of innocence necessitates that the accuser be charged with the duty of proving his accusations. The defendant is not required to produce negative evidence. Charging the accuser with the duty of adducing positive proof is based on the words of the Prophet: "Had men been believed only according to their allegations, some persons would have claimed the blood and properties belonging to others, but the accuser is bound to present positive proof."[57] Another commentator states: "The positive evidence lies on the accuser and an oath is required of one who denies."[58]

A second consequence of the presumption of innocence is that doubt is construed strictly against the accuser. In Islamic law, a conviction must be founded upon assurance and certainty of guilt and not on mere probability. Hence any doubt is resolved in favour of the accused. If the judge has reasonable doubt of guilt based on all the evidence before him, he must conclude that the accused is not guilty. This principle is based on the saying of the Prophet: "Prevent punishment in case of doubt. Release the accused if possible, for it is better that the ruler be wrong in forgiving than wrong in punishing."[59]

GUARANTEES OF THE ACCUSED IN THE INVESTIGATION AND PRIMARY QUESTIONING STAGE

1. Freedom from Unreasonable Searches and Seizures

Because the search of an individual's premises or property involves a curtailment of the right to privacy and infringes upon the inviolability of his house and his need to live in peace, Islamic law has sought to regulate this area of state activity. But such restriction must also take cognizance of the fact that society also benefits from the state's ability to discover the truth wherever it may be concealed.[60] An illustration of that principle in positive law which is in conformity with Islamic law is the Egyptian law defining search as:

> that procedure whereby the legislator has allowed concerned authorities to violate the right of privacy of a given person, because a crime has in fact or probably been committed, in preference of the public interest to that of the

---

[57]Transmitted from Ibn 'Abbas by al Bukhari, Muslim, Ahmad and the authors of AL-SUNAN. *See* 2 MUHAMMAD IBN ISMA'IL AL-BUKHARI, JAMI' AL-SAHIH or SAHIH AL-BUKHARI, (including commentary by al-Sindi and al-Qastalani) 53 (Egypt: al-Matba'ah al-'Amirah, 1913), [hereinafter referred to as AL-BUKHARI]. *See also* 12 MUSLIM IBN AL-HAJJAJ AL-QUSHAYRI, SAHIH MUSLIM BI-SHARH AL-NAWAWI 2 (Cairo: Matba'at Hijazi, 1930), [hereinafter referred to as SAHIH MUSLIM, BI-SHARH AL-NAWAWI].

[58]Quoted by 10 AHMAD IBN AL-HUSAYN AL-BAYHAQI, KITAB AL-SUNAN AL-KUBRA, 253 (Hyderabad, Deccan: Matba'at Majlis Da'irat al-Ma'arif al-Nizamiyah, 1925/26-38); *See also* 6 ABU BAKR AL-KASANI, BADA'I' AL'SANA'I' FI TARTIB AL-SHARA'I' 225 *et seq.*(Egypt: Matba'at Sharikat al-Matbu'at al-Ilmiyah, 1909-1910) [hereinafter referred to as AL-KASANI]; and IBN ABI AL-DAMM AL-HAMAWI, ADAB AL-QADA' 152 (Mustafa al-Zuhayli, ed., Damascus: Majma' al-lughah al-'Arabiyah, 1975) [hereinafter referred to as AL-HAMAWI].

[59]Concerning the application of the principle of avoiding the execution of *Hudud* by doubt, *see* 2 ABU ZAHRAH, *supra* note 3, at 218 *et seq.*

[60]*See* MUSTAFA, *supra* note 56, part 2.

> individual, with a view to discovering some substantial evidence which may contribute in establishing the truth.[61]

Thus, Islamic law has established rules which meet society's need to protect itself from crime and ensure the rights of individuals whom God has honored and favored as His creation.[62] In so doing, Islamic law restrains those who may violate the right to privacy, in particular those officials who could unreasonably search the dwellings of those suspected of involvement in criminal conduct. Consequently individuals, their dwellings, correspondence and property cannot be searched save according to certain requirements and restrictions provided by law.

As to the inviolability of one's dwelling, the *Qu'ran* states:

> O ye who believe! Enter not houses other than your own without first announcing your presence and invoking peace upon the people therein. That is better for you, that you may be heedful . . . and if you find no one therein, still enter not until permission hath been given, and if it be said unto you: 'Go away, for it is purer for you.' Allah knoweth what you do.[63]

Thus, according to this text, entry into the dwelling is prohibited unless by consent of the owner. This prohibition is not limited to places actually occupied by the owner; it applies also to the owner's property during his absence. This is explicit in the verse cited above which precludes entry without "permission," and requires consent. The *Sunna* also is in accord, as seen from the Prophet's saying:

> Three things are not allowed any man. No man who leads a group in prayer should invoke blessing solely upon himself, for if he does, he will have betrayed them. A man should not look inside a house unless he receives permission. If he does so, he would have entered, and a man should not say his prayers when he is congested unless he is relieved.[64]

The Prophet also states figuratively so as to illustrate the right to be free from intrusions into one's privacy that:

> If a person looks at you without your permission and you pelt him with a stone and put out his eye, no guilt will be on you.[65]

This right also extends to one's clothing in that no one has the right to inspect the clothing of another person to determine what may be concealed therein, without reason and without permission.[66] It thereby embodies the proscription against unreasonable searches of the person. The inviolability of the dwelling is linked with the inviolability of the person, for the latter derives from the former as a manifestation of individual freedom. It is meaningless to protect the house

---

[61] Egyptian Cassation on 17/11/1959, Cassation Decisions Collection, Year 10, No. 189, p. 188. cited by SAMI HASAN AL-HUSAYNI, AL-NAZARIYAH AL-'AMMAH LIL-TAFTISH FI AL-QANUN AL-MISRI WA-AL-MUQARAN [THE GENERAL THEORY OF SEARCH IN EGYPTIAN AND COMPARATIVE LAW] 74 (Cairo; Dar al-Nadah al-'Arabiyah, 1972), [hereinafter referred to as AL-HUSAYNI].

[62] 12 MUHAMMAD IBN AHMAD AL-QURTUBI, AL-JAMI' LI-AHKAM AL-QU'RAN, 212 *et seq.* (3rd ed. Cairo: Dar al-Katib al-'Arabi, 1967) [hereinafter referred to as AL-QURTUBI].

[63] *Surat al-Nur* XXIV:27, 28.

[64] 3 'ABD AL-AZIM AL-MUNDHIRI, AL-TARGHIB WA-AL-TARHIB MIN AL-HADITḤ AL-SHARIF, 347 (2d ed. Cairo: Matba'at al-Halabi, 1954).

[65] SAHIH MUSLIM BI-SHARH AL-NAWAWI, *supra* note 57, at XIV:138.

[66] 2 AL-GHAZZALI, IHY'A 'ULUM AL-DIN, part 5, 34 (1st ed. Cairo: Lajnat Nashr al-Thaqafah, n.d.).

without protecting the owner as well.[67]

A person's correspondence is also inviolate. It is thus unlawful to read another's private communications after a clandestine seizure. The Prophet says: "He who reads a letter of his brother without his permission, will read it in hell."[68] The protection against infringing the confidentiality of letters as constituting a violation of the right of privacy extends to intellectual liberties, particularly the freedoms of opinion and expression, as established under Islamic law..

The inviolability of the dwelling is not based on a purely religious foundation; it is also partly inspired by the social policy of protecting individual security and freedom in a manner which does not interfere with the right and duty of the state to take necessary action to investigate crimes. Thus, under Islamic law the inviolability of the dwelling is not absolute but is subject to certain exceptions necessitated to maintain social order and safety. State authorities may enter the dwelling to conduct reasonable searches, and they may search the individual if such activity is reasonably related to the public interest. But the state's right is governed by conditions and guarantees aimed at preventing arbitrary and intimidating searches.[69]

The first restriction on the conduct of the search concerns the official empowered to issue the search warrant. According to Islamic jurists that official is the *Wali al-Mazalim*, the minister of complaints. They are the officials charged with the detection and investigation of crimes. The *Mohtasib*, by contrast, are not within his limited jurisdiction, but rather are within the competence of the *Kadi* or judge.[70] According to the judicial rules of Islam, the judge is not empowered to issue search warrants, nor is he entitled to seek out evidence or proof. His duty is limited to instructing the complainant to furnish evidence to support his allegations.

The search is also restricted by the rule that the warrant should not issue unless sufficient evidence of the crime is obtained, that is, unless there is probable cause that a crime was committed by the accused. Thus, for example, when a trustworthy man informs the authorities that another has tried to kill him, or if he sees a man take a woman aside to commit adultery with her, probable cause exists.[71] The warrant also may issue when the offense becomes perceivable though not seen, as for example, when the smell of alcohol and noise of intoxicated persons emanates from inside a house.[72]

Finally, there must be lawful discovery of sufficiently incriminating proof or existence of the offense. If the discovery is a result of spying (for example, by piercing holes through a door or by eavesdropping), the evidence gained thereby

---

[67] Contemporary laws have followed this approach by equalizing the dwelling with the individual and subjecting both to the same rules pertaining to search. *See* 2 MUSTAFA, *supra* note 56, at 14-15.

[68] JALAL AL-DIN AL-SUYUTI, AL-JAMI' AL-SAGHIR 165 (Egypt: Mustafa al-Babi al-Halabi, 1964).

[69] AL-HUSAYNI, *supra* note 61, at 20.

[70] 'Abd al-Wahhab al-'Ashmawi, Individual Accusation or the Right of the Individual to Criminal Litigation 342, 347-48, 350 (Ph.D. dissertation, Cairo University, 1953), [hereinafter referred to as al-'Ashmawi].

[71] *See* ABU YA'LA, *supra* note 50, at 296: and AL-MAWARDI, *supra* note 51, at 202.

[72] 2 AL-GHAZZALI, *supra* note 66, at part 5, 36-37; quoted by 'Awdah, *supra* note 12, at 504.

cannot be used for incriminating purposes. God says: "And spy not."[73] This is because dwellings and individuals are immune [from infringement] unless the offense is apparent, and they should not be violated or encroached. The *Sunna* is also explicit on this issue.

Islam from its very beginning has observed this rule as illustrated by the following incident. Omar ibn al Khattab once found a group of men drinking wine and burning shacks. He said, "I have prevented you from drinking, but you have drunk. I have prohibited the burning of shacks, but you did." They said, "Prince of the faithful, God ordered you not to spy, but you spied. He ordered you not to enter without permission, but you did." Then Omar said, "These two to those two," and left without questioning them.[74] Abd el-Rahman ibn Awf related another incident:

> Once at night I accompanied Omar on one of his wanderings at Medina. As we traveled we saw the light of a lamp. We went toward it. When we approached it, we found a locked door concealing some people noisily reveling. Omar took my hand and said, "Do you know whose home this is?" I said I did not. He said "It is the home of Rabiaa ibn Omaya ibn Khalef. They are drinking. What is to be done?" I said, "I see that we did what God prohibited. God forbids us to spy." Omar returned and disregarded them.[75]

2. Guarantees of the Accused During Interrogation

Interrogation under Islamic law differs from simple questioning. Besides charging the suspect with a crime, interrogation requires confronting him with the established evidence against him, and discussing that evidence so that he may either refute it or confess because of it.[76] Interrogation is thus an instrument of the investigator to discover the truth either through confession or denial by the accused.[77] The evidence which is secured through interrogation is oral, whereas a search leads to tangible evidence which can be physically examined.[78]

In the middle ages torture was used to secure a confession. It was then regarded as a lawful means of investigation. Modern constitutions and rules of procedure prohibit torture and emphasize fairness to the accused in the interrogation stage by providing many guarantees. Nevertheless, some commentators argue that contemporary interrogation techniques tend to coerce the accused into confessing by means of a flood of critical questions, so that under the pressure of intimidation, he may make incriminating statements which are inherently

---

[73] *Surat al-Hujurat* XLIX:12.

[74] Quoted by ABU YA'LA, *supra* note 50, at 296; and in AL-MAWARDI, *supra* note 51, at 253. However, it is important to note that these accounts differ from one source to another. *See* AWDAH, *supra* note 12, at 503; 'ABBAS MAHMUD AL-'AQQAD, 'ABQARIYAT 'UMAR [THE GENIUS OF 'UMAR] 132 (Cairo: Dar al-Hilal, 1953); also quoted by AL-HUSAYNI, *supra* note 61, at 19. We are of the opinion that the version cited in AL-MAWARDI and ABU YA'LA is closer to the truth and logic.

[75] 'AWDAH, *supra* note 12, at 503.

[76] *See* RA'UF SADIQ 'UBAYD, MABADI' AL-IJRA'AT AL-JINA'IYAH FI AL-QANUN AL-MISRI [FUNDAMENTALS OF CRIMINAL PROCEDURE IN EGYPTIAN LAW] 434 (11th ed. Cairo: Matba'at al-Istiqlal al-Kubra, 1976), [hereinafter referred to as 'UBAYD]; and for a general discussion of interrogation, *see* Muhammad Sami'al-Nabrawi, The Questioning of the Accused (Ph.D. dissertation, Cairo University, 1968).

[77] For further discussion on the subject of confession, *see* AL-MULLA, *suspra* note 1.

[78] AL-HUSAYNI, *supra* note 61, at 49.

unreliable.[79] Such methods clearly do not promote the welfare of society or the rights of the accused. While practical restraints on the investigator's conduct may be difficult to maintain at times, Islamic law provides numerous safeguards, which are discussed in detail below.

The first guarantee during interrogation pertains to the persons responsible for conducting the interrogation. It is established that questioning of the accused should be conducted only by a designated official. Under Islamic law interrogation is conducted by two officials, the Minister of Complaints and the *Mohtasib*. This institution developed gradually. In the early days of Islam, crimes were frequently solved through the securing of confessions by the religious zeal of the converts, but later it was fear of the Ruler which aided in the administration of justice. Then the institution of *Mohtasib* developed with the defined tasks of receiving reports and investigating crimes, whereupon the matter went to the Minister of Complaints who referred it to the judge to adjudicate the facts, render his sentence or dispose of the case by reconciling the parties to the dispute, providing that they agreed to be bound by the decision.[80] The *Mohtasib*, on the other hand, besides his limited investigatory authority was charged with the prosecution of cases before the judge if the complaining parties failed to do so.[81]

The accused is also guaranteed in *Hudud* and *Quesas* crimes from having to take an oath or substituting for the oath by putting up money or other property as a guarantee. In these criminal accusations the investigating authority is not allowed to require an oath from the accused.[82]

A very crucial right of the accused in the investigation of *Hudud* crimes is the right to refuse questioning and the right to remain silent. An accused who exercises this right is guaranteed that his silence will not be used as incriminating evidence against him. *Hudud* crimes can be proved only by means of an avowal or other positive evidence and never by means of the accused's silence. Refusal to answer questions is, therefore, inadmissible evidence to convict the accused. If he is asked to make a statement or give an oath, his refusal to do so will be considered an unreliable confession, for it is no more than silence, and to the silent no statement can be ascribed. Even if it would be considered as giving rise to an inference, it would be equivalent to a naked admission which in Islamic law is deemed doubtful, and in *Hudud* crimes no one can be convicted on the basis of doubtful evidence.[83]

In addition, the accused shall not be subjected to torture or to cruel and inhuman treatment or punishment. Modern constitutions and international human rights instruments place great emphasis on the prohibition against torture or cruel and inhuman treatment or punishment. Islamic law took the lead in the

---

[79] *See* 'UBAYD, *supra* note 76, at 435. *See generally* M.C. Bassiouni, *An Appraisal of Torture in International Law and Practice: The Need for an International Convention to Prevent and Suppress Torture*, 48 REVUE INTERNATIONALE DE DROIT PENAL 17 (1977).

[80] *See* al-'Ashmawi, *supra* note 70, at 342, 348.

[81] *Id.* at 348.

[82] *See* 1 ABU ZAHRAH, *supra* note 3, at 73. This is predominantly the view of Hanafi scholars.

[83] 2 ABU ZAHRAH, *supra* note 3, at 73-74.

introduction and application of this principle fourteen centuries ago and thus discourages the abuse of authority by providing guarantees of fair and humane treatment.

Islamic law expressly prohibits torture, beating, and other cruel and inhumane treatment.[84] The Prophet forbade torture saying: "God shall torture on the Day of Recompense those who inflict torture on people in life."[85] The Prophet also forbade the striking of Muslims.[86] Additionally, Omar ibn el Khattab addressed his governors as follows: "Hit not the Muslims, lest they be humiliated. Deny not their rights, lest they become faithless, and place them not in the jungle lest they be lost."[87]

Al-Gazzali quotes a story revealed by Omar ibn Abdel Aziz which says that Omar ibn el-Khattab asked Mohamed ibn Kaab al-Qortobi to define justice for him. The latter said, "Every Muslim who is older than you, be a father to him. . . . Punish every offender in proportion to his offense, and beware of whipping a Muslim out of wrath; otherwise, you will be in hell."[88]

Another story is recounted in which Audi ibn Arrtaa, one of Omar ibn Abdel Aziz's deputies, sent a letter to Omar asking permission to inflict some torture on those who refused to pay duty to the public treasury. Omar sent a letter forbidding and condemning such measure saying:

> I wonder at your asking permission from me to torture people as though I am a shelter for you from God's wrath, and as if my satisfaction will save you from God's anger. Upon receiving this letter of mine accept what is given to you or let him give an oath. By God, it is better that they should face God with their offenses than I should have to meet God for torturing them.[89]

On the basis of the evidence from the sources and interpretations of Islamic law, Muslim jurists conclude that torture or cruel and inhuman treatment or punishment during the interrogation stage is prohibited and indeed is a sin in the eyes of God.[90]

The Prophet sets forth a factual example for treating the accused fairly and humanely and thereby enabling him to speak freely and encouraging him lest he give a false and misleading confession. A man accused of theft was brought before the Prophet. The Prophet addressed the accused gently saying, "I do not think you stole. Did you?"[91]

---

[84] *See* ABU YOUSSUF , YA'QUB IBN IBRAHIM, KITAB AL-KHARAJ, 115 *et seq.*; 175 (2d ed. Cairo: al-Matba'ah al-Salafiyah, 1933), [hereinafter referred to as ABU YOUSSUF].

[85] ABU 'UBAYD AL-QASIM IBN SALLAM, AL-AMWAL 42-45 (Cairo: Matba'at al-Hijazi, 1934); quoted by FU'AD AL-NADI, MABDA' AL-MASHRU'IYAH WA-DAWABIT KHUDU' AL-DAWLAH LIL-QANUN FI AL-FIQH AL-ISLAMI [THE PRINCIPLE OF LEGITIMACY AND THE RULES OF THE STATE'S SUBMISSION TO LAW IN ISLAMIC JURISPRUDENCE] 100 (1st ed. Cairo: Dar Nashr al-Thaqafah, 1973-4), [hereinafter referred to as AL-NADI].

[86] ABU YOUSSUF, *supra* note 84, at 151.

[87] *Id.*

[88] AL-GHAZZALI, AL-TIBR AL-MASBUK FI NASIHAT AL-MULUK 28-29 (Cairo: Maktabat al-Kulliyat al-Azhariyah, 1968).

[89] ABU YOUSSUF , *supra* note 84, at 119.

[90] Ibrahim ibn Tabataba, quoted by AL-NADI, *supra* note 85, at 108.

[91] ABU YOUSSUF, *supra* note 84, at 176.

Islamic law also guarantees that the accused shall not be coerced into incriminating himself. Any confession by the accused given as the result of coercion, torture or unlawful detention cannot be used to sustain a conviction. A confession under Islamic law must be free and voluntary conduct, whereby the accused ascribes to himself the commission of certain acts constituting a crime, and such confession is nullified by interference with the will of the accused. Omar ibn el Khattab reportedly said that: "A man would not be secure from incriminating himself if you made him hungry, frightened him, or confined him."[92] Mohamed ibn Ishaq reports that al-Zahary once said: "Tariq brought in Syria a man who had been arrested, being accused of theft, and beat him. The accused confessed he was guilty. Tariq sent him to Abdallah ibn Omar asking what to be done. Ibn Omar said not to sever his hand, for he confessed after being beaten."[93]

Islamic law goes further in protecting the accused against his own weakness and indiscretions uttered in the absence of coercion. Islamic jurists maintain that the initial statements of the accused are insufficient to convict him. They hold that his statements and responses should be repeated as many times as the number of witnesses required, and that the confession clearly indicate the commission of the crime, consistently stated by the accused and not contradicted by other evidence. Contrary testimony of a witness casts such doubt on the confession and renders it so unsatisfactory that it must be disregarded.

It is said of the Prophet with respect to Maez's story that when Maez confessed to him that he had committed adultery, the Prophet gave him the chance to retract his confession by saying: "Maybe you only kissed her? Maybe you only touched her?" The Prophet also asked a woman accused of theft: "Did you steal? I do not think you did. Say, no." Thereby giving the accused the opportunity to withdraw the confession.[94] The Islamic judge and the Islamic Ruler as well are bound to follow the *Sunna*. Thus, when a Muslim confesses to the commission of a *Hudud* crime, he must suggest to the accused that he abandon his confession.[95]

The accused also has the right under Islamic law to withdraw his confession at any time prior to the execution of sentence. In that event Islamic jurists agree that a confession cannot constitute positive evidence if the accused withdraws it before the execution of the punishment even though the sentence has been passed. For example, if a man accused of adultery retracts his confession prior to execution of punishment, the execution is to be stopped. This is a unique feature of Islamic law which is absent in other legal systems. It was said that after confessing to the crime of adultery, Maez recanted and tried to escape while being stoned, but the executioners followed him and put him to death. When the Prophet was informed, he said: "Why did not you allow him to repent? God would accept his penitence?"[96]

---

[92] *Id.* at 175.
[93] *Id.*
[94] 2 'AWDAH, *supra* note 12, at 438.
[95] AL-KASANI, supra note 58, at 7; 61 *et seq. See also* 10 IBN QUDAMAH, AL-MUGHNI, 173, 195 (Egypt: Matba'at al-Imam, 1964). In contemporary jurisprudence, *see* 2 'AWDAH, *supra* note 12, at 438 *et seq.*
[96] *See* Mubarak 'Abd al-'Aziz al Nuwaybit, al-Da'wa al-jina'iyah fi al-shari'ah al-Islamiyah wa-al-qanun al-wad'i [Criminal Proceedings in Islamic and Positive Law] 333, (Ph.D. dissertation, Cairo University, 1973).

3. *Rights of the Accused During Preventive Detention*

Preventive detention of the accused is a serious restraint on personal liberty.[97] It is one of the most serious orders that can be given during the investigation stage and is an exception to the general principle that no man shall be deprived of his liberty except for the enforcement of a lawful sentence. Nevertheless preventive detention may be required to protect the investigation, for instance, if the accused may attempt to influence the witnesses while he is free, alter or destroy incriminating evidence or escape.[98] However, this power can be invoked only to promote social order and in the interest of law enforcement. There is, however, some disagreement among Islamic jurists concerning the function of preventive detention. Some have labelled it detention for proving innocence, while others call it confinement for accusation.[99]

Opponents of preventive detention contend that the Prophet and his immediate successor Abu Bakr did not maintain a prison, and did not imprison any person.[100] They also cite the statement of Omar ibn al Khattab who succeeded Abu Bakr that "A man would not be secure and would incriminate himself if you starved, frightened or imprisoned him."[101] Finally, they point out that detention is a *Ta'azir* punishment, which cannot be imposed for a crime until after such crime has been proved and a lawful sentence passed.

A leading jurist, Judge Abu Youssef, Abu Hanifa's friend (a founder of one of the four *Sunni* schools of jurisprudence) was the leading proponent of the view that no one can be convicted on another's accusation, that one should be presumed innocent, that a person accused of a *Had* crime or confessing to it should be admonished against confessing as for the Prophet's *Sunna*, and no confession should ever be the basis of a conviction if it was made under coercion, that the interrogation of an accused should not assume his guilt and thus be acausatory, and finally that it is better to err on the side of leniency than in condemning one that could be innocent. He states:

> The accused will not be punished, for you must not accept the complaint alone as proof of one man against another in murder or theft. He should not be punished for a *Hudud* crime save according to clear and certain evidence or a confession free from coercion. It is impermissible to imprison a man merely as a result of another man's accusation against him. The Prophet did not question the people with accusations. But you must call both the accuser and the accused together. If this produces positive evi-

---

[97] Constitutions and Codes of criminal procedure in various nations provide for preventive detention. But in every case that power is subject to certain conditions and guarantees so as to achieve a balance between individual rights and law enforcement interests. *See, e.g.*, Article 41 of the EGYPTIAN CONSTITUTION; Article 48 of the YUGOSLAVIAN CONSTITUTION; Article 104 of the CONSTITUTION OF THE FEDERAL REPUBLIC OF GERMANY; Article 22 of the INDIAN CONSTITUTION; Article 34 of the CONSTITUTION OF JAPAN; Article 13 of the CONSTITUTION OF ITALY; Article 27 of the CONSTITUTION OF SOMALIA; and Article 27 of the CONSTITUTION OF KUWAIT.

[98] *See* 'UBAYD, *supra* note 76, at 446.

[99] For a discussion of these different views, see 2 IBN FARHUN, *supra* note 30, 316 *et seq. See also* ABU YA'LA, *supra* note 50, at 258.

[100] IBN FARHUN, *id.*

[101] ABU YOUSSUF, *supra* note 84, at 175.

> dence in support of his allegations, the judge will rule for him; otherwise, he will set the defendant free. . . . The friends of the Prophet were so cautious about imposing punishments, for fear they might harm the innocent that they preferred to avoid the penalties . . . They would say to an accused thief 'Did you steal? Say no.'[102]

Unlike some Islamic jurists, Abu Youssef was not a proponent of preventive detention. However, one school of Islamic jurists maintain that preventive detention is permissible, with proper observance of conditions and safeguards to balance the interests between the accused and law enforcement authorities. These jurists base their position on the teachings of the Prophet who detained a man accused of a crime.[103]

Among the necessary conditions and safeguards for preventive detention are that the warrant authorizing that procedure must be issued by the official undertaking the investigation. As cited above both the Minister of Complaints and the *Mohtasib* are charged with this duty. The latter may issue such warrant with respect to cases outside his jurisdiction and under the judge's jurisdiction. If the case is referred to the judge on the case, he is responsible for determining the propriety of preventive detention and release. Some jurists would require that the crime be designated as a grave offense such as murder, manslaughter or infliction of grave bodily injury.[104] Still others require the existence of evidence sufficient to sustain a conviction.[105] Finally, some jurists limit the term of preven-

---

[102] *Id.* at 175-76.

[103] IBN FARHUN, *supra* note 30, at 316-17. *See also* IBN QAYYIM AL-JAWZIYAH, AL-TURUQ AL-HUKMIYAH FI AL-SIYASAH AL-SHAR'IYAH 118 (Cairo: al-Mu'assasah al-'Arabiyah lil-Tiba'ah wa-al-Nashr, 1961) [hereinafter referred to as IBN QAYYIM]. The difference of opinion among jurists centered around the term of preventive detention ordered by the Prophet. IBN FARHUN claims the accused was detained for one hour of daytime then released. IBN QAYYIM quotes Abu Hurayrah specifying that the detention lasted one day and one night.

[104] IBN FARHUN is one of the opinion that:

> the detention of the accused for murder, severe beating which may result in death, or grave wounding is left to the ruler's discretion. The accused may be detained for about one month. If the accusation is strengthened for any reason, the detention is extended. If no positive evidence emerges and the same condition persists, he should be released after one month.

See IBN FARHUN, *supra* note 30, at 330.

[105] For instance if only one witness presents himself, the hearing of the case is adjourned until the required quorum of witnesses is secured and clear evidence is established. In case of two witnesses, the case may be adjourned to verify their impartiality (probity). IBN FARHUN states in this respect:

> if a man accused of a *Had* crime is detained, and one witness testifies in the case, the ruler would have discretionary power to adjourn the case in order to secure the legally required number of witnesses. Also if there are two witnesses, the ruler could adjourn until their impartiality is verified. The term of detention is left to the discretion of the ruler until clear evidence is discovered.

See IBN FARHUN, *supra* note 30, at 330.

The requirement of sufficient evidence to justify preventive detention is emphasized by AL-MAWARDI who says that:

> the state of crime after accusation and before it becomes established and valid is presumed to be true. If a man accused of theft or adultery is brought before a ruler, he would not be influenced by such accusation. The ruler should not confine the accused for discovering or proving innocence prior to hearing the complaint of theft from one credible eyewitness, and until he takes into account his confession or denial.

See AL-MAWARDI, *supra* note 51, at 219.

tive detention to a maximum period. For instance, al Zobairi defines one month as the maximum[106] while ibn Farhon sets the maximum at less than one month.[107]

In conclusion, it is clear from the above discussion that one school of Islamic jurists deems preventive detention to be unlawful *per se*, which is a position favoring protection and safeguarding personal liberties and the right to individual security. Another school considers the measure permissible, but with conditions, restrictions and safeguards which aim at the realization of the necessary balance between the individual right to freedom and security on the one hand and the interest of society in effective law enforcement on the other.

GUARANTEES OF THE ACCUSED DURING TRIAL

A fair and prompt adjudication satisfying all the guarantees and safeguards which enable the accused to exert his right to present a defense and establish his innocence is necessary to sustain a conviction under Islamic law. During his trial, the accused enjoys fundamental safeguards and guarantees. First of all, under the accusatorial system adopted by Islamic law the defendant is shielded by essential guarantees. Secondly, the adoption of legal evidence in *Hudud* crimes involves restrictions on the judge's discretionary power in favor of the accused. Third, the accused has the right to be tried before a competent court and to a fair and impartial trial. The accused also has the right to counsel or to present his own defense. Finally, he is entitled to indemnity for an erroneous conviction.

In all essential respects, the Islamic criminal justice system is accusatorial in nature. While the scope of public accusation is narrow, relative to other legal systems, that function is served by the *Mohtasib* or Minister of Complaints who perform the task of investigation.

The form of the trial and the execution of sentences also are indicative of the system's accusatorial character. If the accused appears guilty, the *Mohtasib* or the Minister of Complaints within their respective jurisdictions submit the case for consideration by the competent judge to determine guilt according to the rules of Islamic law.[108] The private criminal complaint (which in Islamic law is dependent upon a complaint initiated by the victim) includes prosecutions for a number of crimes. Pecuniary crimes under Islamic law are private offenses, so that prosecution is again dependent upon an accusation or complaint by the victim. Also,

---

This same requirement may be deduced from ABU YA'LA'S statement that:

> the ruler may hear the accusation against the suspect from his own assistants without investigating the case. He must inquire whether the accused is of suspicious character and whether he is known to have committed similar acts. If the suspect is cleared, the accusation is alleviated and his release is expedited without faulting him. However, if he has been charged with similar acts, his accusation is strengthened and should be used in the inquiry.

See ABU YA'LA, *supra* note 50, at 258.

[106] Mentioned by AL-MAWARDI, *supra* note 51, at 220; and ABU YA'LA, *supra* note 50, at 258; and IBN FARHUN, *supra* note 30, at 330.

[107] IBN FARHUN, *id.*

[108] *See* al-'Ashmawi, *supra* note 70, at 342, 347 *et seq.* The scope of this complaint is confined to adultery, wine drinking, rebellion and apostasy in addition to discretionary penalties (*Ta'azir*) involving violations of divine rights. 345.

murder and battery are private offenses and subject to the complaint of the victim or his guardian, who may initiate or terminate the complaint or even forgive the accused and thereby discharge him from punishment. They also may achieve reconciliation with the accused even after rendition of sentence.[109] Thus, the rights of the accused, especially those which permit him to prove his innocence, are an integral part of this system.

Concerning *Hudud* and *Quesas* crimes the judge exercises discretionary powers in favor of the accused in determining the admissibility of evidence. The Islamic system is one which operates to determine guilt or innocence by means of legal proof. In rendering judgement, the judge is bound to observe certain categories of evidence as defined and prescribed by the legislator, regardless of his satisfaction with the probative value of the evidence submitted to him. In other words, the satisfaction of the legislator with the probative value of the evidence is conclusive on the judge, if course found to exist. This system of proof is applied to *Hudud* and *Quesas* crimes, but in *Ta'azir* crimes evidence is more liberally admitted and there are no rules of evidence in the submission of proof. The judge is entitled to accept any proof which he assesses in terms of weight and credibility in arriving at his decision.

Rules of evidence and admissibility of evidence in the prosecution of *Hudud* and *Quesas* crimes is confined to tangible evidence to be produced by the accuser or an uncoerced and free confession by the accused. The testimony of four male eyewitnesses is required to prove adultery, and that of two male witnesses in the other *Hudud* crimes and for *Quesas* crimes. The witness must be sane, of legal age, free, not dumb, mute or blind, and must not have been punished for a *Hudud* offense. Also, a witness cannot be related to the accused (his father or son) or be married to the accuser. He also must not bear malice toward the accused, and he must be a person of integrity. The victim's testimony as a witness in his case is disregarded unless supported by oath. Hearsay testimony is inadmissible because of unsupported oaths. The testimony of women is inadmissible (on the irrebutable presumption that they can be easily influenced or coerced).

In order for a confession to be admissible, it must pertain to the offense charged. Although there is a disagreement among jurists as to the number of times the confession must be repeated, by the better view it must be repeated as many times as the number of witnesses.[110]

Moreover, *Hudud* offenses are not punished if there is reasonable doubt as to the guilt of the accused. Consequently the accused is either considered innocent of the crime ascribed to him or he is subjected to a *Ta'azir* punishment. In the latter event the proof of the crime is not subject to particular rules of evidence but is governed by the judge's personal conviction (much as is the case in continental criminal law).

---

[109] *Id.* at 354.

[110] On the confession and its rank among the modes of evidence in Islamic Law, *see* 1 THE MINISTRY OF ENDOWMENTS AND ISLAMIC AFFAIRS, AL-MAWSU'AH AL-FIQHIYAH, 1980, 234-35 (Kuwait, 1980) [hereinafter referred to as AL-MAWSU'AH AL-FIQHIYAH].

The system of proof for *Hudud* offenses involves guarantees for the benefit of the accused against the error and abuse of discretion of the judge. Also, the accused is not sentenced if the prosecutor fails to furnish the required positive proof in terms of kind, number and conditions. The judge is without authority in the absence of such proof to convict and cannot rely on his discretion or personal conviction.[111]

Under Islamic law, it is the judicial authority, in the form of a competent court, that is entitled to determine the truth in all disputes, both civil and criminal.[112] The competence of the court derives from having the accused before it, from the subject matter of the case and from the site of the trial.

With respect to jurisdiction over the person, the judge in the Islamic system is competent to rule on every motion in any criminal case within the territory of an Islamic state. Thus, for example, Ali ibn Abi Talib, as Khalifa of the Muslims, stood before Judge Sharih to resolve a dispute between himself and a Jew as to the ownership of a shield which the Imam allegedly missed when he went out to fight Moawia.[113] We also find al-Mamoun, another Khalifa, who appeared before Judge Yahia ibn Iktham al Saify, Judge of Baghdad, in a dispute between the Khalifa and another man.[114] These examples show that the jurisdiction of the Islamic judge encompasses all people who reside within the territory of the state without discrimination or exception.

However, nothing precludes the establishment of courts of limited or specialized jurisdiction. Only Islamic law recognizes the specialization of the judge for his defined category of cases. For instance, al-Mawardy in al-Akham al Sultania states:

> If two judges are appointed in a city and one of them receives a category of complaints and the other receives another category, such as the payment of blood money to the former and the marriages to the latter, this is permissible provided that each is confined to the judgement of what is under his hand.[115]

There also are gradations of competence within particular categories. Thus, for example, some judges are assigned to simple offenses such as misdemeanors, while others are assigned to felonies. Some judges may hear cases involving a

---

[111] 'ABD AL-WAHHAB HAWMAD, AL-WASIT FI AL-IJRA'AT AL-JAZA'IYAH AL-KUWAYTIYAH [CRIMINAL PROCEDURE IN KUWAIT] 179. (Kuwait: The University of Kuwait Press, 1974). *See also* 1 MUSTAFA, *supra* note 56, at 7-8.

[112] With the exception of the Minister of Complaints (*Wali al-Mazalim*), who possesses a special jurisdiction, two authorities according to Islamic Law receive criminal motions directly: the judge with general competence and the *muhtasib* whose jurisdiction is limited to settling disputes in cases of fraud and swindling in trades and occupations which do not involve denial and do not require positive evidence or oaths. *See* 2 IBN KHALDUN, AL-MUQADDIMAH, 746 (Cairo: Lajnat al-Bayan al-'Arabi, 1957-62). *See also* AL-MAWARDI, *supra* note 51, at 241-42.

[113] 2 MUHAMMAD IBN KHALAF WAKI', AKHBAR AL-QUDAH, 200 (ed. 'Abd al-'Aziz al-Maraghi. Cairo: Matba'at al-Istiqamah 1947-50).

[114] *See* 2 IBRAHIM IBN MUHAMMAD AL-BAYHAQI, AL-MAHASIN WA-AL-MASAWI', (Cairo: Maṭba'at Nahdat Misr, 1961). Cited by IBRAHIM NAJIB MUHAMMAD 'AWAD, AL-QADA'AL-ISLAMI: TARIKHUH WA-NUZUMUH [ISLAMIC JUSTICE: ITS HISTORY AND SYSTEMS] 81-82 (Cairo: Majma' al-Buhuth al-Islamiyah, 1975), [hereinafter referred to as 'AWAD].

[115] AL-MAWARDI, *supra* note 51, at 73.

limited sum of money not exceeding a prescribed amount, while another judge may be assigned to consider cases involving larger sums. It is reported that Omar said to one of his judges: "Be in my stead in litigations of one dirham or two dirhams. Do not let anybody appeal to me in such cases."[116] Also Abu Abdallah al-Zobairi relates: "For a period, people of al-Basra went to a given judge of the mosque to settle their litigations. This judge determined cases of 200 dirhams and twenty dinars and lesser amounts without exceeding what was defined for him."[117]

Islamic law also recognizes the principle that the judge should be required to render his judgements in a defined city or in a part thereof. Thus, he has no jurisdiction in any other place save what is assigned to him.[118] His jurisdiction extends to the actions which occur within his local competence, regardless of whether the litigants are permanent or temporary residents within the jurisdiction of his court. If the parties are from different places, the competent judge will be from the place of defendant's residence. This rule is based on the policy that the defendant is free until his guilt is established. It is deemed unjust to burden the defendant with moving elsewhere to defend himself before the claim against him or his guilt is established.[119] Some authorities hold that the designation of the competent judge should be left to the defendant.[120]

From the foregoing discussion it is clear that the right of the accused to appear before a competent court is ensured under Islamic law and that, in general, Islamic jurists do not disagree on the principles of court organization and judicial competence. Islam also permits the participation of more than one judge in determining a case.[121] Even though Islamic jurists have not known the modern form of judicial process with its various levels of courts, the different methods of

---

[116] MUHAMMAD SALLAM MADKUR, MADKHAL AL-FIQH AL-ISLAMI [INTRODUCTION TO ISLAMIC JURISPRUDENCE], 364-65 (3rd ed. Cairo: Dar al-Nahdah al-'Arabiyah, 1966), [hereinafter referred to as MADKUR].

[117] Cited by AL-MAWARDI, *supra* note 51, at 73.

[118] AL-MAWARDI says:

> If he were appointed to judge those who came to his own house or mosque, it is right, and not permissible to judge outside his own house or mosque, for his jurisdiction and competence is restricted to those who came to his house or mosque . . . hence his judgment therein became a condition.

See AL-MAWARDI, *id.*

[119] MADKUR, *supra* note 116, at 364.

[120] 1 Muhammad Na'im 'Abd al-Salam Yasin, Nazariyat al-Da'wa bayn al-shari'ah al-Islamiyah wa-qanun al-murafa'at al-madaniyah wa-al-tijariyah [The Theory of Motion Between Islamic Law and Civil and Commercial Procedural Law] 224 (Ph.D. dissertation, al-Azhar University, 1972). On the disagreement among jurists on this subject, *see id.* at 321 *et seq.* [hereinafter referred to as Yasin].

[121] *See* MADKUR, *supra* note 116, at 361; *see also* MUHAMMAD FARUQ AL-NABHAN, NIZAM AL-HUKM FI AL-ISLAM [THE SYSTEM OF GOVERNMENT IN ISLAM] 641 (Kuwait: The University of Kuwait Pub., 1974). AL-NABHAN quotes the writer of *Maslak al-absar* saying that:

> Certain serious litigations were considered before four judges. It seems that they used to meet in the mosque of Damascus at the instructions of the Sultan's deputy and deliberate complex questions which could not be properly decided by one judge alone. They would render jointly the required judgment on the disputed issue.

See MAHMUD 'ARNUS, TARIKH AL-QADA' FI AL-ISLAM [THE HISTORY OF JURISPRUDENCE IN ISLAM] (Cairo: al-Matba'ah al-Misriyah al-Ahliyah, 1934).

appealing from judgements and the timing of such procedures, nevertheless the rules of Islamic law do not resist new developments in the judicial process which are compatible with Islamic doctrines.[122]

Islamic law further assures the accused of the right to a just and impartial trial. This is achieved because the judiciary is bound to apply fundamental principles of justice and equality and because of safeguards which guarantee the impartiality of judges.

The pursuit of justice and equality is an ideal rooted in the conscience of the Islamic community from the beginning. That ideal governs the conduct of all state authorities including the judiciary. It is ordained in the *Qu'ran* and the Tradition of the Prophet. God says:

> Oh, mankind! Lo, we have created you male and female and have made you nations and tribes that you may know one another. Lo, the noblest of you in the sight of Allah is the best in conduct.[123]

God also says: "The believers are naught else than brothers."[124] Islam places great emphasis on justice and equality. The word "justice," which implies equality, is used in the *Qu'ran* more than 14 times, and the word *al'quest*, which means justice and equality appears in the holy text more than 16 times.

The Tradition of the Prophet is equally insistent upon universal justice and equality. The Prophet says: "Men are equal as the teeth of a comb. No Arab individual is superior to a non-Arab except in piety." The first constitutional document issued by the Prophet as ruler of the state of El-Medina included nine times the words *al-quest* and *al-adl* meaning equity and justice.[125]

In the message of Omar ibn al-Khattab, Judge Abu Musa al-Ashali was ordered: "To make people equal before you in your sessions and in your justice, lest no noble may look forward to your injustice and no humble person may despair of your justice."[126] Om Salma reports that the Prophet said: "He who is tried among the Muslims must be equal among them..."[127]

On the basis of these teachings, Islamic jurists conclude that the judge is obligated to treat all who come before him in a fair and impartial manner without discrimination between the noble and the humble, between the free person and the slave, or between the Muslim and the non-Muslim.

Finally, many safeguards which ensure the independence and objectivity of

---

[122] *See* MADKUR, *supra* note 116, at 367-68.

[123] *Surat al-Hujurat* XLIX:13.

[124] *Surat al-Hujurat* XLIX:10.

[125] *See* MUNIR HAMID AL-BAYATI, AL-DAWLAH AL-QANUNIYAH FI AL-NIZAM AL-SIYASI AL-ISLAMI [THE LEGAL STATE IN THE ISLAMIC POLITICAL SYSTEM] 116 (1st ed. Baghdad: Dar al-'Arabiyah lil-Tiba'ah, 1979), [hereinafter referred to as AL-BAYATI].

The document of al-Madinah containing 47 articles is published in MUHAMMAD HAMIDULLAH, MAJMU'AT AL-WATHA'IQ AL-SIYASIYAH FI AL-'AHD AL-NABAWI WA-AL-KHILAFAH AL-RASHIDAH [A COLLECTION OF THE POLITICAL DOCUMENTS OF THE PROPHETIC ERA AND THE ORTHODOX CALIPHS] 41-47 (Cairo: Lajnat al-Ta'lif wa-al-Tarjamah wa-al-Nashr, 1956).

[126] *See* AL-MAWARDI, *supra* note 51, at 76.

[127] Cited in Yasin, *supra* note 120, at 11. His sources are: 10 AL-BAYHAQI, *supra* note 58, at 135; and ALI IBN 'UMAR AL-DARAQUTNI, SUNAN, 205 (al-Madinah: Matba'at Kutub al-Sunna al-Nabawiyah, 1966), [hereinafter referred to asa AL-DARAQUTNI].

judges are incorporated into the institution of the Islamic judiciary. These include the protection of the judge from dismissal except for particular reasons,[128] rules and qualifications for the selection of judges,[129] liability of judges for violation of the principles of the Islamic law,[130] and the prohibition against rendering judgement according to personal information.[131] Rather, the evidence must be obtained in accordance with valid procedures.[132] The judge also must base his decision and sentence on definiteness[133] to achieve an impartial judiciary in the Islamic system, with the ultimate goal being to ensure the accused a fair trial.[134]

The right of the accused to obtain counsel or defend himself is guaranteed under Islamic law at the investigation and primary interrogation stages. This right is additional to and reinforces the right to be tried before a competent court by a just and impartial judge. The right to counsel further implements the right of the accused to prove his innocence.[135]

Islamic law guarantees to both the accuser and the accused the right to appoint another person to represent him before the judge.[136] Islamic jurists point out that this right was first discussed as the principle of the *wakil* (agent) in litigation by al-Baihaqi in *al-Sunan al-Kobra* where it is reported: "Ali ibn Abu Talib disliked litigation. In any in which he was a party, he appointed Okail ibn Abi-Talib to represent him. When he grew very old, he appointed me."[137] Jurists conclude that the friends of the Prophet agreed among themselves on the right to obtain counsel from the fact that no one denied the existence of this right once it was effective.

However, jurists disagree as to the scope of the right with respect to *Hudud* offenses.[138] Jurists distinguish between the evidence required to prove *Hudud*

---

[128] For the independence of the judiciary in Islam, *see* AL-BAYATI, *supra* note 125, at 422 *et seq.*

[129] For the bases and prerequisites for selecting judges, *see* AL-MAWARDI, *supra* note 51, at 65 *et seq.*; and ABU YA'LA, *supra* note 50, at 60 *et seq. See also* AL-HAMAWI, *supra* note 58, at 21 *et seq.*

[130] For the liability of judges, *see* 1 IBN FARHUN, *supra* note 30, at 79. *See also* MADKUR, *supra* note 116, at 372.

[131] *See* AL-MAWARDI, *supra* note 51, at 70; and IBN FARHUN, *supra* note 30, at 32 *et seq. See also* 9 MUWAFFAQ AL-DIN IBN QUDAMAH, AL-MUGHNI 53 (Cairo: Matba'at al-Imam, 1964). In contemporary jurisprudence, *see* MADKUR, *supra* note 116, at 353 and AL-MAWSU'AH AL'FIQHIYAH, *supra* note 110, at 243.

[132] If the evidence was collected through spying, for example, it would be inadmissible.

[133] Doubt should be explained for the benefit of the accused in accordance with the presumption of innocence adopted by Islamic Law and in compliance with the principle of repealing *Had* crimes in case of doubt.

[134] Prince of the Faithful, 'Ali ibn Abi Talib, stood before his appointee, Judge Shurayh, in a complaint brought against him by a Jew. Similarly, Harun al-Rashid appeared before his Judge, Abu Yusuf, in a suit brought by a Christian. In both cases, the Judges ruled against the two Caliphs. *See* MADKUR, *supra* note 116, at 359.

[135] On the right of the defendant to obtain counsel under positive law, *see* Hasan Muhammad 'Allub, Isti'anat al-muttaham bi-muhami fi al-qanun al-muqaran [The Defendant's Recourse to Legal Counsel in Comparative Law], (Ph.D. dissertation, Cairo University, 1970), [hereinafter referred to as 'Allub].

[136] On the subject of agency during litigation, *see* Ahmad al-Sammak, Ahkam al-wakalah fi al-shari'ah al-Islamiyah: dirasah muqarinah [The Rules of Agency in Islamic Law: A Comparative Study], (M.A. Thesis, al-Azhar University, 1978), [hereinafter referred to as al-Sammak].

[137] *See* 6 AL-BAYHAQI, *supra* note 58, at 81; quoted by al-Sammak, *id.* at 204.

[138] For a discussion of these different opinions, *see* al-Sammak, *supra* note 136, at 109-12.

offenses and the evidence required to prove *Quesas* and *Ta'azir* offenses.

One view on the right to counsel is represented by the *Shafei*, *Hanbali*, *Hanafites*, some *Imames* and Abul Khattab, one of the *Hanbali* jurists, who contend that the right to counsel does not apply in *Hudud* crimes since their evidentiary requirements are established and in the absence of reasonable doubt of violation of divine right, punishment will not be imposed, as the Prophet instructed.[139]

The *Hanbali* (with the exception of Abul Khattab) and some of the *Imame* contend that counsel is allowed in the trial of all *Hudud* crimes. Their argument is based on the statement from the *Sunna* where the Prophet is quoted: "Go, Anas, to the wife of this man. If she confesses, stone her." This tradition indicates that counsel is permissible for *Hudud* crimes even with respect to punishments for violations of the rights of God, such as the penalty for the crime of adultery. Moreover, proponents of this view argue in response to those who reject the right to counsel that the agent substitutes for the principal in avoiding the doubts which omit the punishment.[140]

Several schools of Islamic jurists maintain, by contrast, that the right to counsel attaches to *Quesas* and *Ta'azir* offenses and to certain *Hudud* offenses like theft and defamation, since all of those offenses involve violation of the rights of men.[141]

All Muslim jurists agree on the major point that the right to counsel applies to *Ta'azir* offenses, whether or not counsel is actually present at the trial, for it is related to man's rights and conviction can be based on the judge's discretion. As to counsel at the stage of execution of *Hudud* and *Quesas* crimes jurists differ. Some say agency, which is the basis of the right to counsel, is present; others say it is allowed in both cases.

The *Hanafit*,[142] and *Hanbali* hold that agency does not arise at the stage of execution of punishment if counsel is absent at the time the punishment is carried out. They argue that it is possible for counsel to confirm the accusation if the punishment relates to the rights of God, and to encourage forgiveness if the punishment pertains to avoidance of blood money or retaliation. These situations imply doubt, and doubt prevents enforcement of the punishment.[143]

But the *Maliki*, Imam Zahiri, and Imam Ahmed, agree with the view of the *Shafei* that counsel is allowed at the enforcement stage, whether counsel is in fact present or not.[144] They point out, first of all, that the judges of the Prophet ruled

---

[139] *Id.* at 109. Al-Sammak's sources are: 2 MUHAMMAD IBN AL-HASAN AL-TUSI, AL-MABSUT FI FIQH AL-IMAMIYAH 362 (Tehran: al-Maktabah al-Murtadawiyah, 1967-8); and 3 AL-DARAQUTNI, *supra* note 127, at 84.

[140] *Id.* at 110. Al-Sammak quotes from 2 AL-BUKHARI, *supra* note 57, at 30; and 5 SAHIH MUSLIM, *supra* note 57, at 121.

[141] *Id.* Al-Sammak's source is 6 AL-KASANI, *supra* note 58, at 21.

[142] The Hanafi view is confined to retaliation and *Hudud* crimes bearing on the rights of individuals, for example, defamation and theft. But as to crimes against the rights of God which do not require litigation, such as drinking and adultery, the Hanafis hold that representation for the execution of punishment is not allowed. *See* al-Sammak, *supra* note 136, at 111.

[143] *Id.*

[144] Some jurists of the Zaydiyah sect absolutely reject representation at the enforcement stage in

in different places and enforced *Hudud* punishments which were abandoned in case of doubt. Secondly, they say that what can be enforced in the presence of counsel can also be enforced in his absence. Whether or not the victim desires to pardon the offender can be expressed through counsel at the time punishment is imposed, or the victim can make his claim himself. In any event, both victim and offender should be entitled to counsel if they feel it is necessary to protect their interests. Finally, there is no danger in bringing the witness to view the punishment of a *Hudud* crime based on the possibility that he might withdraw his confession or say something to change the judge's mind.[145]

The right to counsel also has its origin under Islamic law in the "Theory of Protected Interests." These interests are:[146] (1) freedom of religion (which implies for the Muslim the freedom to practice Islam, for the non-Muslim the freedom to convert to Islam, and for the Christian and Jew the freedom to exercise his faith); (2) preservation and protection of oneself (physical protection and self-preservation); and (3) freedom of the mind (implying all freedoms relating to the functions of the intellect, such as freedom of thought, expression, acquisition of knowledge, and education); (4) the right to procreate (which implies the right to marry, have a family and conduct family life); and (5) the right to property (its acquisition, preservation, and disposition).

These "protected interests" are such by their very nature that may require its beneficiary to rely on the assistance of others to be able to attain his rights and protect them. The "Theory of Protected Interests" is thus founded upon the consideration that every person has the right to do what is in his welfare and resist what is harmful and to use the services of others to accomplish his ends. The companions of the Prophet followed this theory in practice, and many jurists who followed their example adapted the early rules to the particular needs and circumstances of their time in a manner consistent with the letter and spirit of the *Shari'a*.[147] Furthermore, to uphold the "protected interests" Islamic law penalizes their violators.

The preservation of the self according to Islamic jurists implies the preservation of the right to live with dignity. It includes both the preservation of physical well-being and certain moral aspects such as the maintenance of dignity and the freedom from humiliation. It also includes freedom to work, freedom of conscience and freedom to live where one chooses. It assumes that in a civilized society, liberty is the cornerstone of human life, which in turn ensures the security of the individual.[148] It is clear that the principle of preservation of self is enhanced by extension of the right to counsel to those accused of crimes, as it provides the accused with the means to establish innocence and to defend himself.[149] Thus, for example, the accused may be unable to defend himself

---

cases of *Hudud* or retaliation crimes whether counsel is present or not. *See id.*, based on 5 AL-BAHR AL-ZAKHIR, 63.

[145] *Id.* at 11.

[146] *See* 1 AL-GHAZZALI, *supra* note 3, at 277.

[147] See MADKUR, *supra* note 116, at 258.

[148] *See* 2 ABU ZAHRAH, *supra* note 3, at 38.

[149] *See* 'Allub, *supra* note 135, at 49-50.

effectively because he is prone to violent outbursts, or he may lack sufficient comprehension or sophistication to establish his innocence by personally pleading before the judge. If he is denied counsel, his rights are not adequately protected, especially if he is erroneously charged. His failure to demonstrate error or prejudice could result in irreparable harm. These and other difficulties which the accused faces in the contemporary Islamic system of criminal justice necessitate the assistance of a skilled specialist.

Even if it is argued that the right to counsel is not encompassed within the concept of self-preservation, it can be justified as necessary to protect the interests of society in general. If individuals are not assured of personal security, society itself cannot be safe. Thus, to the extent that it is consistent with Islamic doctrine, the right to counsel can be justified on grounds of protecting the greater interest of society.[150]

The importance of adequate legal representation in the judicial process cannot be minimized. The attorney assists in discovering the truth and thereby protects the rights of all parties. His assistance to the judge is also invaluable not only for the time saved in prosecuting cases but also in reaching correct results. The Islamic system, no less than any other system, recognizes the importance of the attorney.[151] This becomes particularly important because under Islamic law the accused is entitled to damages for an erroneous judgement. If the judge intended injustice and rendered an unjust decision favorable to a nobleman or another person in authority, this action constitutes a crime punishable by *Ta'azir* and dismissal. In addition, the property of such a biased judge serves as security for the victim's compensation.

If the error is unintentional, it is necessary to distinguish between charges involving the rights of man and those involving the rights of God. Concerning the rights of man (such as in the case of *Quesas* and *Ta'azir* crimes), if the erroneous judgement is final and executed and the error is due to fraud on the part of the accuser, his property shall be attached and used as security for payment.

If the erroneous judgement concerns the rights of God (such as in a *Had* crime), the compensation is due by the Treasury of the Muslims (*Beit Mal al Muslimin*) and there is no liability on the judge because he acts for the people on behalf of the Muslim state, and performs his judicial function for the public welfare.[152] Thus, to insure a person of that right, a knowledgeable person is necessary and that is usually the attorney.

RIGHTS OF PRISONERS

The history of Islam reveals that confinement could be used as punishment for crimes of *Ta'azir*.[153] Islamic jurists hold different views concerning the lawful-

---

[150] *See* MADKUR, *supra* note 116, at 255-56; and 'Allub. *id.* at 51.
[151] Al-Sammak, *supra* note 136, at 206-07.
[152] *See* MADKUR, *supra* note 116, at 362; and AL-NABHAN, *supra* note 121, at 650-51.
[153] *See* 'AMIR, *supra* note 22, at 361.

ness of imprisonment and the conditions of confinement.[154] However, since imprisonment is legitimized and practiced under Islamic law, the rights of prisoners must be considered. Most jurists agree that regardless of the offense, no prisoner should be insulted, humiliated, beaten, tortured or chained (except to prevent flight).[155]

It is noteworthy that Abu Youssef, the companion of Imam Abou Hanifa, was a strong advocate of the rights of prisoners in early times and did much to protect their interests. Abu Youssef recounts an incident in which a Ruler wrote to his governors concerning the prisoners. The Ruler commanded that no Muslim should be in chains save those of whom it was required for retaliation. Also they were to receive alms sufficient for clothing and food.[156] Abu Youssef then states that it is impermissible to torture or beat prisoners, on the authority of the analogy that the Prophet forbids beating those who pray and even prisoners pray. According to Abu Youssef this *Sunna* implies that prisoners should not be beaten for any crime.[157] Abu Youssef also advocated that monthly salaries should be paid to indigent prisoners, men and women alike, besides providing them with clothing in summer and winter to care for their needs and for their families.[158] Finally, Abu Youssef mentions that if a prisoner dies, the public treasury (*Beit al Mal*) must bear the expenses of his funeral.[159]

THE PRINCIPLE OF LEGITIMACY AS THE CORNERSTONE OF THE RIGHT TO PERSONAL SECURITY IN THE ISLAMIC STATE

The principle of legitimacy, is the principle of supremacy of law. It means that all acts, procedures, dispositions and final decisions of the public authorities at any level cannot be valid and legally binding as to the people they affect, save to the extent they are consistent with the law. If such decisions are issued contrary to applicable law, they are invalid or unlawful. The principle of the legitimacy or supremacy of law is a general principle which is so deeply rooted in modern man's conscience that no civilized society can function effectively without it. This principle governs the interactions of all the authorities of the state and the individual.

---

[154] Ibn Qayyim al-Jawziyah states:

> Legitimate imprisonment is not confinement in a narrow place, but impeding the person and preventing him from his freedom of movement, whether he is placed in a house or a mosque, or charging the plaintiff or his representative with guarding him or appointing him a keeper. This process is called "*tarsim*," and the confined person is called the "prisoner." ... This was confinement during the Prophet's era and that of his successor Abu Bakr. There were no prisons assigned to confine litigants. However, during the rule of 'Umar ibn al-Khattab, when the population increased, he bought the house of Safwan ibn Umayah for four thousand dirhams and made it a prison.

See IBN QAYYIM, *supra* note 103, at 119-20.

[155] Some jurists argue that prisoners should not be deprived of conjugal privileges with their spouses if they so desire. *See* 'AWAD, *supra* note 114, at 274.

[156] *See* ABU YOUSSUF, *supra* note 84, at 150.

[157] *Id.* at 151.

[158] *Id.* at 150.

[159] *Id.* at 151.

Islamic jurists recognize that within the context of Islamic law, the establishment of the principle of legitimacy is a vital safeguard of individual rights. By virtue of this principle, rights are secure from violation by the state and are not affected except in accordance with the law. Thus, the principle of legitimacy is the foundation of the individual's right to security and must be governed by the rule of law.[160]

THE PRECEDENCE OF ISLAM IN ESTABLISHING THE PRINCIPLE OF LEGITIMACY

In medieval Europe and beyond, the state possessed absolute power, and the monarch, as sovereign, was literally responsible only to God. During the Middle Ages, however, the Arabian Peninsula had already witnessed the birth of the first legal state established by Islam some ten centuries earlier. It was unique, satisfying all the requirements of the contemporary legal state. It had a constitution and a uniform body of law to govern the conduct and protect the rights of all the people. The state also was regulated by the principle of legitimacy and the supremacy of law. It thereby recognized public rights and liberties for individuals and furnished sufficient guarantees to maintain them.[161]

EVIDENCE OF THE LEGITIMACY PRINCIPLE IN ISLAMIC LAW

No authority in the Islamic state is authorized to perform any function unless prescribed by law; otherwise these actions are invalid and illegal. The *Qu'ran* provides that the public authorities in the Islamic state are obligated to follow the principle of legitimacy. God says: "The decisions rest with Allah only who hath commanded that ye worship none save him."[162] He also says: "Follow that which is sent down unto you from your Lord, and seek the protection of no one besides him."[163] Also: "So judge between them by that which Allah hath revealed."[164] And: "Whoso judgeth not by that which Allah hath revealed."[165] And: "Whoso judgeth not by that which Allah hath revealed, such are wrongdoers."[166] Finally: "Whoso judgeth not by that which Allah hath revealed, such lead evil lives."[167]

SOURCES OF LEGITIMACY AND THE RANKING OF LEGAL RULES IN ISLAMIC LAW

Islamic jurists are forerunners in the development of the theory of ranking of legal rules, whereby some rules are deemed superior to others and these inferior rules are subject to higher rules. The application of this principle of ranking is significant with respect to constitutional jurisprudence and as a basis for judicial

---

[160] On the principle of legitimacy in positive law in general *see* TU'AYMAH AL-JARF, MABDA' AL-MASHRU'IYAH WA-DAWABIT KHUDU' AL-DAWLAH LIL-QANUN [THE PRINCIPLE OF LEGITIMACY AND THE CONTROLS FOR SUBJECTING THE STATE TO THE LAW] 5-6 (Cairo: Maktabat al-Qahirah al-Hadithah, 1963). *Also* Tharwat Badawi, *The Legal State*, 3 MAJALLAT QADAYA AL-HUKUMAH (1959). *See also* AL-NADI, *supra* note 85. In French law, *see* Charles Eisenman, *Le droit administratif et le principe de legalité*, 11 E.D.C.E. 25 *et seq.* (1957).

[161] AL-BAYATI, *supra* note 125, at 55 *et seq.*

[162] *Surat Yusuf* XII:40.

[163] *Surat al-A'raf* VII:3.

[164] *Surat al-Ma'edah* V:49.

[165] *Surat al Ma'edah* V:44.

[166] *Surat al-Ma'edah* V:45.

[167] *Surat al Ma'edah* V:47.

decision.[168] Islamic jurists point out that the sources of legislation are not equal but follow a ranking from the superior to the inferior, by placing the legal rule derived from a superior source in a rank above the rule derived from an inferior or secondary source. In light of this ranking principle, each legal rule canot be valid save to the extent it is consistent with superior rules. These superior rules, if determined to be valid, restrict the meaning and scope of inferior rules.

The exclusive primary source of Islamic law and the one to which all others are subject is the *Qu'ran*. It is defined by Islamic jurists as follows:

> The Word revealed to Mohamed was communicated to us in a successive order, beginning with Sorat al Fatiha and ending with Sorat al Nas and is compiled between the two binders of the Moshaf (the holy book), revealed to the Prophet in word and meaning to memorize and communicate it to mankind as revealed.[169]

The jurists and students of *Usul* (principles) agree that the *Qu'ran* is the primary and supreme source of all Islamic law. It is the most universally binding source and constitutes the fundamental reference. Thus, it rests atop the legal hierarchy of Islam.

The second most important is the Tradition of the Prophet, the *Sunna*. This source includes his writings, deeds and statements. According to Islamic doctrine, the *Qu'ran* ordains compliance with the *Sunna*. God says: "And whatsoever the Messenger giveth you, take it and whatsoever he forbidith, abstain from it."[170] The *Sunna* follows the *Qu'ran* because the *Qu'ran* revealed all fundamental truths to mankind, as transmitted by the Prophet. Therefore, in case of any apparent contradition between the *Qu'ran* and the *Sunna*, the two must be harmonized if possible; otherwise the *Qu'ran* prevails.[171]

The third source of Islamic law is *Ijma'* the general consensus among Islamic jurists as achieved in a given era after the death of the Prophet concerning the correct legal rule in certain matters.

There is unanimity among Islamic jurists that the general consent to a rule makes it binding. Thus, consensus is considered a source of Islamic law. Any rule which is unanimously agreed upon becomes established and definite, except to the extent it conflicts with rules derived from higher sources, and cannot be violated. The subject matter becomes fixed at the time of consensus and is not subject to the principle of continuity.[172] The basis for the principle of consensus is found in the *Qu'ran*. God says: "And whoso opposeth the Messenger after the revelation of Allah hath been manifested unto him and followeth other than the

---

[168] Some of the most important sources in this field are: MUHAMMAD IBN IDRIS AL-SHAFI'I, RISALAT AL-SHAFI'I FI 'ILM 'USUL AL-FIQH (Egypt: Maktabat Subayh (1909?); IBRAHIM IBN MUSA AL-SHATIBI, KITAB AL-MUWAFAQAT FI 'USUL AL-AHKAM (Cairo: Matba'at al-Ma'arif, 1914); MUHAMMAD IBN 'ALI AL-SHAWKANI, KITAB IRSHAD AL-FUHUL (Egypt: Matba'at al-Sa'adah, 1909); ABU AL-HASAN AL-BA'LI (IBN AL-LUHAM), AL-QAWA'ID WA-AL-FAWA'ID AL-'USULIYAH (Cairo: al-Matba'ah al'Muhammadiyah, 1956).

[169] *See* MADKUR, *supra* note 116, at 200.

[170] *Surat al-Hashr* LIX:7.

[171] MADKUR, *supra* note 116, at 209.

[172] *Id.* at 221.

believer's way, we appoint for him that unto which he himself hath turned and expose him unto hell."[173] The basis of this theory of consensus is the *Sunna* of the Prophet, who says: "My nation do not agree unanimously on straying." He also says: "My nation do not unanimously agree in error." And: "Whatsoever the Muslims see as good, will be good in the sight of God."[174] But as noted, the rules derived by consensus must be consistent with the *Qu'ran* and the *Sunna* and are subordinated to those two sources.

The final recognized source of Islamic law is *Ijtihad* (reasoning by analogy), which applies to jurists and students of *Usul* (principles) who strive by diligent study to deduce rules based on logical inferences and analogy. Not all the rules of Islamic jurisprudence are subject to *Ijtihad*. The rules that are expressed in the *Qu'ran* or the *Sunna*, and the rules confirmed by *Ijma'* in a given era are not susceptible to interpretation by use of *Itjtihad*. The rules which are eligible for the process of *Ijtihad* are those based on a questionable rule or conflicting rules and those matters which neither the *Qu'ran* nor the *Sunna* covered by specific rules.[175] The great feature of *Ijtihad* is that it is the means by which Islamic law can evolve in its application to the needs of an evolving society

Thus, the legal system in the Islamic state consists of a body of rules arranged hierarchically according to the source of each rule and its order in the hierarchy of sources. The basis for this hierarchy is summarized in the message of Omar ibn al Khattab to a judge:

> If you find anything in the Book of God, judge according to it and disregard any other. If any matter is brought before you which is not included in the book of God, judge according to what the Prophet has prescribed. If what is neither in the Book of God nor prescribed by the Prophet is brought before you, judge according to the general consensus of the people, and if what is brought is not in the Book of God or the Prophet's Tradition, and has not been studied by anyone else, then if you want to try your opinion, do so, and if you want to delay, do so. I see that delay is better for you.[176]

EFFECTS OF THE PRINCIPLE OF LEGITIMACY WITHIN THE ISLAMIC SYSTEM

The Islamic system is distinguished from other legal systems by establishing rewards for the Ruler who observes the requirements of the principles of legitimacy. These exist over and above the sanctions imposed on Rulers and citizens who violate it. These rewards are represented by the obedience and support of the Islamic nation. The Ruler who observes the principle of legitimacy and exerts his authority within the limits of Islamic law is entitled to expect obedience from all Muslims, the common and the privileged alike.[177] The exercise of authority in accordance with the law is in turn beneficial to the people in their religious and

---

[173] *Surat al-Nisaa* IV:115.

[174] These Prophetic sayings are cited by MADKUR, *supra* note 116, at 223.

[175] *Id.* at 294.

[176] *See* AL-BAYATI, *supra* note 125 at 130.

[177] AL-MAWARDI, *supra* note 51, at 17, states:

> If the Imam fulfilled what we mentioned of the rights of the community, then he would have satisfied the right of God... and they owe him two duties: obedience and support so long he does not change.

secular affairs.[178]

The basis of such obedience is stated in the *Qu'ran*, where God says: "O ye who believe! Obey Allah and obey the messengers and those of you who are in authority."[179] The *Sunna* gives many indications that make the obedience to the Ruler imperative. The Prophet says: "He who obeyed me, obeyed God, and he who disobeyed me, disobeyed God. He who obeyed my representative, obeyed me, and he who disobeyed my representative, disobeyed me."[180]

However, the duty to obey the Ruler is not absolute under Islamic law. Rather it depends on the observance of Islamic law by the ruler. Obedience is given only to the just Ruler. The Ruler who is unjust in his judgements and violates individual rights and liberties loses his right to demand the obedience of his subjects. Indeed, obedience to such a Ruler is prohibited by Islamic law. Warning that those who obey a disobedient Ruler will suffer the punishment of hell, God says: "And they say: Our Lord! Lo! We obeyed our princes and great men, and they misled us from the way of our Lord! Oh give them double torment and curse them with a mighty curse."[181] The Prophet says: "Obedience is the duty of the Muslim. Concerning what he likes and what he dislikes unless he is ordered to disobey, if he is ordered to carry out an unlawful action, no obedience is required."[182] He also says: "No obedience shall be required of a person in a matter involving disobedience to the creator."[183]

Besides the duty of obedience, Muslims are under obligation to support the Ruler and stand by him against any danger to his legitimate authority. If a revolt against the Ruler is caused by some unjust actions on his part, he must refrain promptly from such behavior or lose the support of the people. An uprising due to oppression and injustice by the Ruler or a challenge to his continued authority to rule is not considered impiety.[184]

Islamic law prescribes various sanctions and penalties for violations by public authorities of the principle of legitimacy and the obligation to observe the law. The first such sanction, according to Islamic jurists, requires that every action taken by public authorities in violation of binding Islamic rules shall be considered legally invalid as to the Islamic community.[185] Another sanction is dismissal of the Ruler. Islamic law provides many reasons for dismissal of an Islamic Ruler. Certain of those reasons are encompassed within the general category of violations of the principle of legitimacy.[186]

---

[178] *See* AL-NADI, *supra* note 85, at 225.

[179] *Surat al-Nisaa* IV:59.

[180] *See* AL-NADI, *supra* note 85; citing 9 AL-BUKHARI, *supra* note 57, part 9, at 77.

[181] *Surat al-Ahzab* XXXIII:67-68.

[182] *See* AL-BUKHARI, *supra* note 57, part 9, at 78.

[183] *See* SAHIH MUSLIM, *supra* note 57, part 10, at 227.

[184] *See* A. SANHOURY, LE CALIFAT, SON EVOLUTION VERS UNE SOCIETE DES NATIONS ORIENTALES [THE CALIPHATE: ITS EVOLUTION TOWARD A SOCIETY OF ORIENTAL NATIONS] 233-34 (Paris: Paul Geuthner, 1926), [hereinafter referred to as SANHOURY].

[185] For further detail, *see* AL-NADI, *supra* note 85, at 238-40.

[186] Jurists agree that the principle of dismissing the ruler is necessary; however, they disagree as to the reasons for which a ruler must be dismissed. *See* AL-BAYATI, *supra* note 125, at 377 *et seq.*

There is wide agreement among Islamic jurists that the Ruler who violates specific texts and the general rules of Islamic law should be dismissed, for he rules according to what God has not revealed, and such action is prohibited by Islamic law.[187]

The right of the Muslim nation to dismiss their Ruler is founded on the principle that the object of the Ruler's duty in the contract of *al-Baia* (election) consists in his being bound by Islamic law to enforce the rules and judgements of Islam. If he breaches that duty, the Muslim nation is entitled to terminate his *Baia* (election) and dismiss him. Moreover, the Muslim nation is constrained to forbid what is improper, and that includes the dismissal of the ruler for serious reasons.[188] El Shafei says that the debased or the corrupt Ruler has no authority; hence his authority is null by the force of law.[189] In addition, a number of modern and earlier jurists, including ibn Hazm, hold that the Islamic nation is entitled to overthrow the oppressive Ruler even if this requires armed revolution.[190]

Thus, we find that Islam was the forerunner in establishing the principle of legitimacy. Islam not only established this principle but expanded it by setting forth practical and effective guarantees which prevent the public authority from violating this rule. In this manner, Islam assures the protection of individual rights and liberties against transgression on the side of authority.

CONCLUSION

The right to individual security is firmly established in Islamic law. The principles of Islamic jurisprudence resemble a shading tree which spreads justice and ensures peace to those under its protection. It is based on the proper and legitimate rule of the Legislator and is guided by the light of reason. Both derive from piety, for the man to whom Allah gives no light, has no light.

---

[187] *See* SANHOURY, *supra* note 184, at 196 *et seq.*

[188] *Id.* at 195 *et seq.*

[189] *Id.* at 196.

[190] For the reasoning behind this argument, *see* AL-NADI, *supra* note 85, at 261 *et seq.*

THE RIGHTS OF THE ACCUSED UNDER ISLAMIC CRIMINAL PROCEDURE

Awad M. Awad

INTRODUCTION

The administration of justice in any modern society is one of the State's many powers. It is intertwined with other state powers, yet enjoys a certain measure of independence in all developed systems. Moreover, contemporary legal systems assign criminal cases to specialized courts, even though most systems do not provide judges who specialize in criminal cases. Typically, criminal justice decides or disposes of criminal cases only, but exceptions are made with regard to related areas, particularly claims of compensation for injury caused by crime. Criminal courts, therefore, possess various types and degrees of jurisdiction differing mainly in terms of the nature of the crime and the character of the accused.

Like other divinely inspired legal systems, Islamic *Shari'a* seeks a number of temporal goals, the most important of which is the pursuit of justice. Both the *Qu'ran* and the *Sunna* repeatedly demand justice and condemn injustice, associating the former with reward and the latter with punishment. Thus, Islamic *Shari'a* is designed to implement those goals by prescribing the punishment corresponding to defined crimes. In other texts it permits punishment to be imposed as a matter of judicial discretion for those acts deemed criminal in the sense of violating the public interest. For any case, no law can be applied except through the judiciary.

Historically, aside from defining substantive crimes and their punishment, the *Shari'a* did not set forth a detailed system of criminal procedure since such a system falls within the province of delegated interests, *i.e.*, those which the ruler has the authority to organize according to his personal reasoning, consistent with particular circumstances of time and place, and inspired by the spirit of the *Shari'a* and its general principles.[1]

---

[1] In this context the Islamic state, during the Prophet's rule, and subsequently during the rule of the rightly-guided *Caliphs* (*al-Rashidun*), and the *Umayyads* and the *Abbasids*, undertook to organize justice as a judicial system, and to organize its function in trying and adjudicating lawsuits. It is apparent that the particularities of this system did not remain fixed, but changed with time and place.

The administration of criminal justice in the Islamic state was historically distributed among several offices: the Caliphate, the Office of Complaints (*Mazalim*), the emir or military commander, the chief of police, the market inspector, and the judge (in the narrow sense of the term). The province of these offices did not remain continuously fixed but often fluctuated. Some of them at times expanded to include extra functions. In particular, the governor and the chief of police were usually concerned with capital or high crimes, such as those of *Hudud* and *Quesas*,* while the market inspector** specialized in *Ta'azir* punishments for crimes injurious to the public welfare.*** The jurisdiction of the judge, by contrast, was not primarily over criminal cases. Instead, his original jurisdiction was confined to civil disputes and matters relating to personal status (private law). Some jurists expressed this distinction by saying that whereas the purpose of the military governor's office was to prevent corruption in the world and to eradicate crime, the purpose of the office of judge was to redress injuries to private rights.[2]

THE DIVISION OF THE CRIMINAL ACTION INTO TWO STAGES: INVESTIGATION AND PROSECUTION (TRIAL)

Procedural systems which have dominated legislations throughout the ages

---

**Ed. note: See* Bassiouni, *Crimes of Quesas*, at 203.

***Ed. note:* Trial Judge.

****Ed. note: See* Benmelha, *Ta'azir Offenses*, at 211.

The system at first was simple, reflecting its contemporary socio-economic life. Then, with the development of society and expansion of the state, and perhaps in part due to increasing Muslim contact with other deeply rooted cultures, the system began to change. The ability of *Shari'a* to adapt to the changes which the judicial system underwent during different historical periods while remaining faithful to fundamental principles is one of the most distinguishing features of the system. IBN AL-QAYYIM, AL-TURUQ AL-HUKMIYYA [THE METHODS OF JUDGEMENTS OR JURISPRUDENCE] — hereinafter referred to as AL-QAYYIM — lists the different ranks of the judiciary prevailing in the Eastern state (*Mashriq*) during the 8th Century (H). He states that adjudicating or arbitrating between people with regard to matters which did not involve legal claims was called *hisba* and the official in charge of such cases was called the market inspector. Also, the institution of *Mazalim* courts was established through special officers in charge of complaints called *Sahib al-Mazalim* (The Official in Charge of Grievances). Civil disputes and matters of personal status were, however, placed under the jurisdiction of the judge or arbitrator. As an after-thought, ibn al-Qayyim adds that this name applies to any arbitrator or judge with jurisdiction over two litigants, thus encompassing all other legal functions. Other jurists, such as ibn Khaldun, al-Mawardi and ibn Taymiyya, have also discussed the judicial offices of their times and described the jurisdiction of each one.

Ibn al-Qayyim suggested that there is no provision or decision in the *Shari'a* itself which prescribes that all legal matters be assigned to one particular person or one particular office. Rather, the arrangement is purely political and is left to the discretion of the authorities. It is possible to divide legal jurisdictions among several offices or to aggregate them all in one. The only condition for one who is assigned the responsibility of practicing law is that he should be competent and should possess the qualifications prescribed by the *Shari'a* which entitles him to carry out his duty.

[2] AL-QAYYIM, *supra* note 1, at 122. The office of the judge under Islamic law was traditionally accusatorial in form, first of all, because the judge was obliged to follow strict rules of evidence which imposed strict standards of proof and limited types of admissible evidence. Secondly, the judge had scant administrative assistance. By contrast, other judicial agencies possessed certain investigative powers, and these paved the way for the development of the inquisitorial system in criminal cases. *See infra* note 3 and text accompanying. The social and cultural causes for this differentiation in the powers of judicial authorities, with special reference to the jurisdiction and function of the office of chief of police, is discussed in 2 IBN-KHALDUN, AL-MUQADDIMA [THE INTRODUCTION] 35-37 [hereinafter referred to as IBN-KHALDUN].

are of three kinds: the accusatorial, the inquisitorial and a mixed system which combines aspects of both. The accusatorial system is the oldest, and its most salient feature is its view of criminal action as a common dispute between two parties of equal legal status. Within this system the case is presented directly to the judge who is precluded from engaging in judicial investigation beforehand. The role of the judge is to balance the evidence presented by each of the litigants, without influencing or interfering in its discovery.

With respect to the inquisitorial system, the case proceeds through a pre-trial stage wherein evidence is gathered, and investigation and indictment are carried out by a judicial magistrate. The indictment office is endowed with certain powers to assist it in carrying out its function by authorizing it, within certain limitations, to place restrictions on the freedom of the accused and other key individuals in the case. Furthermore, the judge plays a positive role by gathering evidence for both the defense and the prosecution, regardless of the conduct of the litigants.

Unlike either the accusatorial or the inquisitorial systems, the guiding principle of Islamic *Shari'a* is *siyasa al Shari'a*.* This principle means that in the administration of criminal justice, the Sovereign's reasoning in relation to circumstances of time and place with preference given to the system is deemed to be in the public interest. *Shari'a* jurists distinguish between legal and political questions pertaining to the administration of criminal justice. In this regard the statements of ibn Khaldun reflect the careful differentiation made by jurists between discretionary and mandatory legal determinations.[3] Sacred law cannot concern itself except with imposing legal punishment prescribed for the crime; whereas, it is the duty of the political authorities to establish procedures for the investigation and prosecution of crime. By this Khaldun means that even though sacred law prescribes penalties for criminal acts, it does not specify the means used to apprehend the offender and bring him to justice. Such matters are left to the political authorities to establish in accordance with the best interests of society. Thus, procedures for investigation and prosecution are considered to be within the political realm (*siyasa*), or that of delegated powers.

Thus, it can be said that Islamic *Shari'a* does not require the administration of justice to be combined into one office or divided into many. Rather, it leaves this matter to the discretion of the state provided that its decision serves the public interest. The only requirement of the *Shari'a* is that there be an office to apply the law, and that the person occupying it satisfy certain requirements which ensure the proper execution of religious legal injunctions and the realization of justice.

Secondly, concerning the investigation of a case, determining the office entrusted with that function, the regulations which govern the office, and the procedures and powers it employs to discover the truth all are matters of admin-

---

**Ed. note:* The philosophy (and policy) of the *Shari'a*.

[3] IBN-KHALDUN, *supra* note 2.

istrative justice and the policies to implement that goal, and are not matters of *Shari'a*. At the same time, the *Shari'a* sets down general principles and ordinances which limit that organization to protect the rights and security of people, even though it is permissible to restrict these rights as required by and within the limits of necessity and the broad guidelines of *Shari'a*.

THE RIGHTS OF THE SUSPECT DURING THE INVESTIGATION STAGE

THE INDICTMENT

At that stage suspect is a person presumed in fact to have committed a crime based on a quantum of evidence as prescribed by law. Suspicion alone is inconsequential, unless it leads to indictment, which is a procedural function carried out by a specific agency. The indictment consists of charging a person with a crime either by confronting him with the accusation thereof or by subjecting him to certain steps taken only against suspects, such as apprehension (arrest) and preventive detention. In the language of the *Shari'a*, jurists use the term 'defendant' (*mudda'a alayhi*), or the litigant against whom a claim is made, to describe the person brought by his adversary before a judge, and the term *mathum* (the accused) is used if he is brought before the governor or the chief of police. What follows applies the treatment of persons brought before one of the latter offices and often indicted or accused by public officials.

In principle, the indictment limits the rights and freedoms of the accused. This is common to all inquisitorial systems although they differ in the degree of limitation placed on the rights and freedoms of the accused. Under Islamic law, the reason for this difference stems from the conflict of two principles. The first is that since every man is innocent until proved guilty, his rights should not be forfeited until such proof is established. Accusation alone does not invalidate this presumption, since accusation by nature is not devoid of doubt, and doubt does not negate certainty; whereas, the accused's prior innocence is a certainty.

The second principle results from the necessity to ascertain the truth. Bringing indictment against the suspect may lead to placing restraints on his liberty and other rights. Since every case seeks to do justice, this principle justifies the proper official's infringement of the suspect's liberty and other rights.

The conflict between the two principles puts the jurist in a delicate position, for he must strike an uneasy balance, which is not always possible in the face of the multitude of practical considerations that a judge confronts daily. While moderation in the application of either principle is usually essential to a just resolution, it is a relative notion and thus not succeptible of unambiguous rules instructive of its use.

To forestall abuse of the accused's rights, he enjoys a number of primary and secondary rights. His primary right is the right of lawful defense, which attaches independently by virtue of the mere fact that he is the accused. Secondary rights are related to the powers which are granted to the examination or investigative authority and represent the restrictions placed upon those powers. From the perspective of the accused, these restrictions represent guarantees which might be broadly called rights.

THE RIGHT OF DEFENSE

The right of defense is a principal right which attaches at the accusation stage. It enables the accused to deny the accusation, either by showing the insufficiency or invalidity of the evidence on which it is based or by submitting evidence, such as an alibi, to prove innocence. By its very nature accusation requires defense in a logical and imperative way, for accusation not countered by defense becomes a verdict. Thus in reality, they represent both sides of the same question. By its very nature, accusation implies doubt, and the extent of that doubt will reflect upon the scope of the defense. By juxtaposing defense with accusation the truth emerges, which is the goal of the investigation. Neither of the two, however, is capable of uncovering the truth by itself. For this same reason defense is not considered to be the absolute or clear right of the accused alone, which he is free to accept or reject; it is also the right and obligation of society. Thus, if the accused has the right not to be judged guilty when innocent, society has no less of a right, because legal justice and social interest require that only the criminal be punished. Otherwise, society suffers a twofold injury: the innocent receives undeserved punishment while the criminal eludes his.

In theory, the accused must take personal charge of his defense, although he is allowed to enlist others to assist him.* Naturally, the role of the representing attorney is to shield his client with every available right, but the presence of an attorney does not eliminate the role of the defendant *qua* defendant and does not prevent him from presenting evidence in his own defense. For he is the primary party to the defense, and the attorney is only his agent or representative.

There are several aspects to the right to present a defense. First, the accused must be informed of the act attributed to him and of the evidence against him, and of the procedures taken to adduce, verify and clarify such evidence. This assumes the right to be informed of the time and place of each proceeding, to be present at such proceedings, and to be informed of any affirmative evidence in the possession of the prosecution. Each of these rights must be preserved. Thus, for example, it is not permissible to bar the defendant from the investigation without guaranteeing him sufficient subsequent knowledge of what transpires in his absence in a timely manner so as to permit him to prepare for trial. What applies to the accused in this respect also applies to his attorney.

Second, the defendant must be given the opportunity to present his defense to the investigator, whether it includes matters of fact or law, negates incriminating evidence, or proves his innocence. From the right to a defense stems the right of the accused to present petitions and pleadings, to appeal decisions, to retain an attorney, technical expert or witness, and to move for an inspection of documents. As a related right, the defendant must be permitted to meet and correspond in private with his attorney and to cross-examine and confront other accused persons or witnesses.

**Ed. note:* This is the basis of the right to counsel.

GUARANTEES TO THE ACCUSED

These guarantees represent the restraints placed on the authority of the investigator in limiting the freedom of the accused and in the restriction of his rights. The investigator, in order to reveal the truth or secure the investigation, is empowered to arrest the accused and to search his home and person, to record his private conversations, to seize his letters and belongings, and to hold him under preventive detention. However, each of these powers is subject to certain limitations. For example, no procedure may be utilized by the investigator which infringes upon the rights of the accused (as discussed above) unless based on an explicit law allowing it, since the authority of the investigator in this respect is not a principle, but an exception to a principle.

Furthermore, the meaning of the law must be interpreted narrowly. Therefore, the accused may not be tortured in order to secure his confession. Indeed, he should not be coerced into giving any involuntary answers to the investigator's questions. Also, the investigation should proceed in accordance with prescribed rules governing agency jurisdiction, the form of the investigation, the circumstances calling for it, the manner of its execution and the admissibility of evidence. Thus, if the investigator undertakes a proceeding outside his jurisdiction, or in circumstances or conditions other than those legally specified, or if he delegates its execution to any unauthorized agent, the proceeding is void and the accused is not bound to abide by its outcome. Such abuse of authority might also lead to finding the investigator liable for the abuse on civil, administrative, or criminal process.

THE RIGHTS OF THE ACCUSED IN THE INVESTIGATION STAGE

A central theme of this article is that there is no mandate in any source of Islamic law establishing the existence of an investigation stage. It is a matter of administrative justice (*siyasa*) and not of *Shari'a*. Historical precedents do not indicate that this stage was always recognized in criminal cases. This does not mean however that adjudication took place without investigation, but that investigation was not (always) an independent phase conducted by a competent authority other than the court. Thus, the investigative phase (as it was known, or) in its present form is an ordained part in the Islamic system of criminal justice.

Nevertheless, it can be said that cases which were not decided by a judge or an arbitrator, but by a governor, market inspector, or chief of police, did include a stage of investigation prior to trial. However, the division between the judge and the investigator was not a confirmed practice. Often the official deciding a case was also the same person who undertook to investigate and prepare it and gather supporting evidence. It is for this reason that books on jurisprudence do not speak independently of the rights of the accused during the investigative phase and at trial. Fortunately the general principles of Islamic *Shari'a* and some relevant works on jurisprudence allow the modern jurist to ascertain those rights separately and present them coherently.

THE RIGHT OF DEFENSE

As it is in positive law, the right to a defense in Islamic *Shari'a* is fundamental to the concept of accusation. Moreover, it guarantees the right itself and not merely its exercise, since the accused might fail to invoke this right, even though he may be able to do so. Consequently, the judge is not faced with the choice of deciding the case on the basis of incriminating evidence alone. *Shari'a* jurists do not analyze the right of defense as a general theory, nor do they discuss its elements in detail; however, they closely consider a number of its applications in different areas of their writings. It remains true, nevertheless, that many of the doctrinal precepts of the *Shari'a* lack foundation and conceptualization, and need an additional measure of both.*

There is much evidence for the need to guarantee the right to a defense. It is said of the Prophet that, when he granted 'Ali governorship of the Yemen, he said to him:

> O 'Ali, people will appeal to you for justice. If two adversaries come to you for arbitration, do not rule for the one, before you have similarly heard from the other. It is more proper for justice to become evident to you and for you to know who is right.

Additionally, historians relate that the Caliph, 'Umar ibn 'Abd al-Aziz, advised some judges by saying, "If an adversary whose eye had been blinded by another comes to you, do not rule until the other party attends. For perhaps the latter had been blinded in both eyes." It is agreed in Islamic jurisprudence that enabling the accused to defend himself is a matter of right under *Shari'a*, and not simply of policy. Thus, the accused may never be denied this right.

In order for the accused to be able to defend himself, he must be informed of the crime charged against him and of the known incriminating and exonerating evidence. This requires that the investigator apprise him of such facts.** Jurists are unanimous about this aspect of the right to a defense, particularly with respect to cases to be decided by an arbitrator or judge. If informing the accused of the suit brought by his adversary is necessary in civil cases of personal status, it is even more crucial in criminal cases. In any event, the real issue is not that a legal system granted the accused the right of self-defense, and then withheld from him knowledge of the act attributed to him and the evidence established against him. Rather, the question here is whether it is the right of the accused to know of all these matters during the process of investigation. Here Islamic jurists are not unanimous. Further, it is probable that these opinions are a matter of *Ijtihad* (independent reasoning), since the differences do not the concern the necessity of informing the accused, but rather the accuracy and the timeliness with which he is informed.

Another aspect of the right to a defense is that the accused be capable in fact of defending himself. An inability to defend oneself is effectively identical to the

---

**Ed. note:* Which *Ijtihad* can provide.

***Ed. note:* This concept of "equality of arms" is known in contemporary western European systems and reflected in the "discovery" procedures in U.S.

state's preventing one from so doing. *Shari'a* jurists were stricter in this respect than contemporary jurists of positive law. The Hanafis, for example, prohibit the infliction of penalties for capital crimes on mute offenders even where conclusive evidence is demonstrated against them. The Hanafis reason that, had the mute individual been capable of speech, he might have been able to raise a doubt that would have invalidated his guilt. Since such a person cannot express everything in sign language, it would be unjust to inflict the *Had* penalty on him given the possibility that reasonable doubt of his innocence has not been eliminated.

With regard to the right of the accused to retain an attorney to assist in his defense the *Shari'a* is not explicit neither does it appear that this right was widely practiced. Perhaps this is due to the fact that judges formerly consulted closely with jurists on legal problems so that the accused had no significant need for independent legal advice.* It is noteworthy, however, that the role of the attorney has never been so limited. It also includes the presentation of favorable evidence, the safeguarding against improper incrimination, and the overseeing of the execution of criminal judgements.

Despite actual practice, the sources of the *Shari'a* are not contrary to the right of the accused to be represented by an attorney. This view is supported in various ways, some based on logic and some on tradition. From a logical viewpoint, there is no reason to limit the availability of the right to a defense to the accused alone. On the contrary, such a restriction might hinder the defense because the accused might be unable to defend himself. Even if he were capable of doing so, the symbolic and psychological impacts of the indictment might deprive the accused of clarity of mind and cause him to falter in his defense. Besides the absence of a specific text explicitly prohibiting the accused from retaining an attorney, the spirit of Islamic *Shari'a* and its general principles would not forbid the accused from seeking any legitimate help he deemed necessary, for Islam exhorts assistance to those in distress. Being charged and taken to court for what might lead to one's death is the epitome of distress.

The right to a defense also is stated in the *Sunna*:

> Since I am only human, like all of you, I might, when litigants come before me to decide between them, rule in favor of the more eloquent of them. If I should thereby transfer to him what is rightfully his brother's, I warn him to take not that which is not his, or I shall reserve for him a piece of Hell.

This *Hadith* suggests that the judge, perceptive though he may be, might be misled by a clever and well-versed litigant into confusion and consequently rule incorrectly. The Prophet found this repugnant and warned against it, and modern jurists understand this warning to be consistent with allowing the accused, incapable of adequately defending himself to enlist the aid of an attorney to present his case and thereby permits the defendant to seek the help of those who are more knowledgeable and experienced. Such help ultimately aids the judge in fulfilling his primary purpose of discovering the truth.

It might be argued that representation by a skillful attorney might impede

---

**Ed. note: See* Abdel-Malek, *The Right to Individual Freedom*, at

justice by misleading the judge into ruling against the innocent.[4] Although that possibility exists, the alternative is worse. Because a judgement is necessarily based on the judge's perception of the truth, it is unjust to deprive one of the parties of an adequate defense. Thus, if a balance or a choice must be made between limiting the right of defense and granting more than minimal protections, the scale should tip in favor of the latter.

Nevertheless, some jurists would restrict the right of the accused to be represented by an attorney. Writing on the duties of the judge, al-Mawardi suggests that only if the judge urges one of the litigants to find someone to represent him during the investigation stage is such aid permissible. This viewpoint derives from *Ijtihad* (independent reasoning) and thus is not based on an explicit text. Further, the *raison d'être* for attorneys would appear to be to achieve equality between parties. It is possible to dispute the soundness of this purpose, for adjudication by its nature seldom leads to such equality. In most cases, the process itself can only lend a formal equality, since litigants always differ in their ability to present their arguments and defend themselves.

Even if the argument in favor of the limited right to counsel is applied in civil cases and cases of personal status, still there is no basis for accepting it in criminal cases. Most criminal matters cases focus on transgressions against divine right, with the remainder equally divided between transgressions against man's divinely received rights and other private rights. This requires facilitating, even liberalizing, the accused's right of defense, since the reason for practicing law — to achieve equality between litigants—unquestionably is otherwise negated. In effect, the accused faces the public prosecutor as his adversary, especially in contemporary procedural systems which do not contradict the *Shari'a*. Thus, it is because the prosecutor is more capable of obtaining evidence by virtue of the public authority he possesses than the accused, that the right counsel must be closely guarded and rigorously enforced in criminal prosecutions.

GUARANTEES TO THE ACCUSED

Islam is concerned with protecting man's basic rights. In this Islam does not discriminate between Muslim and non-Muslim. More precisely, there are minimum rights which all persons enjoy by virtue of being human beings. These can be abridged only by reason of some higher interest that transcends these protections. We find this imperative in the words of God, "Verily we have honored the children of Adam." The rights which are acknowledged and protected by Islam

---

[4] Al-Khushani relates the following story: two men took their dispute before Judge Ahmad ibn Baqi who observed that one of the men was very eloquent, while the other could not express himself. So the judge said to the second, "Would it not be better if you were represented by someone who can match the verbal skills of your opponent." The man answered, "But I only speak the truth." Replied the judge, "How many men have perished telling the truth!" If this venerable judge found it necessary to encourage the litigant to seek the assistance of a competent attorney in a case which involves merely financial matters, then the spirit of the *Shari'a* and the force of logic will require the seeking of such help in matters which might involve the shedding of one's blood or an injury to one's honor, reputation or physical well being. AL-KHUSHANI, TARIKH QUDAT QURTUBA (or KITAB AL-QUDAT BI-QURTUBA) [THE HISTORY or BOOK OF JUDGES OF QURTUBA]—[hereinafter referred to as AL-KHUSHANI].

are many, the most important of which being the rights to life, bodily safety, honor of self and women, individual freedom, right to own property and home, and the right to privacy. *Qu'ranic* verses and *Hadiths* provide overwhelming proof of the existence of these basic rights. Safeguards for these rights are thus fundamental to the *Shari'a*, and the state is responsible for protecting them through the implementation of the *Shari'a*.

However, in contraposition to this principle is another which provides that all rights can be limited or even violated when necessary. A universal precept in Islamic jurisprudence is that necessity knows no law (or necessity renders prohibited things permissible).*

The conflict between the two principles in the sphere of criminal justice results in limiting the rights and freedoms of the accused to the extent that such limitations are "necessary" in the interests of truth and justice. The extent of this limitation is indicated by the degree of authority granted to the investigator. It is an exception, rather than the application, of the principle that no man can be arrested or jailed, his home or private life violated, or his money confiscated. If the necessity of uncovering the truth and of doing justice requires limiting some or all of these rights, an exception will be recognized to the principle but only if it does not go beyond the dictates of necessity. Thus, the encroachments allowable on the rights of the accused are checked by limitations on the authority of the investigator. These limitations are considered, from the accused's point of view, to be his guarantees.

It can be argued that, from the perspective of the *Shari'a*, the two above-mentioned principles are not in conflict. Instead, harmonizing between them is a matter of criminal justice administration and policy in such a manner that neither principle is totally abrogated. Herein lies the flexibility of the *Shari'a*, for it does not set forth a rigid list of rights that may be limited and the extent or conditions of those limitations. Instead it delegates the matter to those in state power and allows them the authority to administer it according to their perception of public interest. Thus, for example, Islamic jurists find different views as to the nature and extent of the permissible limitations upon the rights of the accused during the investigation stage, *i.e.*, the scope of the authority delegated to the investigator.

It is instructive to present some of the opinions of the *Shari'a* jurists on this subject.

1. Categories of Accused Persons

For purposes of subjecting the defendant of investigative procedures, *Shari'a* jurists divide suspects into three categories: (1) the accused is from the pious and righteous group; (2) he is among the disobedient and immoral; or (3) his character is unknown though neither righteous nor immoral. The importance of this classification becomes clear when dealing with crimes unsupported by legal

---

**Ed. note:* The doctrine of "necessity" is based on "public policy" and "public welfare"; it is not based on the whim of the Ruler or judge and is limited by the *Shari'a*. *See* Kamel, *Principles of Legality*, at

or circumstantial evidence. In the opinion of most jurists, members of the first group are not liable nor should their rights and freedoms be restricted simply on the basis of verbal or hearsay accusations against them. Some argue that *Ta'azir* punishment might be applicable in this case, but this view is not widely accepted. As for the other two categories, it is permissible to limit the rights and freedoms of such defendants to the extent required by the necessity to discover the truth. The basis for this is the concept of *Istishan*, which refers to a continuance or the presumption in the law of evidence that a state of affairs known to exist in the past continues to exist until the contrary is proved. *Shari'a* jurists use this concept well and were sensitive to the distinction between its role in the sphere of punishment and the sphere of procedure.

As to punishment, the principle of presumed innocence makes every man immune from punishment until evidence of guilt is established. This presumption is not negated by any degree of doubt.

Islamic jurists suggest that mere accusation against pious and righteous people should carry no weight; whereas, accusation against the sinful and immoral is more likely to be true because of the style of life they have led. As for the unknown of character, accusations against them carry no presumption of truth or falsity. The majority of jurists have held that this category belongs with that of the immoral; thus, they could be held subject to the same investigative restrictions.

Some jurists have confused the substantive and procedural effects of the principle of presumed innocence, and have argued for non-interference with the rights of the accused until the establishment of legal evidence proving guilt. They assume that any interference with his rights before proof of guilt is a violation of the principle of presumed innocence.

Despite the humanistic appeal of this presumption, its unrestricted adoption does not comport with a sound understanding of the *Shari'a* and fails to preserve the balance between individual and community rights. If the balance tips too far in favor of the accused, the state will seek to reestablish equilibrium and may overreact by unnecessarily restraining defendants' rights. Thus, many state officials have in the past inflicted unwarranted exemplary penalties on suspects on the assumption that the matter was purely political (or administrative) and not a matter for the *Shari'a*. They wrongly believed it was their right and duty to regulate such matters without restrictions.[5] Their ignorance of the true meaning of the *Shari'a* caused grave injustice and impermissible changes in administrative practice and policy (*siyasa*) which were either falsely attributed to the *Shari'a* or blatantly substituted for it. They have further claimed that the *Shari'a* was

---

[5]Ibn Taymiyya attacked both groups and was followed by ibn al-Qayyim who quoted him saying:

> To my knowledge, none of the Muslim Imams says that the accused may be set free after having been sworn, without imprisonment or other measures. This is absolutely not the opinion of the Four Imams nor of any other Imam. And whoever claims, in an absolute or general manner, that this is what the *Shari'a* stipulates, is gravely mistaken and stands in contradiction to the teachings of the Prophet and the consensus of the Imams.

AL-QAYYIM, *supra* note 1.

inadequate and failed to protect the public welfare and thereby replaced it with generalities that contradict sound *Shari'a* teachings and precepts. In the *Qu'ran* God enjoins people to do justice. He does not permit accusing the truthful with falsehood nor denying the evidence which manifests the truth. He ordered the verification of accusations and testimony given by impious persons, and never to ignore them, until sufficient evidence is presented. Should this evidence support the truth of the testimony, it becomes admissible, but if it proves the testimony to be false, then the testimony is rejected. Thus, passing judgement on a defendant is closely linked to the truth. In the past many state officials intruded upon *Shari'a* by using inadmissible evidence to support certain legal decisions and to promote limited political ends while others ignored obvious admissible evidence which they considered inadequate to justify other legal decisions.

2. The Permitted Extent of Preventive Detention

Shari'a jurists hold that in principle man is guaranteed the freedom to move as he pleases. Ibn Hazm cites the following *Qu'ranic* verse as the source of this principle: "He it is Who hath made the earth subservient unto you, so walk in the paths thereof and eat of His providence."[6] Jurists have condemned the violation of this principle by forbidding arrest except when necessary. When they speak of *habs* (imprisonment), they intend its wider meaning which includes both arrest and preventive detention, according to the terminology of positive law. Thus, ibn al-Qayyim defines *habs* not as imprisonment in a narrow sense, but as detention and deprivation of personal liberty.

An indication of the intense concern which jurists have for personal freedom is the conditions they posit to ensure the legality of arrest. All jurists would require the judge, upon initially assuming his post, to inspect the prisoners and release any who had been jailed unjustly. Having done that, he should next look into trusteeships, and the palace treasury, and only then begin to decide cases before the court.[7]

Preventive detention is recognized by Islamic jurists as a legitimate state function. Some call it "precautionary arrest" (*habs ihtiyati*), others "trial (or examination) arrest" (*ikhtibar*), and still others "discovery and acquittal arrest" (*kashf wa istibrah*). In his al-Mabsut, Sarakhsi, a Hanafi jurist, suggests that when witnesses accuse a person of adultery, the judge, if unfamiliar with the suspect, should keep him under arrest until the truth of the testimony is

---

[6] *Surat al-Mulk* LXVII: 15.

[7] It is stated that in order for a judge to jail a man legally, he must record his name and that of his father and grandfather, the reason for his imprisonment, and its date. When a judge replaces another, the new judge should ask the one he replaces about the prisoners and the reasons for their imprisonment. He also must ask the prisoners themselves about these reasons, and hold meetings with them and their opponents together. AL-FATAWA AL-HINDIYYA [THE RULINGS].

Another jurist states that a new judge should inspect the prisoners and release those unjustly held. The prisoner who confesses to his crime remains in jail. When a prisoner claims unjust treatment, his accuser is recalled to renew litigation and reestablish that the deposed judge had ruled justly in his favor. Should the prisoner express ignorance of the reasons for his imprisonment, his accuser is recalled. If the accuser fails to appear, then the prisoner is released. If an accuser has since disappeared, the prisoner claiming to be wronged should also be released. AL-GHAZZA, AL-WAJIZ [THE CONDENSED OR MANUAL].

established.[8] Otherwise, the accused may escape the jurisdiction of the courts. Precautionary arrest is not limited to cases of adultery but applies to all cases where it is necessary to detain the accused in order to guarantee that he does not escape or in order to execute the judgement as soon as it is handed down.

Jurists differ, however, as to who is authorized to make an arrest, who can be arrested, and for how long. Al-Mawardi says that the authority of the investigator varies with his title.[9] A judge or an arbitrator cannot arrest someone who stands accused before him of theft or adultery while such official determines his guilt or innocence. However, if the accusation is brought before an *amir* (commander) or *wali al-jara'im* (official in charge of criminal offense), then they are authorized to arrest the accused if the accusation is serious, but not in cases of minor offenses. A less serious charge may be upgraded to a graver offense through information gathered by the commander's aides regarding the temperament and character of the accused or other types of evidence.

Al-Mawardi further details his view by suggesting that the commander may order his aides to uncover evidence concerning an accused and may rely on their reports concerning whether he is of a suspicious background or has a history of conduct similar to that with which he is accused. If they deem these factors to be inapplicable, then a serious charge is mitigated and the detained suspect must be released. However, if they also accuse a suspect with what has been attributed to him, then the charge is aggravated and the commander proceeds with discovery. The commander also may consider evidence of circumstances and the character of the accused in determining the strength or weakness of the charge. In cases of theft, if the suspect is reproachable or bears the scars of beating or is caught with a pick or other digging tool when apprehended, then the charge is deemed strengthened, and with such accusation, the commander may hasten the arrest in order to determine his status and verify his innocence or guilt.

As to the period of imprisonment, al-Mawardi says that, "There are different opinions. Some say one month, others say it is undetermined and should be left up to the *Imam's* view and his independent reasoning—the last is more likely."[10] Al-Mawardi is inclined to restrict the authority of the judge and to expand the power of those who, by virtue of their functions, can show leniency in matters where sacred law simply defines the interest. These are matters not provided by text and not dealt with through *Ijma'* (consensus) since, "the sovereign is concerned with administrative policy and the judges with the legal judgements."[11]

Thus, it appears that preventive detention is, in general, permissible in the *Shari'a*, but its purpose is limited, as are the powers of the authority who orders it and the conditions giving rise to the order, and its duration. *Shari'a* policy (*siyasat al-Shari'a*) plays a great role in determining these controls and systematizing their rules. Nothing in the general theoretical bases of the *Shari'a* nor in its

---

[8] The Hanafis are joined in this opinion by the Shafe'is, Malikis and Hanbalis.

[9] AL-MAWARDI, AL-AHKAM AL-SULTANIYYA [THE RULINGS]. Many other jurists concur.

[10] *Id.*

[11] *Id.*

specific texts prevents an approach to these matters that permits variation of time and place as required by public interest.

3. Searches and Eavesdropping

According to the *Qu'ran*, God honors man in order to protect his inviolability. There is nothing more inviolable than man's person, home and private life. *Qu'ranic* verses and *Hadith* are numerous in this respect. The *Qu'ran* states:

> O ye who believe! Enter not houses other than your own without first announcing your presence and invoking peace upon the folk thereof. That is better for you, that ye may be heedful.
>
> And if ye find no one therein, still enter not until permission hath been given. And if it be said unto you: "Go away again," then go away, for it is purer for you.[12]

And, in the *Surat* of the Private Apartments, God says, "O ye who believe! Shun much suspicion; for lo! Some suspicion is a sin. And spy not..."[13] The Prophet said "All of the Muslim is prohibited to another Muslim, his blood, wealth, and honor."* The Prophet also stated: "If the *amir* (Ruler) creates mistrust among people, he corrupts them." And, "Whoever listens to people's conversations without their permission will have melted lead poured in his ears on the Day of Judgement." Also, it was said to ibn Mas'ud, "The beard of Walid ibn 'Uqba is dripping wine," to which he responded, "We have been prohibited from spying, but if we see something, then we will believe it."[19] Another story is told of Umar ibn al-Khattab who, when told that Abu Muhjin al-Thaqafi was drinking wine in his home with some of his companions went to see. But when he entered the house, he found that Abu Muhjin was only with one man, whereupon Abu Muhjin said, "This is forbidden unto you, God forbade you from spying." A similar story is related by 'Abd al-Rahman ibn 'Awf, who said:

> One night, I was on guard duty with 'Umar ibn al-Kattab in Medina. We noticed a night-light through an open door, where we heard the loud and noisy voices of some people. 'Umar said: "This is the residence of Rabi'a ibn 'Umayya ibn Khalaf, and they are drunk. What do you think?" I said: "I think we have done a forbidden act. God has stated: Do not spy and we have." 'Umar left them alone.

These texts establish the principle under Islamic law that man's inviolability must be protected. This is conditioned, however, on the absence of reasons requiring the restriction or suspension of those rights. This condition is implicit in the *Qu'ranic* verse which declares only some forms of suspicion to be criminal, but not others.[14] Jurists suggest that suspicion in this sense means accusation. Thus, what is prohibited is baseless accusation, such as accusing someone of adultery or drunkenness without evidence. The proof that what is intended by

---

**Ed. note:* That was part of the Prophet's "farewell speech," *Khotbat al-Weda's*, which means that the rights of a Muslim are a limit to another's right.

[12] *Surat al-Nur* XXIV:27-28.

[13] *Surat al-Hujurat* XLIX:12.

[14] *Id.*

suspicion is accusation lies in the imperative, "And spy not...,"[15] for it might occur to someone initially to accuse a person of some wrongdoing so as to spy on him. The Prophet condemned such practice. One might say that what distinguishes objectionable from other types of suspicion is that suspicion not based on strong evidence and apparent cause should be avoided and ignored if the suspect is discreet, righteous and publicly honest. Suspecting such persons of corruption and impiety is prohibited, unlike suspicion of indiscreet persons who openly engage in wrongdoing. Thus eavesdropping is not permissible, nor are searches of the person or his home and private conversations when based on the mere belief that he has committed a crime deserving punishment. Mere belief is suspicion and is not a substitute for truth. Suspicion can be considered by the judicial authorities only if supported by evidence. The opinion of the jurists on this matter is consistent with their view on arrest and preventive detention, for they distinguish between pious and righteous people and those who are disobedient and immoral. They prohibit spying on the former but do not object to spying on the latter. It appears that permitting the violation of the rights of members of the second category because of mere accusation is a matter of doctrinal interpretation and is open to objection. The range of opinion allows for the argument that spying should be absolutely prohibited, whether through searching the person or his house or through recording his conversation, unless there is factual evidence in support and whether the accused is pious and righteous. This view opposed to spying is supported by the account, summarized above, in which Umar ibn al-Khattab ceased from spying on Abu Muhjin al-Thaqaft and Rabi'a ibn 'Umayya, both of whom were well known for their drinking habits.

It is significant here that the *Shari'a* prohibits the search of person and home, and the invasion of privacy for the purpose of verifying the occurrence of a crime unless there is independent corroboration. This rule is essential to the *Shari'a*. However, determining the strength of the evidence and its degree of sufficiency is left to the duly constituted authority.

Since it is established that restricting the rights and freedoms of the accused is an exception to a principle, such restrictions must not exceed certain limits as determined by the purpose for which the exceptions were allowed, namely to uncover the truth. Whatever is not required as necessarily promoting that end remains prohibited. Furthermore, in the process of investigation, Islamic ethics governs the limitations when necessity requires restricting the freedom or the rights of the accused. Thus, if a man is to search an accused woman, he is not permitted to touch her private parts, a condition which is axiomatic in the *Shari'a*.

This principle is confirmed in the story of Hatib ibn Abi Balta'a. It is related in the books on the Prophet's life that when he decided to conquer Mecca and informed the people of his decision, Hatib wrote to the Meccans a letter about the Prophet's intention, and sent it with a woman he trusted. When the Prophet discovered this, he sent 'Ali ibn Abi Talib, al-Zubayr, and al-Miqdad to stop her

---

[15] *Id.*

and retrieve the letter. When they overtook her, they asked her to produce the letter, but she denied that she had it. Having searched her camel and not finding the letter, they then said to her that the Prophet does not lie, and that she must produce the letter, or they would strip her naked. Realizing they were serious, she took the letter out of her belt (others say her braid). Thus, the three companions did not search the woman's person first, but searched her belongings and stopped short of searching her. Then they frightened her into producing the letter, without actually touching any of her private parts.

4. *Right of the accused to speak or remain silent*

Under *Shari'a* the accused has the absolute right to answer or refuse to answer the investigator's questions. If he answers, he is not obligated to speak the truth. If he admits guilt, he has the right to change his mind. Should he do so, his admission becomes invalid and cannot be used as evidence at trial.

It is universally agreed among Islamic jurists that the accused cannot be forced to admit guilt. Ibn Hazm suggests in *al-Muhalla* that neither the *Qu'ran*, nor the *Sunna*, nor *Ijma'* (consensus) allow examination by beating, imprisonment or threats. And the Malikis require that admission be voluntary, otherwise it is invalid even if it would have led to the recovery of the victim in a murder or of stolen goods in a robbery. The Hanafis also reject as unjust an admission obtained by torture or threats even though it might be true. However, some later Hanafi jurists would permit coerced admissions. Thus, ibn 'Abidin in his *hashiya* (commentary) relates that al-Hasan ibn Ziyad allowed the beating of the accused to force him to admit guilt, provided this did not lead to wounding the flesh and exposing the bones. Ibn 'Abidin adds that without beatings, it is rare to get confessions of guilt, arguing that there is a special need for this measure during interrogation due to the spread of corruption. However, those who hold this opinion qualify it by limiting it to the known evil and immoral men.*

Some jurists adopt a middle view by not permitting involuntary confession while admitting its true results (except in *Hudud* crimes). Among these are ibn al-Quayyim[16] and ibn Hazm.[17] Ibn al-Qayyim points out that if the accused is tortured in order to obtain his confession of stealing, but he does confess and the stolen money is found in his possession, then his hand should be severed. This is not punishment on the basis of the confession he was forced to make, but rather the fact that he was caught with stolen possessions. Ibn Hazm expresses this opinion more clearly and logically, arguing that such forced confession by itself has no legal weight according to the *Qu'ran*, *Sunna* or *Ijma'*. The skin, blood and honor of the accused are inviolate and cannot be otherwise affected except by text or consensus. If there is evidence consistent with the accused's confession, then he deserves the *Had* punishment for whatever the crime (*Had* or *Ta'azir*). On the

---

**Ed. note:* This is positively prohibited in *Hudud* crimes, and only the very few jurists mentioned in this school would allow this in any crime.

[16] AL-QAYYIM, *supra* note 1.

[17] IBN HAZM, AL-MUHALLA.

other hand, the accused has the right of redress against those who ordered his torture, whether this be the Ruler or any other person in authority, since beating him unnecessarily is an illegal and oppressive act. The fact that he committed a crime does not negate the fact that an illegal act was committed against him, nor does the commission of a crime deprive him of his basic rights.

The opinion of ibn Hazm leads to a legal dilemma, for he does not rely upon the invalidity of the involuntary confession, but at the same time he does rely on its results as self-sufficient evidence and a valid basis on which to base a conviction. Nevertheless, ibn Hazm, with the intuition of a jurist, tries to balance the requirements of justice necessitating the punishment of the guilty and the protections afforded by the *Shari'a* against harming a person to obtain a confession.

An assessment of these views suggests that the majority opinion is more consistent with the *Shari'a*. The second opinion clearly stands on a weak and unsound foundation, and the fact that it is result-oriented conflicts with the *Shari'a*, which requires that the means and the objective be equally legitimate. The third view is defensible, and its practical benefits may be justifiable. However, it is indefensible for two reasons. First, it conflicts with the established doctrine of the *Shari'a* as expressed by jurists using it as a basis for several secondary judgements. The rule states that "right cannot arise out of wrong" (*jus ex injuria non oritur*) and "the source determines the offshoot."

The second reason is that the use of illegal means to achieve legal ends requires the exclusion of what is obtained through coercion because reliance on the result of an involuntary confession will tempt weak souls to torture the accused. Furthermore, the accused is not protected sufficiently from this danger simply by affording him a subsequent opportunity to retaliate against his torturers. His injury may not be adequately redressed in that manner. He is better protected if involuntary confessions are held invalid and their results or consequences are nullified.

Confessions obtained by deceit were, however, allowed and preferred by ibn Hazm, since no coercion is involved. On this question he criticized Imam Malik by commenting that deceit is not forbidden. Ibn Hazm attributes the use of trickery to the Prophet and 'Ali, who used it to obtain the confession of certain suspects. Ibn Hazm argues that trickery is not like force, for force is that which harms a person's body or belongings or threatens him or his family. No such harm is effected by trickery. Thus, trickery is not coercive.

However, Malik's view seems the more acceptable, for it is not true that the investigator's resort to deception and deceit is not prohibited. Furthermore, coercion nullifies a confession by invalidating the element of choice (the will) and negating the voluntary nature of the confession which is a requirement of its validity. This defect is likewise present in a confession obtained through trickery. Thus, the latter must be considered the same in effect as an involuntary confession. Ibn Hazm viewed harm or the threat of harm as the defect of involuntary confessions. While a confession gained through deceit is not without harmful consequences, it is more important to recognize the effect of the means employed as the means of coercing the accused to submit the will of the confessor.

GENERAL PRINCIPLES OF CRIMINAL EVIDENCE IN ISLAMIC JURISPRUDENCE

Ma'amoun M. Salama

INTRODUCTION

The principles which govern proof in any legal system reflect, to a great degree, the intellectual achievement and cultural values of the society. Since anyone may be accused of committing a crime, the rights of the accused must be respected. However, these rights must be balanced against the right of society to impose punishment. It is the system of criminal evidence which achieves this balance. Furthermore, advanced criminal systems recognize the necessity of final judgments in providing legal certainty. Consequently, a judgment must be an expression of truth thereby precluding the need to reopen a case. Such a principle requires a system of evidence which minimizes, and ideally eliminates, all contradictions between facts and legal conclusions.

Islamic *Shari'a* by systematizing the principles of criminal evidence has endeavored to harmonize the rights of the accused with the right of society to impose punishment. The purpose of this study is, first of all, to set forth the general rules of criminal evidence developed by Islamic jurisprudence, and second to discuss the kinds of evidence recognized as required means of proof which must be demonstrated before punishment may be inflicted.

GENERAL PRINCIPLES OF CRIMINAL EVIDENCE IN ISLAMIC JURISPRUDENCE

THE PRINCIPLE OF INNOCENCE AND ITS IMPACT ON THE BURDEN OF PERSUASION

The principle that the accused is presumed innocent is fundamental in Islamic law. Whoever claims otherwise must prove it. The corollary to this principle is that the burden of proof is on the complainant.

These rules are revealed in the *Qu'ranic* verse: "And those who produce not four witnesses to support their allegation, flog them with eighty stripes." *Surat al Nur* XXIV:4. God also warns every man who falsely accuses his wife of adultery: "Give proof or you will receive a *Had* penalty on your back." The rules are also found in the following *Hadith* of the Prophet: "If men were to be granted what they claim, some will claim the wealth and lives of others. The burden of proof is on the proponent; an oath is incumbent on him who denies." The Prophet also stated: "Your evidence or his oath." These fundamental principles run throughout Islamic law. They are especially important in Islamic criminal law as they embody the presumption of innocence and place the burden of proof on the accuser.

MODES OF EVIDENCE: THE RESTRICTED AND LIBERAL VIEWS

The manner in which the judge may reach his opinion and the types of evidence on which he may rely is a subject of disagreement among Islamic jurists. The focus of the controversy is the evidence which the proponent must present in order to prove his claim and to which the judge is bound in prescribing the penalty. One view is represented by the Shafi'i, Hanafi and Hanbali schools. Those jurists maintain that evidence (*Bayyina*) means the testimony of witnesses (*Shahada*) and point out that the *Qu'ran* considers such testimony as the basis of proof in many situations, including transactions between people, matters of personal status, and wills. They find additional support from the *Qu'ranic* verses quoted above concerning the accusation of adultery. Those verses, it is argued, clearly demonstrate that evidence means primarily the testimony of witnesses.

The second view is presented by ibn Taymiyya, ibn al-Qayyim and ibn al-Ghars. They hold that evidence which appears in the *Qu'ran* is a general form of proof and is not limited by the testimony of witnesses. Such limitation, they argue, is not justified. As ibn al-Qayyim points out, in the words of God and his Prophet, evidence is a name for whatever manifests the truth. Thus, it is more general than the evidence of jurists who restrict it to the testimony of two witnesses or of one witness and an oath, and to assert that the words of God and the Prophet are limited only to witness testimony is a misunderstanding of texts. Examples from the *Qu'ran* clearly indicate that evidence is not limited to witnesses is evidenced by the following quotes:

1. "Our apostles came to them with clear evidences (*bayyinat*)." *Surat al-Ma'edah* V:32.

2. "Nor did the People of the Book make schisms, until after there came to them clear evidence." *Surat al Bayyinah* XCVIII:4.

3. "Say: Surely I have clear evidence from my Lord." *Surat al An'am* VI:57.

4. "Has not there come to them a clear evidence of what is in the previous books?" *Surat Taha* XX:133.

Advocates of the general view also cite the Prophet's question, "Do you have evidence (*bayyina*)?" as well as Umar's statement, "the burden of proof is on the plaintiff." Thus, the Lawgiver intended evidence to be whatever brings forth the truth, whether it be witnesses or general proof and by whatever signs and testimony that make such manifestation possible. Truth manifested through evidence cannot be rejected. The statement that the burden of persuasion is on the plaintiff implies that the claimant must submit whatever evidence is needed to prove the truth of his claim. If the truth is somehow established then the decision will be in his favor.

The second view aims at freeing the means of proof from all limitations in both criminal and civil cases. The first view does not, however, confine proof to witness testimony alone; it equates evidence with the testimony of witnesses, while allowing other methods of proof to be used only in non-criminal matters. In criminal, particularly in *Hudud*, proof is limited to confession (*iqrar*) and the testimony of witnesses. The two schools also differ with regard to the admission of presumptions as proof. The first argues against it, but the second favors such admission, albeit without textual support, provided such presumptions meet the criteria of legal proof, as discussed below.

CAN THE JUDGE RENDER A DECISION ON THE BASIS OF PERSONAL KNOWLEDGE?

In order for the judge's conviction to be valid, civilist and common law systems require that his decision be supported by evidence established by documents and/or testimony of witnesses and that it be made public during deliberations by the opposing contenders in the courtroom. The underlying policy is to prevent a judgement based on the judge's personal knowledge. Civilist and common law systems also require the judge under certain circumstances to disqualify himself when he has extrajudicial knowledge of the case. This was not a universally accepted principle among Islamic jurists who treated the problem from the perspective of searching for truth. They reasoned that justice might not be achieved by prohibiting the judge from passing judgement on the basis of prior knowledge.

Jurists expressed three viewpoints on this matter. The first prohibited the judge from ruling on the basis of pre-trial and extrajudicial knowledge as to any criminal or non-criminal matter. This view is founded on the *Sunna* of the Prophet and on the following statement by Umar ibn al-Khattab: "If you wish, I can testify but not render judgement, or I might judge but not testify." This was his response to a request that he arbitrate a dispute with which he was familiar. Judging on the basis of prior knowledge is, by this view, simply rendering judgement without evidence. This is the view of Abu Bakr, Umar, Ali, ibn Abbas, Abd al-Rahman ibn Awf, and Mu'awiya. It is also held true in the teachings of Malik, al-Shafei, Hanbal al-Shu abi, al-Bukhari, ibn al-Qayyim, and the later Hanafis.

According to the second view, the judge is allowed to rule in accordance with prior knowledge in criminal as well as non-criminal matters. This view is based on the following *Qu'ranic* verse: "O ye who believe! Stand out firmly for justice as witnesses to God..." *Surat al-Nisaa* IV:135. Thus believers, including judges, are enjoined to do justice, and it would be unjust if a judge, knowing one of the adversaries to be guilty, fails to punish him. In addition, a judge's ruling based on the testimony of two frequently unreliable witnesses, would be less often correct than if he ruled on the basis of personal, tough certain, knowledge. Furthermore, the judge evaluates the credibility of the witnesses according to his own familiarity with them. Thus he should also be permitted to decide truth or falsity according to his personal knowledge. This is the view of al-'Athra, Abu Thawr, al-Shafei, ibn Hanbal and ibn-Hazm al-Zahiri.

Proponents of the third view would prohibit the judge from making decisions according to prior knowledge only in the cases of *Hudud*, crimes which are prescribed by the right of God. This is inspired by the prophetic *Hadith* concerning a woman accused of *li'an* (sworn allegation of adultery) about whom the Prophet said: "Were I to stone without evidence, I would stone her." This *Hadith* states that the judge is prohibited from judging according to personal knowledge in case of adultery. This rule applies to all the *Had* penalties and reflects the related precept of forgiveness. This view derives additional support from the *Hadith*: "Doubt nullifies *Hudud*." Thus, the judge's personal knowledge does not inspire confidence in the public, but instead breeds doubt. The *Hudud* are applied by the Imam as God's representative, without any other individual demanding them (*i.e.* a complaining witness) which might make the judge's motives suspect were he to rule on the basis of personal knowledge. Also, a *Had* is nullified if the confessed retracts his admission, in which case the judge cannot inflict the fixed penalty upon him. Therefore, a *Had* penalty may not be inflicted on the basis of the judge's personal knowledge if the confessed denies the confession. The Shafi'is and Abu Hanifa, and the followers of Abu Youssef, and Muhammad ibn al-Hassan all have adopted this view.

It seems clear that Islamic jurisprudence favors prohibiting the judge from ruling according to personal knowledge in criminal matters. This is turn protects the public interest by inspiring confidence and trust in the judge's decision.

CONDITIONS WHICH EVIDENCE MUST MEET TO BE THE BASIS FOR CONVICTION

In order to support a conviction, the first condition that evidence must satisfy is that it must be conclusive. This means that the evidence must clearly and explicitly prove the occurrence of the criminal act without any need for explanation or interpretation. The fundamental principle on which this is based is that certainty can only be negated by another certainty. And since every man is inherently innocent, only clear and convincing evidence can overcome that presumption. On this Abu Hanifa al-Shafi'i, Malik and ibn Hanbal all concur. Thus, for example, if the act in question is adultery, the testimony of every witness must clearly and explicitly prove the act of adultery. The criminal act must be described explicitly by each witness so as to substantiate each element. Applying these rules, Umar ibn al-Khattab imposed the *Had* penalty for defamation on three witnesses who testified against a person accused of adultery when the testimony of the fourth witness clearly failed to corroborate theirs.

In order to achieve conclusiveness in evidence, the time and place of the crime must be specified, and must be consistent with the other evidence adduced by the judge pertaining to the circumstances of the crime. This is also true of evidence obtained through confession. It must be clear and explicit as to the commission of the crime and consistent with all other evidence. As a result of this condition, the judge in Islamic law (*Shari'a*) has the authority to evaluate the evidence, despite the principle of restricting the evidence that can be considered. The principle of restriction generally requires the judge to render a decision, not whenever some of the evidence would be sufficient, but rather when he believes all the evidence clearly and convincingly proves the commission of the crime. The burden of proof is consistent with the Prophetic *Hadith*: "Doubt nullifies *Hudud*," *i.e.*, legal punishment will not be imposed in case of doubt, and conflicting evidence precludes a *Had* punishment. For example, proof of virginity is a conclusive defense even when the witnesses testify to adultery, or if the accused confesses. It is essential, therefore, that the judge strictly and conscientiously evaluate the evidence.

The second condition necessary to support a conviction requires that the evidence remain conclusive until the execution of punishment. If the evidence loses it conclusiveness during any of stage of the trial prior to sentencing, as when the witness changes his testimony and deprives it of its clear and convincing quality, or when the confessor retracts his confession, then neither the evidence nor verdict based thereon is valid. The same is true when the evidence loses its conclusive quality after sentencing but before execution. If the witness changes his testimony, if the accused retracts his confession prior to execution, or if new facts not known to the judge during sentencing come to light which might have cast doubt on the testimony of witnesses or the validity of the confession, then the evidence lacks credibility and the verdict must be reversed. If punishment has been imposed, it must cease.

The third condition is that the presentation of evidence should not be delayed. Some jurists have raised the issue of delay of evidence as equivalent to doubtful evidence which is sufficient to preclude punishment for *Hudud* crimes.

Islamic jurists have approached this problem from four distinct perspectives. The first, as represented by Muhammad ibn al-Hasan, considers testimony inadmissible if the witness fails to come forward and submit his testimony within a specified period of time. This applies to all *Hudud* crimes. Confessions are always admissible except of the crime of drinking. The second view also considers testimony inadmissible when it is delayed and applies to all *Hudud* crimes. However, a confession is never nullified in crimes of *Hudud*, including drinking, because delay does not affect the validity of the evidence. The third view holds that any delay in the presentation of the confession and testimony creates sufficient doubt so as to invalidate the evidence in *Hudud* crimes. As for other crimes the evidence can be used irrespective of time.

These three viewpoints are based on the theory that where the rights of God are affected, testimony is the providence of God. Concealment is a necessary element in crimes which predominantly violate the rights of God. Therefore, if the witness hesitates before the two commands of God not to withold testimony in order to prevent corruption in society and apply the *Hudud* of God, and to protect believers by preventing the spread of evil, then this testimony becomes suspect. Although he may hesitate because of just concern for those who inadvertantly fall into disobedience, it creates the suspicion that behind his motivations lie ulterior motives whose source is hatred or enmity. Umar ibn al-Khattab has stated: "Those who testify to a *Had* without being eye-witnesses testify out of hatred and their testimony is invalid." Thus, such testimony is inadmissible if it is suspected of being motivated by hatred. And while delay of testimony in cases involving the rights of men does not affect its admissibility, such delay in cases of crimes of *Hudud* leads to the nullification of delayed testimony because of the principle of invalidating convictions of *Had* based on doubt. For example in cases of theft, the *Had* penalty may not be inflicted, even though restoring the stolen possessions to the rightful owner is permissible.

In addition, jurists who maintain that delay of confession casts doubt on the *Had* of drinking reflect the consensus that the *Had* is proved only when the drunkard is caught smelling of wine. Obviously, delay necessarily attenuates all signs of intoxication. 'Abd Allah ibn Mas'ud made it a condition of proving drunkeness that the culprit be brought to him while drunk.

Those who consider that a delayed confession nullifies all *Hudud* penalties except defamation, deterrence is impossible unless punishment is imposed at the time of the crime or as quickly thereafter as possible. In addition, delay of confession encourages repentance, which, according to some jurists, constitutes grounds for repeal of the *Had* punishment. As for the *Had* of defamation, it is unaffected by delay in testimony or confession because defamation involves the rights of men. This right encompasses the protection of man's honor and the exoneration from the accusation of adultery. This can be achieved only by inflicting the penalty on the defamer.

Finally, the fourth view expressed by many jurists, including Malik, al-Shafei, and Ahmad ibn Hanbal, suggests that delay of testimony or confession does not necessarily cast doubt on the evidence. Proponents of this view claim that delay of confession or testimony does not directly affect any rights because proof by testimony or confession is based on their inherent credibility, which is a question determined by the judge. Thus testimony or confession cannot be nullified presumptively by mere delay but is left to the judge to determine its credibility.

It is noteworthy that Hanafi jurists equated the results of doubtful evidence due to delay with those of delay in the execution of sentence. They regard such delay as grounds for prohibiting the infliction of the *Had* punishment and argue that the decision to punish is the consequence of the content of the testimony. The witnesses, as testimony givers, and the ruler, as punishment-executor, represent society. Due to the strong connection between testimony and execution, whatever is true of the one becomes true of the other. Thus, if delay affects testimony on which judgment is based, then delay affects execution in the same manner. However, the majority of jurists hold that the *Had* penalty is not nullified by delay of execution, because it is determined and established by judgment. Its delay is considered merely a partial impairment of the *Had* penalties.

When Does Delay Bring Evidence into Doubt?

Islamic jurists have expressed three views concerning Abu Hanifa's analysis of the extent of the delay required to invalidate the evidence or render it doubtful. First, recognizing that societies differ, it is left to the discretion of the judge to determine the proper extent according to his knowledge of the circumstances and customs of the people. The second view is that a period of limitations is six months long. The third view is that the period of limitations is one month. This last view is that of Abu Youssef based on the authority of Abu Hanifa. These periods of limitation apply to all *Hudud* crimes, except drinking, where delay is determined by the absence of the smell of alcohol.

It is important to note that causing doubt does not include excuses acceptable to the judge, such as travel, sickness, distance, and mental distress due to threats and terror, although the effect of such factors is for the judge's evaluation. According to the Hanafis and sometimes the Shafi'is, the trial judge must verify the evidence himself. Generally, the trial judge is not permitted to consider evidence sent to him by another judge, since the trial judge cannot make a personal evaluation in the light of the totality of evidence. This would constitute a form of transmitted testimony (hearsay) which is inadmissible in *Hudud* and in most other crimes. However, Imam Malik allows judges to render judgment on the basis of transmitted testimony in *Hudud* and other crimes. Similarly, Imam Ahmad ibn Hanbal admits this type of evidence, but only in *Hudud* crimes and in some *Quesas* crimes.

In any event all schools of jurisprudence agree that the judge must be convinced on the basis of the evidence submitted during the criminal proceedings. The fact that the majority of jurists restrict criminal evidence to testimony and confession does not mean that the judge is constrained to impose punishment once the legal elements of proof have been established, for the judge still has the authority to evaluate the persuasiveness of the evidence. He may discard the testimony of witnesses if he is not convinced of its validity, credibility, or reliability and he may reject confessions if they are inconsistent with the facts revealed during the proceedings. There is, however, disagreement among jurists as to inflicting the *Had* penalty for defamation where the judge rejects the testimony of a witness due to conflict with the testimony of other witnesses or other substantive differences. Some believe in applying a *Had* punishment to that witness; others do not, and a third group leaves the matter to the judge's discretion. In other words if there is perjured or false testimony it is a matter for the discretion of the judge.

MODES OF CRIMINAL EVIDENCE

INTRODUCTION

Criminal evidence in Islamic jurisprudence consists essentially of testimony. It was clearly indicated earlier that the majority of jurists restrict evidence to the testimony of witnesses. In addition to testimony there are confessions. Evidence outside of these two types takes the form of evidentiary presumptions (*qarain*). The following discussion will consider the conditions which all these modes of evidence must meet.

TESTIMONY

Abu Hanifa, al-Shafei, and Ahmad ibn Hanbal hold the view that the witness must begin his testimony with the word *ashhadu* ("I testify"), since it indicates bearing witness (seeing with one's own eyes) and being certain of one's testimony, in addition to taking the oath. No other word can be substituted because it would be less affirmative, and a cast doubt on the testimony, and thereby requires it to be rejected in accordance with the principle "Doubt nullifies the *Had* punishment." However, Imam Malik did not require that testimony begin with these words so long as the substance indicated direct eyewitnessing.

1. The Stipulation of the Number of Witnesses

Jurists generally agree that for *Hudud*, including homicide and *Quesas*, at least two witnesses must provide consistent testimony, except in cases of adultery and the nullification of the defamation penalty, wherein four witnesses are necessary. However, ibn Hazm argues that judgment should be allowed on the basis of one witness and the oath of the plaintiff in homicide and *Quesas*. In cases of *Hudud* he does require such stipulation. His view is contrary to the majority of jurists, who maintained that judgment can be based on the testimony of one witness and an oath in property disputes and related matters.

There is also no requirement that the witness be male, except in the case of adultery. Here the testimony of two women may equal that of one man.

2. Conditions of Testimony

Testimony must meet certain general criteria in all crimes, in addition to special ones in the case of adultery.

General Criteria

A witness must possess the following:

Maturity The testimony of a minor is inadmissible even if he understands the nature of his testimony. However, in homicide cases Malik allowed the testimony of adolescents against other minors, provided they are rational and there are no other witnesses. It is also reported that Ahmad ibn Hanbal allowed the testimony of minors in cases of assault and battery if their testimony was heard prior to completion of the crime.

Reason The witness must be mentally sound, he must be in possession of his mental faculties both when he observes the incident and when he testifies to it.

Memory The witness must be capable of understanding what he is testifying about and possess sufficient memory to retain and recollect his observations. Persons notorious for bad memory or lethargy are not competent as witnesses.

Speech The witness must be able to speak. There is divergence of opinion concerning the testimony of deaf-mutes. Malik finds it acceptable if the mute has some means of communication. Ahmad accepts him as a competent witness only if he is capable of writing and can write his own testimony. The Hanafis reject the testimony of deaf-mutes whether written or through sign language. The Shafi'i are split on this question.

Visual and Audible Perception The witness must be capable of having visually observed the incident to which he testifies. The testimony of the blind is inadmissible according to most jurists. In addition, the Hanafis require that the witness have sight when he gives testimony. Should a person become blind after witnessing the act, his testimony would not be admissible in court. Concerning perception, the Hanafis reject the testimony of the blind, whereas Abu Youssef allows it in all cases and Zufar limits it to crimes other than *Hudud* and *Quesas*. The Malikis, some of the Shafi'i, and Imam Ahmad generally accept the verbal testimony of a blind witness so long as he is capable of hearing. As for perception of actions, the blind person's testimony is accepted concerning all acts witnessed prior to becoming blind, so long as he recognizes the accused by name and family relations. The Zahiris, however, would allow the testimony of the blind in all cases, whether as a witness to words or deeds and regardless of whether the witness was blind when witnessing the event or when testifying.

Good Character The witness must be of good character. Moral integrity, according to the Hanafis, is achieved when the religion and reason of the witness overcome whim and lust and when he avoids grave and venial sins. Such a person's credibility, righteousness and sense of honor should be beyond question.

To the Malikis and the Shafi'i, good character means the persistent avoidance of grave and venial sins in addition to being trustworthy and having good relationships with people. To the Hanbalis, good character is achieved through religious probity by fulfilling religious religious duties and avoiding both grave and minor crimes; and through manliness, by which valor and chivalry are attained and dishonor and disgrace avoided. Manliness is considered one of the basic elements of good character by all Islamic schools although there are differences in definition.

There are two theories on proving good character. Abu Hanifa and the Zahiris assume that the witness is of good character unless proven otherwise, but the judge is not required to test the probity of the witness. The second opinion which is held by the Malakis, the Shafeis, the Hanbalis, and Abu Youssef requires the judge to verify the good character of the witness even if his competence is not challenged by one of the litigants.

Authenticity Jurists differ with regard to the requirement of authenticity, by which the witness must have realized or noticed the event with his own senses. First of all, Abu Hanifa and al-Shafei argue that witness testimony must be authentic. Thus, transmitted or second-hand testimony (hearsay) is inadmissible due to doubt. The second view, as expressed by Malik and al-Shafei on another occasion, accepts transmitted testimony in *Hudud* and other crimes, providing each authentic witness is replaced by two ordinary witnesses, one of whom at least must not be a direct observer. For adultery, four indirect witnesses may replace four direct witnesses. In all cases, the number of witnesses must not be less that the number of direct ones. The third view, represented by Imam Ahmad ibn Hanbal, rejects indirect testimony in *Hudud* but accepts it in *Quesas*, homicide and defamation cases. In any event, indirect testimony is admissible only if authentic or direct testimony cannot be presented due to death, sickness or travel.

Islam Jurists agree that acceptance of the Islamic faith is a precondition to permitting a witness to testify. This view is based on the verse: "And call to witness two just men among you." *Surat al-Talaq* LXV:2. However, the Hanfis admitted the testimony of one non-Muslim against a Muslim but the Malikis, Shafi'is and most Hanbalis rejected that practice. Ibn Taymiyya and ibn al-Qayyim permitted the testimony of the non-Muslim against the Muslim only when no Muslim witnesses exist. This view is supported by the verse: "O ye of faith, when death is about to come to you, have two just witnesses to your will from among you, or two from another faith if you are travelling and the catastrophe of death strikes you." *Surat al-Ma'edah*, V:106.

Legal Disqualifications of Testimony

Any of the following attributes disqualifies the testimony of a witness:

Blood relation The majority of jurists with the exception of some Shafi'is argue that the testimony of the major and minor branches of families for each other is inadmissible. Abu Hanifa, Malik and Ahmad ibn Hanbal disqualify spouses from testifying for or against each other, but the Shafi'is do not.

Enmity The majority of jurists agree that enmity between a witness and a party to a case arising out of worldly matters disqualifies the witness. Enmity by reason of matter involving the rights of God does not disqualify a witness if he possesses the quality of *'adl* (justness or fairness).

Partiality A claim of partiality exists when there is a relationship between the witness and one of the parties which suggests partiality or a personal interest that may be advanced by the witness through his testimony. This is the position of all jurists, but the Zahiris do not consider this a qualification if the witness is a just person (*adel*).

Special conditions of Testimony in Cases of Adultery*

In addition to the previous criteria, testimonial evidence in cases of adultery must meet additional requirements.

The Number of Witnesses Four competent witnesses are necessary to prove adultery, otherwise the crime is not proven and the witnesses become guilty of defamation. There is some disagreement among the schools on this point.

Males and Females Prosecution witnesses in cases of adultery must all be males. All jurists reject the testimony of women. However, the testimony of women is accepted as evidence for the defense, and in some cases it is a condition that witnesses be women. Nevertheless, 'Ata', Hammad, and ibn Hazm find admissible the testimony of women in proving adultery, provided that there are two women for each man. There is disagreement among jurists concerning the admissibility of the husband's testimony. Malik, Shafeis, and Ahmad ibn Hanbal would not accept the husband's testimony as one of the required number of witnesses. Abu Hanifa would allow such testimony if the husband meets the other necessary qualifications as a witness. Ibn Hazm distinguishes between the husband who accuses his wife of adultery (*quadhf*) and the husband who is a witness to it. In the former case he is not considered a witness, but in the latter he is if he is deemed otherwise qualified.

The Forum Malik, Abu Hanifa, and Ahmad ibn Hanbal maintain that the witnesses to adultery must present their testimony at the same legal session,

---

**Ed. Note:* Because of the seriousness of the penalty the evidentiary requirements were circumscribed—in fact, proof of adultery is so difficult that some jurists believe that the purposes of the punishment are designed to have a general deterrent effect even though seldom applied. Another observation is that the nature of such rigorous proof makes it a crime of public indecency rather than adultery.

while al-Shafei finds testimony presented at separate sessions acceptable. In the majority of views when the hearing is concluded the absent witness is not allowed thereafter to present his testimony, and the accuser who does not have all four witnesses to support his claim is considered a defamer. Malik and Abu Hanifa further argue that all witnesses must be present when the testimony of each one of them begins.

CONFESSION

Confession is the admission by the accused of having committed the act that incurs punishment. It is the second form of evidence which Islamic jurisprudence admits as a means of proving criminal guilt.

1. *Conditions for the Admissibility of a Confession in Criminal* Evidence*

The confessor must be of age, mature,** sane, capable of self-expression and acting of his own free will. Jurists have no disagreement on the first three factors. As for capability of self-expression, the Hanafis argue that it should be verbal and not in writing or sign language. Thus the mute could not make a legally effective confession. However, al-Shafei, Ahmad ibn Hanbal, and in general, Malik, would admit the mute person's confession if his signs are intelligible. All concur that confession by the blind is admissible.

Free will The confessor must confess with a free and conscious will. Any pressure, torture or deception by the judge nullifies the confession. Thus the judge is not allowed to mislead the accused during cross-examination so as to elicit his confession. The judge must not encourage confessions.

Unequivocal The confession must be unequivocal, clear, and explicit as to the crime. The confessor must detail the act he committed in such a way that leaves no doubt (*shubha*). The *Sunna* precludes doubtful confessions.

Forum The confession must take place in and during a legal hearing. According to Abu Hanifa, if it takes place outside the court, it is invalid. However, Malik, al-Shafei, and Ahmad ibn Hanbal would accept an extra-judicial confession if it is witnessed by two people. Malik and al-Shafei apply this to all cases. Ahmad ibn Hanbal, however, requires four witnesses in the case of adultery. If the confessor retracts his confession, Malik considers it a withdrawal of the confession that nullifies it, but Shafei does not consider it withdrawn unless the confessor contradicts himself in his confession.***

Repetition of the Confession The Hanafis maintain that the accused must repeat the confession the same number of times as that of the required number of

---

**Ed. Note:* The rigid requirements set forth herein are intended to limit confessions and make their admissibility subject to stringent rules.

***Ed. Note:* Maturity whereas capacity to understand what is being admitted to and its legal consequences.

****Ed. note:* Withdrawal of a confession in a *Had* crime is always permissible up to the execution of the punishment. The views differ on *Quesas* crimes. The same applies to extra-judicial confessions in *Hudud* and *Quesas*—in *Hudud* crimes the confession must be in open court and if doubtful it must be rejected. No testimony of an extra-judicial confession is admissible unless as corroborative of other testimony. The views differ on *Quesas* crimes. The difference is based on the seriousness of the crime and the punishment.

witnesses. Thus, if four witnesses are necessary, as in the case of adultery, then four separate confessions are necessary. In the case of defamation, however, one confession is sufficient. Abu Hanifa says that the *Qu'ran* requires this rule only with reference to adultery; as for other *Hudud* crimes he sees no need for repeating the confession since it is not specifically required by the *Qu'ran*. Al-Shafei does not require repetition, even in adultery cases. In general, jurists who support the repetition requirement also argue that they should be made on different occasions, even though within the same legal proceedings. While insistence on the confession is one of the legal requirements for a conviction based thereon, its repetition has no apparent value since the confessor can withdraw it any time before execution of sentence irrespective of its repetition.

Corroboration The judge must find in other circumstances corroboration of the facts confessed for.

2. The Effect of the Confession

A confession only implicates the accused but not his accessories or co-conspirators; this derives from the principle of individuality of responsibility. Thus, confessing to adultery with a certain woman does not render her guilty, if the legal evidence against her is not present. The confessor is the only person to be punished in such circumstances. It is related that a man confessed to the Prophet of adultery with a woman whom he named. Upon asking the woman, she denied the man's allegation. The Prophet inflicted the *Had* penalty on the man but left the woman alone.

3. The Jurisdiction of the Judge in Evaluating Confession

Confession proves guilt and incurs penalties only when the judge is convinced of it. This requires that the confession meet all the legal criteria set forth above, and that it be corroborated by other circumstances inferred by the judge. Thus if it is proven that the accused confessed under duress or if the woman accused of adultery is proven a virgin, the confession is inadmissible. Some jurists hold the view that the judge should suggest to the accused the possibility of retracting his confession, as the Prophet did in the case of a confessing adulterer and a woman accused of theft.

4. Retracting the Confession

The accused may withdraw his confession at any time before or after sentencing or during execution of sentence and in so doing nullify the judgement if it is based solely on the confession. Withdrawal of confession may take a public form or simply the form of the convicted person's escape from punishment. Although some jurists such as al-Hasan, Sa'id ibn Jubayr, and ibn Abi Layla believe that retraction or denial after proof is of no consequence and that the *Had* punishment must be applied, the prevailing view is that the withdrawal of confession at any time halts execution, since withdrawal introduces doubt (*shubha*), and doubt nullifies *Hudud*.

PRESUMPTIONS (*QARA'IN*)

Qarina (presumption) is the logical inference to be drawn from something done, or from circumstances. A presumption may be weak or strong evidence; sometime it is considered conclusive while other occasions it might only be probative.* Only when it is strong is it significant as criminal evidence. Jurists define *qarina* as that by virtue of which the matter becomes definitive, a sign which makes the matter certain. The underlying concept is that a *qarina*, like the other methods of evidence, must meet the condition of certainty and conclusiveness.

Islamic jurisprudence admits presumptions as evidence in a number of diverse situations, but jurists did not assign to them an independent category. The failure to do so became a source of disagreement among later jurists. Some argued that a judgment can be based on presumptions, while others argued that it should not.

Jurists express three views as to the use of presumption for crimes of *Hudud* and homicide. In the first view, the Shafi'is, Hanafis, and, with one exception, the Hanbalis reject the use of presumptions in *Hudud* cases, allowing only witnesses and confession as evidence. This view is based on the following statement by the Prophet: "Were I to stone anyone without evidence, I would stone so-and-so (*fulana*), for her speech, appearance and cohabitation which raise suspicion." This reinforces the rule that doubt nullifies *Hudud*. Since a presumption is always doubtful it cannot be the basis for judgement in *Hudud*.

The second view would permit certain types of presumptions to be used in proving *Hudud* cases. Thus, for example, pregnancy is an evidentiary presumption applied in cases of adultery, provided that the woman has no husband and has not claimed rape. The smell of alcohol or regurgitated wine presumptively proves drinking. This is the view of Malik and reportedly of Ahmad ibn Hanbal and is based on statements by Umar ibn al-Khattab, 'Uthman ibn 'Affan, and 'Ali ibn 'Abi Talib who said: "Adultery is public when pregnancy appears or confession is made."

The third view freely recognizes the validity of evidence by presumptions in all *Hudud* cases. It is argued that evidence is whatever brings the truth to light including presumption.** This view is based on the decision of the Companions of the Prophet and the four Caliphs following the Prophet who imposed *Had* penalties for adultery when pregnancy resulted and for drinking wine on the basis of odor and vomiting. Also stolen property found in the possession of the thief constitutes rebuttable proof of theft. In contrast to the second view expressed above, they reason that if a presumption is susceptible of doubt, so is the testimony of witnesses and it should therefore be judged in the same manner. Indeed testimony is more susceptible to illusions, lies, and error than presumptions. Thus presumptions have at least as much validity as testimony. This is the opinion of ibn al-Qayyim and ibn al-Ghars.

**Ed. Note:* The difference between conclusive and probative is the same as irrebuttable and rebuttable presumptions except that it is based on the legal logic of the fact and not by operation of law.

***Ed. note:* Provided that in *Hudud* it is not doubtful.

CONCLUSION

The system of the criminal evidence in Islamic law seeks to harmonize and balance the rights of the accused with those of society. If the public interest lies in eradicating corruption from society and deterring wrong-doers, it is also in the interest of the individual and the community that no innocent person should be punished. For those reasons the Islamic rules of criminal evidence take great care to require consistency between these sometimes contradictory concerns. The right of a person not to be judged guilty of a crime unless there is proof requires that the evidence be both conclusive and certain as is demonstrated from this discussion of the rules of evidence and standards of proof. These considerations also explain the differences among jurists as to the use of evidentiary presumptions in criminal law.

It is also clear that the strict requirements for proving certain crimes is a confirmation of the individual right to the presumption of innocence, dignity, and good reputation requires safeguarding unless there is specific and certain evidence to justify the loss of those rights. Finally, along with the emphasis of criminal evidence in confirming the presumption of innocence, human dignity, and good reputation, Islamic law leaves the evaluation of evidence to the judge but not without providing him with clear standards to guide his decision.

BIBLIOGRAPHY

ABU AL-FUTUH, ABU AL-MAATI HAFIZ. AL-NIZAM AL-IQABI AL-ISLAMI: DIRASAH MUGARINAH (THE ISLAMIC PENAL SYSTEM: A COMPARATIVE STUDY). Cairo: Dar al-Ansar, 1976.

ABU ZAHRAH, MUHAMMAD. AL-JARIMAH WA-AL-UQU-BAH FI AL-FIQH AL-ISLAMI (CRIME AND PUNISHMENT IN ISLAMIC JURISPRUDENCE). Cairo Dar al-Fikr al-Arabi, 1974.

AWDAH, ABD, AL-QADIR. AL-TASHRI AL-JINAI AL-ISLAMI (ISLAMIC CRIMINAL LEGISLATION). Cairo: Maktabat Dar al-Urubah, 1960-63.

AL-BAHI, AHMAD ABD AL-MUNIM. MIN TURUQ AL-ITHBAT FI AL-SHARIAH WA-AL GANUN. (Methods of Evidence in Islamic and Positive Law.) Cairo: Dar al-Fikr al-Arabi, n.d.

IBN FARHUN, IBRAHIM IBN ALI. TABISRAT AL-HUKKAM FI USUL AL-AGDIYAH WA-MANAHIJ AL-AHKAM. Cairo: al-Matbaah al-Bahiyah, 1882.

IBN HAZM, ALI IBN AHMAD. AL-MUHALLA. Egypt: Matbaat al-Imam, 1964.

IBN AL-HUMAM, MUHAMMAD IBN ABD AL-WAHID. SHARH FATH AL-QADIR. Cairo: al-Maktabah al-tijariyah, 1937.

IBN QAYYIM AL-JAWZIYAH, MUHAMMAD IBN ABI BAKR. AL-TURUQ AL-HUKMIYAH FI AL-SIYASAH AL-SHAR'IA. Cairo: Matbaat al-Sunnah al-Muhammadiyah, 1953.

IBN QAYYIM AL JAWZIYAH, MUHAMMAD IBN ABI BAKR. I'LAM AL-MUWAQQIIN AN RABB AL-ALAMIN. Cairo: Dar al-Kutub al-Hadithah, 1969.

IBN QUDAMAH, MUWAFFAQ AL-DIN. AL-MUGHNI. Egypt: Matbaat al-Imam, 1964.

AL-JASSAS, AHMAD IBN ALI. KITAB AHKAM AL-QURAN. Egypt: al-Matbaah al-Gahiyah al-Misriyah, 1928.

AL-KASANI, ABU BAKR IBN MAS'UD. BADA I AL-SANAI FI TARTIB AL-SHARAI. Egypt: Matbaat Sharikat al-Matbuat al-Ilmiyah, 1909-10.

MALIK IBN ANAS. AL-MUWATTA. Egypt: Mustafa al-Babi al-Halabi, 1920-21.

AL-SARAKHSI, MUHAMMAD IBN AHMAD. KITAB AL-MABSUT. Egypt: Matbaat al-Saadah, 1906-12.

AL-SHAFII, MUHAMMAD IBN IDRIS. AL-UMM. Cairo: Maktabat al-Kulliyaat al-Azhariyah, 1961.

SHALTUT, MAHMUD, and AL-SAYIS, MUHAMMAD ALI. MUGARANAT AL-MADHAHIB FI AL-FIQH (A COMPARISON OF THE SCHOOLS OF ISLAMIC LAW). Cairo: Muhammad Ali Subayyh, 1953.

AL-SHIRAZI, IBRAHIM IBN ALI. KITAB AL-MUHADHDHAB. Cairo: Matba'at Isa al-Babi al-Halabi, 1924.

Part Two

Criminal Responsibility, Crimes and Punishment

THE BASIS OF ISLAMIC PENAL LEGISLATION

Muhammad Salim al-'Awwa

INTRODUCTION

There are two categories of crime and punishment in Islamic legislation: determined and discretionary. Determined crimes and penalties are those provided for in the *Qu'ran* or the *Sunna* (the tradition of the Prophet Muhammad) where both the form of the criminalized conduct and its assigned punishment are specified. A crime or a penalty is discretionary when neither *Qu'ranic* nor *Sunna* text render the act in question criminal. Rather, its criminalization results from the implementation of general legislation by the competent authority of the Islamic state.

Crimes of the first category are of two kinds: crimes of *Hudud* (offenses to which a *Had* punishment applies), and crimes of retribution (*Quesas*) and compensation (*Diyya*). The function of *Hudud* crimes and punishments is to protect public interests in Muslim society, public property and security (theft and banditry), family structure, conjugal and familial relations (adultery), and personal reputation (defamation or false accusation of unchastity). Furthermore, the prevailing tendency in Islamic penal law is to consider crimes related to the protection of the public religious order in Islamic society (apostasy) as crimes of *Hudud*. Also included in this category are crimes related to the protection of the psychological welfare and moral conduct of individuals, such as the prohibition against drinking wine.

Unlawful rebellion against the political system of the Islamic state as punishable by *Had*. These offenses have been termed crimes of *Hudud* (determined offenses) because Allah (the Lawmaker) has irrevocably and permanently specified their punishment.

Crimes of retribution and compensation (*Diyya*) involve homicide, bodily injury or other forms of harm committed against the physical security of the person. They are labelled as such because the punishment imposed is either a retributive penalty equivalent to the injury inflicted on the victim, or takes the form of pecuniary compensation (ransom) for the victim's injuries and is imposed only if retribution is not executable or the victim waives his right to demand it.

Similar to crimes of *Hudud*, offenses of retribution and compensation are also prescribed by the *Qu'ran* and *Sunna*. However, they differ in that the victim or the political authority of the State may not grant pardon for crimes of *Hudud*. The victim or his legal guardians, on the other hand, may do so in cases of retribution and ransom. The *Had* penalties may not be mitigated, aggravated or suspended. However, if the victim or his guardians waive the retribution or ransom claim, then the applicable verdict is left to the discretion of the tribunal.

Discretionary offenses, commonly known as crimes of *Ta'azir* (corrective punishment), are numerous in Muslim states since all such criminal acts and corresponding penalties outside the framework of crimes and penalties of *Hudud* and retribution are considered discretionary. The system of discretionary crimes in Islamic penal law represents the means through which society protects its political, economic and social systems, and preserves its cultural continuity by prescribing penalties for infringement or disruption of the system, *Qu'ranic* and *Sunna* sources abound with examples of *Ta'azir* penalties. But of greater importance is the conclusion reached by some contemporary studies that the *Qu'ran* and the *Sunna* prescribe the general principles of the *Ta'azir* system, suggesting thereby an integrated theory covering the legislative sources, societal functions and judicial applications of *Ta'azir*. This theory has challenged if not laid to rest the widespread view that the *Ta'azir* system is one of incrimination and punishment totally governed by the unrestrained discretion of the ruler.[1]

The divisions of the Islamic penal system, as described above, rest upon a number of fundamental principles. Some relate to the sources of this system; others can be described as objective or substantive principles, and still others pertain to rules of procedure. The basic principles of each division are discussed below.

FUNDAMENTAL PRINCIPLES RELATED TO THE SOURCES OF THE ISLAMIC PENAL SYSTEM

THE RELIGIOUS CHARACTER OF ISLAMIC CRIMINAL LEGISLATION

The Islamic penal system is characterized by direct reliance in its general foundation, universal principles and many summary provisions upon divinely inspired *Qu'ranic* and *Sunna* texts. Thus, Islamic *Shari'a* has been defined as "the collection of *ahkam* (legal provisions) divinely revealed to the Prophet." In addition to classifying Islamic rules of law into categories on the basis of their subject matter, they also may be grouped according to their sources. One such grouping derives from the source of divinely inspired texts, including the *Qu'ran* and the prophetic *Hadith*.

The *Qu'ranic* sources for the *Had* penalties are found in various texts. The *hukm* (fixed judgement) of inheritance is based on the *Qu'ran*. "Allah chargeth you concerning...your children: to the male the equivalent of the share of two

---

[1]*See* 3 M. A. AL-'AWWA, FI USUL AL-NIZAM AL-JINA'I AL-ISLAMI [THE SOURCES OF THE ISLAMIC PENAL SYSTEM] ch. 4 (1979).

females . . .";[2] the *hukm* for theft: "As for the thief, both male and female, cut off their hands. It is the reward of their own deeds, an exemplary punishment from Allah . . .";[3] the *hukm* for defamation: "And those who accuse honorable women but bring not four witnesses, scourge them (with) eighty stripes . . .";[4] the *hukm* for banditry or highway robbery: "The only reward of those who make war upon Allah and His messenger and strive after corruption in the land will be that they will be killed or crucified, or have their hands and feet on alternate sides cut off, or will be expelled out of the land";[5] and the *hukm* for adultery: "The adulterer and the adulteress, scourge ye each one of them (with) a hundred stripes. And let not pity for the twain withhold you from obedience to Allah. . . ."[6] Jurists have recorded approximately 500 *Qu'ranic* verses and 4000 prophetic *Hadith* stipulating similar legal decisions or judgements.

The second category of crimes and punishment has as its direct source the *Ijtihad* (independent reasoning) of Muslim jurists who for centuries have taken legal decisions on matters for which guidance in the *Qu'ran* or the *Sunna* is not specially provided. *Ijtihad* is generally regarded as the legal framework applicable in procedural matters, in imposing certain punishments as required by different schools of Islamic jurists, and in *Ta'azir*. This category includes, for example, most doctrinal judgments such as the mandatory death penalty for joint perpetrators of a homicide. Thus, Caliph Umar ibn al-Khattab rendered such a decision during his reign when two convicts were brought before him and jointly charged with murder. Initially he hesitated to inflict punishment on both offenders due to God's statement: "And we prescribed for them therein The life for the life. . . ."[7] Upon consulting with Ali who advised him to put both men to death, Umar issued his verdict and ordered capital punishment. Another example of *Ijtihad* rulings is the decision by the Companions of the Prophet stipulating that artisans pay compensation for damages to goods which they were charged to manufacture. This decision was justified on grounds of being in the public interest. They also determined that wives were being divorced on their death beds for the purpose of depriving them of their inheritance rights. Therefore, they ruled that in such divorces the wife does not forfeit her inheritance.

The various schools of Islamic jurisprudence continued to rely on *Ijtihad* where sacred texts were silent. As a result, a juridical and doctrinal heritage emerged which today continues to guide the legal reasoning of *Shari'a* scholars and to serve as a source from which they develop Islamic theories in all areas of law.

The religious character of both *Had* and *Ijtihad* is equally apparent. The first group's judgments are taken directly from divinely inspired text, be it the *Qu'ran* or the *Hadith*. In the second doctrinal *Ijtihad* takes two courses. One consists of

[2] *Surat al-Nisaa* IV:11.
[3] *Surat al Maeda* V:38.
[4] *Surat al-Nur* XXIV:4.
[5] *Surat al-Maeda* V:33.
[6] *Surat al-Nur* XXIV:2.
[7] *Surat al-Maeda* V:45.

deducing the judgment from an inconclusive source, *i.e.*, where the views of the *mujtahidin** differ regarding its validity. The other consists of proving the decision by logical means, including by analogy to a conclusive judgment in an existing text, by juristic preference, by taking the public interest and custom into consideration (*Istihsan*)* or by other methods of deduction treated in detail by Islamic scholars.[8]

If the basis of a doctrinal decision lies in *Ijtihad's* interpretation of a purportedly applicable text, then the matter presents no problem, since the decision in reality rests upon divine text, and *Ijtihad* is merely a tool to facilitate the understanding of what is decreed by text. And if the method of reaching a doctrinal decision is one of the approved methods of deduction and in the absence of text, then the religious character of judgments reached through such methods is also evident, since these methods derive legitimacy from their explicit or implicit confirmation by the *Qu'ran* or *Sunna*.

In this regard, the words of al-Shafei are instructive: "For everything that affects the life of a Muslim, there is prescribed in the *Qu'ran* a guide to lead him on the right way." He also said, "For everything that befalls a Muslim there is an obligatory *hukm* and a guide to lead him on the right way."[9] These words indicate that God has prescribed for man binding and irrevocable judgments applicable to particular situations and that He has established specific methods through which men can reach a decision in the absence of a specifically designated decision. Thus, it is clear that Islamic legal decisions, including those of a penal nature, are religious judgments based explictly on divine inspiration, or reached indirectly through divinely inspired and sanctioned methods of deduction.

Important consequences flow from the religious character of the provisions of Islamic penal legislation. The most significant of these are as follows:

1. Conformity to and application of Islamic penal decisions are inseparable from faith in God. Thus, for example, with regard to usury, which is a *Ta'azir* crime, God says, "O ye who believe! Observe your duty to Allah, and give up what remaineth (is due to you) from usury, if ye are (in truth) believers."[10] On the subject of adultery and the necessity of public punishment for it, the *Qu'ran* says: "The adulterer and the adulteress, scourge ye each one of them (with) a hundred stripes. And let not pity for the twain withhold you from obedience to Allah, if ye believe in Allah and the Last Day. And let a party of believers witness their punishment."[11] The following prophetic *Hadith* demonstrates the impact of faith on abstinence from unlawful things: "A believer neither steals nor commits adultery."[12]

**Ed. note:* Those scholars who engage in *Ijtihad*, independent reasoning.

**Ed. note:* Reasoning toward the "better rule."

[8] For further detail on methods of deduction, see 1 S.M.M. SHALABI, USUAL AL-FIQH AL-ISLAMI [THE ROOTS OF ISLAMIC JURISPRUDENCE] 188-365 (1973).

[9] *See* A. SHAKIR, RISALAT AL-SHAFE'I USUL AL-FIQH [THE MESSAGE OR PHILOSOPHY OF AL-SHAFE'I IN THE PRINCIPLES OF JURISPRUDENCE] 20, 477 (1937).

[10] *Surat al-Baqara* II:278.

[11] *Surat al-Nur* XXIV:2.

[12] *See* 1 MISHKAT AL-MASABIH 23.

2. Islamic criminal law provides for both earthly punishment and punishment in the hereafter. Thus, after specifying the temporal punishment to be inflicted upon bandits, God says: "Such will be their degradation in the world, and in the Hereafter theirs will be an awful doom."[12a] As for murder, the Almighty says: "Whoso slayeth a believer of set purpose, his reward is Hell forever. Allah is wroth against him, and He hath cursed him and prepared for him an awful doom."[13] With regard to the necessity of obedience to God and prohibition against insubordination and sin, He says:

> Whoso obeyeth Allah and His messenger, He will make him enter Gardens underneath which rivers flow, where such will dwell forever. That will be the great success.
>
> And whoso disobeyeth Allah and His messenger and transgresseth His limits, He will make enter Fire, where such will dwell forever: his will be a shameful doom.[14]

3. The association between legal decisions and faith on the one hand, and between obedience to them on earth and eternal reward or punishment, on the other, has always been the motivation to abide by the rules of Islamic penal law. It is widely recognized that the government of a state and its security forces, regardless of how effective, inevitably fall short of deterring all violations of law in that society, since they are incapable of preventing all offenses by exerting external control over individual conduct. However, if the element of religious restraint is added, each person becomes in effect his own judge, with his faith in God preventing him from indulging in forbidden pursuits and doing injury to the rights of others.

4. The enforcement of Islamic penal law by Islamic states is considered an obligatory function of Islamic government, from which the Islamic state may not waiver. Adherence to the Islamic faith is not complete, as God demands, unless accompanied by the temporal application of Islamic law.

The religious character of Islamic criminal law is considered one of its most remarkable attributes, distinguishing it from other contemporary penal systems. Differences too numerous to mention within the present discussion stem from that fundamental distinction. It is sufficient to note that this religious character is not restricted to Islamic criminal legislation, but also extends to other branches of Islamic lawmaking.

THE PROTECTION OF MORAL VALUES IN ISLAMIC CRIMINAL LEGISLATION

The age-old problem of the relationship between law and morality, the compatibility which can exist between legal and moral principles has always concerned jurists and moral philosophers. Some of the most serious debate takes place among the scholars of criminal law due to its role in imposing moral values on society or at least in presupposing their existence and protecting them through

---

[12a] *Surat al-Maeda* V:33.
[13] *Surat al-Nisaa* IV:93.
[14] *Surat al-Nisaa* IV:13-14.

the criminalization of contrary acts.

Penalizing certain acts regarded as immoral by the criminal law, jeopardizes the legal rights of those penalized. For this reason, most legal systems recognize the necessity of confining the scope of the criminal law as narrowly as possible. John Stuart Mill, a proponent of this view argued that, "while moral laws represent the maximal limit of perfection, legal principles are its minimal limit of which the rules of criminal law are the essential part."[15] Lord Devlin points out that "the only purpose for which power can rightfully be exercised over any member of a civilized community, against his will, is to prevent harm to others."[16]

The relationship between law and morality, as expressed in the criminal law was further highlighted in Britain after the publication of the Wolfenden Report in 1957 by a committee established by the British House of Commons to study homosexual offenses and prostitution. Soon afterwards, there occurred the famous case brought before the Central Criminal Court of London, in which a Mr. Shaw was accused and convicted of conspiracy to corrupt public morals. In 1961, the House of Lords upheld the verdict of guilty rendered by the Court. Thus, the debate shifted from the level of philosophical discussion and assumed a practical character.

While there has been significant polarization among western scholars on the extent to which the criminal law should intervene in protecting moral values and punishing immoral conduct, a similar schism never existed in Islamic thought because of the integral relationship between religion and morality in Islam.

The relationship between Islamic religious doctrines and Islamic legal principles is clear. Thus, the rules of both Islamic *Shari'a* and Islamic penal law are replete with measures designed to protect the moral values of Muslim society. The *Qu'ran* justifies the prohibition of certain acts on the basis of their moral consequences. For example, concerning wine-drinking and gambling, it states: "Satan seeketh only to cast among you enmity and hatred by means of strong drink and games of chance...."[17] It prohibits adultery, as stated in *Surat Bani Isra'il*: "And come not near unto adultery. Lo! It is abomination and an evil way."[18] Furthermore, a number of *Qu'ranic* texts are justified on the basis of their power to sanctify souls and purify hearts, two ways of instiling upright character and moral behavior.

The *Qu'ran* explictly mentions two *Had* crimes which are directly connected with individual and social morals: fornication (unlawful sexual intercourse) and defamation (false accusation of unchastity). Also under *Ta'azir* the moral values of society are protected by defining penalties for all other forbidden conduct not provided for in the *Qu'ran* or *Sunna*. Accordingly, the Islamic legal system has been aptly described as the law of moral precepts.[19] This is confirmed by the fact

---

[15] J.S. Mill, On Liberty 15 (1859).

[16] Lord Devlin, The Enforcement of Morals 25 (1959).

[17] *Surat al-Maeda* V:91.

[18] *Surat al-Israa* XVII:32.

[19] One commentator has stated in Islam "all acts and relationships are measured by a scale of moral evaluation." N. Coulson, A History of Islamic Law 83 (1972).

that punishment for violating Islamic law is not merely a temporal punishment but also is punished in the hereafter. Thus, if a Muslim commits a forbidden act and somehow escapes worldly punishment, he will not evade eternal punishment except through genuine and sincere repentance, which is the act of turning away from sin and resolving never to return to it. True repentance combines with the temporal policy of rehabilitation to strengthen the link between criminal law and moral principles.

The preservation of moral principles by the Islamic penal system is not simply a doctrinal deduction. Rather it forms an integral part of Islamic lawmaking, as confirmed by the prophetic *Hadith*: "I was sent to perfect moral goodness."[20] Thus, there is no dichotomy in the Islamic legal system between criminal law and moral principles. the former is always used to confirm, protect and enforce respect for the latter. This represents the distinctive character of the Islamic legal system, with its origin in divinely inspired texts simultaneously governing religious, moral and judicial principles.

FUNDAMENTAL OBJECTIVE PRINCIPLES

The cornerstone of contemporary Islamic criminal law upon which individual rights and freedom is built is the principle of legality (*Shari'a*). That principle (*Nullum crimen nulla poena sine lege*) essentially provides that there is no crime or punishment unless established by law. The protection of rights and freedoms in the Islamic or any other legal system depends upon the system's recognition of the legality principle.

Among the most important components of the principle is the non-retroactivity doctrine of criminal law. That doctrine prohibits the infliction of punishment on an individual, unless the crime of which he is accused has been specifically criminalized or had a penalty prescribed for it in existing law at the time it was committed. The Islamic penal system has been criticized on the grounds that it does not adequately recognize the principle of legality and its consequences. Even some commentators who maintain that the Islamic penal system takes the principle of legality into consideration have expressed doubts over the purportedly limited scope of the non-retroactivity principle. Those objections will first be addressed, and then the principle of equality in the execution of criminal law will be considered.

THE ISLAMIC PENAL SYSTEM AND THE PRINCIPLE OF LEGALITY

An examination of both fundamental sources of Islamic *Shari'a*, the *Qu'ran* and the *Sunna*, clearly indicates the absence of an *expressis verbis* of the principle of legality. It is not difficult to conclude, however, from *Qu'ranic* and *Sunna* sources and from basic principles of the *Shari'a* that Islamic law provides for everything that the legality principle implies.

---

[20] A confirmed *Hadith* commented by Imam Malik in A. MALIK, AL-MUWATTA' 504 (n.d.).

[21] For further details on the principle of legality, see Al-Awwa, 1 AL'MAJALLA AL-ARABIYYA LIL-DIFA'A AL-IJTIMA' [THE ARAB REVIEW OF SOCIAL DEFENSE] 11 *passim* (1978).

The *Qu'ran* states: "We never punish until We have sent a messenger."[22] Also: "Never did the Lord destroy the townships, until He had raised up in their mother (-town) a messenger reciting unto them Our revelations."[23] And: "Tell those who disbelieve that if they cease... that which is past will be forgiven them...."[24] In prohibiting certain forms of conduct, God "excepts what hath already happened...."[25] And: "Allah forgiveth whatever... may have happened in the past, but whoso relapseth, Allah will take retribution from him."[26]

Among the *Hadith* of the Prophet which confirm the principle of legality, there is the verse from the Prophet's discourse at the farewell pilgrimage:

> "Any blood-guilt traced back to the period of ignorance *(jahiliyya)* should be disregarded, and I begin with that of al-Harith ibn 'abd al-Muttalib the usury practices during al-jahiliyya has also been erased, and I begin with that of my uncle al-'Abbas ibn 'abd al-Muttalib."

Similarly, he said to Amr ibn al-'As, "Islam annuls what preceeded it."[27]

The *Qu'ran* and *Hadith* of the Prophet thus make clear that punishment may not be inflicted on a person for certain types of conduct unless prohibited by a preexisting law criminalizing such conduct and specifying a penalty for it.

On the basis of these and other texts and *Hadith*, jurists have extracted the two fundamental components of which the principle of legality is comprised. The first is that no obligation exists prior to the enactment of legislation, and the second is that all things are presumed permissible. The application of those rules to the criminal law signifies that no punishment shall be inflicted for conduct which no text has criminalized and that punishment for criminalized conduct is restricted to instances where the act in question has been committed after the legislation takes effect.

The application of the legality principle to Islamic criminal law is equally important as its confirmation. Indeed, as will be demonstrated the principle is embodied in each of the three categories of crime: determined crimes *(Hudud)*, crimes of retribution *(Quesas)* and discretionary crimes *(Ta'azir)*.

Hudud crimes, or those for which the punishment is clearly specified in the *Qu'ran* or *Sunna*, leave no room for the judge to resort to *Ijtihad* or to any discretionary authority. In the sacred texts, each is specifically criminalized and the corresponding punishment prescribed. *Quesas* crimes are those which involve assault resulting in homicide, wounding or battery. Such offenses and their corresponding penalties are defined in the *Qu'ran* and *Sunna* and further elaborated in the works of the leading authorities on Islamic jurisprudence. *Ta'azir* offenses are those having neither a fixed penalty nor an expiation. Their related material sources usually define the crime but leave the penalty to the discretion of the

---

[22] *Surat al-Israa* XVII:15.

[23] *Surat al-Naml* XXVII:59.

[24] *Surat al-Anfal* VIII:38.

[25] *Surat al-Nisaa* IV:22.

[26] *Surat al Maeda* V:95.

[27] A sound *Hadith* related by Imam Muslim. *See* 2 AL-NAWAWI, SHARH 'AL-SAHIH MUSLIM [COMMENTARY ON THE SAHIH OF MUSLIM] 136-139.

competent state authority, its prescription to the legislative authority, and its infliction to the judiciary. All such discretionary acts must be within the framework of sanctions permissible under *Shari'a*. It is clear, therefore, that both modes of imposing punishment under Islamic penal law must be consistent with the principle of legality. The mandatory penalties applied under *Hudud* and *Quesas* as well as the flexible penalties of *Ta'azir* are thereby restrained from arbitrary or unreasonable infringement upon individual rights.

Furthermore, through the system of *Ta'azir* the legislative authorities of contemporary Islamic states fulfill their duty of protecting social interests and prescribing appropriate penalties. All jurists agree, however, that the authorities may not impose such penalties retroactively, nor inflict penalties for previously non-criminalized acts or without giving due notice of the punishment. In this regard, Judge Abu Ya'la described as follows the ruler's right to inflict punishment on acts not explictly criminalized by *Qu'ranic* or *Sunna* texts: "Denial should be advanced... and punishment should not be imposed without warning."[28]

Some contemporary scholars consider that the application of the principle of legality encroaches upon divine law and thereby attempts to supersede it by positive law and that *Ta'azir* is a substitute for the principle itself. Those who subscribe to this view assume that the purpose of the legality principle is to annul certain rules of Islamic criminal law and replace them with a system of codification on the model of western legal systems.[29] That view fails, however, to properly consider *Qu'ranic* and *Sunna* texts which impart to Islamic law the elements of the legality principle. Furthermore, the principle derives from the broader constitutional principle which provides that the state shall be governed by the rule of law which thereby prevents all branches of government from behaving arbitrarily in discharging their duties. The Islamic state is governed by law which developed from *Qu'ranic* and *Sunna* texts.[30] Thus, the state and its duly constituted authorities are constrained to apply the criminal law in accordance with the principle of legality. Therefore, the obligation to convict and punish can only be exercised in accordance with the rule of law.

The principle of legality in the Islamic state applies not only to the sphere of *Hudud* and *Quesas* crimes, but also to *Ta'azir* offenses. Its application to *Ta'azir* suggests that the judge does not have unlimited discretion to create new crimes or to inflict unprescribed penalties. Therefore, the assertion that *Ta'azir* punishment "takes the place of punishment without law" is incorrect. Jurists have

---

[28] A. YA'LA, AL-AHKAM AL-SULTANIYYA 277 (n.d.).

[29] This assumption is fundamental in Dr. Wasfi's comparison between the punishment prescribed for unlawful sexual intercourse in the Islamic system and that prescribed for adultery in the criminal laws of both capitalist and communist legal systems. M. Wasfi, Legality Between Islamic Shari'a and Criminal Law 3-8 (1976) (A report submitted to the Second Symposium of the Criminal Justice Organization). Based on this erroneous view, Wasfi called for the abrogation of the legality principle in Islamic law for fear that it might "encroach on [divine] text of the Lawmaker." But as demonstrated herein, Islamic *Shari'a* acknowledge the existence of the legality principle.

[30] For further detail *see* M.S. AL-AWWA, THE POLITICAL ORGANIZATION OF THE ISLAMIC STATE (2d ed. 1977). Compare with these, sources of western constitutional jurisprudence: A.V. DICEY, AN INTRODUCTION TO THE STUDY OF THE LAW OF THE CONSTITUTION 207 *passim*; I. JENNINGS, THE LAW AND THE CONSTITUTION 51.

criticized the practice of judicial power to determine punishment because they perceive the authority of the judge to be restricted by the *Shari'a* provisions concerning determined penalties. The personal or independent reasoning (*Ijtihad*) of a judge in choosing the applicable penalty is restricted by what is in the best interest of Muslims. Otherwise, his conduct is contrary to consensus (*Ijma'*).[31]

It also is erroneous to conclude that in Islamic penal law certain acts cannot be classified as criminal or otherwise beforehand.[32] Proponents of this view find support from *Ta'azir* which can only be imposed in manner consistent with the public interest. However, that view conflicts with the view presented here that no punishment may be inflicted for such offenses before the act in question has been criminalized. Thus, it is not the criminalization of the act but the timing of the punishment which determines whether the application of *Ta'azir* in a particular instance complies with the legality principle.

THE ISLAMIC PENAL SYSTEM AND THE CONSEQUENCES OF THE PRINCIPLE OF LEGALITY

The principle of legality has a number of inescapable consequences for Islamic law, among which the doctrine of the non-retroactivity of penal sentences is the most important. Thus, conceding that the criminalization of certain conduct prior to adoption of an express rule criminalizing it requires that the act in question be criminal even though it could not have been legally construed as such at the time of its occurence. Such a result is inconsistent with the legality principle.

Some contemporary scholars argue that the application of the non-retroactivity principle in Islamic *Shari'a* is subject to the exception that retroactivity can be applied to penal provisions in cases of serious crimes which affect public security or order or the established structures of the state. These scholars argue that the penalties for defamation and banditry, and the rulings concerning *zihar*—a form of repudiation in pre-Islamic times which consisted of using the formula, "You are for me (as untouchable) as the back *(zahr)* of my mother"—have all been applied retroactively. Thus, punishment was imposed for certain acts committed long before the prophetic revelation defining those crimes and penalties. In the course of this debate, some jurists have recently added a forth legal decision, namely that of *li'an* (the procedure by which a husband affirms under oath that his wife has committed adultery or by which he may repudiate paternity of a child born to his wife).

These four *ahkam* (rulings) are examined below in order to demonstrate that no exception to the principle of non-retroactivity exists in Islamic penal legislation, save for mitigation of punishment.

1. *The Crime of Defamation (False Accusation of Unchastity)*

The penalty for committing the offense of defamation is prescribed in the

---

[31] 3 IMAM AL-QARAFI, KITAB AL-FURUQ (1939), 16-20 and vol. 4, at 182.
[32] 1 A. ODEH, ISLAMIC PENAL LEGISLATION 161 (1969).

Qu'ranic Surat of Light:

> "And those who accuse honorable women but bring not four witnesses, scourge them (with) eighty stripes and never afterwards accept their testimony. They indeed are evil-doers. Save those who afterward repent and make amends. Of them Allah is forgiving and merciful."[33]

In the same *Surat*, verses 11-20, God reveals the innocence of al-Sayyida 'A'isha of the falsehood of which some people had accused her. The Prophet then imposed on the slanderers the *Had* penalty of flogging for defamation.[34]

Some scholars maintain that the *Had* penalty for defamation was revealed through the falsehood of unchastity brough against Sayyida 'A'isha and therefore, the Prophet must have imposed it on an act committed prior to its revelation, *i.e.*, retroactively. However, scholars concur that the revelation regarding 'A'isha is found in the ten verses beginning with, "Lo! They who spread the slander are a gang among you. Deem it not a bad thing for you; nay, it is good for you," and closing with, "Had it not been for the grace of Allah and His mercy unto you, and that Allah is clement and merciful, ye had been undone."[35]

The origin of this revelation is similarly suggested in books of authentic *Sunna*. Hence, the verses revealing the *Had* penalty of defamation preceded the teaching set forth in the verses which vindicate al-Sayyida 'A'isha. Given this and the application of the principle of legality as defined in the *Qu'ran* and *Sunna*, the view that the penalty for defamation was applied retroactively in the first instance must be rejected. It appears, therefore, that the Prophet inflicted punishment upon those who slandered 'A'isha for an act which they committed after the *Qu'ran* had already criminalized it and prescribed the corresponding penalty.

2. The Li'an *Ordinance*

Li'an is an allegation under oath by a husband whereby he accuses his wife of an act of adultery to which he is the sole witness. The purpose of *li'an* is to protect the husband against the *Had* penalty of defamation where he accuses his wife of unchastity without producing witnesses should his wife successfully refute the accusation. The law governing *li'an* is revealed in the *Surat* of Light where one of the Companions accused his wife of adultery. The Prophet asked him to submit his evidence, *i.e.*, produce four witnesses, or be subject to the mandatory penalty for defamation. The original sentence entailed eighty lashes for the husband just as for any other slanderer. However, this was mitigated subsequently in the husband's interest by legitimizing the act of *li'an*.

Thus, it appears that applying the way of *li'an* to such an accusation made prior to the revelation of the relevant verses suggests the imposition of a mitigated punishment even though the legislation followed the commission of the act in question, a practice known in contemporary criminal jurisprudence as the

---

[33] *Surat al-Nur* XXIV:4-5.

[34] 6 IBN KATHIR, TAFSIR AL-QU'RAN AL-AZIM [COMMENTARY ON THE HOLY QU'RAN] 32.

[35] *Surat al-Nur* XXIV:11-20.

retroactive application of the law in a manner which benefits the interest of the accused. It also constitutes a recognized exception in many contemporary penal systems to the principle of non-retroactivity of criminal legislation. However, one cannot infer from the application of the *li'an* ordinance to an act committed prior to its legislation that Islamic *Shari'a* acknowledges an exception to the principle of non-retroactivity. It is, nevertheless, correct to conclude that retroactivity of the more suitable law is permissible where it mitigates the penalty or abrogates the criminalization of the act. Thus, the act of *li'an* is criminalized with respect to prior conduct but for reasons of policy, a form of mitigated punishment was deemed proper to impose.

3. The Ordinance of Zihar

Zihar takes place where a man tells his wife, "You are for me as untouchable as the back of my mother." In pre-Islamic times, this form of repudiation rendered the wife "forbidden" to her husband and thereby prevented her from returning to him or marrying another man. God abolished that practice, which had been widely used by the Arabs of *jahiliyya*, and replaced it with *zihar*. Thus, a man who pronounces *zihar* may not approach his wife until he atones for his *zihar* through one of three practices: freeing a slave, fasting for two consecutive months, or feeding sixty needy people. Should he fail to do so, and his wife meanwhile has taken her case before a judge, the judge shall compel him to make amends in the prescribed manner or else grant the wife a divorce.

The *Qu'ranic* law governing *zihar* is thus less harsh than the pre-Islamic law, and by applying the *Qu'ranic hukm*, the Prophet has shown clemency toward both husband and wife. Therefore, it is incorrect to infer from *zihar* and its corresponding *Qu'ranic* revelations the possibility of retroactive legislation. However, the mitigated punishment applies, which thereby supersedes the earlier harsher penalty.

Furthermore, it seems improper to conclude from the *zihar* judgment that criminal legislation is an example of retroactivity, for the reason that *zihar* is a question of personal status or family laws which is unrelated to criminal ordinances. Instead, one must refer to specific criminal texts in Islamic *Shari'a* or to those defining general penal principles. Thus, the ordinance of *zihar*, regardless of the manner in which it is applied, is outside of the framework of Islamic criminal legislation.

4. The Penalty for Banditry (Highway Robbery)

Hiraba or banditry is one of the *Had* crimes in Islamic *Shari'a*. The Holy *Qu'ran* defines its sentence in these words:

> The only reward of those who make war upon Allah and His messenger and strive after corruption in the land will be that they will be killed or crucified, or have their hands and feet on alternate sides cut off, or will be expelled out of the land. Such will be their degradation in the world, and in the Hereafter theirs will be an awful doom;
>
> Save those who repent before ye overpower them. For know that Allah is forgiving, merciful. [36]

---

[36] *Surat al-Maeda* V:28, 33-34.

The response to those who claim that these penalties were applied retroactively is that they were originally revealed in order to deal with the conflict of a group of people who settled in Medina and subsequently became ill and dissatisfied. The Prophet sent them to the place where the charity livestock (those destined for alms) grazed. Once recovered, they killed the herdsman and took over the herd. Upon hearing this, the Prophet became angry and sent for them. When they appeared before him the above quoted verses were revealed, and the Prophet inflicted upon them the punishment prescribed therein.

It is true that these people were the subject of this revelation, but the verses were revealed in fact after they were punished. The object of the revelation was to determine the penalty for *hiraba*, as mentioned in the *Sahih* of al-Bukhari (the *Musnad* of Ahmad and the *Sunan* of Abu Da'ud) on the authority of ibn Sirin. Al-Bukhari observes that: "This [their punishment] has occured prior to the revelation of the assigned penalties (*Hudud*)." However, the verses dealing with *hiraba* in the *Surat* of the Table Spread were never applied to this group of people. Instead they were punished on the basis of general texts assigning a penalty commensurate with the act of aggression. God says, "The guerdon of an ill-deed is an ill the like thereof."[37] And, "If ye punish, then punish with the like of that wherewith ye were afflicted."[38]

It is evident, therefore, that *hiraba* is not an exception to the doctrine of non-retroactivity, and the principle of legality remains intact in Islamic penal legislation. Furthermore, as illustrated by *li'an*, criminal provisions may not have a retroactive effect unless beneficial to the person against whom a penalty is threatened.

Recognition of the non-retroactivity principle is not only evident with regard to assigned penalties prescribed in the Holy *Qu'ran*, *Sunna* and general principles of *Shari'a*, but it was equally obvious to the jurists who determined matters of *Ta'azir*. In his treatise, *al-Ahkam al-Sultaniyya*, Judge Abu Ya'la al-Hanbali stated that whenever a judge imposed a *Ta'azir* punishment, "priority should be given to denial. And punishment should not be inflicted prior to warning." Thus, the clear weight of authority compels the conclusion that the Islamic judge may not give retroactive effect to any penalty prescribed by law irrespective of the source of law.

EQUALITY OF TREATMENT BEFORE THE LAW

Commentators on contemporary criminal law are unanimous concerning the necessity of applying the law uniformly to all who violate it if the law is to successfully achieve its goal. As has been expressed, "The law is one and the same for all people."[39] And the principle of fair and evenhanded application of the criminal law, is considered part of the principle of equal protection of the law which was first recognized in contemporary legal systems with the Declaration of

[37] *Surat al-Shura* XLII:40.
[38] *Surat al-Nahl* XVI:126.
[39] HOGAN & SMITH, CRIMINAL LAW 10-11 (1976).

the Rights of Man and of the Citizen during the French Revolution of 1789.

The principle is much older in Islam. At the dawn of the Muslim era society was governed by rival people and factions in matters of lineage (kinship), wealth, reputation and power. This rivalry in its myriad forms dominated all aspects of Arab life. Discrimination was evident in the sphere of criminal law. Thus, for example, the ransom paid for a murdered nobleman (*sharif*) or lord (*sayyid*) was several times that paid for an ordinary person. The nobility and lords were satisfied with punishing the killer but insisted on applying the law of retribution to his whole tribe. This inequality in applying rules of criminal law became the direct cause of several prolonged wars among Arab tribes.

Islam abolished these tribal customs by establishing a principle which held that with the revelation of the *Qu'ran*, distinctions among people with respect to the application of Islamic decrees, whether religious or judicial would no longer be made. The *Qu'ran* addresses these words to all people: "O mankind! Lo! We have created you male and female, and have made you nations and tribes that ye may know one another. Lo! The noblest of you, in the sight of Allah, is the best in conduct."[40] The Prophet also has said, "O mankind! You worship the same God, you have the same father. The Arab is not more worthy than the Persian, and the red is not more deserving than the black, except in godliness."[41]

The principle of equality before the law under Islam is manifest in its system of criminal justice. Thus, for example, the Prophet has determined a uniform amount of ransom for all people, without distinction among criminals, victims or anyone's socio-economic status. Similarly, the laws of retribution are defined in the *Qu'ran* and the *Sunna* in such a way as to allow for their application without discrimination on economic, political or social grounds.

The Prophet also has warned against discrimination in applying *Had* penalties by enforcing them as against the common people while exempting the nobility. The Prophet stated that if his own daughter, Fatima, committed theft, her kinship ties (*nasab*) would not save her the *Had* punishment.

Jurists have further concluded from the Prophet's decision to inflict the penalty for defamation on those who slandered his wife, 'A'isha, that the equality principle as applicable to the infliction of penalties extends throughout the Islamic penal system. According to al-Suhaili this indicates, "equality between the noblest person next to the Prophet and the one with the lowest degree of faith. Defamers receive eighty lashes . . . no more and no less."[42]

It is clear, therefore, that Islamic *Shari'a* consistently acknowledges and applies the principle of equality in its criminal texts. This principle arises not only explicitly from the general provisions of the *Shari'a* which impose criminal penalties such as those for retribution, theft, ransom, and defamation, but also implicitly through the Prophetic application of those provisions.

---

[40] *Surat al-Hujurat* XLIX:13.

[41] Related by Iman Ahmad with sound documentation (*sanad sahih*).

[42] 2 IBN HISHAM, SURAT AL-NABI CCV [THE SAYINGS AND DEEDS OF THE PROPHET].

FUNDAMENTAL PRINCIPLES OF PROCEDURE

To properly consider the basis of Islamic penal law, two basic issues of criminal procedure are worthy of examination. One pertains to the right to commence criminal action and the extent to which this right can be guaranteed to the victim in certain crimes. The second question deals with the duty of a criminal judge to ensure the competence and credibility of evidence submitted in a criminal case in order that the penalty for the crime in question be justly imposed. Those questions fall under the topic of the abrogation of *Had* penalties in case of doubt.

THE VICTIM'S RIGHT TO COMMENCE CRIMINAL ACTION FOR CERTAIN CRIMES

Muslim jurists divide acts enjoined or prohibited by legal obligation into three categories: 1) the absolute rights or claims of Allah; 2) private and divine claims, with the latter being predominant; and 3) both divine and private rights, but where private claims predominate. First of all, acts or omissions which are criminalized as violative of a right of Allah are those whose commission or omission are proscribed as contrary to the public interest. Those proscriptions, besides covering the first category, involve the second category as well, where the private and divine claims coincide but the latter claim predominates. As for acts which are prohibited as a private claim, their justification is based on furthering private interests and benefiting the individual.

Distinguishing between forms of criminalized conduct on the basis of an infringed right has procedural consequences. When there is an injury to the right of the community, *i.e.*, to divine right, then the state or its competent authority has the right to commence criminal action. Jurists also agree that the Imam is empowered to carry out the penalty. The victim in such cases has no rights to intervene at any state of the criminal process, either in commencing the action or in the indictment, both of which are exclusively left to the prerogative of the state. Where the victim has a right to damages, he may so claim without prejudicing the criminal action. Thus, for example, in cases of theft where both public and private rights are affected, the right of the state to inflict punishment on the perpetrator is unaffected by the victim's right of compensation or restitution, whether he chooses to exercise it or not, although differences in procedural detail among Islamic schools of jurisprudence exist.

These offenses in Islamic penal law are analogous to certain crimes in other modern legal systems where the state assumes the exclusive right to determine and demand punishment. Persons appointed by law are entrusted with the duties of investigating the crime, conducting the trial, prosecuting and rendering a verdict with no intervention permitted by the victim or his representatives.

The procedural consequence involving crimes considered by Islamic penal law as violative of private rights are much different. There, by contrast, prosecution may not be initiated against the accused except upon the victim's demand. In crimes of assault against the person (crimes of retribution and ransom), crimes of defamation (where false accusation of unchastity is viewed as injurious to the defamed person), and crimes of *Ta'azir* (which are considered violative of the victim's private right), the competent state authorities may not intervene to conduct an investigation or trial except upon the victim's demand. It is noteworthy, however, that the scope of the victim's demand is limited to commencing criminal action, and the findings of the court are in any event subject to the proof, based on Islamic rules of evidence, established during the proceedings.

The victim's request to commence criminal action is known in certain contemporary penal systems by the term "ester in judgment," *i.e.*, the right to submit a complaint or to terminate criminal proceedings initiated by the victim's complaint. However, such crimes do give rise to the restricted right of the state to inflict punishment. Making the victim's complaint a prerequisite to the right of the state to inflict punishment stems from the view that the victim's private interest is paramount to the public interest which the state represents and protects. Thus, despite the consistency between Islamic penal jurisprudence and contemporary systems of criminal procedure requiring the victim to make a complaint before the state commences proceedings, it is apparent that the two systems differ as to the crimes for which such complaints must be lodged. This difference is due to the distinctions made among crimes on the basis of the rights infringed and in determining which interests, whether public or private, are to be protected according to text or legislation. Yet in spite of this difference and its consequences, the requirement of the conditional complaint in both Islamic and contemporary systems rests on the same principle, namely, that the private interest of the victim takes precedence over the public interest.

It is also significant in this regard that all procedural matters, except for the few rules prescribed in the *Qu'ran* and *Sunna*, fall within the purview of *Ijtihad* whereby the competent authority of the state is granted broad discretion to determine that which constitutes good and sufficient procedure as well as their methods of application and consequences.[43]

Furthermore, the rules of criminal procedure in the Islamic penal system allow flexibility to serve the ends of justice. The rules of criminal procedure are essentially the means which guarantee the state its right to punish criminals without jeopardizing the fundamental guarantees granted the accused in proving his innocence. Therefore, as prominent jurists have expressed, these rules are a method of achieving justice and truth. Stated differently, it is difficult to imagine the task of deductive rules being restricted to only one mode while ignoring others, particularly if the goal for which the rules are established is considered.

---

[43] In this context, Al-Jawziyya states that:

> God Almighty has sent his Prophets and revealed His scriptures so that people might carry out justice, the same justice in which the earth and heaven were created. So if the signs of justice become manifest and if it materializes in any way, then God's law and religion are realized. God Almighty is more knowing, wise, and just than to attribute something to the ways of justice and its manifestations and then to negate what is even more apparent, evident and manifest, and not to judge according to them when they are present and established. God Almighty might have revealed, through his legal ways, His purpose of establishing justice among the believers and enjoining people to carry out justice. Therefore, any means through which justice and equity are deduced is in conformity with religion and not contrary to it.

Q. AL-JAWZIYYA, AL-TURUQ AL-HUKMIYYA 16-17.

This procedural difference, which has been characterized as limiting judicial discretion as to the range of possible sanctions, may be the most important procedural difference resulting from the classification of crimes according to those which violate collective rights and those which violate private rights. There also exists another difference which emanates from this classification, namely, the right of the victim's successors for crimes violative of private rights, to inherit the right to litigate or commence criminal action upon the death of their decedent. Jurists unanimously include in this classification *Quesas* crimes (generally crimes of assault against the person resulting in death or serious bodily injury). Some consider defamation as a graver infringement of the right of a slave than that of the community and so include it too. *Ta'azir* offenses which impair individual rights might also be added. The victim's heirs, it is argued here, inherit the right to commence criminal action for all such crimes.

Survival of the right to lodge a criminal complaint could never arise with respect to crimes of aggression against the right of the community (divine right) because a similar end to the life of the community is inconceivable. Even if the specific person competent to conduct criminal proceedings in the community (a judge or a prosecutor) happens to die, the claim for penalty is not nullified because it is linked only to his capacity as a representative of the state and manager of the state's claims as a delegated power and not to him personally.

NULLIFICATION OF THE *HAD* PENALTY BY DOUBT

The practice of nullifying *Hudud* crimes in case of doubt is based on a doctrinal rule which prevents a judge from imposing a fixed penalty should doubt or uncertainty exist in his mind as to whether the accused has committed a crime to which a *Had* punishment applies.[44] In certain situations, it is possible for the judge to impose a *Ta'azir* punishment instead. Although doubt might lead to the acquittal of the accused or the dismissal of charges, it might also lead to reformulating the indictment so as to convict the accused of a crime other than the one for which he was brought to trial.

If in cases of theft, the requirements of *hirz* (taking custody of personal property) and that of *nisab* (minimum value of stolen property) are not fulfilled, the judge may not impose the *Had* penalty of amputating the offender's hand. By the same token, if the condition of *'ihsan* (immunity from the defamation penalty of free Muslims who were never convicted of unlawful intercourse) in cases of defamation is not met, then the accused may not be sentenced to eighty lashes (the *Had* for defamation), although an alternative penalty may be imposed. However, if the defense and prosecution present conflicting evidence, or if the prosecution evidence in a criminal case fails to meet the burden of persuasion, then the judge must acquit the accused who then shall not be subjected to any further punishment, inlcuding *Ta'azir*.

---

[44] For an analytical study of the principle of repealing fixed punishment in cases of doubt, see 'Awad, *The Theory of Doubt in Legal Doctrine,* 1 AL-MAJALLA AL-'ARABIYYA LIL-DIFA' AL-IJTIMA'I 9 (March, 1979).

The avoidance of *Had* penalties in case of doubt also is closely linked to the presumption of innocence and the requirement that guilt be proved beyond reasonable doubts which Islamic *Shari'a* has adopted as standards in both the civil and criminal law. However, Islamic penal law applies this principle only to *Had* and *Quesas* offenses but not to *Ta'azir*. This aspect of Islamic penal law must be considered with respect to the rules of criminal justice and related matters, particularly as it relates to the principle in question here.

1. *The Substance and Basis for the Principle of Nullifying Had Penalties by Doubt*

Because of stringent penalties for *Hudud* the admissibility of evidence in the trial of *Hudud* offenses is limited by the following rules: (1) the requirement of two witnesses in most crimes and four in cases of unlawful intercourse; (2) the requirement of eyewitness accounts instead of hearsay; (3) the condition that testimonial evidence must be stated in clear and unambiguous terms: and (4) requiring the moral integrity of witnesses, their prompt testimony, and their adherence to it. Each of these requirements is based either on text or doctrine and innumerable applications in the practice of the Companions and their judges and governors.

Concern over restricting the scope of *Had* penalties is evident in the prevailing doctrinal trend which accepts the principle of nullifying such penalties in case of doubt. As suggested above, this principle requires the determination of *Had* penalties (or the infliction of punishment) only where the proof dispels all reasonable doubt that the accused committed the crime charged. The principle of nullification is a clear application of the Islamic doctrinal presumption of innocence (or presumption of freedom from debt). Through application in the criminal law, this principle gives rise to another doctrine, namely that "The human body is innocent of *Quesas* and *Had* penalties and *Ta'azir* punishment . . . and of all utterances and all acts."[45] The presumption of innocence under Islamic law is identical to the principle recognized by contemporary penal systems and embodied in most constitutions and many international human rights conventions.[46] It considers crime a form of abnormal or irregular conduct, and thereby suggests prudence and caution in attributing such conduct to a particular person. Thus the person is presumed innocent until it becomes unreasonable to consider him otherwise.

The presumption of innocence is a necessary component in every legal system in order to protect individual freedoms from the threat of procedural abuse or other injustice. However, many contemporary systems limit its operation. By contrast, the presumption of freedom from debt under Islamic law exists in all branches of law both religious and secular. Consequently, neither criminal nor civil liability may be imposed on a person unless the requisite quantum of evi-

---

[45] 1 I. 'ABD AL-SALAM, QAWAED AL-AHKAM FI MASALI AL-'ANAM 32 (1968).

[46] R. 'UBAYD, MABADI' AL-IJRA'AT AL-JINA'IYYA [THE PRINCIPLES OF CRIMINAL PROCEDURE] 676 (1976).

dence is presented. In particular, no person can be subjected to a *Had* penalty unless the evidence proves his guilt beyond a reasonable doubt.

The presumption of innocence is the foundation of the rule requiring that *Had* penalties be nullified in case of doubt, and in that respect contemporary legal systems are no different from the Islamic system. In fact, by applying the presumption, some tribunals in Arab countries have purposely based their administration of justice upon Islamic doctrinal principles, despite the fact that the penal systems in force in those countries do not derive the presumption of innocence from Islamic doctrine.

The presumption of innocence also is related in Islamic legal doctrine to the principle that certainty is not abrogated in case of insufficient doubt, or in case of uncertainty indubitable proof is not abrogated. Some jurists have considered this principle as a corollary to the presumption of freedom from debt, while others consider the latter as derived from the former. In any event it seems clear that Islamic jurisprudence applies the principle that certainty is not abrogated in case of doubt which is less than reasonable, to all branches of the law to the same degree as it does the presumption of innocence.

Imam al-Suyuti writes, "I realize that this principle enters all branches of jurisprudence, and the questions inferred from it constitute three quarters of *Fiqh* or more." With regard to penalties, he states that if the judge doubts whether "it should be a *Had* of flogging or lapidation, then a *Ta'azir* punishment replaces the *Had* penalty. If he hesitates between two penalties, assuming neither one involves the death penalty, then both are dropped in favor of *Ta'azir* punishment."

Another consequence of the principle that certainty is not abrogated by insufficient doubt is the consideration given to the minimum age of liability with regard to *Hudud* offenses. Since as a rule the young are not criminally liable, someone should not be charged with a crime unless he is of age. This practice derives from the rule that indubitable evidence may not be nullified in case of doubt, it thereby avoids the potentially harsh consequences of the rule and is analogous to the principle found in many contemporary legal systems that the accused is entitled to the benefit of the doubt. It also has been codified in the constitutions and rules of criminal procedure of various countries.[47] It is a logical result of the presumption of innocence that the accused be given the benefit of a doubt, which is manifested procedurally by requiring the state to prove every element of the crime charged beyond a reasonable doubt. This requirement corresponds with the aforementioned tendency in certain segments of Islamic jurisprudence to base the principle that certainty is not abrogated by doubt on the presumption of freedom from debt.

The judiciary in Arab countries, no less than in western countries, have in innumerable cases interpreted doubtful evidence in a light favorable to the accused. The words of Imam al-Shafei stated long ago remain true, that guilt must

---

[47] *See, e.g.*, the SUDNAESE CONSTITUTION, art. 69, and the Sudanese Law of Criminal Procedure of 1974, art. 3.

rest upon the "application of that which is convincing, the rejection of doubt, and not founding judicial decision-making on that which is prevalent (or popular) but on that which is proven valid." Thus, the Egyptian Court of Cassation confirmed the agreement between the two views by requiring rigid standards for admitting evidence of guilt in crimes of adultery and by basing its conclusions upon the sound principle of the abrogation of *Had* penalties in case of doubt.[48]

The conclusions reached by Islamic jurisprudence in applying the principle of the avoidance of *Had* by doubt are virtually identical to those reached by contemporary systems in applying the two procedural rules of the presumption of innocence and resolving doubtful propositions generally in favor of the accused. The fundamental difference, though, between the position of Islamic penal jurisprudence and contemporary systems lies in the scope of the application of the principle. The predominant view among Islamic jurists holds that the principle of nullifying *Had* by doubt applies only to *Hudud* and *Quesas* crimes but not to *Ta'azir*. By contrast, other contemporary legal systems apply the presumption of innocence and the principle of favoring the accused in case of doubt to all classifications of crimes. The extent to which the predominant Islamic doctrine as outlined above, is applicable in order to determine if doubt nullifies other crimes is the final topic of discussion.

2. *Can Ta'azir Be Abrogated in Case of Doubt?*

The possibility of applying the principle of nullification of penalty in case of doubt to non-*Hudud* crimes has long been the subject of debate. The prevalent view among Islamic jurists is that the application of this principle is restricted to crimes of *Hudud* and *Quesas* but does not extend to *Ta'azir*. One commentator disagrees, however, stating that:

> There is nothing to prevent the application of this principle to *Ta'azir*, because the rule was established with the purpose of insuring justice and guaranteeing the interests of the accused who is in need of securing these two considerations whether he is accused of a *Had* crime or one of *Ta'azir*.[49]

Ta'azir crimes are in effect conduct viewed as harmful or dangerous by society, and the principles of *Shari'a* impose certain penalties therewith. Such penalties aim at inflicting harm upon the offender to deter him from further crime and to deter others from committing similar violations. Therefore, punishment which inflicts injury on a person may not be imposed by a judge unless he is convinced of that person's guilt. Consequently, it can be suggested in conclusion that founding the principle of nullification of *Had* in case of doubt upon the presumption of innocence and the principle of indubitable evidence, as presented above, requires the application of this principle to *Ta'azir* crimes in addition to crimes of *Hudud* and *Quesas*. When one considers the vast number of *Ta'azir*

---

[48] Judgement of Nov. 12, 1930, Egyptian Court of Cassation, 2 Collection of Judicial Rules 155 n. 129 (1930) (cited by R. 'UBAYD, *supra* note 46, at 681).

[49] *Supra* note 32, at 216.

convictions, it becomes clear that the interests of justice and the rights of the accused cannot be secured unless these basic principles apply to all categories of crimes. The failure to extend them to *Ta'azir* offenses is also inconsistent with the principle of equality of all persons before the law.

THE PRINCIPLE OF LEGALITY AND ITS APPLICATION IN ISLAMIC CRIMINAL JUSTICE

Taymour Kamel

> Ye are the best community that hath been raised up for mankind. Ye enjoin right conduct and forbid indecency. . . .
>
> *Surat al-Imran* III:110

INTRODUCTION

The principle of legality in crime and punishment—in Roman Law, "*Nullum Crimen Nulla Poena Sine Lege*"—constitutes a fundamental guarantee of individual freedom by precisely and clearly delimiting the domain of forbidden activity. The principle protects against the abuse of power or the arbitrariness of judges, guaranteeing the security of individuals while informing them of what is permitted or forbidden. Each person must be forewarned of illegal acts and their legal punishments. This is a right of individuals and a duty of society.[1]

Under the legality principle, no act may be considered a violation of law by a judge if it has not been explicitly anticipated in a penal law in force at the time the act was committed. The law may punish only those acts committed after their prohibition by law; the judge may inflict upon the criminal only those penalties which are sanctioned by law.

In the history of western law, the French Revolution consecrated the individual right as a basis for legality. Judges had possessed an extensive power in criminalizing deeds which were not anticipated in written texts, and were capable of choosing at will the most suitable punishment available "as the case may require." But the Declaration of the Rights of Man (1789) proclaimed the legality

---

[1]On this point, *see* R. MERLE AND A. VITU, TRAITE DU DROIT CRIMINAL 221 (3rd ed. 1978); *see also* M. C. BASSIOUNI, SUBSTANTIVE CRIMINAL LAW 28-31 (1978); and M.C. BASSIOUNI and V. V. SAVITSKI, THE CRIMINAL JUSTICE SYSTEM OF THE USSR 130-144 (1979).

principle in order to negate the arbitrariness of judges. Individual freedom became one of the foundation-stones of the new judicial structure in the West. The principle of no crime or penalty without law appeared, according to M. J. Magnol, as "a definitive conquest of modern public law." It has been expressly acknowledged by all states, with the exception of common law countries following the English tradition where the judge nevertheless is bound constantly by judicial precedents.

Ostensibly, according to western views, the principle of legality was invented in Europe, and Islamic criminal law is not based on such a principle. European countries which have occupied Islamic lands have in general hastened to apply to the indigenous population penal laws governed by French law or models of European codes (Turkey and Egypt as early as the 19th century, and Tunisia since 1903). Though these codes respected such Islamic institutions as retribution and legal settlement (*Diyya*) (Art. 171 of the Ottoman Penal Code; Art. 216 of the Egyptian Penal Code, and Art. 216 of the Tunisian Penal Code of 1921), the spirit of these codifications is Occidental. Their authors apparently believed that the essence of the matter was not found in the *Shari'a*.

This western attitude reflects only an arrogantly narrow European understanding of Islamic penal law. Long before the Declaration of the Rights of Man, the Islamic system of criminal justice operated on an implicit principle of legality. No Muslim would be surprised by this. Given its divine origin, Islam inevitably bears witness to a more precise understanding of man's nature, his aspirations—whether legitimate or not—and his objectives. Furthermore, the teachings of Islam are called upon to last forever.

Islamic law in its entirety may be linked to a general or universal principle, the obligation to require what is good and to forbid what is evil, as the *Qu'ran* states: "And let there be from you a nation who invite to goodness, and enjoin right conduct and forbid indecency."[2] This principle, through its application in criminal matters, produces modalities which are implicitly based on a concept of legality. In order for an act to constitute a crime, the *Shari'a* requires that it involve the commission of a prohibited act or the omission of a required act under penalty of law or public authority.

On the other hand, beginning late in the 19th century western law began to react to the rigidity of punishment in most penal laws.[3] Inflexibility of punishment indeed did not enable the judge to exceed the limits of the text. But it also might not allow for the adequate protection of society against dishonest conduct. Facing a gap (*lacuna*) in the law, many individuals still managed to escape criminal punishment when the acts they had committed did not strictly fit the definition of the offense given by the penal laws in force at the time of the act. Also, rigidity of the principle did not enable the judge to adapt the punishment to the varying personalities of criminals and the danger which the criminal before

---

[2] *Surat al-Imran* III:104.

[3] For further detail, see Saint-Hilaire, The Crisis of the Principle of Legality of Crime and Punishment 43 *et seq.* (Doctoral Course, University of Cairo, 1967).

him posed to society. To meet these needs, modern law has introduced analogy. Specific crimes are defined in quite general terms, and judges may extend the charges established by law to contiguous deeds which present an essential and predominating similarity to those acts explicitly forecasted by law. Further, the authority of the judge has been expanded by the individualization of penalties—punishments with a set maximum and minimum level, within which the judge determines a specific sentence—plus the consideration of extenuating circumstances, reprieve, pardon, or the commutation of punishment.

Again, centuries before, the Islamic criminal justice system avoided such inflexibility. Analogy has always been an important source of Islamic legal development. And the *Shari'a* acknowledges freedom for the judge in inflicting punishment for certain categories of offenses (*Ta'azir* offenses, below).[4] The sanctions available to the judge include the penalties and measures of social defense now recognized by modern western penal laws. In other words, what western law has been struggling toward since the French Revolution—a criminal justice system based on a principle of legality but tempered with some freedom for judicial flexibility based on the needs of society—has been present in Islamic law since its inception.

The purpose of this study is to present the characteristics of the principle of legality in Islamic law. Defining this principle in the *Shari'a* requires an investigation of its sources, meaning, and scope of application. The results of such an investigation should broaden the knowledge of western jurists. The *Qu'ran* enjoins Muslims to graciously receive all those who desire to engage them in dialogue: "And speak kindly to mankind . . ."[5] and "Reason with them in the better ways . . ."[6] and "Argue not with the People of the Scripture unless it be in [a way] that is better, save with such of them as do wrong."[7]

SOURCES

In western legal traditions, the public authority is the giver of law. If, to adhere to a principle of legality, a written law must anticipate offenses and penalties, then the sources for such written laws are the enactments of the public authority: law in the narrow sense—proper law, voted by a parliamentary body—and administrative regulations.

In Islamic law, properly speaking, there is only one giver of law: God. "The decision is for Allah only. He telleth the truth and He is the best of deciders."[8] The law is a decision by God in the form of a communication regarding human actions, either demanding, authorizing, or prohibiting them.[9] The sources of Is-

[4] Discretionary penalties, *i.e.* penalties not determined by sacred law.

[5] *Surat al-Baqara*, II:83.

[6] *Surat al-Nahl*, XVI:125.

[7] *Surat al-Ankabut*, XXXIX:46.

[8] *Surat al-An'am*, VI:57.

[9] S. MAHMASANI, FALSAFAT AL-TASHRI' FIL-ISLAM [THE PHILOSOPHY OF JURISPRUDENCE IN ISLAM], 17, 23, 138 (Beirut, 1961).

lamic law are those communications from God, the injunctions of the Divine Legislator. The legal penal order in Islam thus rests on four sources: The *Qu'ran*, the *Sunna* (traditions of the Prophet), *Ijma'* (consensus of Islamic jurists), and *Qiyyas* (analogy with the *Qu'ran* and *Sunna* drawn by jurists). Some of God's injunctions are expressly enacted in the *Qu'ran* or the *Sunna*. Others are only implied in those texts; hence, the necessity for jurists who make deductions and inferences.[10] Over the centuries, four schools of *Sunni* law have developed. All schools acknowledge the *Qu'ran*, the *Sunna*, and consensus as sources of Islamic penal law.[11] They differ with regard to analogy.[12]

To properly appreciate the meaning and scope of the legality principle in the Islamic criminal justice system, it is first necessary to understand something of these sources of law.

THE *QU'RAN*

The *Qu'ran* is the Holy Book of Islam and, for Muslims, the Word of God, which He has revealed in order to guide all of mankind and secure its happiness both on earth and in the hereafter. It contains 114 *Surats* (chapters), including 6,342 verses, of which 500 verses deal with legal matters (*khitab*). Each of these judicial verses bears an injunction—either an order (*'amr*) or a prohibition (*nahi*). Out of each judicial verse, a decision (*hukm*) arises which is analogous to a judgment and is a specific legal rule.

What characterizes *Qu'ranic* prescriptions is their general formulation. The *Qu'ran* is a code which governs religious and social life. It has foreseen everything, so that all is implicitly or explicitly regulated. When a new situation arises, or a new need is found, it is met with the help of the principles which are laid down in the *Qu'ran*. In its entirety, the *Qu'ran* aims at prohibiting all acts detrimental to society.

The true reading of the *Qu'ran* is not possible except by resorting to its commentaries (*tafsir*). Drawing practical, religious or judicial rules out of a *Qu'ranic* verse or narrative is a task reserved to scholars (*'alim*), who are solely capable of shouldering such a responsibility. In the perception of Muslim jurists the *Qu'ran* includes decisions (*hukm*) by the Law-Maker, Allah, whose essential purpose is to qualify human actions according to God's will and to determine the consequences. Such acts include disobedience to edicts or prescriptions given by God as obligatory, and which, consequently, are or might be punished on earth first, then, should the criminal fail to repent, in the hereafter. For example, voluntary homicide has an immediate penalty on earth—retribution—in addition

---

[10] A. ṢHARAF AL-DIN, *Islamic Law and Islamic Doctrine*, 47 BULLETIN DU CENTRE DE DOCUMENTATION D'ETUDES JURIDIQUES ECONOMIQUES ET SOCIALES (Cairo, 1978).

[11] On this point *see* O. PESLE, 8 LES FONDEMENTS DU DROIT MUSULMAN [THE FOUNDATION OF ISLAMIC LAW] 141; M. Hamidullah, *Source of Islamic Law: A New Approach*, I ISLAMIC QUARTERLY 4 (1954). The four schools were formed at the beginning of the *Abbasid* period (the third century after the *Hijra* or *Hegirah*). They were led by such prominent jurists as: Abu-Hanifa, Malik, al-Shafe'i and ibn-Hanbal. These schools are equally "orthodox" and are acknowledged on an equal footing in Sunni Islam.

[12] A. ODEH, AL-TASHRI' AL JINAI' AL ISLAMI, [ISLAMIC PENAL LAW] 165 (2d ed. 1969).

to punishment in the hereafter. Similarly, fornication, usury and apostasy have two penalties.[13]

Qu'ranic prescriptions are distinguished by their open formulation, which allows each new case to be adequately integrated in Islamic Law.

THE *SUNNA*

Sunna is the collective word for the mass of texts which tell of the Prophet's spoken words, or are an account of acts or the absence of acts attributed to him. These comprise the tradition, or more literally, the path of the Prophet which a Muslim strives to follow.[14] *Sunna* have, since the first century of the *Hijra* ("Hegira," the emigration from Mecca to Medina in 622 C.E.), assumed the form of a narrative or story (*Hadith*) providing information on a certain deed or decision attributed to Muhammad.

The *Sunna* provide a second source for law, a source which is outside revelation, yet still sacred and divinely inspired.[15] The importance of following Muhammad's decisions and example is confirmed by several *Qu'ranic* verses, *e.g.*: "Obey Allah and obey the Messenger. . . ."[16] And "They will not believe [in truth] until they make thee judge of what is in dispute between them and find within themselves no dislike of that which thou decidest, and submit with full submission."[17] With the growth of Islam after the Prophet's death, *Sunna* acquired tremendous importance. Since the time of the Umayyads *Hadith* have been employed for new decisions complementing the *Qu'ran*.

Hadith generally take one of three forms:

Sunna uttered by the Prophet For example, Muhammad has enumerated the cases where the death penalty is applicable: "It is not lawful to shed the blood of a Muslim except in three cases: if he denounces religion after being a believer, if he commits adultery after marriage, or in the case of unjustifiable murder." Similarly it is through *Hadith* that Muhammad has communicated the punishment for fornication ("As for the virgin, one hundred lashes, and banishment for one year") and wine drinking ("The one who drinks wine, scourge him—and if he drinks again, then scourge him").

Sunna by reported facts about the Prophet As one example, Muhammad applied the penalty of stoning to death in cases of admitted adultery, and inflicted the amputation of the right hand in cases of theft.

Sunna by the confirmation of the Prophet, who validates an act either ex-

---

[13] Hell (*Gehenam*) as a retribution is a terrible punishment. An apostate is one who converts from Islam to another religion.

[14] The term which we translate as "Tradition" is *Sunna*, or *Sunnat al-Nabi*, *i.e.*, his practice, life style and conduct. It might acquire a broader meaning: for example, *Sunnat*-Allah, the practice (or behavior) required by God, or *Sunnat al-Awwalin—i.e.*, the traditional behavior of the ancients. However, in its sound usage, *Sunna* means the tradition which must be followed, as lived and taught by the Prophet. *See* L. GARDET, L'ISLAM RELIGION ET COMMUNAUTE 47, 48 (1970) [hereinafter cited as GARDET, ISLAM].

[15] L. MILLIOT, INTRODUCTION A L'ETUDE DU DROIT MUSULMAN 106 (1925).

[16] *Surat Ibrahim*, XXIV:54-56.

[17] *Surat al-Nissaa*, IV:65.

pressly or through his silence For example, independent judicial reasoning was validated in a *Hadith.* When Muhammad sent Mu'adh ibn Jabal as a judge (*qadi*) to Yemen, he asked him: "How will you decide when a question arises?" He replied: "According to the Book of God." "And if you do not find the answer in the Book of God?" "Then according to the *Sunna* of the Messenger of God." "And if you find the answer neither in the Book nor in the *Sunna*?" "Then I shall come to a decision according to my own opinion without hesitation." Then Muhammad slapped Mu'adh on the chest with his hand saying: "Praise be to Allah who has led the messenger of the Messenger of Allah to an answer that pleased him."

The *Sunna* became a means of developing the principles found in the words of the *Qu'ran* and thus is the most important source for understanding the *Qu'ran*, in the development of dogma as well as for judicial norms.

If a *Hadith* narrative, like a *Qu'ranic* verse, gives general application to a special case, it has the force of a principle for all similar cases.[18] However, if despite the generality of its terms, its formulation intimates that it has been laid out only for the specific case, then it should not give rise to a principle which would extend to other circumstances.

Modern jurists or scholars, like Chehata or Linant de Bellefonds, sometimes maintain that the *Sunna* can no longer be considered a formal source of law.[19] But the *Sunna* simultaneously comprises the words of the Prophet, judgments delivered by him in specific cases, and his conduct in a given situation. It constitutes, therefore, next to the *Qu'ran*, which it often happens to complement or interpret, a source of the first order. The *Sunna* has the same legal weight as a *Qu'ranic* text; it is equivalent to a text of formal law.[20]

IJMA'

Ijma' is the unanimous consensus of the community through its competent representatives. The community is viewed as all Muslims living at a given time, linked by the same faith and the same submission to the legitimate sovereign. *Ijma'* is a dynamic consensus which might be formulated at any point in time.

When one is faced with an obscure *Qu'ranic* passage or apparently contradictory texts, or is in a position where no available *Hadith* explains or anticipates the situation, Islam finds the solution in the form of a collective action. This is the legislative process called *Ijma'*, the consensus of the Prophet's Companions, and later of their disciples, and their followers and those who follow. Those who knew Muhammad were the most qualified to suggest solutions in accordance with his thinking and to pass this capacity on to their respective students. Later, the consensus of the jurists of a specific period became acknowledged as a solution reached by *Ijma'*. Agreement by silence on a certain subject was also admitted, *i.e.*, if no objections are raised against a certain opinion, then

---

[18] MILLIOT, *supra* note 15, at 35.

[19] C. CHEHATA, ETUDE DE DROIT MUSULMAN 35, 36, 44 (Paris: PUF, 1971); 1 Y. LINANT DE BELLEFONDS, 33 TRAITE DE DROIT MUSULMAN COMPARE (Paris, 1965).

[20] IBN 'ABIDIN, RADD AL-MUKHTAR ALA AL-DURAR AL-MUKHTAR 402 (3rd ed. Cairo, 1255 H.).

the scholars are held to have reached unanimity on the subject.[21]

Ijma' follows from the emphasis upon the community of Muslims in Islam. "Ye are the best community that hath been raised up for mankind. Ye enjoin right conduct and forbid indecency; and ye believe in Allah."[22] In various *Hadith* Muhammad has said: "My community shall never unite upon error..." "Whoever separates himself from the community (*jama'a*) removes the bond of Islam [off his neck]. Whoever dies after withdrawing from the community, he dies as done prior to Islam." "Everlastingly until the will of God intervenes, there shall be some in my community who will not cease to solemnly uphold the truth without the opposition of their enemies hurting them."[23] Should the community (*'umma*), in the sense of a nation or people, be unanimous in a particular assertion, then its rightness is guaranteed.[24] The unanimous opinion of jurists enjoys as a consequence the same weight in Islamic law as *Qu'ranic* texts and the *Sunna*.

It was during the second century of the *Hijra* that the modalities of texts which serve as a basis for the notion of *Ijma'* were extricated from the *Qu'ran* and *Hadith*.

Ijma' is a rational source of judicial norms which provides a modicum of certainty (*yaqin*) with regard to a verse or a *Hadith*. *Ijma'*, however, is a somewhat inferior authority since it is revocable by a new consensus, and so unstable.

Solutions based solely on *Ijma'* as a source are few. For example, it was on the basis of the consensus of the Prophet's Companions that jurists of the different schools of doctrine have commonly agreed that the *Diyya* for a woman is half of that for a free man. Also, *Ijma'* does not exclude the possibility of abrogating a *Qu'ranic* text or a *Hadith*. Under the right of *'Umar*, the penalty of banishment which is linked to bastinado, and which is prescribed for adultery in the *Qu'ran*, *Surat* XXIV:2, was revoked by *Ijma'*.

Ijma' is also the source which underlies the laws, regulations, and decrees of an Islamic state. A parliamentary body may be considered competent representatives of the community. Penal laws may be among the provisions proceeding from the authority which a legislature exercises at the proper moment, regularly undertaken, and promulgated and proclaimed in the conditional forms. These provisions are called laws in western terminology if they are announced by a Parliament, or regulations or orders (in-council) if they are proclaimed by the executive authority or its agencies. These laws, regulations and decrees also make up Islamic law.

QIYYAS

Qiyyas, analogical reasoning, may be used to broaden the application of an existing rule of law derived from a decision (*hukm*). Systematic reasoning, disci-

---

[21] MILLIOT, *supra* note 15, at 100.

[22] *Surat al-Imran*, III:110.

[23] AL-BUKHARI quoted by Hassan Soufy, Le "Periculum rei Venditae" en Droit Romain et en Droit Musulman 35 (These, Paris, 1953).

[24] GARDET, ISLAM at 185.

plined by the rules of analogy, projects the rule beyond its immediate application onto a different plane. For example, the solution to a case at hand may be found by analogy to a similar case found in the *Qu'ran* or the *Sunna* and thus already settled by text. Or, occasionally, a solution may be proposed by looking to the general spirit of the rules laid down by law envisaged in its entirety, and deriving thereby an analogy.[25]

Analogical reasoning in Islamic law is not an autonomous source of law since it depends on the existence of a model case, or a model body of rules, in either the *Qu'ran* or the *Sunna*. Also, *Qiyyas* is a specifically Semitic mode of logic, using only two terms. It operates simply from like to like, from like to contrary, from more to less, or from less to more, without a universal intermediary term as in the typical Aristotelian syllogism, and here always referring to the argument of the Supreme Authority who furnished the text.[26]

In the development of Islamic Law, the role of *Qiyyas* has been vigorously contested. Its opponents argued on the basis of revelation: "We have neglected nothing in the Book..."[27] It was not for fallible human reason, they maintained, to make up the deficiency of God's silence. But proponents of *Qiyyas* noted the *Hadith* (quoted above) in which the Prophet approved Mu'adh ibn Jabal's determination to do his best to decide questions not covered in the *Qu'ran* or the *Sunna* by his own opinion. Without the use of some form or reasoning, they pointed out, the system would be absurd. For example, injury to the skull which lays the bone bare is punished by *Hadith*, but without *Qiyyas* lesser injuries would be left unpunished. The *Qu'ran* also states: "So learn a lesson, O ye who have eyes [to see]!"[28] These became the foundations of the principle of analogy. Perhaps the most powerful argument in favor of analogy is the necessity of having recourse to it, in order to infer from the few explicit texts all that they might encompass.[29]

The use of *Qiyyas* in penal law is carefully limited. Most jurists prohibit the application of analogy in the realm of the seven strictly prescribed offenses (*Hudud*, see below), in retribution (*Quesas*, below) and in compensation, by virtue of explicit texts in the *Qu'ran* and *Sunna*.[30] On the other hand, it is from *Qiyyas* that the five classsifications of acts—obligatory, recommended, indifferent, reprehensible, and forbidden—derive. The *Shafi'i* school uses analogical reasoning, for example, to inflict the penalty of stoning for sodomy.[31] Other jurists hold that the legal definition of fornication includes sodomy, and so reach

---

[25] MILLIOT, *supra* note 15, at 134.

[26] GARDET, ISLAM, *supra* note 14, at 184 *et seq.*

[27] *Surat al-Ana'am*, VI:38.

[28] *Surat al-Qamar*, LIX:2.

[29] MILLIOT, *supra* note 15, at 155.

[30] M. AL-SHAWKANI, NAYL AL-AWTAR, 305 (2d ed. 1344 A.H.), quoted by Gamal al-Din, *De la legalite criminelle*, REVUE DE SCIENCES JURIDIQUES ET ECONOMIQUES, 448 (1974).

[31] M. ABU ZAHRA, AL JARIMA WAL-UQULIA FIL-ISLAM [CRIME AND PUNISHMENT IN ISLAM] 295 (n.d. *circa* 1950).

the same result without analogy.[32]

Qiyyas, together with *Ijma'*, offers a criterion to determine positive law. They involve rational interpretation of the normative written law from which they themselves derive. *Ijma'* is a collective task, whereas *Qiyyas* is largely a process of individual initiative by a jurist. Analogy permits the derivation of a new solution from an already accepted one.

THE PRINCIPLE OF LEGALITY

Islam encompasses all knowledge relating to man's relations with invisible and transcendant realities in addition to his relations with his fellow man. The *Qu'ran* states: "He it is Who hath revealed unto thee [Muhammad] the Scripture wherein are clear revelations... None knoweth its explanation save Allah. And those who are of sound instruction say: only men of understanding really heed."[33] Islam, whose doctrine is in full agreement with science, reason and thought, may apply adequately to ever-changing conditions imposed by the march of time, and permits the furnishing of appropriate answers to any question.

It is, however, indispensable in Islamic dogma to establish a distinction between general principles which allow neither alteration nor change, and particular details or provisions which apply those general principles. The latter may undergo modifications in compliance with changes of public interest and the evolution of morals. The *Qu'ran* formulates general principles, and thus is a constitution and an organic law which concerns fundamental rights. These general principles are immutable. But particular provisions may be modified as long as they remain subordinate to the spiritual interest of the community.

A principle of legality, balanced against the public good, is precisely one such general principle.

The founders of the various schools of Islamic law and their disciples did not at first construct a general theory of the principle of legality and punishment. They have, however, continuously studied each violation and each penalty. From those studies, three categories of crime and punishment have emerged:

1. crimes of *Hudud*, offenses punished by fixed legal penalties.

2. crimes of *Quesas* and *Diyya*, offenses punished by retribution or compensation.

3. crimes of *Ta'azir*, offenses punished by penalties left to the discretion of the judge.

Western scholars have noted the apparently arbitrary nature of the second and third categories, and have concluded that no principle of legality underlies Islamic law. But the same scholars have failed to investigate the basic documents, defeated perhaps by their diversity and the difficulty of making use of them. All

---

[32] Al-Husaini, *La base du droit de punition, dans la doctrine musulmane et la doctrine arabe*, REVUE DE SCIENCES JURIDIQUES ET ÉCONOMIQUES, 404-405 (1971).

[33] *Surat al-Imran*, III:7.

Islamic law, including criminal law, is bound by the general principles laid down in the *Qu'ran*. And among those principles are the essentials of a modern concept of legality. The first is the concept that no act shall be considered criminal unless and until men have been fairly notified and warned. The second is the basic concept of enjoining right conduct and forbidding indecency within the Islamic community, which binds all, both those who act and those who would judge their acts, to a principle of the public good.

THE EXISTENCE OF A LAW AS ESSENTIAL TO CRIME AND PUNISHMENT

Formal principles theoretically affirm the legality of crime and punishment in Islamic law. They are not based on human reason, but rather upon divine decrees. In the *Qu'ran*, the Divine Legislator has declared:

"We never punish until We have sent a Messenger...[34] And never did thy Lord destroy the townships till He had raised up in their mother [-town] a messenger reciting unto them our revelations...[35] This *Qu'ran* hath been inspired in me, that I may ware therewith you and whomsoever it may reach."[36] He has also said: "Allah tasketh not a soul beyond its scope."[37] And God addressed these words to the Prophet: "Tell those who disbelieve that if they cease [from persecution of believers], that which is past will be forgiven them."[38]

In the same way that God does not inflict punishment upon men prior to informing them about it through his Messenger, so it follows from those texts that within Islam there is no crime without explicitness, and no penalty without warning.

Further, this principle was specifically expressed in several acts of legislation in the time of the Prophet. The *Shari'a* was opposed to several practices which were allowed among Arabs in pre-Islamic times. Each of the prohibitions of these practices, however, included a statement that no penalty for the practice would be retroactive. For example, in pre-Islamic Arabia a son was allowed to marry the ex-wife of his father, and could even inherit the paternal *conjugium*. Islam intervened to prohibit this practice, but the *Qu'ranic* verse specifically excludes any such marriages made before the time of the Prophet's announcement of the prohibition: "And marry not those women whom your fathers married, except that hath already happened [of that nature] in the past. Lo! It was ever lewdness and abomination, and an evil way."[39] Also, during the era of paganism, Arab men married their sisters. Legislation against that practice included a similar exception: "Forbidden unto you [for marriage] are your... sisters ... except what hath already happened."[40] The *Qu'ran* thereby made an exception for what has been concluded in the period of paganism.

---

[34] *Surat Bani Isra'il*, XVII:15.
[35] *Surat al-Qasas*, XXVIII:59.
[36] *Surat al-Ana'am*, VI:19.
[37] *Surat al-Baqara*, II:286.
[38] *Surat al-Anfal*, VIII:38.
[39] *Surat al-Nisaa*, IV:22.
[40] *Surat al-Nisaa*, IV:23.

Similarly, the Prophet did not punish crimes of blood or acts of usury which had occurred prior to Islam, but he applied the prohibition starting only with the Islamic Revelation. In his farewell pilgrimage address, he indicated: "Any blood-guilt traced back to the period of ignorance should be disregarded, and I begin with that of al-Harith ibn 'Abd al-Muttalib; the usury practiced during that period has also been erased starting with that of my uncle, al-'Abbas ibn 'Abd al-Muttalib." The interest collected during the age of ignorance did not have to be refunded, but that which remained due after the Islamic Revelation did not have to be paid.

Clearly the principle of non-retroactivity of penal laws embodied in Article 8 of the Declaration of the Rights of Man, and endorsed by several modern constitutions and codes, was already acknowledged and applied centuries before in the *Shari'a*. It follows from sacred texts and the practices of the Prophet. Thus modern jurists conclude that non-retroactivity is one of the basic principles (*qa'ida 'usuliyya*) of the *Shari'a*: "There is no legal status for liable actions prior to the establishment of a text."[41] That is to say, the acts of an accountable human being may not be considered as prohibited if there is no text which anticipates this prohibition. "Permission is the fundamental legitimation of acts."[42] One cannot incriminate an act if there is no text which prohibits its commission or omission. In essence, there can be no crime and no punishment unless there has first been a law.

BINDING THE COMMUNITY TO THE PUBLIC GOOD

The Community of Islam has received from God the essential task of enjoining good and prohibiting evil. "Ye are the best community that hath been raised up for mankind. Ye enjoin right conduct (*ma'ruf*) and forbid indecency (*munkar*)."[43] *Ma'ruf* includes what is known as decent (or proper); *munkar*, that which is hateful, disapproved and blameworthy. The appropriate task of the Islamic community (*'umma*) is to watch over the practice of what is good and decent, and to prohibit that which is evil and blameworthy. Being true to this task entails as a predisposition the accomplishment of "good deeds," and such will be the essence of virtue.

No *Qu'ranic* text provides an exhaustive list of what is *ma'ruf* or *munkar*; one finds instead different listings which complement each other.[44] But the principle of legality in Islamic law proceeds out of this command to enjoin good and forbid evil, because it is a perpetual principle of reform within the Islamic city. This is a task in which all believers must participate; each believer is responsible for each of his brothers and also for those who secure the functions of the community. The same principle is recorded in the following *Hadith*:[45] "Whoever among you sees a reprehensible thing must change it with the hand; if he is

---

[41] ODEH *supra* note 12, at 115.

[42] Permission is that which is allowable or licit.

[43] *Surat al-Imran*, III:110.

[44] GARDET, ISLAM, *supra* note 14, at 137.

[45] AL SAHIH AL-MUSLIM.

incapable of doing so, then by word of mouth; and if this is impossible for him, then let him do it with his heart. This last method is the minimum degree of religion."[46] This means that the duty of struggle on "God's path" in order to expand the frontiers of Islam (*jihad*) is "like a light puff of wind over the rough sea."[47]

While all believers are called to realize this principle, the duty of actualizing it falls particularly on those who hold power. The *Shari'a* allows those who hold power to legislate matters affecting both the community as a whole and the interests of the individual.[48] The legislative authority in an Islamic country may punish an allowable act if the public interest necessitates it; it may inflict a discretionary punishment (*Ta'azir*) upon an incriminated act, and may also limit or expand the authority of the judge if required by the public interest. A Muslim scholar, ibn Qayyim al-Jawziyya, said that "The law of God is where the public good lies." Ibn 'Aqii completed these words by adding: "Even if no revelation has been handed down on [the particular] subject and if the Prophet hasn't said a word about it."[49] With the emphasis on the community and its task to require good and prohibit evil, no other conclusion is possible. But, under Islamic law, the laws, regulations and decrees promulgated by those who hold power must be applied so that they do not contradict express texts of the *Qu'ran* or the *Sunna* or its general principles, nor oppose the spirit of the law in the *Shari'a*. If a law is contrary to a principle of the *Shari'a*, then it becomes a nullity.[50]

The *Qu'ran* orders that justice may not discriminate on the basis of religion, race, color, kinship, or even hostility. It proclaims the dignity of man as God's lieutenant on earth, and on the other hand man's servitude to God, whereby all men and even all creatures are equally subjects of God. Islam condemns all enmity, hatred, contempt and oppression based on personal motives among men. No law which arbitrarily discriminates or oppresses can be promulgated by an Islamic state, and no arbitrary penalties can be imposed by Islamic justice. The Islamic state, like the Islamic community as a whole, is bound to the public good. Finally, as established above, it is a general principle of the *Shari'a* that no act can be considered a crime prior to the existence of a law. Therefore, no Islamic state could promulgate a law, and no Islamic judge impose a penalty, contrary to the public good or the legality principle.

The concept of enjoining right conduct and forbidding indecency which binds the public authority to the public good also binds it to a principle of legality. One may not consider an act as forbidden except by virtue of an explicit text of the law or the public authority which anticipates the prohibition, whether legal (*hadd*) or

---

[46] Commentators explain the term "with the hand" as the use of a stick as necessary. *See* GARDET, ISLAM, *supra* note 14, at 294.

[47] *Id.*

[48] "Oh, ye who believe! Obey God, and obey the Apostle, and those charged with authority among you." (*Surat al-Nisaa* IV:59).

[49] THE RIYADH CONFERENCE ON ISLAMIC DOCTRINE AND HUMAN RIGHTS IN ISLAM 19 (The Ministry of Justice, Riyadh, Beirut, Lebanon: Dar al-Kitab al-Lubnani, 1972).

[50] ODEH, *supra* note 12, at 181.

with punishment at the discretion of the judge (*Ta'azir*). The public authority must act to promote good and punish evil, but it cannot act capriciously or arbitrarily. It can therefore only act fairly, with fair warning and no retroactive punishments, and in the public good.

SCOPE OF APPLICATION OF THE LEGALITY PRINCIPLE

The scope of application of the legality principle in Islamic law is broad, but varies with the offense. Seen as a whole, however, the Islamic criminal justice system provides a basis of legality balanced by degrees of judicial flexibility, similar to the functioning of the legality principle in modern western law.

Islamic law is the laying down of the code of life for the Muslim community, covering religious obligations (*ibahat*) as well as social relations (*mu'amalat*). Thus, law (*fiqh*) plays a more vital role in Islamic society than that played by modern or secular law in western societies.[51]

In Islamic law acts subject to punishment are either the reprehensible (*makruh*) or the forbidden (*haram*), with only the latter requiring corporal punishment. Offenses are divided into three categories according to a complex criterion which combines the gravity of the penalty with the nature of the crime. Each obligation essentially corresponds to a penal sanction. The few penalties distinctly called *Hudud* are limits imposed upon man's action which he may not transgress without being penalized by the community. Crimes of *Quesas* and *Diyya* are those which man may not commit without being penalized by private individuals. Crimes of *Ta'azir* are acts for which the *Shari'a* did not establish precise penalties; it is the duty of the judge (*qadi*) to decide and establish the penalty.

The *Shari'a* employs and applies the principle of legality to all offenses, though not in a uniform manner. The scope of its application differs depending on whether crimes of *Hudud*, *Quesas* and *Diyya*, or *Ta'azir* are in question. In general, crimes of *Quesas* and *Diyya*, though left to individuals (and families) to punish, show their basis in a principle of legality by being bound to specific procedures and appropriate penalties in the process of retribution or compensation. Crimes of *Hudud* are firmly based on a principle of legality, with precise determination of both crime and punishment, yet with some flexibility for the judge depending upon the intent of the accused and the quality of the evidence. Crimes of *Ta'azir*, on the other hand, allow a great deal of flexibility to the judge, yet are still implicitly tied to the general principle of legality in the *Shari'a*.

QUESAS AND *DIYYA*

The crimes of blood are punished by retribution or legal compensation. In crimes of this kind, only the victim or his representatives possess the right to prosecute the criminal; the public authority has no power to intervene as in

---

[51]GARDET, ISLAM, *supra* note 14, at 182.

western law.[52] This method of punishment provides for both specific and general deterrence, and for a reparation to the victim or his avenger which terminates the conflict between the criminal and the injured party.[53]

Voluntary homicide, with or without premeditation, is normally punished by retribution; it may be punished by legal compensation with the consent of the representatives of the victim. Assault resulting in homicide (blows dealt and wounds inflicted voluntarily, without intent to cause death but causing it in fact) and quasi-voluntary homicide are normally punished by legal compensation; they may be punished by retribution if the criminal refuses to consent to compensation. Retribution consists of having the criminal undergo the same injury or the same form of death which he caused to the victim.[54] In legal compensation, the family of the victim may demand the payment of, in effect, a ransom for the lost life or injury during the period when the exercise of retribution is still possible.

The institution of retribution is of course not a *Qu'ranic* innovation. The *Qu'ran* itself states that this law was equally prescribed to Jews in the Torah: "The life for the life, and the eye for the eye, and the nose for the nose, and the ear for the ear, and the tooth for the tooth, and for wounds retaliation."[55] But the principle of both retribution and compensation is clearly adopted in the *Qu'ran*:

> O ye who believe! Retaliation is prescribed for you in the matter of the murdered. The freeman for the freeman, and the slave for the slave, and the female for the female. And for him who is forgiven somewhat by his [injured] brother, prosecution according to usage, and payment unto him in kindness. This is an alleviation and a mercy from your Lord. He who transgresseth after this will have a painful doom.[56]

The same is summarized in a *Hadith* reported by al-Tirmidhi: "If a man is murdered, his parents have two choices: either to kill the murderer, or, if they prefer, to accept compensation."[57]

Any compensation, however, must have the consent of the perpetrator, as indicated by the following Prophetic *Hadith*: "The possessions of a Muslim are not legally appropriated except through his consent. Thus, if the murderer prefers to undergo the infliction of retribution, the rightful claimants of the victim may not impose upon him instead the payment of any ransom whatsoever."

However, two of the schools of law, the Shafi'is and Hanbalis, maintain that a murderer is obliged to pay compensation if the representatives of the victim demand it. This they justify as a ransom to buy back his life, on the analogy to the

---

[52] A.F. Sorour, *Les orientations acutelles de la politique criminelle, des pays arabes*, 2 ARCHIVES DE POLITIQUE CRIMINALLE, 176 (Centre de recherches de politique criminelle, 1977). *See also* MILLIOT, INTRODUCTION, *supra* note 15, at 745.

[53] 6 TABYIN AL-HAQA'IQ 97 *et seq.* (Cairo: Bulaq, 1315 A.H.); AL-MAWARDI, AL-AHKAM AL-SULTANIYYA, 219 *et seq.* (E. Fagnan trans.); ODEH, *supra* note 12, at 78 and 663.

[54] *See* Krautter-Bordenet, al-Qisas. [Islamic Talion] 150 (Paris, 1973) (Ph.D. dissertation); Sharaf al-Din, *Le Talion en Droit Egyptien et Musulman*, REVUE DE SCIENCE CRIMINELLE 393, 401 (1954); A.F. BAHNASSI, LE TALION EN DROIT MUSULMAN, (Cairo, 1964).

[55] *Surat al-Maeda*, V:45.

[56] *Surat al-Baqara*, II:178.

[57] A. SALIT, L'HOMICIDE VOLUNTAIRE 85 *et seq.*

necessity to buy food if one is at the point of death. To fail to do so would be suicide.

While "the punishment of murder is retaliation,"[58] retaliation is not considered appropriate when a father murders his son, a free Muslim murders an infidel or a slave, or in cases where murder was committed by several perpetrators, carried out indirectly, committed abroad, or where the rightful claimant of the victim in unknown. Where retaliation is inapplicable, another punishment is substituted, usually pecuniary compensation.[59] This independent settlement of legal prescriptions is not linked to any fixed amount. In classical Islamic times, arbitrators were often employed by both families to reach a settlement. Even when the avenger pardons the criminal, the pardon is presumed to apply only to retribution and not to legal compensation unless contrary evidence is established.[60]

Whether retaliation still exists in modern Islamic countries is a point of some debate. In Egypt, for example, retaliation certainly existed until 1883;[61] the question is whether it survived the penal code of French origin introduced in that year.[62] Though retaliation is not specifically mentioned, article 7 reserves personal rights consecrated by Islamic law.[63] In practice, however, retaliation no longer is applied in any case.

HUDUD

The principle of legality is observed most strictly in crimes of *Hudud*, which are offenses punished by fixed legal penalties. "*Hudud* are penalties established by God for the purpose of preventing the commission of forbidden acts or the omission of prescribed regulations."[64] Crimes of this category are of a grave nature because they bring about injury to the primordial interest of Islamic society. There are seven such offenses: theft, fornication, false accusation of fornication, brigandage, drinking of wine, apostasy, and rebellion against the legitimate authority. Even here, however, legality is somewhat tempered by concern for the public good, and questions of, for example, intent in theft, or evidence in fornication, allow a judge at least minimal discretion in the imposition of the fixed penalties.

"*Theft* indictable by *Had* (the singular of *Hudud*) is the fraudulent taking

---

[58] For further detail *see* A. Salih, l'Homicide Voluntaire et l'Homicide Preintentionnel en Droit Penal Musulman et en Droit Romain: Etude Comparative 77-78 (These, Paris, 1977).

[59] AL-SARAKHSI, 26 AL-MABSUT 61 (Cairo, 1324 A.H.); AL-KASANI, 7 BADA'I' AL-SANA'I 241 (Cairo, 1328 A.H.).

[60] AL-HAKIM, LE DOMMAGE DE SOURCE DELICTUELLE EN DROIT MUSULMAN SURVIVANCE EN DROIT SYRIEN ET LIBANAIS 31, 32 (2d ed. Paris, 1971).

[61] This period begins with the conquest of Egypt by Islam during the seventh century (639) and extends to the nineteenth century (1883).

[62] The period during which positive laws derived from European legislation were applied. A. Abu Haif de la Compensation (These, Cairo, 1932); A. CHERON AND A. BADAWI, NOUVEAU CODE PENAL EGYPTIAN EN ANNOTE (Cairo, 1939).

[63] A. IBRAHIM, Le Talion en Droit Penal Musulman et dans le Droit Penal Egyptien (These, Cairo, 1944). We are in full agreement with the opinion of M. Sharaf al-Din, *supra* note 54, at 397.

[64] AL-MAWARDI *supra* note 53; E. TYAN, HISTOIRE DE L'ORGANI JUDICIAIRE EN PAYS D'ISLAM 568 (2d ed. Leiden 1960).

away, out of custody, of someone else's property, whose value is at least 20 dirhams."[65] The basic principle appears in the *Qu'ran*: "As for the thief, both male and female, cut off their hands; it is the reward for their own deeds, an exemplary punishment from Allah."[66] The *Sunna*, however, clarifies the conception. Above all, intent to steal must be reasonably established; if there is a reasonable dispute over ownership, amputation would not be levied. This is an application of the *hadith*: "Actions are appraised according to the intents." Another tradition limits amputation to those cases where "the value of the stolen object is worth at least 20 dirhams of silver." Finally, by the *Sunna*, proof of an act must be established through the testimony of two honorable men (*'adl*). The penalty must not be imposed if there is any doubt.

It is the severity of this penalty in Islam which safeguards the peace for everyone, preserving both the life of the victim and, by its deterrent power, the hand of the thief as well. This penalty is only executed in public in order for the punishment to serve as an example. The need for proof of intent and of the value of the stolen object by the testimony of two honorable men insures that the penalty cannot be applied capriciously or absent reasonable doubt of guilt. Thus, in countries which apply the *Shari'a* today, such as Saudi Arabia, theft has almost disappeared, while in the cities of western countries man does not feel safe for his possessions or his life.[67]

Fornication carries different penalties depending on the status of the guilty party. When committed by a married person, the penalty is death by stoning. An unmarried person receives one hundred lashes and may also be banished for a year. "And come not near to adultery . . . as for those of your women who are guilty of lewdness, call to witness four of you against them. And if they testify [to the truth of the allegation] then confine them to the houses until death take them or until Allah appoint for them a way [through new legislation]."[68] A *Hadith* amplifies on this *Qu'ranic* text: "As to the virgin, one hundred lashes and banishment for one year, the married woman, one hundred lashes and the penalty of stoning to death." In practice the additional penalties of banishment for the single person, and flogging for the adulterer, may not be applied.[69] The basic penalties are flogging for fornication and stoning for adultery; the additional penalties depend on the circumstances of the case.

Imposition of those penalties is further restricted by the evidentiary requirements. Only when four witnesses known for their honesty and integrity declare that they have assisted in the perpetration of the sexual act, or at least witnessed

---

[65] MILLIOT, *supra* note 15, at 123.

[66] *Surat al-Maeda*, V:38.

[67] Most offenses of theft in the West are committed by force, and as a result, they are often accompanied by murder. In armed attacks against banks and restaurants in order to rob their safe-boxes, one should ask first of all: Why feel pity for the hand of the thief instead of the head (life) of the robbery victim?

[68] *Surat Bani Isra'il* XVII:32; *Surat* IV:15.

[69] 'ALI IBN KHALIL AL-TARABULSI, MU'IN AL-HUKKAM [ON FLAGELLATION AND LAPIDATION] 182 (Bulaq ed. Cairo, 1300 A.H.); *see* IBN RUSHD, BIDAYAT AL-MUJTAHID 363, 367, cited by 'Abd al-'Aziz 'Amir, Ta'zir in Islamic Shari'a 77 (Thesis, Cairo, 1955).

it so that they can testify to it according to the traditional formula ("like a brush in a pot of glue") will the accused be punished.[70]

In practice, bringing charges is also limited by the fact that *slanderous accusation of fornication* is punished by eighty lashes. "And those who accuse honorable women, but bring not four witnesses, scourge them with eighty stripes, and never [afterward] accept their testimony—they indeed are evildoers."[71] The definition of the crime includes not only such slander against either married or marriageable women, but also denial of someone's legitimacy of paternity, even if only by allusion or innuendo. Eighty lashes is the penalty for free men and infidels, forty for a slave.[72]

Brigandage is subject to a range of punishments depending on the gravity of the crime. "The reward for those who wage war upon Allah and His Messenger, and strive after corruption in the land, will be that they will be killed or crucified, or have their hands and feet on alternate sides cut off, or will be expelled out of the land."[73] An unrepentant bandit must be killed if he has committed murder, and may be sentenced to death even if he has not. Amputation and banishment are otherwise imposed at the discretion of the *Imam*. However, if the bandit surrenders voluntarily, demonstrating his repentance, these penalties do not apply. He would, however, remain subject to retribution or compensation relative to those he has injured.

Drinking wine is normally punished by eighty lashes. "They question thee about strong drink and games of chance. Say: in both is great sin, and some utility for men, but the sin of them is greater than their usefulness. . . . Strong drink and games of chance, and idols and diving by arrows, are only an infamy of Satan's handiwork. Leave it aside in order that ye may succeed."[74] The schools differ on whether all beverages whose consumption impairs the senses are prohibited, or only wine and an intoxicating beverage extracted from fermented dates or raisins. The penalty, eighty lashes, apparently reflects a decision of the Caliph 'Umar in consultation with the surviving Companions of that time. The Shafi'i school, however, sets the penalty at forty lashes.

Apostasy, the turning away from Islam after once having embraced it, is

---

[70] It is not sufficient, for example, for the witnesses to have seen the accused naked and one on top of the other. Since the beginning of the Islamic Predication and during the lifespan of the Prophet, there has never been a single case of adultery proven by the deposition of four eyewitnesses. Whatever was verified in matter of adultery, it was through the free admission of the criminal who must purify himself in this life in order to avoid punishment awaiting him in the hereafter. This was the case when a suspect came to the Prophet to admit his crime and ask to undergo the penalty of stoning to death. The Prophet turned away from him and refused to listen to him. The act had been perpetrated in secrecy, resulting in no injury whatsoever to the public order and morality; thus, the affair depends on the criminal himself, who, in his soul and conscience, must do nothing but seek pardon from the Lord. The man nevertheless insisted on undergoing punishment, but at the point of execution he regretted his statements and escaped but was recaptured. Then the Prophet made his famous remark: "Why didn't you let him live. He would have repented and God would have shown his mercy."

[71] *Surat Ibrahim* XXIV:4.

[72] *See* M. MUSTAFA, PRINCIPES DE DROIT PENAL DES PAYS ARABES 9, 11 (Librairie general de droit et de jurisprudence, 1972).

[73] *Surat al-Maeda,* V:33.

[74] *Surat al Baqara,* II:219; *Qu'ran, Surat al-Maeda* V:90.

punishable by death. The crime stems from the *Qu'ran*: "Those among you who turn away from their religion and die as unbelievers: vain are your deeds in this world, and in the hereafter ye are the companions of the fire, to dwell therein [forever]." The penalty stems from *Hadith*: "Whoever changes his religion, kill him," in addition to the consensus of the Companions.[75]

Rebellion against the Imam and the community, by practicing a prohibited rite, is punishable by death.[76]

> If two parties of believers fall to fighting, then make peace between them. And if one party of them doeth wrong to the other, fight ye that which doeth wrong till it return unto the ordinance of Allah. Then, if it returns, make peace between them justly and act equitably. Lo! Allah loveth the equitable.[77]

The companions agreed to put rebels to death if they have first been warned to cease their rebellion and continue fighting in spite of such warning. In practice, penalties short of death have been inflicted.

TA'AZIR

The Islamic principle of legality is at its most flexible in *Ta'azir* offenses, offenses left undetermined by religious law. In this category, the criminalization of acts and the punishment given for them is left to the discretion of the judge or public authority.[78]

At first glance, it would appear that a principle of legality does not operate for the offenses. Indeed, the authority of a judge acting under *Ta'azir* is considerable. In some cases it would be fair to state that in this category the judge creates the offense, selects the penalty, and inflicts it. But a concept of legality is lacking only if the category is judged by a wholly western, individualistic standard. Muslims are bound, individually and collectively, to a community whose task is to promote right conduct and forbid improper conduct. The judge in a *Ta'azir* offense acts legally under that fundamental principle of the community in the interest of the public good.

Admittedly, Muslim jurists have overwhelmingly preferred to study crimes of *Hudud* and their prescribed penalties, the clear reflections of the Divine Will whose elements and consequences do not change. They have failed to investigate in detail the elements and consequences of *Ta'azir*.[79] This may have helped to create the Western impression that the legality principle is absent from this category.

In fact detailed study by jurists was not necessary. *Ta'azir* offenses are the necessary complement to *Hudud*; they are the acts not specifically mentioned by the Divine Lawgiver, the punishment of which is entrusted to the community.

---

[75] IBN RUSHD, BIDAYAT AL-MUJTAHID 383; IBN QUDAMA X AL-MUGHNI 274; 2 AHKAM AL-QU'RAN (*fil-qisas*) 286; AL-SHAWKANI, 7 NAYL AL-AWTAR 98-100.

[76] ODEH, *supra* note 12, at 10.

[77] *Surat al-Nur*, XVIX:9.

[78] *See* 'ABD AL-'AZIZ 'AMIR, LE TA'AZIR, 15 *et seq.*; MILLIOT *supra* note 15, at 746.

[79] ODEH, *supra* note 12, at 343-44.

The *Shari'a* does not determine in a restrictive manner the offenses of *Ta'azir*.[80] Nevertheless it is clear from the sources that offenses of *Hudud*, *Quesas* and *Diyya* are not the only offenses which the Islamic community was expected to punish. According to al-Mawardi's definition, *Ta'azir* consists of chastisement for errors unpunishable by *Hudud*.[81] Theoretically, the crimes of this category are those acts which bring injury to the social order as a result of the trouble they cause. Some unquestionably would be held by any society or any judge at any time or place to be criminal: false witness, corruption, extortion. But the divine plan left their precise determination to the community and its representatives, to allow for changes over time in the needs of that community. God and His Messenger called all Muslims to enjoin right conduct and to forbid indecency, and both trusted the Islamic community to understand that call and consistently strive for better implementation. This is most obvious in the standing which *Ijma'* (consensus) and *Qiyyas* (analogical reasoning) have as sources in Islamic law. They provide rational sources of positive law through the representatives of the community, both collectively (*Ijma'*) and individually (*Qiyyas*). *Ta'azir* provides a similar role for the community, through its representatives, in the ongoing elaboration and application of the principles of Islamic law. The sovereign or public authority and the individual judge have the flexibility to determinine a range of criminal acts and their penalties beyond those which the Divine Lawgiver has specified. It does *not* free those representatives from the fundamental principle of legality in Islamic law; the sovereign and the judge still can only act fairly, with fair warning and no retroactive punishments, and in the public good.

In practice, of course, at certain times and places Islamic judges have not lived up to their task. Thus, some Muslim jurists have said that "For some a wink of the eye is sufficient to reform, while for others bastinado is indispensable."[82] However, for the most part the discretion of the judge in a *Ta'azir* offense has not been and was never designed to be total. The judge is a delegate of the sovereign, and the sovereign's regulations determine or define the punishable acts. In the absence of a specific decree from the sovereign, custom (*'urf*) supplied or augmented the list of crimes.

The judge's freedom in this category exists primarily in the application of the penalty anticipated by law in light of the gravity of the incriminated act. The judge must consider objective culpability, the nature of the crime, and subjective culpability, the situation of the delinquent. Nor is the judge free to invent any conceivable penalty *sua sponte*. Furthermore, implicit recognition of the principle of legality appears in the position of three of the schools which held that the penalties of *Ta'azir* must always be inferior to those of *Hudud*.[83] The penalties available are: exhortation or reprimand, reparation (compensation for injury),

---

[80] *See* TYAN, *supra* note 64, at 569.

[81] AL-MAWARDI, *supra* note 53, at 224.

[82] MILLIOT, *supra* note 15, at 762.

[83] DAMAD AFANDI, MAJMA; AL-ANHUR 609 (Ahmad ibn 'Uthman, ed.); IBN NUHAYM, AL-BAHR AL-RA'IQ 40, cited by TYAN, HISTOIRE, *supra* note 64, at 570.

imprisonment, flagellation, and banishment. The Shafi'i school, however, believes that even the death penalty is available if necessary to the judge in a *Ta'azir* offense.[84] Also, many cases of *Ta'azir* result from the commission of acts forbidden by religious law in which the victim has remitted the legal penalty to which he is entitled under *Quesas* or *Diyya* offenses. If the victim foregoes his rights, the state may intervene under *Ta'azir*. In such cases, the judge will be strongly influenced by the determined penalty.

In short, the judge has wide authority in *Ta'azir*, but not, if properly understood, beyond the bounds of legality. The discretion of the judge is confined by the guidelines described above in ascertaining the crime and setting the penalty. As a general principle, a Muslim knows that he and his community are expected to act rightly and that the community will consider it necessary to punish him if he fails to do so. The representatives of the community know that they are expected to warn fairly before punishment and to act to promote the public good. The judge is a delegate of the sovereign and restricted by him, his decrees, the demands of custom, and some limitations on the penalties at his disposal. Sanctions also may be imposed on the judge for abuse of official duty. For these reasons, the presence of the legality principle is felt as strongly in the category of *Ta'azir* offenses as in any of the superior categories. *Ta'azir*, like the other crime classifications of Islamic law, is not based on a principle of legality formulated in express terms like that in all contemporary western legal systems, but all which that principle represents is embodied in the *Ta'azir* category of offenses.

CONCLUSION

The western struggle with the principle of legality may be summarized briefly as follows: strict legality emerged from the French Revolution as a means of protecting the individual from the unfettered discretion of judges; since then, western legal systems have gradually restored some discretion to the judge to better protect the interest of society against the criminal. These systems seek a balance between the injustice of no principle and the injustice of inflexible regulations, between the rights of individuals and the needs of the community.

God Himself imbued Islamic law with the proper balance centuries ago. If the perfectly judicious character of the provisions of the *Shari'a* have an analogy with a main principle of modern legislation, this is not an analogy by nature but simply one of modality. Modern law, however much it is revered, is precarious, because it springs solely from the human will and is alterable by that same will. The fundamental principles of Islamic law spring from the Divine Will and are immutable. Some ask today if the *Shari'a* is applicable to the conditions of the modern world. The Muslim faithful remain unmoved by such pseudo-problems. The real question is when will those who assault the *Shari'a* both from without and from within realize that the *Shari'a* even now possesses the true justice which western law still seeks, but as yet can only approximate.

---

[84] *ibid.*

Islamic law rests upon a principle of legality, but also upon the principle that the community should, must, and will demand right conduct and forbid indecency of its members. It balances individual, family, and community rights by categories of offenses which grant the authority to punish variously to the family of the victim, to the community under the specific command of God, and to the representatives of the community under general guidelines laid down by God. Of these categories, one is based on specified retribution, one on explicit legality with minimal discretion for the judge, one on implicit legality with maximal discretion for the judge. Individual, family, and community are all protected; justice is achieved. Unlike western law, Islamic jurisprudence has not lost sight of the value of the community in a headlong rush to protect the individual. Its principle of legality stems from its concept of community, and ultimately protects the individual because he is a member of the community. Islamic jurisprudence steadfastly refuses to elevate the human above the divine. When other legal systems realize the value of the timelessness of divine command, perhaps they too will find the proper balance of true justice.

CRIMINAL RESPONSIBILITY IN ISLAMIC LAW

Ahmad Fathi Bahnassi

INTRODUCTION

In Islamic law we find different schools of thought concerning the bases of criminal responsibility. The *al-Jabriyah* (fatalism) school, for instance, holds that man does not freely choose his own actions. He is not endowed with a will or power of choice. Rather, his actions are directed by God and are attributed only secondarily to man. There also are the *Mu'tazilites* in Iraq who believe that man is the author of his own actions, both the good and the evil, and therefore, he deserves reward or punishment in the hereafter. They also believe that God, as the perfect Being, does nothing evil or unjust. Man has a choice in all he does and has legal capacity. One of the most prominent supporters of this view was Ghaylan al-Dimashqi, also called al-Qadari, the fatalist. Proponents of this view have been called fatalists because of their absolute denial of fate. They were divided into twenty groups each accusing the other of heresy.[1] Finally, there are the *Ash'arites* who believe that although man has a will, it cannot prevail over the power of God. Man performs actions determined by God, but man's will also prompts his own actions. Hence, he is considered to exercise choice (albeit predestined) in his actions. This school of thought has been traced to al-Ash'ari who was very prominent in his time and was given the title "Imam of the Sunnis" by the *'ulama* (religious scholars). However, he had many opponents. Most important among them was ibn Hazm who considered al-Ash'ari a fatalist for his view on the great sins, because he postponed the passing of judgment on anyone until the Day of Judgment.

According to Islam, God is omnipotent. As the creator of all that is in heaven and on earth, his power is total. He knows what is unknown, what is in the heart and what is in the womb. Hence, he also knows what actions a person may take,

---

[1]On the subject of fate and divine decree *see*: ABU MANSUR 'ABD AL-QAHIR AL-BAGHDADI, AL-FARQ BAYN AL-FIRAQ 18, 93 (Cairo: Dar al-Ma'arif, 1910); and 'ALI IBN AHMAD IBN HAZM, KITAB AL-FISAL FI AL-MILAL WA-AL-AHWA' WA-AL-NIHAL, Part III, 51 (Cairo: al-Matba'ah al-Adabiyah, 1899-1903).

be they good or evil. Islam also teaches that God has endowed man with reason and will and made him capable of thinking according to his perceptions and his understanding. Naturally, God knows what good or evil deeds each creature will do, but each person is free to make it. The thief steals, the adulterer commits adultery; but each sin is prompted by the sinner's desires and lusts. He commits such sins by his own will, not to realize a predestined fate but rather to satisfy a forbidden desire. Such acts are known to God beforehand since He is omniscient. In Islam, therefore, a person is totally responsible for his actions—a responsibility brought upon him by his reason, his will, inclinations, and choice.

Bearing this theological foundation in mind, the following discussion of criminal responsibility in Islamic law (*Shari'a*) is divided according to:

1. responsibility and the physical act;
2. responsibility and the mental state; and
3. reasons for vacating responsibility.

Reasons for permissibility and those for withholding responsibility will also be discussed.

RESPONSIBILITY AND THE PHYSICAL ACT

Only the perpetrator of a crime is held responsible for it. But when a crime can be considered to have been the result of the defendant's act and when it resulted from someone else's act gives rise to the problem of establishing causation for purposes of imposing criminal responsibility.

CAUSATION

Most Islamic jurists insist that there be a causal relationship between the act committed and the resulting death. Islamic law holds a person responsible for the result whenever it is possible to trace its source back to the act which leads to it. In ibn Hazm's *al-Muhalla* it is stated: "It is homicide for someone to open up a river dam thus drowning people, or to spread fire, or destroy a building." Similarly, Ali has said:

> If someone opens up a river dam and a group of people drown, and if the act was performed with the intention of drowning people, the person is liable to retribution and indemnities for the killing of a group. If the opening up of the river dam was done for some benefit or for no benefit, if the person had not realized that it would injure any of those who died, then this is a case of accidental homicide. Indemnities are to be paid by his clan; penance is upon him for each soul that perished; and, in all this, he is liable for all damage to property that he caused. If one channels water onto a wall and the water, in destroying the wall, causes death, as stated above, the same rule applies equally here without any distinction because in each case the person is the physical cause of the damage.[2]

It is stated in *Nihayat al-muhtaj*:

---

[2] 11 'ALI IBN AHMAD IBN HAZM, AL-MUHALLA, 19 (Cairo: Idarat al-Tiba'ah al-Muniriyah, 1927-32).

> He who intentionally injures a man who remains bedridden until his death, deserves retribution. If someone kills a sick man in the last throes of death, his act deserves retribution.[3]

It is clear from the above that Islamic law does not require that the act of the assailant be the only cause that brings about the result. It is sufficient that the act be the principal and uninterrupted cause that brought about the result. But if there is no relationship between the act and the result, then no responsibility is imposed. This is illustrated in an example from ibn Hazm:

> A man was traveling with his mother when another man came on a horse galloping at a high speed. The donkey was frightened as a result of the horse and jumped. The woman fell off the donkey and was killed. The man appealed to 'Umar ibn al-Khattab for assistance. 'Umar asked, 'Did he hit the donkey?'. The man answered, 'No'. 'Umar asked, 'Did the horse injure the donkey in any way?'. The man answered, 'No'. So 'Umar said, 'Your mother's time had come, so resign yourself to God's will'.[4]

Abu Muhammad ibn Hazm has also said in this respect:

> The story about Umar, even if not correct in all details due to the way it has been transmitted, is generally correct. We accept it because if someone does not order or oversee the execution of an act, he cannot be held liable. If an animal jumps due to fright, then the person who made it jump cannot be blamed unless he intentionally made the animal jump. If he had made the animal jump, then the person would be liable for retaliation for whoever it has killed if by doing so he had intended it to trample the one it hit. If, however, his act was unintentional, then this would be a case of accidental homicide. Indemnities are paid by the clan, and penance is upon him. In either case, he is liable for payment if he intentionally made it jump because he controls its movement.[5]

SEQUENTIAL CAUSATION

If a person's wall falls on another's wall and the second wall falls on a man thus killing him, then the owner of the first wall is liable because the falling of his wall began an uninterrupted chain of events. If, however, a man falls and is injured in the debris of the second wall, then the first man is not liable for his injury since removal of the debris is not his responsibility. Neither is the owner of the second wall liable unless he had knowledge of the falling of his wall and did not remove the debris in an appropriate time.[6]

If a snake attacks a person and, in being pushed away, falls onto a second person who in turn throws the snake onto a third person who is bitten and dies, then who would be held liable for the death? Abu Hanifa answered thus:

> The first person is not liable because the snake did not hurt the second

---

[3] 7 SHAMS AL-DIN AL-RAMLI, NIHAYAT AL-MUHTAJ, 16 (Cairo: al-Maktabah al-Islamiyah, 1939).

[4] 11 IBN HAZM, AL-MUHALLA, 9.

[5] *Id.*

[6] 7 ABU BAKR IBN MAS'UD AL-KASANI, BADA'I' AL-SANA'I' FI TARTIB AL-SHARA'I', 276 (Cairo: Sharikat al-Matbu'at al-Ilmiyah, 1910).

> person. Neither is the second liable, or the third and so on if there were more persons involved. As far as the last person in the chain is concerned, if the snake falls on him and he is bitten as soon as the snake falls on him, thus giving him no time to throw it away, then the person who had thrown the snake on the last person is liable to the heirs of the deceased. If, however, the snake does not bite him immediately, then the person who had thrown the snake is also not liable.[7]

Additionally, Abu Hanifa insists that it is necessary to consider the instrument used in the homicide in the causal analysis. If the instrument does not usually kill, then according to Abu Hanifa, this breaks the causal relationship between the act and the death. And a person is, therefore, not held responsible for the act of intentional murder.

This view is further supported by the following quote from *al-Mabsut*:

> If a man drowns another in water, according to Abu Hanifa, he is not subject to retribution. His argument is that water cannot be viewed as a weapon in that it does not cause the destruction of body parts. It is in this respect similar to a stone or a stick. He further explains that a drowning man draws the water himself. It is as though he is bringing it upon himself and this would constitute a doubt which results in avoidance of retaliation. According to Abu Hanifa, a causal relationship is broken if any outside nonessential cause interferes in bringing about the death.
>
> If a person injures a boy in his abdomen with a knife so that his intestines are exposed, and if someone is brought in to close the wound and return the intestines to their place but is unable to do so except by widening the wound, and if he does so by permission of the boy's father, but that same night the boy dies, in this case, the person who inflicted the wound pays half the indemnities since the second act (the widening of the wound) was consented to.

Muhammad, Abu Hanifa's friend, disagreed on this point, as stated in *al-Mabsut*:

> If someone throws an insect at a man and that insect bites him, then he is liable because he intentionally caused this injury. It cannot be said that it was not direct, namely, the scorpion's sting or the snake bite, because that is not valid to maintaining the verdict. This will not interrupt the chain of causation from the act of throwing in the same way as a man accidentally walking and falling into a well that another had dug. This will not abrogate the implied causation in the digging for purposes of imposing liability.

CAUSATION AND THE COMMISSION OF AN INTENTIONAL CRIME IN A PASSIVE MANNER

It is required of whoever abstains from offering food or drink with the intention of torture that if he does not give water to a traveller, knowing that his abstention is not justified and that the traveller would die if not offered water, such a person shall be executed for the traveller—even though this person has not killed him (the traveller) with his own hands. On the face of it, a person is

[7] 5 MUHAMMAD AMIN IBN 'ABIDIN, HASHIYAH [COMMENTARY ON AL-DURR AL-MUKHTAR OF AL-HASKAFI] 551 (Cairo: Mustafa al-Babi al-Halabi, 1966). [Also known as RADD AL-MUHTAR 'ALA AL-DURR AL-MUKHTAR.]

sentenced for the death of another if he intended by his abstention to kill him or to torture him. And so in this respect is the case of the mother. If a mother denies milk to her son, with intention of killing him, then she should be sentenced to death. In other words, she shall not be sentenced on the grounds of abstention unless that abstention is accompanied by an intention to kill. Analogous is the case of the father, who while beating his child, had the intention of killing and torturing. If there was no intention to kill, then indemnities are paid by the clan.[8]

RESPONSIBILITY FOR THE ACT OF ANOTHER

A person is not criminally responsible for a crime which he has not committed since punishment is personal. However, an individual's mistake or neglect may be a cause for holding him responsible for another's criminal act. A merchant, for example, is responsible for the actions of employees in his store for violation of the laws when governing pricing. This is equally true of the owner of a car when he gives his car to someone else to drive without a driver's license.

A person who owns an animal or is otherwise in charge of it may be criminally responsible for homicide or for the injuries arising from the acts of the animal if he commits certain mistakes. Similarly, the owner of a building may be responsible if he interferes in the work or if he takes over the management or supervision of the work of an unqualified and untrained person.

In Islamic law a person may be held responsible for the following:

1. *For the acts of others*
   An employer may be civilly liable for the practices of his subordinates, be that subordinate a son, a hired hand or an apprentice.
2. *For what buildings he owns and what he does to public roads*
   It was said of one who left his garbage in the street so that it injured a person, that he is liable for the injury because the injury occurred as a result of his intentional placing of the garbage. Muhammad has suggested that when the man placed the garbage at the end of the road on which he lived, he would be held liable for the injury because this was a common road shared by the residents. Each of the residents had a right to benefit from the road just as they would from a common area if they shared a house.[9]
3. *For animals*
   A person also may be held responsible for the animals he owns.

   The rider of an animal is responsible for all that it treads on and all that it injures on the public road. But if he is riding on his own land when the injury occurs, he is not liable. If he rides on land owned by another with the owner's permission, then too he is not liable. But if he does not have the owner's permission, he is liable.[10]

---

[8] 4 MUHAMMAD AL-DASUQI, HASHIYAT AL-DASUQI 'ALA AL-SHARH AL-KABIR OF AL-DARDIR 215 (Cairo: al-Matba'ah al-Amiriyah, 1900).

[9] *See further* 7 AL-KASANI, BADA'I' AL-SANA'I' 243, and 3 AL-FATAWA AL-'ALAMKIRIYAH... AL-HINDIYAH, 467 (Egypt: al-Matba'ah al-Amiriyah, 1892-93).

[10] 2 'ABD AL-WAHHAB AL-SHA'RANI, AL-MIZAN, 153 (Cairo: Maktabat al-Babi al-Halabi, 1940).

a. *For a dog*

A person is responsible for what animals in his possession do. If a vicious dog is kept with the intention of killing a particular person and the dog kills him, then retribution is due whether or not the person was warned against keeping the dog. If the dog kills someone other than the intended victim, then indemnities are due. If the dog is taken in to kill an unspecified person and it kills someone, then indemnities are due whether or not the owner gave a warning.

If, however, a person keeps a dog with no intention to harm anyone and the dog kills a person, then, if the owner kept it in for a justifiable reason, indemnities are due only if a warning had been given to him by the ruler or other authority before the killing. Otherwise, the person is not responsible. But, if he keeps the dog for some unjustifiable reason, he is liable for damages whether or not he was warned about the dog since he knew that it was vicious.

b. *For bees and birds*

Some jurists argue for liability in the case of bees that consume other people's fruit. Diverting the bees from other people's property is not required according to some commentators, but it is required by others if the damage arises from what *al-fatwa* (religious council) specifies.[11]

c. *For other harmful animals*

It is stated in *Bada'i al-sana'i*: "If a snake or a scorpion is thrown on a road and it bites someone, then the person who threw it is liable, because his act of throwing was intentional unless the snake or scorpion moves from the place in which it was thrown to another." Al-Ramli was asked about a man who borrowed a bull knowing that it had a tendency to gore. The man drove the bull which gored another person to death. Is the liability then on the borrower of the bull, the lender, or both, or neither? He answered that the borrower's clan is liable for indemnity because there was neglect on the part of the borrower in letting the bull go. Such a bull must be tied up.[12]

RESPONSIBILITY AND THE MENTAL STATE

Responsibility ultimately means the assumption of the consequences for one's act. For a person to be criminally responsible, he must be of the age of discretion and be able to exercise choice in what he does. In addition, he must be at fault. Fault is the basis of criminal responsibility. If no fault is found, a person cannot be held responsible for what has happened. Fault may be determined from deliberate intent, which is called criminal intent, or it may arise unintentionally as through a mistake.

---

[11] 5 IBN 'ABIDIN, HASHIYAH 427.

[12] 4 FAKHR AL-DIN AL-RAMLI, *al-Fatawa al-khayriyah*, 43 (Cairo: Matba'at Bulaq, 1854); and 7 AL-KASANI, BADA'I' AL-SANA'I' 273.

CRIMINAL INTENT

Intent in criminal matters is the inclination of one's will toward the performance of a punishable act or toward a punishable omission. Thus, in this respect criminal intent does not differ as between Islamic and positive law. Intent as it has been described by jurists can be divided into two categories, general and specific intent.

Some commentators say that the Imam Malik does not require specific intent for murder because he does not recognize murder with quasi-deliberate intent. For him, there are only two types of homicide: premeditated murder and accidental homicide. He considers any act done with the intention of aggression to be premeditated murder even if the killing of the victim was not intended. General intent alone is sufficient, according to Malik, to establish a crime of premeditated murder.[13] However, it is arguable whether Malik's position on murder, that it is either premeditated or accidental, means that he fails to recognize specific intent. This becomes clear from the following text:

> In some cases of deliberate intent no retaliation is due as in the case of those wrestling with each other and those throwing at each other in a game or one person tripping up another person in play. In cases like these, the clan pays a fifth of the accidental indemnities. If, however, in doing the above the persons involved intended to kill, then retribution is due.[14]

What this means is that the deliberate intent for which no retribution is due does not include specific intent. And since this is the case, it is not punishable by retribution since retribution requires intent to kill. This can be better understood from what was mentioned in *Hashiyat al-Dasuqi on al-sharh al-kabir*:

> A father does not murder his son if he deliberately kills him, so long as he did not intend to kill him. A father shall not be sentenced to death for killing his son even if he killed him deliberately unless he intended his death. Beating, as far as the necessity for retribution is concerned, is like strangling or withholding of food or drink whereby death is intended. If the victim dies, retribution is exacted. If his intention was merely to torture, then indemnity is required.

Similarly, the mother who intentionally refrains from nursing her child until he dies will be sentenced to death; otherwise, her clan pays indemnities.[15] The Malikites then distinguish cases of a parent intentionally killing a child from those where the parent kills his child unintentionally as when, for example, the parent throws a piece of iron or a sword at the child intending only to discipline the child. In this case the father is not sentenced to death. But the father who intends to kill his son would be sentenced to death if he uses any instrument, even a stick.

PRACTICAL APPLICATION

1. With respect to crimes infringing upon the security of the state, juriscon-

---

[13] 'ABD AL-QADIR 'AWDAH, AL-TASHRI AL-JINA'I AL-ISLAMI MUQARANAN BIL-QANUN AL-WAD'I [ISLAMIC CRIMINAL LEGISLATION COMPARED WITH POSITIVE LAW] 414 (Cairo: Maktabat Dar al-'Urubah, 1960).

[14] 8 AHMAD IBN IDRIS AL-QARAFI, AL-DHAKHIRAH 387 (Cairo: Matba'at Kulliyat al-Shari-'ah, 1961).

[15] 4 AL-DASUQI COMMENTARY 215, 237.

sults distinguish between the traitor, whether Muslim or non-Muslim, and the foreign spy. The Muslim and the non-Muslim traitors are both executed if they had specific intent—the intent to harm a Muslim. But if their criminal intent was general, that is, does not include harming a Muslim, they are punished by some means other than death. As for the foreign spy, he is executed for spying and for perjury whether his intent was general or specific. In short, the criterion for killing or not killing is intent. If the traitor's intent is specific, he is sentenced to death. If it is general, he is not sentenced to death, but receives some lesser punishment, unless he is an alien in which case he is sentenced to death no matter what his intent was.

2. The crime of infringing upon the security of the state from within is called in Islam *al-baghi*, and those who commit it are called *al-bugha(t)*. They are believers who rebel against the authority of the Imam and seek to overthrow him because of their contrary views. They may be so powerful that an army may be needed to supress them. This crime requires specific intent, but one which must be made public.
3. The crime of bribery requires a specific criminal intent on the part of the person offering the bribe. It is a promise of payment or the actual payment with the intent that the receiver do something or refrain from doing something in return for the payment.
4. The crime of apostasy is to some extent similar to the crime of attempting the destruction of the social system in western jurisprudence—*e.g.*, by anarchism or other destructive ideologies—since both influence society. For this to be a crime, a specific criminal intent must be present. The apostate must have the intent of becoming an infidel. The intent in such a crime is that of practising apostasy. Thus if a person burns the *Qu'ran* in order to heal a sick man as conjurers do, he is not considered an apostate.
5. The criminal intent in a premeditated murder is the intent of bringing about death. The texts in Islamic jurisprudence are so contradictory in this respect that some modern jurists believe that some schools of thought do not insist upon premeditation to kill, and they cite text written in support.[16] From *al-Khirshi*:

> The meaning is as follows: the condition of murder requiring retribution is that the murderer should deliberately have the intent of striking. That is he has the intent of bringing about the death. The intent to kill is required only in the original crime. If the intent is to strike with something that usually kills and the victim dies from the blow, then retribution is due. Similarly, if the intent is to strike with something that does not usually kill and the victim dies from the blows, then retribution is also due.[17]

[16] Ahmad Muhammad Ibrahim, Al-Qisas 65 (Ph.D. dissertation, 1944).

[17] 7 MUHAMMAD IBN 'ABD ALLAH AL-KHIRSHI, SHARH AL-KHIRSHI 'ALA MUKHTASAR KHALIL 7 (Cairo: al-Matba'ah al-Amiriyah, 1897).

From *Takmilat fath al-qadir*:

> Because deliberateness is the intent, a conclusion to this effect can only be reached upon evidence which is the use of the deadly weapon in which case the perpetrator will be said to have intent.

RESPONSIBILITY FOR CRIMES OF MURDER BY POISONING

Jurists disagree concerning cases where a person gives a deadly poison to another who dies thereby. The Hanafites believe that if someone serves poisoned food to another, the person is not liable for the victim's death so long as the victim had taken the food voluntarily. The reason they give is that the victim had a choice in eating the poisoned food. But the perpetrator must be punished because he has committed at least a crime of *Ta'azir*. Had the perpetrator fed the victim the poison himself, an indemnity would have been imposed.

According to al-Shafei, Ahmad and Malik, such a person is subject to retribution. Ibn Hazm believes, however, that neither retribution nor indemnities are required of him or of his clan unless he had forced the victim to eat, in which case retribution is due. The disagreement is due to what occurred in the prophetic traditions where a Jewish woman poisoned a ewe and offered it to the Prophet hoping to kill him. The Prophet and some of his friends ate from it and one of his friends died. So the Prophet was asked: "Shouldn't we kill her?" He said: "No." This supports the argument that no indemnities are due from a person who poisons another's food and serves it to him in the hopes of killing him.

In another version attributed to Abu Hurayra, the Prophet sent for the Jewish woman and asked her: "What made you do what you did?" She said: "If you were a prophet, it would not have hurt you; if you were a king, I would have relieved the people of you." So the Prophet issued his order and she was executed. Disagreement among jurists stems from those different versions of the *Hadith*.[18]

Jurists also disagree as to whether retribution is to be carried out by the use of the sword or by using the same method of poisoning as the murderer used. The use of the sword in the execution is preferable.[19]

RESPONSIBILITY IN ABORTION

If a person hits a woman so as to cause an abortion or if she aborts the fetus herself by using medicine or some other means, responsibility for harm to the abdomen due to the beating is unrestricted. Even if the defendant hits her head or if she treats her vulva, they are held liable in both cases. If someone yells at a woman and the fetus is aborted, he is not liable. But if he threatens her with beating, he is liable. The difference is that if a woman aborts due to someone's threats, that person is the source of the act and so he is held responsible. If the abortion is due to someone's yelling, it is her own fear that leads to the abortion.

---

[18] For further detail *see* BAHNASSI, AL-MAS'ULIYAH AL-JINA'IYAH FI AL-FIQH AL-ISLAMI [CRIMINAL RESPONSIBILITY IN ISLAMIC LAW] 138 (Cairo: Dar al-Qalam, 1961).

[19] 19 AL-DASUQI COMMENTARY 236.

Islamic law in this respect is not identical to secular laws in that Islamic law avoids the requirement that the perpetrator have the intent to cause an abortion.

RESPONSIBILITY IN CRIMES OF BATTERY

General criminal intent is sufficient in these crimes no matter how different they may be. We must, however, not confuse intent with motive. Criminal intent is considered to be present whenever a perpetrator commits an act of battery knowing that his act will affect another person's physical integrity. No consideration is given to motive.

According to Islamic jurisprudence, a physician is not held responsible if he was granted permission to give treatment by the guardian of the patient. If he has permission from the guardian to treat the patient but is incompetent, then he is held responsible for any mistake. He is also held responsible for premeditation if he has the intent to harm the patient. The burden of proof is on the plaintiff.

CRIMINAL INTENT IN MONETARY CRIMES

Embezzlement can only be established if there is an intention of unlawful possession. This is the specific intent which constitutes the requisite criminal intent. For a crime of theft, the hand is severed. However, theft and betrayal of trust must be distinguished, as in betrayal of trust the intention is to cheat or to possess something in order to permanently deprive its rightful owner of it. Thus, the hand is not cut off in that case.

TYPES OF INTENTIONALITY

1. *Specific intent*

   A perpetrator is said to have specific intent if he intends a definite result as, for example, if he wants to kill someone and does so. Such a person is punished for premeditated murder. In a case of nonspecific intent, the perpetrator commits an act which leads to a number of results all or some of which were intended by the perpetrator without any discrimination. For example, if a person throws a bomb into the middle of a crowd, he definitely knows that it will kill some and injure others even though he had not intended harm to any specific persons. In Islamic jurisprudence we find that only some jurists believe that the defendant should be punished for his nonspecific intent.

2. *Probable intent*

   Even though Muslim jurists do not mention the theory of probable intent, their collective views would establish one of the most modern theories dealing with this problem. Thus, for example, we read from al-Mughni:

   > If someone deliberately creates a hole in a ship loaded with people—an act which usually sinks a ship—and if those aboard the ship die in it because they are in a deep sea or because they cannot swim, retribution is due on that person if someone for whom retribution is due had been killed. He is also liable for the ship as well as what it carries in terms of money and people.[20]

---

[20] 8 MUWAFFAQ AL-DIN IBN QUDAMAH, AL-MUGHNI 345 (Cairo: Matba'at al-Manar, 1921).

Ibn Abidin has further suggested that the intent to kill is not a precondition for the murder to be considered premeditated. If the offender sought to injure only a man's hand (*i.e.*, had not intended to kill) and injures his neck (*i.e.*, the man dies), then the murder is premeditated; but if he injures another person's neck (*i.e.*, someone else dies), then it is a case of accidental homicide. From *al-Sharh al-Kabir* by al-Dardir:

> A crowd not conspiring against one person would be sentenced to death if they beat him deliberately and unjustly and he dies immediately or is carried away while unconscious and remains so until he dies. A group conspiring to kill or beat someone is also sentenced to death on the basis that they all intended the beating even though only one of them dealt the fatal blow, since if it were the case that the particular perpetrator had not dealt the blow, surely one of the other non-perpetrators would have dealt it.[21]

Thus even though one had not dealt the blow, he had intended the death of the victim, and, therefore, it must have been part of his probable intent that another's aggression with his consent would lead to the death. He would, therefore, be responsible for premeditation for the murder committed by another. It is a fiction that allows the court to reach the result of imposing criminal responsibility. This is analogous to the concept of being an accessory to a crime in western jurisprudence.

3. *Criminal intent as to degree of premeditation*
Jurists speak in terms which almost assume premeditation or deliberation even though it was never indicated. A Muslim shall not be killed for a slave or a non-Muslim (*al-dhimmi*) except in the case of assassination (*al-ghila*). This is murder in order to take the victim's money whether the murder was committed by stealth as, for example, if the perpetrator lures the victim to some place and kills him there to take his money, or if the murder is committed in the open in such a way that help could not have been sought. The latter, however, may be called *hiraba*. Thus, the Imam Malik has said: "In these cases there is no pardon and no reconciliation. The reconciliation of a subject is rejected and judgment concerning the case is left up to the Imam."[22]

RESPONSIBILITY FOR MISTAKE

It is appropriate to waive Divine Right if a violation occurs as a result of a person's mistaken interpretation. Mistake constitutes grounds for doubt as far as punishment is concerned so that the mistaken person would not be held guilty and would not be subject to legal punishment. For example, if a woman other than his wife is brought to a man on his wedding night and thinking she is his wife, he has sexual intercourse with her, the man would not be legally punished nor would he

---

[21] 4 AHMAD IBN MUHAMMAD AL-DARDIR, AL-SHARH AL-KABIR 217 (Beirut: Dar al-Fikr, n.d.). Non-conspirators are those who do not agree to participate with or aid others in committing a crime.

[22] The view of Ahmad ibn Hanbal is similar to that of Abu Hanifa and al-Shafei. *See* 9 IBN QUDAMAH, AL-MUGHNI 235. For Malik's view *see* Ibn Sahnun's version of 11 MALIK, AL-MUDAWWANAH AL-KUBRA 230 (Cairo: Matba'at al-Sa'adah, 1940).

be considered to have committed adultery; and so he is not punished by retribution (*Quesas*). Similarly, if a man sees a person far away and thinking it is game, he shoots and kills him, the man is not considered to have committed premeditated murder and retribution is not due from him. Mistake, however, is not an excuse as far as the rights of people are concerned (as opposed to the rights of God). A person who makes a mistake is liable for his aggression if he accidentally causes damage to another's property as, for example when he sees an object far away and thinks it is wild game but it is in fact a ewe which belongs to someone else. Indemnity is due for a mistake because a person's rights are affected.[23]

If a mistake is committed against something other than a human being, then the defendant is required to pay a fine (*al-'arsh*). If the fine due comes to or exceeds half the tenth of the indemnity due for a male, which is one tenth that due for a female, the fine is paid by the clan. The clan, however, does not pay anything below that amount as it does not pay for what is required in a crime against non-humans. This would be paid out of the perpetrator's property.[24]

REASONS VACATING RESPONSIBILITY

If one of the three elements of a crime, the physical, the mental or the legal element, is not present, then there is no responsibility and no punishment. The reasons that vacate or mitigate responsibility are provided in Islamic law. These include (1) reasons for permissibility, which encompass the use of one's right, the performance of a duty and self-defense, and (2) reasons for withholding punishment–cases of insanity, unconsciousness, coercion, necessity and infancy.

REASONS FOR PERMISSIBILITY

1. *The Use of One's Right*

Perhaps the best example in this category is a husband's disciplining of his wife. This matter is governed in Islamic law by God's words: "As for those from whom ye fear rebellion, admonish them and banish them to beds apart, and scourge them. Then, if they obey you, seek not a way against them."[25] Jurists agree that this right is restricted by two conditions for which the husband's failure to comply renders him an aggressor. The use of the right to discipline must conform to the wisdom behind this legislation since it is a means of reforming the wife. This means would not have been prescribed if there was any doubt as to its effectiveness. Some permissible harm may befall the wife as a result of the disciplining. However, excessive harm is prohibited.

If the husband exceeds his legal right so that his beating leaves marks, he is held responsible on both criminal and civil grounds, depending on the severity of the injury, and is severely restrained (by *Ta'azir*) depending on the wife's

---

[23] 'ABD ALLAH IBN AHMAD AL-NASAFI, KASHF AL-ASRAR FI SHARH AL-MANAR 99 (Cairo: al-Matba'ah al-Amiriyah, 1886).

[24] *Id.* 2:90.

[25] QUR'AN, *Surat al-Nisaa*, IV:34. (*Nushuz* is disloyalty or violation of marital duties.)

condition.[26] Also, the wife who is harmed has, according to the Imam Abu Hanifa, the right to ask for a divorce. According to the Shafi'i, if a husband mistreats and injures his wife, for example, by beating her for no cause, and if he ignores the judge's warning, then the judge may separate them until the husband agrees to treat her fairly. The husband remains obligated to support her during this period.

2. *Disciplining the Young*

It is basic to Islamic law that the father, the grandfather, the guardian, and the instructor, be he a teacher or a master of a trade, have the authority to discipline a minor. If the father or the guardian beats a boy and he dies, jurists disagree as to the responsibility of the father or guardian. According to Imam Abu Hanifa, he is liable because in disciplining, murder is not intended. However, according to al-Sahiban, he is not liable because the act is legal just as if the Imam restrains a person and the person dies.

If the instructor beats the boy and the boy dies, then, if the father or guardian had not granted permission for the beating, the instructor is liable as an aggressor. If permission had been granted for the beating, then he is not liable. But if the instructor beats the boy unjustly for a purpose other than disciplining or if he oversteps the usual bounds of disciplining, he is liable for whatever injury he causes.

As for the mother, jurists disagree as to the consequences of her beating her son for the purpose of discipline. Abu Hanifa says that she is liable. Others say she is not. Still others say she is liable because the beating has been inflicted upon a person over whom she has no authority.[27]

3. *Injuries in Sports*

Islam encourages participation in sports. However, the law will impose responsibilities in this context too. For example, we find in *al-Dhakhira* by al-Qarafi the Malikite:

> Among the premeditated acts are those for which no retribution is due as is the case of the wrestlers or those shooting at each other in play or one person tripping up another in play. For such acts, one fifth of the indemnity for accidental homicide is due from the clan. If, however, in doing so they have the intent to kill, then retribution is due.
>
> If one of them does that in play and the other was not playing and does not throw at him, then no retribution is due. This has been said by Malik, and it was reported of Abd al-malik that he said this is like an accidental homicide.[28]

If the game involves horseplay, then responsibility is total. It was mentioned in *Tabsirat al Hukkam*:

---

[26] MAWLA KHUSRAW, DURAR AL-HUKKAM (Cairo: al-Matba'ah al-Wahbiyah, 1874); II: 77 and 5 IBN 'ABIDIN, HASHIYAH 295.

[27] 8 MUHAMMAD IBN HUSAYN AL-TURI, TAKMILAT AL-BAHR AL-RA'IQ, (Cairo: al-Matba'ah al-Ilmiyah, 1891) 293.

[28] AL-QARAFI, AL-DHAKHIRAH, 387.

> In *Mukhtasar al-Wadiha,* Asbagh said: "If a man throws a poisonous snake onto another, then the one who threw the snake is sentenced to death if the snake kills that other man." And his statement: 'I was playing because they know what is in their hands,' was rejected.[29]

4. *The Performance of One's Duty*

The performance of one's duty may require certain acts that carry with them different responsibilities as where a physician treats a patient or someone rescues a drowning man. The rule of Islamic law on this matter is, according to Malikism, that there is no responsibility on the part of the doctor or the person who performs circumcision if they treat their patient and he dies as a result. If they were knowledgeable and made no mistake in what they did, none of them is liable for payment, nor is the clan liable for payment. If, however, any of them has made a mistake in what he did and if he is knowledgeable, then indemnities are due from his clan. If he was not knowledgeable, he is punished.[30] Ibn al-Qasim and Malik differ as to whether the indemnity is to be paid out of the defendant's own money or that of his clan.

Concerning the rescue of a drowning man, it stated in *al-Dhakhira* by al-Qarafi:

> Ibn Qasim said: If in trying to rescue a drowning man you fear for your life and you let him go, then you are not liable. If in teaching someone to swim you fear for your life and let him go, you are liable for his indemnity but you are not liable for him just as in the case of the drowning man. If someone falls into a well and asks you to lower a rope for him and you try to pull him up but when it proves too much for you, you let him go and the man dies, then you are liable for his death.
>
> Al-Qarafi further states: If you hold a rope for a man in a well to hold on to and the rope breaks, then you are not liable because it is not your doing. If the rope slips from your hand, you are liable.[31]

5. *Self Defense*

Self-defense is a person's natural right, and its legality has been approved in Islam since ancient times. According to Islamic law, self-defense that vacates one's responsibility is subject to several conditions:

1. The occurrence of an act which is considered a crime against a person or property
2. The use of force necessary only to repel aggression
3. The impossibility of relying at the crucial moment on protection by public authorities.

First, the act in question must involve a crime against oneself or one's property, or against another person or his property, or against honor. This is

---

[29] 2 IBN FARHUN AL-YA'MURI, TABSIRAT AL-HUKKAM FI USUL AL-AQDIYAH WA-MANAHIJ AL-AHKAM 167 (Cairo: al-Matba'ah al-Bahiyah, 1882).

[30] 4 AL-DASUQI, HASHIYAT AL-DASUQI 26-26; 7 ABU AL-WALID AL-BAJI, AL-MUNTAQA: SHARH AL-MUWATTA' 76 (n.p., 1912).

[31] 8 AL-QARAFI, AL-DHAKHIRAH, 366.

based on what Sa'id ibn Zayd relates that the Prophet has said: "He who fights to protect his family or property and is killed is a martyr." If a man seizes another's goods, you may kill him in order to retrieve the goods and return them to their rightful owner. The same principle has been expressed by Abu Hanifa. Concerning the thief who takes someone's goods, he said: "You may pursue him until you kill him if he does not return the goods." Muhammad said: "Abu Hanifa had said about the thief who breaks into houses that killing him is permitted."

Some jurists do not require the amount of the thing stolen or about to be stolen to reach the minimum value required for amputating the hand, although the contrary is the more prevalent opinion. As for honor, Ahmad said: "Concerning a woman who, in protecting herself, kills a man as he tries to take her against her will, if she knew that the only thing he wanted is to take her so she kills him to protect herself, she is not liable."

Second, the force used must be only that necessary to repel aggression. If an armed man enters a house and the person in the house orders him to leave but he refuses, the person has the right to beat him with whatever makes it easiest for him to drive off the intruder. Thus, if he knows that the intruder can be repelled by the use of a stick, then it is not justifiable for him to beat the intruder with a piece of iron because to do so would amount to the use of excessive force. If the intruder escapes, then he has no right to deal him a second blow because the intruder can do no further harm. If he strikes him with a blow that severs his right hand, and the man runs but he deals him another blow which cuts his leg, then he is liable by retribution or indemnity for cutting the intruder's leg because the intruder was in a situation where striking him was no longer justified. The victim cannot, in short, administer a beating once he repels the initial attack, for then the victim is viewed by the law as the aggressor. However, he is not liable for cutting off the intruder's hand.

Third, it must have been impossible to rely at the critical time on protection from public authority. It is mentioned in ibn 'Abidin:

> If the person being stolen from knows that if he yells at the thief, he would leave his property yet he still kills the thief, then retribution is required of him for killing him with no cause. This is like a person being usurped if he kills the usurper, he is required to pay indemnities on the ground that he could have righted the wrong by appealing to the Muslims and the judge[32]

REASONS FOR WITHHOLDING RESPONSIBILITY

Here the issue is the reasons for vacating responsibility, which are attributed to the personality of the perpetrator on the basis of his inability to choose or discriminate. A person is not held responsible under such conditions because one of the elements necessary for establishing criminal responsibility is necessarily missing. Reasons for withholding responsibility include:

1. insanity
2. unconsciousness

---

[32] 5 IBN 'ABIDIN, HASHIYAH, 383.

3. coercion and necessity
4. infancy.

1. Insanity

Insanity is a derangement in one's power to discriminate between what is good and what is bad, or in the ability to know such a choice exists. Insanity, whether from birth or later, deprives one of reason and the ability to discriminate and suspends perception. Insanity may be total; in other words, it may completely block one's rational and discriminatory capabilities and totally vitiate one's perception. This is called prolonged insanity. Insanity may also be interrupted (sporadic); that is, it may attack the person intermittently and if interspersed by lucid periods, during the periods in which the defendant is insane, criminal responsibility is vacated, but he is held responsible during those periods when he regains his sanity.

The law further recognizes the condition of feeble-minded and mentally retarded persons as those who are confused in speech and mismanage their affairs regardless of whether born with such a condition or whether it was brought about later due to some disease.[33] Emotionally and mentally disturbed patients, if they lose their sense of discrimination, also are not held responsible. If their loss of discrimination is total, as in the cases of epilepsy, then they are also relieved of total responsibility.

<u>The Status of Insanity</u>

Criminal responsibility is completely vacated in the case of a totally insane person, if he commits a crime for which the person must otherwise be held responsible—crimes like adultery, false accusation, theft or drinking of alcoholic beverages. Criminal responsiblity also would be vacated in cases of interrupted insanity if the person commits the crime during a period of insanity. If, however, he commits a crime while sane and then becomes insane, he should be punished for his crime. Insanity does not vacate responsibility in the following cases:

Insanity Before a Verdict The Hanbalis and the Shafi'is believe that insanity subsequent to a crime is not grounds for dismissing the case or suspending trial. The Malikis and the Hanafis believe that insanity prior to a verdict is grounds for suspending the trial until the person recovers from his insanity. This is because a person must possess legal capacity in order to be punished and an insane person does not possess this capacity at the time of the trial.

Insanity After the Verdict The Hanbalis and the Shafi'is believe that insanity subsequent to the verdict is not grounds for suspending its execution if the crime has been proved by evidence. But if the crime has been proved by confession, the verdict is suspended due to the defendant's insanity. This is because a person convicted of a legally punishable crime has the right to retract his confession at the time the verdict is executed. Insanity may prevent the convicted person from retracting his confession.

---

[33] *Id.* 294.

According to Malik, insanity is grounds for suspending the execution of a verdict unless the punishment is retribution. According to one view, the verdict is suspended in this case and is replaced with payment of indemnity and according to another view, the verdict of retribution is executed if requested by the executor of a blood feud.

According to Abu Hanifa, legal punishment is not administered in case of interrupted insanity because, in his view, if witnesses are disqualified after their testimony and before the execution of the verdict, punishment is not administered because it is fraught with doubts that might vacate legal punishment. It is, therefore, more reasonable that if the person to be punished is disqualified as far as his legal capacity is concerned, that punishment should not be administered. In the case of retribution, it is preferable, according to Abu Hanifa, that the verdict of retribution be changed to indemnity even though analogy (*Qiyyas*) necessitates retribution (*Quesas*).[34]

The Status of Mental Retardation

The rules applying to juveniles apply equally to the mentally retarded because, according to Islamic law, a juvenile in the early stage of his youth does not possess reason, thus, the comparison between an insane person and a juvenile. In the late stages of his infancy, the youth's reason is imperfect; hence, the comparison between the mentally retarded and a juvenile in these stages. Some jurists have said that it is not right to generalize about the mentally retarded person making him in all cases a discriminating juvenile. But what is right is that his actions should be judged according to his mental condition and the extent of his comprehension. If his ability equals that of a discriminating juvenile, he should be treated like a nondiscriminating juvenile. Thus, it is stated in *al Fatawa al-Hindiyya:*

> In *al-Muntaqa* it is mentioned that a man killed another and then turned into an imbecile. Witnesses testified to the murder while he was an imbecile. I prefer not to sentence him to death and to require the payment of indemnity out of his money. It is also thus *in al-muhit.*[35]

2. Unconsciousness

The crucial question here is how we punish a person who is unconscious or has no choice in what he does at the time he commits an act, if unconsciousness is due to any kind of drug, given to the defendant forcibly and unknowingly. Included in this is unconsciousness resulting from drinking different kinds of alcoholic beverages.

Intoxicants

Intoxication deprives a person of his reason. Al Hamawi has said that drinking alcohol veils the mind, but unlike insanity, alcohol does not destroy it. There

---

[34] *Id.* 198.

[35] 4 AL-FATAWA AL-HINDIYAH, 6.

are three views concerning actions committed by an intoxicated person. One view invalidates the acts of the drunkard whether or not he had an excuse in becoming drunk and regardless of the substance that intoxicated him. This view is held by ibn al-Qayyim, Al-Tahawi, al-Karkhi, Abu Youssef and Zafar among the Hanafis and al-Muzani and ibn Shurayh from the Shafi'i. According to ibn Hazm, no retaliation is due against an intoxicated person for damage he causes while intoxicated, nor are indemnities imposed on him, nor is he liable in any other way. He is imprisoned, however, until he desists from further harm and becomes sober.

Most jurists do not examine intoxication in itself but rather its causes, and whether it results from choice or by coercion. If intoxication is by choice and is due to a forbidden substance such as alcohol, then all of the acts of the accused are held to be valid so that he might refrain from breaking the law. If intoxication is due to coercion, then he is not held responsible for any of his acts. This is also true if intoxication is due to a permitted substance.

The third view looks at the matter from the standpoint of the intoxicated person's fitness and holds that intoxication due to a forbidden drink does not invalidate a verdict since the requirements that the person be of age and of reason are both met. The person is, therefore, obligated to assume all expenses and correct his behavior, and his acts would be considered to have been valid whether he had been coerced to drink or drank voluntarily. That is because the verdict is based on normal circumstances.

The view which seems to accord best with public interest is that an intoxicated person be held criminally responsible for what he does if he is intoxicated voluntarily, provided that punishment is executed after the effects of intoxication wear off.

Narcotics

A person may become unconscious by taking narcotics. To what extent would he be held responsible in such case? And what rules govern the taking of narcotics in Islamic law? Alcohol is a fluid which leads to quarrelsome and belligerent behavior. A drunk becomes more aggressive and easily enraged. Narcotics, by contract, are substances which render the mind inactive and ultimately destroy it; they also induce a prolonged state of lethargy. For those reasons, the views of jurists are divided along three lines.

It must be understood at the outset that the disagreement among jurists is not over the basis of punishment but rather as to imposing punishment on a person for taking narcotics in the same manner as for drinking alcohol or whether to impose it in accordance with *Ta'azir*. This is because the prohibition against taking drugs is explicitly stated in the text. Imam Ahmad Hanbal has said this in *al-Musnad* as has Abu Da'ud in his *Sunna* based on genuine transmission from Umm Salma, who said: "The Prophet, may God's prayers be on him, has proscribed all that intoxicates and numbs." The scholars also have said: "That which numbs is anything that leads to numbness of the limbs."[36]

---

[36]'Abd Allah ibn Ahmad ibn al-Baytar, al-Durrah al-bahiyah fi manafi' al-abdan al-insaniyah 146

Proponents of the first view hold that intoxication due to an anesthetic (*banj*) or any other type of narcotic requires legal punishment. The leading proponent of this view is ibn Taymiyya whose argument, as presented in *al-Siyasa al-Shar'a*, is:

> that legal punishment is required for the use of hashish made out of hemp leaves. He who smokes it is whipped as the one who drinks alcohol is. It is worse than alcohol in that it impairs one's reason and disposition so that one becomes effeminate and of suspect moral character and of other corrupt qualities.

Proponents of the second view contend that taking narcotics is forbidden but intoxication due to narcotics requires restraint (*Ta'azir*) rather than legal punishment. Al-Rafi'i said in *al-'At'ima* and *Bahr al-Madhhab* that mildly intoxicating plants are forbidden for anyone to eat, but legal punishment is not imposed on whoever eats it. We know of no disagreement in this respect.

The third view distinguishes between taking narcotics for medical reasons, in which case taking the necessary amount for the treatment is permitted. But if it is taken for pleasure, then it is forbidden, and he who takes it is then restrained (by *Ta'azir*), though not legally punished (by *Had*). However, it is worth noting that firstly, drinking is explicitly forbidden in the *Qu'ran* and is punished. Secondly, taking narcotics also is forbidden explicitly in the *Qu'ran*. There is, however, disagreement as to whether the punishment is legal punishment (*Had*) or restraint (*Ta'azir*). The importance of this question becomes evident if we assume the view that the penalty for taking narcotics is legal (*Had*) punishment. It would follow then that it should take on all the characteristics of legal punishment, the guilty individual is necessarily punished without the chance to be pardoned or to have others intercede for him.

If we assume, however, the view that the penalty for taking narcotics is restraint (*Ta'azir*), then the focus is upon the possibility of its being atoned for and pardoned by the ruler. This is not allowed in any way in cases of legal punishment (*Had*). Assuming this view, however, allows the positivist legislator to impose penalties in accordance with the act committed by the defendant. Thus, if the accused is a first offender, a penalty would be imposed on him which would be of a lesser degree than that imposed on a repeater. The judge also would be able to penalize narcotics dealers with such severe penalties as capital punishment or hard labor. This is the trend the contemporary positive laws follow.

Fainting

Fainting is regarded by Islamic law as a disease and not the loss of one's mind as with insanity. Fainting is one degree above sleep insofar as necessitating the delay of a verdict and the suspension of acts of worship. Fainting is valid as an excuse for waiving certain divine rights, unlike sleep which does not qualify as an excuse for waiving such rights, because fainting, as a disease, lessens strength.[37]

(n.p., n.d.). and 1 DA'UD IBN 'UMAR AL-ANTAKI, TADHKIRAT ULI AL-ALBAB WA-AL-JAMI' 78 (Cairo: al-Matba'ah al-Azhariyah, 1906); and 2 MAWLA KHUSRAW, DURAR AL-HUKKAM 70; and 5 IBN 'ABIDIN, HASHIYAH 170.

[37] 2 'ALI IBN MUHAMMAD AL-MAWARDI 1399.

Sleep

The law regards sleep as a diminution of one's awareness and outer senses, whereas one's inner senses do not subside during sleep. Furthermore, voluntary movements produced by one's intent and choice cease during sleep, unlike involuntary movements such as respiration or muscle spasm. A sleeping person is not held responsible for his actions or his behavior, but he is held responsible on civil grounds if his acts inflict harm on others.[38] The Prophet has said: "The pen is lifted from three [among whom a person asleep is mentioned]."

Forgetfulness

Forgetfulness is a state which involuntarily overpowers a person and results in a failure of memory. Forgetfulness is said to be a sudden state of ignorance. It is also said to be a person's ignorance of what he used to know due to learning too many other things. As such, it is not a disease. But, it is said also that it is a disease that affects the mind preventing memories from registering therein. Forgetfulness has two meanings:

1. To omit something due to bafflement and inattention as mentioned in *Hadith:* "The Almighty God has exempted by people from punishment arising from mistakes, forgetfulness and that which they were forced to do."
2. To leave something out deliberately and intentionally in which case there is total responsibility.

3. *Coercion and Necessity*

Coercion

Legally, coercion is the compelling of someone to do something by suggestion and threat. Coercion to remove responsibility, is governed by certain conditions. They are:

1. The compellor must be capable of carrying out the threatened harm. That is why Abu Hanifa says that coercion can only be carried out by a person in power (authority).
2. The compelled person must believe that if he does not comply with the compellor's demands, the harm promised by the compellor will be inflicted upon him.
3. The coercion does not look to the violation of property or other legal rights such as the selling or damaging of one's property or the damaging of someone else's property or accusing him falsely, or drinking alcohol, or committing adultery.
4. What the person is being compelled to do must injure one's self or unlawfully induce a sense of fear.

---

[38] MAS'UD IBN 'UMAR AL-TAFTAZANI, SHARH AL-TALWIH 'ALA SHARH AL-TAWDIH LI-MATN AL-TANQIH 269 (Cairo: Dar al-Kutub al-'Arabiyah al-Kubra, 1909).

Rules Governing Coercion

Murder According to Abu Hanifa, Muhammad and a statement by al-Shafei, no retribution is due on the compelled person, but he is restrained (by *Ta'azir*). Retribution (*Quesas*), however, is due on the compellor. Abu Youssef believes that retribution is not due on either but indemnity is due from both. According to Zafar and another statement by al-Shafei, retribution is due on the compellor but not the person compelled. Finally, a third statement by al-Shafei, as supported by Malik, suggests retribution is due on both.

Adultery If a man or a woman is forced to commit adultery, no legal punishment is imposed on either, provided that the coercion was total.

Apostasy If a person is totally coerced into drinking alcohol, whether by threat, beating, or by having his mouth opened and alcohol poured down him, he should not be subjected to legal punishment. If however, it is a case of partial coercion, then legal punishment is due, because partial coercion does not change the nature of the act from what it was before the 'coercion.' Hence, it does not require a change of sentence.

Theft Similarly, legal punishment should not be imposed on a person totally coerced into stealing.

Coercion into Confessing to a Crime

In Islamic jurisprudence, there are two views concerning the validity of a coerced confession. The first view holds that a confession coerced by beating or the like is invalid, on the basis of what has been related by Sa'id about Umar, namely, that a man can no longer be entrusted with his own self if you starve him, beat him, or tie him up. Ibn Shihab said about a man who confessed after he was compelled by whipping: "He is not subject to legal punishment."

The second view suggests that the coerced confession from a defendant known for his acts of inequity and immorality such as theft, highway robbery and murder is valid, because in this case beating him to obtain a confession is justifiable.

Malik found it objectionable that the ruler should trick a defendant by saying, "Tell me and you are immune," and not mean it. According to Malik, if a judge, a ruler or a representative of a ruler coerces someone into confessing to a crime by threatening to incarcerate, chain or beat him, the accused would not be liable at all, even if he is found to have the stolen items in his possession, because of the possibility that such stolen items may have fallen into his hands from somebody else. The same is true if he is compelled to confess to murder even if the body is discovered on his premises as in *al-Mudawwana*, because of the possibility that someone else might have murdered the victim there. So such a person's hand shall not be severed in the case of theft, nor will he be sentenced to death in the case of murder, unless he confesses theft or murder after the coercion is removed as in *al-Mudawwana*.[39]

---

[39] 8 MUHAMMAD IBN 'ABD AL-BAQI AL-ZURQANI, SHARH AL-ZURQANI 106-107 (Cairo: Matba'at Bulaq, 1873).

Necessity

Necessity is a state that makes a person violate the law in spite of himself to prevent an inescapable evil befalling him, even though it is in his power not to violate the law and allow the evil to befall him or someone else. Islamic *Shari'a* exempts such a person from penalty. Examples of this abound: "But if one is forced by necessity, without willful disobedience, nor transgressing due limits, then he is guiltless." "He has explained to you in detail what is forbidden to you—except under compulsion of necessity." "But if any is forced by hunger with no inclination to transgression, God is indeed oft-forgiving, most merciful." A person who must drink alcohol, therefore, is not punished if it is to ward off choking. Similarly, if a man or a woman is forced to commit adultery and the conditions for necessity obtain, neither is punished.

Examples of Necessity

Ibn al-Qayyim mentions some instances which constitute a proper case of necessity. A person sees someone's ewe or some other edible animal of his dying and so slaughters it in order to save the owner his money. Someone sees a flood pouring toward a house and hastens to tear down the wall to divert the flood so that the house will not be destroyed. Someone hires a boy and a gangrenous sore develops on one of the boy's limbs, so that if he does not cut off the limb, the gangrene will spread. If he amputates, he would not be liable.

4. Infancy

According to Islamic *Shari'a,* a child passes through three stages:

Prior to the age of discretion This stage extends from birth to the age of seven. In this stage, the law regards the child as non-discriminating. Like the insane person, he is considered unfit and is not held responsible if he commits an act which requires legal punishment or one which requires *Ta'azir*. But he would be held responsible on civil grounds as far as his money is concerned so that others may not be harmed by whatever harmful acts he might commit against others.

The age of discretion This is the period between seven years of age and the onset of puberty. It is determined by age, by the signs of puberty, or both. The child at this stage has the same status as a mentally retarded person in all rulings. Al-Zayla'i has suggested that premeditation on the part of a child and an insane person should be regarded as mistake, and its indemnity is to be paid by the clan. No penance is required nor is disinheritance since the mentally retarded is like a boy at this stage.

Al-Shafei has commented that premeditation at this stage is treated like ordinary premeditation. Therefore, indemnity is to be paid out of the child's money because premeditation is a form of intent which contradicts a mistake. Thus, the child is disciplined and restrained. And restraint (*Ta'azir*) is for something done intentionally and not by mistake. Retribution (*Quesas*) should have been required but is vacated due to doubt since the child is not fit for punishment. Yet, if a child at this age steals, though his hand is not severed, he must be held liable for the property he stole, and he is fit for pecuniary fine. For a murder, he is disinherited.

The stage of puberty If a boy or a girl reaches the age of puberty and is of sound mind, according to the rules, he or she can be held criminally responsible.

CONCLUSION (BY EDITOR)

Islamic jurisprudence has since its earliest time established detailed rules for criminal responsibility as illustrated above. While the examples may not always fit contemporary instances they nonetheless represent the application of principles which can very well fit contemporary needs.

It is interesting to note that the doctrinal basis for principles of criminal responsibility and their application while deriving from Islamic sources as discussed in other contributions in this book, are nonetheless the product of a historical evolution similar to that of the common law and which in the course of time acquired the force of precedent (*stare decisis*). Nothing, however, precludes the codification of these principles in the general part of a criminal code, thereby transposing into positive codified law that which is now diffused throughout the writing of numerous scholars whose works span hundreds of years.

HUDUD CRIMES*

Aly Aly Mansour

INTRODUCTION

Punishment is necessary to maintain the peace, security and stability of any society. All societies have penal laws, regardless of their level of development. The main purpose of punishment, however, must not be retribution but specific and general deterrence. The more effective the penalty is in fulfilling that purpose, the more successful it becomes in combating serious crime. This is a rationale for enforcing severe penalties for the more dangerous crimes, so that the severity of the penalty will prevent the recurrence of similar conduct.

What distinguishes the penalties of *Hudud* from crimes in other systems is their great effectiveness in combating serious crime, since they cause great physical pain as, for example, by flogging, or by leaving a permanent scar (in the case of amputating the hand), or through imposition of the death sentence. Because these penalties have a tangible effect, they are more fearsome to habitual offenders than are less severe penalties, like imprisonment, in which case criminals often become accustomed to the penalty itself. They become morally exhausted and lose all sense of responsibility. *Hudud* penalties are not meant to frighten Muslims but to prevent the growth of a climate favorable to the existence and spread of such crimes. Thus, the incidence of such crimes becomes the exception. The penalties of *Hudud* are only intended to deter those who have a tendency to commit crime, or those who are easily tempted. In the majority of cases, such people will not be restrained except by very severe penalties.

Crimes of robbery represent the most serious crimes against property, and these, in turn, are considered to be the worst because of their evil purposes and adverse consequences. The crime of robbery will lead, in most cases, to other crimes like homicide, to the extent that some robbers may kill close friends or family during commission of the primary offense. Professional robbers also may become experts in blackmailing and embezzlement, devising new methods to achieve their goals and using the stolen property to further other criminal ends such as prostitution and narcotics traffic. By severing the hand of the robber, Islam gets to the root of evil; it extracts the rotten seeds in order to purify and protect society and the individual from destruction. Those who protest amputation should consider the welfare of society, since the occasional use of that sanc-

---

*This contribution is excerpted from a larger contribution on the Religious Bases of Islamic Penal Legislation, and the application of these bases to the crimes of *Hudud*, *Quesas* and *Ta'azir*.

tion has proven to be an effective deterrent in Islamic societies. Those who contend that such penalties are excessively harsh must consider the harmful effects on both the individual and society. Such criticism must be temepred with the recognition that these penalties are essentially deterrent in nature and that they have effectively reduced the incidence of serious crime in Islamic societies.

God has explicitly forbidden adultery and has established a severe penalty, but only after allowing the Muslim man to marry two, three or four wives (provided however that he be fair and equal to each and all). Similarly, in forbidding robbery, God required the establishment of a public treasury of monies collected from *Zakat* (the religious tax on Muslims) and of proceeds collected from natural resources to help the disabled, the sick, the old and the poor. Such entitlements were not only restricted to Muslims, but were available to Christians and Jews—*ahl al-Dhimma* (people of the book)—living in Muslim countries, who in return paid another tax, the *Jizya*.

Islam does not sever the hand of the robber who is hungry or needy, for in this case the blame is attributed to the injustice of society or the ruler. Islam teaches that God is more merciful to us than we are to ourselves. A religion that commands that no animal should be left to die from hunger is *a portion* more merciful to humans. It is said that a woman went to hell because she kept a cat closed up until it died; and a man went to paradise because he took off his shoes and tied them with a rope which he suspended into a well to get some water for a dog that was dying from thirst. When asked whether people were blessed if they acted favorably toward animals, the Prophet replied affirmatively.

Thus, the *Hudud* penalties imposed by Islamic law are intended to preserve the peace, security and stability of society. Punishment also is an act of mercy to those who have a tendency to commit crime. If the penalty is not an effective deterrent, people will commit crime without fear and will encourage others to do so. If the penalty is severe but just, criminals will fear the consequences of their acts. When the chances for crime decrease, potential wrongdoers will forget altogether about crime, and channel their energies toward the improvement of their society. Thus, Islam has made it possible for individuals to satisfy their basic needs in an honest way and by legal means. Islamic society thereby guarantees a free and honorable life, and consequently, removes the incentive to crime. Islam established *Hudud* penalties to safeguard the institutions of society. The fact that Islam has set forth severe punitive measures for serious crimes is evidence of the great concern which Islam has for the proper conduct of the individual in relation to God and society. It is concerned not only for man's soul but also for the welfare of society.

By making penalties severe for the above mentioned crimes, Islam also intends that they be morally condemned apart from the religious motivation which Islam seeks to instill in its believers. This will also contribute to the suppression and elimination of criminal activity.

It is not asserted that the application of *Hudud* penalties will completely suppress crime. There is, however, a high probability that such measures will decrease criminal activity to a minimum. Crime will evade light in search of darkness, and consequently, it is hoped, will suffocate and vanish. There is a critical difference between crime that is rarely committed by weak and sick people who are unable to be socially restrained, and crime being publicly and openly committed with great frequency.

HUDUD CRIMES AND PENALTIES

Apostasy (Ridda) The penalty is set forth in the *Qu'ran* as follows:

> And whoever of you turns from his religion and dies disbelieving, their works have failed in this world and the next. Those are the inhabitants of fire: therein they shall dwell forever.[1]

Apostasy is to reject Islam by word, deed or omission. Turning against Islam by word is, for example, to deny the existence of God, the Prophets and the angels; or by rejecting any part of the *Qu'ran* or its principal teachings like prayer and alms-giving (*Zakat*). Rejecting Islam by deed is to act contrary to its teachings, as in the case of committing adultery. Rejecting Islam by omission is to refrain from doing an act required by the *Qu'ran.* In such a case the offender is considered an infidel. The prerequisite for committing an act of apostasy is to intend the act or omission with the awareness of the penalty. A person who commits apostasy is allowed a certain time to repent but the length of time is not agreed on by jurists. Some say three days, and others say it is left to the ruler's discretion. After this period lapses, if the offender fails to repent, the *Had* for *Ridda*, or death penalty, is imposed.

Transgression (Baghi) The punishment for transgression is defined in the *Qu'ran*:

> If two parties among the believers fall into a quarrel, make ye peace between them, but if one of them transgresses beyond bounds against the other, then fight ye all against him who transgresses until he complies, then make peace between them with justice, and be fair. For God loves those who are fair (and just).[2]

Jurists disagree on the definition of transgression and its prerequisites, but the general and common definition agreed upon by the majority refers to transgression as rising against the legitimate leader (*Imam*) by use of force (equivalent to treason and armed rebellion). The uprising could be groundless or it could be based on specific interpretation of certain rules which the uprising Muslims rely upon in their revolt against the ruler. These claims however and the conduct of the uprising participants are such that they compel the *Imam* to overcome them by force. The *Imam* however should not take the initiative and fight them unless he knows their arguments and calls on them to stop the uprising. If they refuse, he is allowed to fight them with armed force until they surrender or are defeated. If any one of the transgressors is killed in the fighting, he will be considered as having been punished by *Had*. Those who are unable to fight or those who surrender or are arrested should not be punished by *Had* but may be punished by

---

[1] *Surat al-Ma'eda* V:35
[2] *Surat al-Hujurat* XLIX:9

Ta'azir. Those who fight until subdued are subject to the death penalty as a *Had*. It must be noted however that if their claims are just and the *Imam* deviated from Islam then he is the transgressor, and the uprising participants will not be subject to punishment.

Theft Allah says:

> As to the thief, male or female, cut off his or her hands, a punishment by way of example, from God for their crime.[3]

The *Had* for theft is to sever the right hand of the thief. A requirement for such punishment is that the thief must commit the theft with clear intent to acquire the stolen property, without the consent of the victim. Also, he must carry the property away from the place where it is usually kept. The thief must also have broken into the safe or any other money container. Furthermore, the property stolen should be of value in Islam.

The penalty is cutting off the hand. There is no amputation of the hand for stealing property which is not valued in Islam, such as alcohol or pork. The value of the property stolen should reach the minimum value (*nisab*) in order to apply the penalty of amputation. If the value of the stolen property is less than the minimum, the thief should be punished by *Ta'azir*.

Jurists disagree as to the minimum amount of the property that must be stolen. Some say it is a quarter of a golden dinar or three silver dinars; others say it is ten silver dirhams, and still others say 40 dirhams. Such differences are due to the different interpretations of the value of a *mizan* (a certain monetary value), for the Prophet says in a *Hadith*:

> The hand of the thief should not be cut off except if the value of the property stolen is worth the price of *mizan*.

The hand should not be severed unless the stolen property is owned by others at the time of the theft, and if it is later learned that the property is owned by the offender, the penalty cannot be imposed.

The penalty of severing the hand involves a great deal of uncertainty and doubt. Islamic jurists have mentioned several cases in which this penalty was avoided or not applied. The rule holds that the penalty should not apply in case of doubt. In that case the thief will be punished by *Ta'azir* if necessary.

Highwaymanship (Haraba) This penalty is defined in the *Qu'ran* as follows:

> The punishment of those who wage war against God and his Apostle, and strive with might and main for mischief through the Land is execution, or crucifixion, or the cutting off of hands and feet from opposite sides or exile from the Land.[4]

Some Islamic jurists call *Haraba* either fatal theft or highway robbery. The offense occurs in any of the following situations:

---

[3] *Surat al-Ma'eda* V:38

[4] *Surat al-Ma'eda* V:33

1. The victim is only confronted but not robbed.
2. Property is forcibly taken from the victim.
3. The victim is murdered but not robbed.
4. The victim is murdered and robbed.

Jurists disagree as to whether these punishments are to be applied alternatively or applied differently according to circumstances. Amputating hands and feet from opposite sides is understood to mean the right hand and the left foot. Similarly, jurists have interpreted exile from the land to include imprisonment.

Adultery (Zena) The penalty for adulterers is flogging with 100 stripes for the unmarried and lapidation for the married person. The flogging of the unmarried person is based on the Prophet's saying:

> The woman and the man guilty of adultery or fornication, flog each of them with a hundred stripes. Let not compassion move you in their case; in a matter prescribed by God, if ye believe in God and the last day, and let a party of the believers witness their punishment.[5]

The stoning of the married person is based on the Prophet's *Hadith*:

> Take from me as for fornication. Flog both of them with 100 stripes and keep them away from Muslim society for a year. As for a woman and a man guilty of adultery, flog them with 100 stripes and stone them.

During his life the Prophet ordered the stoning to death of a man and a woman found guilty of adultery.

As a prerequisite for applying the *Had* of adultery *(Zena)*, the crime must be witnessed by four eyewitnesses or confessed to by the adulterer himself, who must give full details of the act. It is nearly impossible to satisfy the prerequisite for eyewitnesses, unless the act is performed openly and publicly. In such case the *Had* penalty is not exacted unless the adulterer confesses to having committed adultery and requests the penalty. As with other *Had* penalties, in case of doubt, the penalty cannot apply. The evidentiary requirements are exacting.[6]

Slander (Badhf) This is based on the *Hadith* of the Prophet:

> And those who launch against chaste woman, and produce not four witnesses to support their allegations, flog them with 80 stripes and reject their evidence even after, for such men are wicked trangressors.[7]

The penalty for slander is flogging with eighty stripes. Slander in this sense means the false accusation of adultery, sexual abnormality, or defamation of a married Muslim, who is sane, pure and physically capable of committing what he is accused of. If the offender is impotent or weak, the penalty becomes *Ta'azir* and not slander.

Drinking Alcohol (Shorh al-Khamr) The habit of drinking wine prevailed among the Arabs when Islam appeared, so a complete prohibition was not im-

---

[5] *Surat al-Tur* LII:2

[6] *See* Salama, *General Principles of Criminal Evidence in Islamic Jurisprudence*, at 109.

[7] *Surat al-Baqara* II:219

posed immediately, but gradually. It is stated in the *Qu'ran*:

> They ask thee concerning wine and gambling. Say, in them is great sin, and some profit, for men. But the sin is greater than the profit.

At a later time another teaching was revealed in the *Qu'ran*:

> Ye who believe, approach not prayers with a mind befogged, until ye can understand all ye say.[8]

In order to act according to this teaching, it was impossible to drink wine at any time of prayer from dawn until sunset; consequently, people stopped drinking wine. Later Islam became more stringent in forbidding wine, as evidenced in the verse:

> O ye who believe, intoxicants and gambling, (idolatry), and divination by arrows, are an abomination and Satan's handiwork. Avoid them so that you may prosper. Satan's plan is but to create enmity and hatred in you, with intoxicants and gambling, and to hinder you from the remembrance of God and from prayer. Will ye not then abstain?[9]

Consequently, Muslims complied with the order of God and disposed of all the wine they had in their possession. Moreover, the following *Hadith*: "He who drinks wine, whip him," applied to all who drank wine in the days of the Prophet.

THE POLICY OF *HUDUD* CRIMES

The *Hudud* penalties are designed to avoid unreasonable limitations on individual freedom to the extent that they are "bodily penalties." They are executed for a limited duration and cause momentarily severe physical pain to the criminal and remain unforgettable to him so that in most cases, he will refrain from future criminal conduct. These penalties contrast with prison sentences which the criminal becomes accustomed to, having experienced them for long periods of time. Thus, imprisonment soon loses its deterrent effect and prisoners lose their sense of responsibility. Often after being released, they return to prison to serve a longer sentence. The execution of the "bodily penalty" allows the criminal to resume his work immediately thereafter; he is also not prevented from supporting himself and his children. Similarly, Islam teaches that to undergo the *Hudud* punishment is in itself an act of penance and remission after which the offender resumes his normal life as a good citizen. Living with one's family keeps it intact and united. This differs from imprisonment whereby the offender is deprived of earning a living for himself and his family, which in turn may force the family into crime because of need. Furthermore, the absence of the head of the family may lead the other members of the family into delinquent and criminal behavior. This is over and above the heavy expenses which governments have to incur to support prisons and prisoners. In addition, prisons dehumanize and corrupt the imprisoned and house habitual and experienced criminals alongside impressionable first offenders.

---

[8] *Surat al-Nisaa* IV:43

[9] *Surat al-Ma'eda* V:91, 92

Thus, despite the hope that imprisonment will have a beneficial effect on society in suppressing crime, law enforcement officials have failed to successfully combat violent crimes, while prisons serve as a training ground for youthful offenders.

By contrast, in Islamic society, the reliance on *Hudud* penalties brings about peace, stability and security. When these were abandoned in favor of foreign theories of penology, Islamic societies experienced increased crime rates. Thus, Islamic societies have wronged themselves by failing to use *Hudud* penalties. As stated in the *Qu'ran:*

> These are the limits ordained by God; so do not transgress the limits ordained by God.[10]

Also,

> And any who trangresses the limits of God, does verily wrong his own soul.[11]

A vivid present-day example of the effectiveness of the *Hudud* penalty against robbery is the case of Hijaz (in Saudi Arabia) which was at one time one of the worst places for violent crimes and highwaymanship. When Saudi Arabia adopted *Hudud* penalties for crimes against property and highwaymanship, such crimes ceased and criminal gangs were disbanded. Saudi Arabia is now an example of a country in which theft and highway robberies rarely occur. The number of amputations during the last 25 years (the reign of King Abdel Aziz Al Saud) was only 16. Comparing this number to the number of robberies which took place in Egypt, for instance, we find that 1038 robbery cases were sentenced to imprisonment in 1938, and in 1968 the number was approximately 30,000. This means that within 30 years the number of prison sentences for robbery increased 33 times. This is significant evidence suggesting that imprisonment may be an inadequate sanction. The only remedy may be to enforce the sentence of amputation ordained by God in the *Qu'ran*:

> Should he not know, He that created? And He is the One that understands the finest mysteries and is well-acquainted with them.[12]

Nevertheless, imprisonment should not be completely discarded as a criminal sanction, but its effectiveness in reducing or controlling major crimes is certainly an open question. Loss of liberty may be recommended if reasonably applied to specific crimes and to keep the criminal away from society, either for his incorrigibly bad conduct or to reeducate and rehabilitate criminals where crime is determined to be the result of mental illness and is not susceptible to the usual Islamic legal sanctions. Special care should be given to organize prisons and to the duration of sentences, so that they will fulfill the two purposes previously mentioned to the best advantage.

---

[10] *Surat al-Baqara* II:229
[11] *Surat al-Talaq* LXV:1
[12] *Surat al-Mulk* LXVII:14

QUESAS CRIMES

M. Cherif Bassiouni

The word *Quesas* means "equality" or "equivalence." It implies that a person who has committed a given violation will be punished in the same way and by the same means that he used in harming another person. Many western writers refer to *Quesas* as retaliation, which connotes more vindictiveness or revenge than the redress of a wrong by equalizing the harm.

There are five *Quesas* crimes:

1. Murder
2. Voluntary killing (similar to intentional killing or voluntary manslaughter)
3. Involuntary killing
4. Intentional physical injury or maiming
5. Unintentional physical injury or maiming

These crimes are defined both in the *Qu'ran*[1] and the *Sunna* and both establish two types of sanctions: retaliation, the principle of "talion," or *Diyya*, compensation.

For all practical purposes, crimes of *Quesas* fall into two categories, the first being homicide and the second, battery. Both intentional and unintentional homicide are included but the sanctions are different. The term killing includes unjustifiable and inexcusable homicides and for which there is either an element of intention or recklessness.

In contemporary non-Muslim criminal law these crimes would be considered murder, voluntary and involuntary homicides or manslaughter.[2]

The categories of battery include the infliction of intentional and uninten-

---

[1] Thus, for example, *Surat al-Baqarah* II:178 provides:

> O ye who believe! Retaliation is prescribed for you in the matter of the murdered; the freeman for the freeman and the slave for the slave, and the female for the female. And for him who is forgiven somewhat by his (injured) brother, prosecution according to usage and payment unto him in kindness. This is an alleviation and a mercy from our Lord. He who transgresseth after this will have a painful doom.

See also Surat al-Maeda V:45.

[2] *See* M.C. BASSIOUNI, SUBSTANTIVE CRIMINAL LAW 230-282 (1978).

tional bodily harm which result in serious or permanent injury to the person and thus is more than the technical physical contact of battery. It also includes maiming and other forms of physical disfigurement.

Quesas crimes are considered violations of the rights of individuals, which as a result provide the basis for the need to satisfy and compensate the victim or his family.

The sanctions prescribed for *Quesas* crimes are either the *Quesas*—that is the talion or the equivalent infliction of physical or bodily harm against the person who committed the act—or alternatively the payment of *Diyya* for compensation.[3] However, there are provisions in the *Qu'ran* concerning other penalties for the crimes of *Quesas*. These include, for example, exile, prohibition from inheritance and prohibition from the right to dispose of one's property by testamentary disposition.

To properly understand *Quesas*, one must consider the historical context of its divine revelation in the *Qu'ran*. It should be recalled that according to Islam, the *Qu'ran* continues the tradition of the Judeo-Christian teachings concerning the talion or the law of an eye for an eye and a tooth for a tooth.[4] The policy supporting the Judeo-Christian Islamic principle of talion is essentially twofold. First, it does not allow the victim or his family to exact a greater level of retribution against the person committing the violation or from his family. By so limiting the punishment, the infliction of greater vindictive harm upon the perpetrator of the crime or members of his famly or tribe is precluded. That practice proved very effective in preserving social order in the early period of Islam when there was no organized system of criminal justice whereby institutions and official personnel carried out penalties, which as a result were imposed by the victim or his family.

The second principle involves the equivalency of treatment inflicted on the offender.[5] The principle of *Quesas* as revealed in the *Qu'ran* was designed to limit the harm to be inflicted against certain wrongdoers to the equivalent harm

---

[3] The principle of *Diyya* is set forth in the *Qu'ran* in *Surat al Nisaa* IV:92, wherein it is established that if one person unintentionally kills another, the family of the deceased is entitled to compensation.

[4] *Surat al-Maeda* V:45 states:

> And we prescribed for them therein: The life for the life, and the eye for the eye, and the nose for the nose, and the ear for the ear, and the tooth for the tooth, and for wounds retaliation. But who so forgeth it (in the way of charity) it shall be expiation for him Who so judgeth not by that which Allah hath revealed: such are wrong-doers.

See also Surat al-Nisaa IV:94 and *Ayat* 135, which states:

> O ye who believe! Be ye staunch in justice, witness for Allah, even though it be against yourselves or (your) parents or (your) kindred, whether (the case be of) a rich man or a poor man, for Allah is nearer unto both (than ye are). So follow not passion lest ye stray (from truth) and if ye stray or deviate, Allah is ever knowing and informed.

[5] Thus, *Surat al-Baqarah* II:186 states:

> Allah asketh (or burdeneth) not a soul beyond what it can bear. It has (receives) what it has earned, and owes (only) what it has deserved. Lord do not condemn us for what we have forgotten or for what we have mistaken. Lord do not impose upon us the burdens you have imposed on those before us. Lord do not impose upon us that which we cannot bear..."

inflicted on the victim. Thus, one of the policies of *Quesas* is to limit the consequences of certain categories of wrongdoing. Furthermore, there are provisions in the *Qu'ran* indicating that the infliction of *Quesas* must be in the manner least likely to cause pain.[6] This principle satisfies the general tendency of vindictiveness on the part of the victim and members of his family and tribe while precluding unnecessary harm[7] This sense of vindictiveness also can be satisfied by the state or the community acting for and on behalf of the victim, as most contemporary systems of criminal justice aspire to do. There is, however, an alternative penalty called the *Diyya* (or compensation) to be paid by the wrongdoer or his family to the victim or his family.[8] The principle of *Diyya* finds analogous expression in the contemporary science of victimology, whereby victim compensation emphasizes decriminalization of the act and compensation of the victim as an alternative to the traditional punishment of incarceration.

As between retaliation and *Diyya*, the *Qu'ran* clearly indicates a preference for the *Diyya* and for forgiveness, which negates the application of *Quesas*. Such preference illustrates the bond of continuity between the temporal law and religion since the forgiver will be rewarded in heaven, which for the Muslim is a much greater reward than any other.[9] Thus, the combination of *Diyya* and forgiveness produces a powerful material and spiritual inducement to forsake *Quesas* as retaliation. Consequently, one must interpret the crimes of *Quesas* as being based on a general deterrence policy which recognizes the victim's sense of vindictiveness against his aggressor, while limiting the consequences of the penalty to the harm done and establishing the alternative remedies of victim compensation or outright forgiveness. It is, therefore, incorrect to consider individual retaliatory *Quesas* as a requirement of the *Shari'a*. On the contrary, the purpose of the *Shari'a* is to develop a system of criminal justice, which permits the establishment of institutions and the training of officials to carry out specific penalties. Such a view is expressed by several interpretations of the penalty of *Quesas*, all of which assert that the person carrying out the talion penalty have certain expertise and experience acquired through training.

In light of these general observations, it is significant that in several schools of jurisprudence, the crimes of *Quesas* for which the penalty of talion is applicable is limited to only intentional killings and intentional infliction of serious and

---

[6] *See* for Penalties.

[7] *Surat al-Baqarah* II:179:

> And there is life for you in retaliation, O men of understanding, that ye may ward off (evil).

[8] *Surat al-Nisaa* IV:58:

> Lo! Allah commandeth you to restore (or return) that which you have been entrusted with to their owners and if you judge between the people judge justly...

[9] *Surat al-Omran (or al-Imran)* III:159 states:

> It was by the mercy of Allah that thou wast lenient with them (O, Muhammad), for if thou hadst been stern and fierce of heart they would have dispersed from round about time. So pardon them and ask forgiveness for them and consult with them upon the conduct of affairs, And when thou are resolved,then put thy trust in Allah. Lo! Allah loveth those who put their trust (in Him).

permanent bodily harm and maiming, and that acts of unintentional killing and unintentional bodily harm or maiming are only subject to the payment of *Diyya*, or victim compensation.

Because of the seriousness of the talion principle, however, a variety of evidentiary requirements exist which must be satisfied before such punishment can be applied. These rules apply, for example, to the proof of the commission of the crime. If the crime cannot be proved in accordance with the evidentiary requirements established by the various schools of jurisprudence, then the talion punishment cannot be imposed, and only *Diyya* can be obtained. Again, one sees the operation of a criminal justice policy intended to make the application of talion more difficult and to encourage victim compensation. Facilitated by these evidentiary rules, the policy of limiting the application of equivalent harm to crimes of intentional killing and maiming (or serious bodily harm having permanent effects) recognizes the individual's right to vindication in such circumstances but does not promote broader application because of the adverse effects on the social order. Thus, other forms of involuntary killing, or even homicide arising from excessive use of force in self-defense and other forms of battery are not governed by the equivalency principle of retaliation but such offenses are punishable by payment of *Diyya*. It is also significant that if proof is insufficient and if the crime is less than that which is established for the crimes of *Quesas*, then the *Ta'azir* category of crimes could be applied.

Concerning rules of evidence, the Islamic system of criminal justice recognizes the concept of hierarchy of crimes and of lesser included offenses. Thus, for example, if in the area of *Hudud* crimes, a given crime may not be proved in accordance with the evidentiary requirements for any of the seven *Hudud* crimes, a lesser included crime or the penalty could be based on the principles of *Ta'azir* offenses which have less exacting standards of evidence, and for which the penalty is deemed to be rehabilitative and correctional rather than being purely punitive or mandatory in nature. The same is true for the crime of *Quesas*; thus, for example, a physical touching or technical battery not resulting in physical injury or maiming would not be considered a crime of *Quesas*, and therefore, the talion or *Diyya* is not imposed. Instead the *Ta'azir* penalty can be applied which can include a lesser penalty, or a principle of victim compensation, in accordance with the type of harm suffered.

Another important aspect of the principle of *Diyya*, though analogized herein with that of victim compensation, is that it is not regarded purely as victim compensation in the same manner as civil damages, for *Diyya* also has a punitive damage component which gives it criminal characteristics. It is akin to the setting of the fine for a particular crime, which is different from civil damages, except that in the case of *Diyya* the fine goes to the member of the victim's family rather than to the state. That is why the *Diyya* was fixed in kind by several juris consults.

It is also important to understand the criminal justice policy behind the concept which permits the state to become part of the process as a substit ute for a victim's family in order to secure from the perpetrator or his family the payment of the *Diyya*, and thereafter to provide the victim or his family with the necessary compensation. Thus, it is not necessary for the *Diyya* to be paid directly to the family of the victim or the victim exclusively. It can go through the state in the form of a fine provided that the state assumes the responsibility of being able to satisfy the needs of the family. Many authors have in fact also established a graduated system of *Diyya* by providing for mitigation and aggravation as determined by the intention of the perpetrator and the harm produced.

The principle of *Diyya*, according to certain authors, also embodies a concept of collective responsibility. There is, however, disagreement among the four major *Sunni* schools of Islamic jurisprudence as well as their subschools concerning responsibility for the payment of the *Diyya*. Because the principle of individual criminal responsibility is fundamental in Islam, there is an apparent inconsistency between that principle and that of making payment of *Diyya* the duty of family members of the perpetrator. In this situation, however, the overriding policy is one of social solidarity by which the family knows that it has responsibility for its members. Such a policy leads to a system of social compliance by having family members exert control over one another since all fear a certain financial responsibility for the deeds of each individual member of the family.

The various schools of Islamic jurisprudence have developed a variety of rules concerning, for example, who may carry out the penalty of *Quesas*, and on whom may it be inflicted, and who bears the duty of paying *Diyya*. The different schools distinguish between youthful offenders and youthful victims, between sane and insane persons whether victims or perpetrators, and between the physically healthy and the infirm. Such factors are considered in determining the rights and duties of the parties with respect to *Diyya*.

Islamic criminal law also prescribes rules for the use of talion. One such rule requires that a person shall not inflict a greater degree of harm than that which has been inflicted. Another requirement is that the person who inflicts the talion must have the knowledge and competence to be able to inflict it and that there be certain conditions which must be satisfied with respect to the person who inflicts it. It is noteworthy in this regard that some schools consider that the talion applies to the person who intentionally kills another even in a state of necessity or a state of coercion, thus eliminating those defenses as an excuse or justification for the killing of another. Another important rule is that if the talion would otherwise be applicable to a male who has killed a female, then because the male is usually the breadwinner of the family, the family of the deceased must pay the family of the executed perpetrator the equivalent of one half of the *Diyya* that would have been paid to them had he been killed and had they been entitled to *Diyya* for his death. Thus, the family of the perpetrator who is killed in retaliation is afforded an opportunity for economic survival after his death.

The various schools of jurisprudence distinguish between the killing of a male and female, the killing of an infant and an insane person, usually by providing for less harsh penalties in the cases of women, infants, insane persons or persons who are physically handicapped while placing the higher penalty for the killing or infliction of great bodily harm on the male Muslim. That distinction is justified by the traditional role of men as the economic foundation in Islamic societies.

Thus, the distinction is not justified in terms of absolute equality but rather in terms of criminal justice policy as it pertained to the times when the male Muslim enjoyed a more prominent social and economic role than he might in contemporary society.

Finally, talion law does not apply to a person who kills or maims another while in a condition of intoxication. Also, according to some schools talion is not applied if the individual who was killed was impious or was in the process of committing a particular crime, such as the situation of the paramour who is caught in the adulterous act by the husband. In that case, the killing of the paramour will not entail talion, but only *Diyya* on the part of the husband.

Most schools recognize that the right to talion belongs to the parents in ascendancies of the male of the victim. Thus, the father or grandfather has the right to demand talion or to forgive; other than that, the rest of the family is only entitled to agree on the payment of *Diyya*.

Concerning evidentiary requirements in general proof of the *Quesas* crime must be by at least one eyewitness, or by a confession, but there are many distinctions depending upon the various schools. The same general rules of confessing in the case of *Hudud* crimes apply here (which according to some with less rigidity) namely that the person who makes the confession does so voluntarily with understanding and discernment as well as out of his free will with no compulsion or coercion. Testimony in the case of homicides must be by two men, or by one man and two women and must be accompanied by the sermon or oath, if requested by the accused. The accused also can represent by oath that the facts asserted by the witnesses are not correct. Witnesses to collateral facts also can be obtained and their number will differ.

The following is a summary of the rules governing the crime of *Quesas*:

1. The accused must be an adult who is of sound mind and understanding at the time of the act, and the act must have been done intentionally.
2. The victim must be a male Muslim or a *Dhimmi* (Christian or Jew), or according to a majority of writers, a *Musta'amin* (a non-Christian or non-Jew who has entered the Land of Islam pursuant to a peace treaty or guarantee of safe conduct).[10]
3. Only the male blood relative (father or grandfather) in line of ascendancy can claim *Quesas* in case of the death of the victim. Only the victim can claim it in case of maiming, although some jurists require that the ascendant male parent agree.
4. A Muslim or *Dhimmi* cannot be executed or maimed (based on the equivalency principle) for the killing or maiming of someone not *ma'asoum* (immune), that is in the case of a *Kafir* (an idolater, not a *Musta'amin*), one who has abandoned Islam, or a rebellious Mulsim (one

---

[10] Bassiouni, *The Protection of Diplomats Under Islamic Law*, 74 AM. J. INT'L L. 609 (1980).

who commits the *Had* crime of rebellion as set forth under Islamic law).

5. According to most jurists, the *Had* crime must be inflicted with the sword (the weapon known in early Islam to be swiftest and least capable of inflicting more pain than necessary).
6. The infliction of the *Quesas* must be in the least painful manner.
7. As responsibility is personal, the death of the offender extinguishes all other claims.
8. Pardon or forgiveness extinguishes *Quesas* but not *Diyya*, according to some jurists, while others say it also extinguishes *Diyya*.
9. If the offender is a minor or is insane there is no *Quesas* but only *Diyya*, which a majority of jurists impute to his family. Others say that there also is no *Diyya* if the aggressor is a minor or insane.
10. Female Muslim victims or their families are only entitled to *Diyya*, the amount being equivalent to half that of the male. This rule exists by analogy to the rule that the male's inheritance is twice that of a female.
11. Reconciliation is encouraged between the parties even before adjudication, although the collectivity retains the right to impose a *Ta'azir* penalty.[11]
12. The *Diyya* is otherwise applicable to all other forms of killing and maiming and to those cases in which the requirements of *Quesas* are not met. The *Diyya* does not require that the victim or aggressor be an adult, sane or male. No *Diyya* is payable for one who is not a *ma'asoum* (see *supra* number 4).
13. An exception to *Quesas* is made in the case of *Quesama* (oath), that is when fifty members of the community, who are adult, sane and devout Muslims, swear that the accused could not have committed the crime.[12]

---

[11] For a discussion of the *Ta'azir* crimes, see Benmelha, *Ta'azir Crimes*, *infra*, at 211.

[12] *See* generally A.F. BAHNASSI, MADKHAL AL-FIQH AL-JINAI [AN INTRODUCTION TO THE JURISPRUDENCE OF ISLAMIC CRIMINAL JUSTICE] (1972); A. ODEH, AL-TASHRII AL JINAI AL-ISLAMI [ISLAMIC CRIMINAL JUSTICE] (1969).

TA'AZIR CRIMES

Ghaouti Benmelha

INTRODUCTION

The efficacy of individualized punishment has long been debated in criminal science. Every society reacts against the behavior of individuals which infringes upon public interest, and it is universally believed that acts which provoke social disturbance or which upset the harmony of social relations must be penalized. When an antisocial act is committed or attempted, its perpetrator must undergo a systematic investigation in order to determine if criminal responsibility exists. The judge who finds that certain conduct is criminal, must impose a sanction and in so doing he must consider the extent of the social harm, the seriousness of the offense and the personality of the delinquent.

In Muslim society, writers of the four major legal schools of thought have observed that Islamic criminal law is based on individualizing punishment.[1] The

---

[1] Islamic as well as western commentators have long recognized the system of individualized punishment under Islamic law. Thus, one scholar states: "Preceding Europe by twelve centuries, Islam acknowledges the criminal and personal liability of single individuals endowed with intellect." R. CHARLES, LE DROIT MUSULMAN (1965). Elsewhere he asserts that, "Muslims have revealed principles (the individualization of punishment through *ta'zir* or discretionary punishment) which our legislations did not know till long afterward." R. CHARLES, HISTOIRE DU DROIT PENAL (1963). Another commentator emphasizes that Islamic law:

> has further organized for the adult a system which might to a certain extent already be called a system of social defense. Aside from the seven major crimes which are defined and foretold by the Qur'an, a certain number of offenses were left to the discretion of the judge, who must bear in mind, all at once, the infraction committed, and circumstances under which the crime has been committed, and the personality of the delinquent.

M. ANCEL, LA DEFENSE SOCIALE NOUVELLE 44 (1971). Finally, an eminent Egyptian magistrate writes:

> It is my duty to observe that this great power of appraisal (or judgement) resting with the judge in matters of punishment, and the freedom of action granted him in choosing adequate penalties, have for a long time been sanctioned by the *Shari'a* which has established a system of punishing offenses without determined legal penalties. This system allows the judge to select an adequate penalty and to determine the quantum or amount of punishment. Far better, the *Shari'a* assigns the judge a role no less important than that of a legislator. In effect, it does not determine any penalty whatsoever for these offenses; instead it offers a general list of penalties such as banishment, expulsion, reprimand and seclusion. The judge is then authorized to determine the penalty which he finds appropriate to the circumstances of each case and to the status of the accused....

'Abd al-Salam, *The Social Aspects of the New Penal Code of the United Arab Republic*, REVUE DE SCIENCES CRIMINELLES ET DE DROIT PENAL COMPARE 101 (1967).

structure of that system is the subject of this article.

There are three categories of crime *(jara'im)* in Islamic criminal law. The first includes those crimes termed *Hudud*. These are enjoined in the *Qu'ran* with penalties laid down in the *Qu'ran* or in the teachings of the Prophet Muhammad. Both the constituent elements of the crime and the penalty incurred are specified therein, and these crimes are considered offences against God. The list includes apostasy, fornication or *zina*, (sexual relations outside marriage), adultery, blasphemy, and wine drinking. Also included are certain crimes against man, God's creation, as for example, false accusation of fornication, theft and brigandage.

Crimes classified within this first category are punished with penalties called *Hudud* (plural of *Had*). The term *Had* means a limit or constraint in the case established by Allah, to prevent the commission of acts which He has forbidden. These crimes are based on the belief that human nature is often tempted by situations which provide immediate gratification but obscure the rewards and threats of the hereafter. The *Had* is a legal or mandatory penalty in contrast to the discretionary penalty of *Ta'azir*, which is left to the assessment of the ruler or judge.

The second category is concerned more specifically with crimes against persons, including for example, voluntary homicide, mayhem and battery. The penalties for these infractions are called *Quesas*. They are determined also by law, but they are imposed in the interest of the victim and therefore can be substituted by the *Diyya* which is called today victim-compensation.

The two categories differ, however, because penalties which sanction a breach of obligations toward God (*Had*) may never be abrogated, either by the individual or by society through its duly constituted authorities, while in crimes of the second category *(Quesas)*, punishment may not be inflicted if the victim forgives the accused (usually after being compensated).

The third category is that of a *Ta'azir* which encompasses all offenses for which the *Shari'a* does not prescribe a penalty. Punishment of these crimes proceeds instead from the discretionary authority of the sovereign as delegated to the judge.[2]

Ta'azir has several connotations. The word literally means chastisement in the widest possible sense. In its legal sense, however, it signifies criminal punishment which is not legally fixed. Jurists consider *Ta'azir* discretionary correction, rehabilitation or chastisement. Al-Mawardi,[3] for example, defines *Ta'azir* as:

> punishment inflicted in cases of offenses for which the law *(Shari'a)* has not enacted written penalties. The rules relating to it differ depending upon who is inflicting it and upon whom it is inflicted. It has this point in common with written penalties: it, too, is a means of reprieve and repri-

---

[2] Some writers attempt to add to the category the same dual distinction of penalties restraining those acts which infringe divine right and those which violate the rights of men, by maintaining that those offenses which do not fulfill certain conditions in the first two categories fall within the scope of the third category. M. ABU ZAHARA, CRIME AND PUNISHMENT IN ISLAMIC LAW 87 (n.d.).

[3] Al-Mawardi died in 1058 in Baghdad, where he exercised the functions of judge (*qadi*). He has left several works; among them: AL-AHKAM AL-SULTANIYYA, translated into French by E. Fagnan.

> mand which varies with the nature of the offense; however, it differs from them in other respects . . .[4]

Based on this definition, this study of *Ta'azir* will first develop the scope of the penalty and thereafter its material or essential rules relative to the conditions of its infliction and matters which affect punishment.

THE SCOPE OF *TA'AZIR*

Offenses arising under the first and second categories set forth by Islamic criminal law encompass acts which are prohibited by the *Shari'a*. Both the criminalization and the punishment of such offenses proceed from legal rules found in the *Shari'a*. Most often this involves a *Qu'ranic* verse or a prophetic *hadith* (a rule or a norm laid down by the Prophet). Also with regard to *Hudud* and *Quesas* crimes, the principle of the legality *(nullum crimen nulla poena sine legge)* of crimes and penalties is observed in Islamic criminal law.

Crimes of *Ta'azir*, by contrast, are not subject to the principle of legality in the same manner. Islamic law has not specified all violations subject to *Ta'azir* to the same extent as for other crimes. However, it considers that regardless of circumstance, all acts which infringe private or community interests of the public order are subject to *Ta'azir*. It is the duty of public authorities to lay down rules penalizing all conduct which seems contrary to the interests of the community, to social tranquility or to the public order. These rules must, however, draw their inspiration from the *Shari'a*.

According to this broader formulation, *Ta'azir* is consistent with the principle of legality and is fundamental to a system of social defense. Also, based on this wider scope of *Ta'azir*, a twofold classification of penalties exists, one being a function of the criminalized act, and the other related to the nature of the penalty imposed.

TA'AZIR IN RELATION TO THE CRIMINAL ACT

1. *Punishment for Offenses of Commissions and Omissions*

Offenses which relate to obligations or prohibitions imposed by Islamic law where no fixed or expiatory[5] penalty is prescribed are punished through *Ta'azir*. While these obligations or prohibitions are set forth on behalf of divine right, or out of respect for community rights, social tranquility or public order, their fundamental purpose is to protect the individual.

There are three types of discretionary penalties in this category. First, there are criminal acts which must by their very nature be sanctioned by penalties which relate to *Hudud*. These include, for example, simple robbery (theft in the absence of aggravating circumstances) or that of larceny (petty theft) and attempted robbery. There is also attempted adultery, or illicit cohabitation.[6] Khalil

---

[4] *Id.* at 504.

[5] Expiation consists of fasting continously for two successive months, the equivalent of sixty poor people fasting at once, or freeing a slave.

[6] *Idem.* MUSLIM CODE 591 art. 1939 (trans. N. Seignette. 1878).

declares that: "Unnatural contacts between women are not classified as fornication, but the perpetrators are liable to a reformatory penalty left to the discretion of the magistrate."[7] In all such cases, the violation is not so grave as to require the infliction of *Had*.

The second type includes criminal acts which are normally punished by *Hudud*, but by reason of doubt or because of the situation of the accused, as in the case of theft among relatives, the *Had* penalty is replaced by *Ta'azir*.

Finally, all acts which fall under the provisions of the law and which are not punished by *Had* are subject to *Ta'azir*. This applies, for example, in case of the consumption of pork, the breach of trust by the public treasurer or a testamentary guardian, false testimony, usury, slander, and corruption.

2. Ta'azir *Punishment for Injuries to the Public Interest of the Public Order*

The very notion of public interest allows severe sanctions to be used to ensure the protection of the community and the safeguarding of its welfare against dangerous elements. Punishment plays a deterrent role in this context, but its application is subject to certain limitations. First, it is necessary that one of the following conditions be fulfilled: a) the perpetrator must have committed an act which caused actual damage to the protected interest or public order; or b) the danger posed by the individual must represent a threat to the public interest or the public order.

Second, due to the broad and somewhat vague notion of public interest or public order, the substantiation of the penalty must justify the penalty itself. The discretionary authority of the judge is not absolute since he must classify acts as contrary to the public interest or the public order. Islamic Law has designed an implicit check on the discretionary power of the judge in determining *Ta'azir* penalties.[8] Finally, the justification for the penalty on the basis of public interest must flow from flexible rules adaptable to each situation, thereby permitting adequate and appropriate protection of the public interest.[9]

3. Ta'azir *Penalties in Different Schools of Muslim Jurists.*

In the hierarchy of crime under Islamic law, there are obligatory acts whose omission invokes sanctions, and forbidden acts whose commission is penalized. On the other hand, there are acts which are merely reprehensible or recommended. Jurists are divided as to the proper judicial attitudes toward individual conduct in this last category. According to one view, when reprehensible acts are repeatedly committed, or when the individual constantly neglects to fulfill recommended

---

[7]Khalil ibn Ishaq (d. 1365) was a famous *Maliki* jurist and author of *al-Mukhtasar*.

[8]This problem of control over the discretionary power of the judge has attracted the attention of contemporary authors, each from the viewpoint of his respective legal system. 3 & 4 REVUE INTERNATIONALE DE DROIT PENAL, 221-279 (1956) (Reports presented to the Internation Congress of Penal Law).

[9]It is undeniable that the state has the right and even the duty to attempt to deter crime, but the precise limits on state repression—the point beyond which the ends no longer justify the means—is beyond the scope of this article. That question will doubtless be the subject of endless debate in the annals of political science.

acts, then *Ta'azir* punishment should be inflicted.

TA'AZIR PENALTIES

With regard to the infliction of *Ta'azir,* Islamic law retains the traditional division between deprivation of liberty and pecuniary penalties. Besides these categories of punishment, there are other penalties which are designed to instill morality.

1. *Traditional Penalties*

Corporal Punishment

Some of the corporal penalties applicable in matters of *Ta'azir* are the death penalty (which is rarely imposed) and flagellation.

The Death Penalty In principle, Islamic penal law imposes the death penalty for acts which violate the duties incumbent upon Muslims toward God. These are encouraged by the *Had* penalties. The death penalty is also reserved for crimes of blood, and related to the classification of *Quesas.* However, jurists have suggested that criminal acts which also seriously harm the public interest ought to be similarly punishable in order to protect society against dangerous and incorrigible individuals. For example, acts which incur the death penalty in *Ta'azir* could be espionage and heresy, and could also be imposed on habitual criminals who pose a serious danger to society. But rehabilitation, which is the overall purpose of *Ta'azir,* should be kept in mind.

The death penalty is rarely inflicted as *Ta'azir.* Its sphere of application is naturally limited because the judge's discretionary authority is not very broad. The sovereign determines criminal acts which are punishable by death, but only if absolutely necessary. For example, the death penalty is proper in the case of the incorrigible criminal only when it is indispensable to protect society.

Hanafi writers,[10] consider the death penalty inflicted within *Ta'azir* as a necessary measure to ensure political order. Islamic penal law, on the other hand, has adopted an intermediate position with regard to the interests of society vis-à-vis the death penalty, and it has determined that crimes punishable by death can be inflicted only with great restraint.[11]

Flagellation This penalty is recommended most often on the grounds that

---

[10] These include the disciples of Abu Hanifa, a jurist born in Kufa, Iraq (d. 767 A.D) and considered the founder of the school of *fiqh* which bears his name. He was a matchless jurist, often called the Praetor of Baghdad. He laid down in his methodology the fundamental distinction between principles and applications. He taught more than he wrote, and his disciples collected his teachings and preserved his doctrine which spread widely in Iraq and the Ottoman Empire. Among his disciples are famous Imams: al-Shaibani (d. 805), author of AL-JAMI' AL-KABIR, and Abu Youssef Ya'Qub (d. 798).

[11] Louis Milliot wrote:

> One might observe [in the Islamic law of punishment] a general tendency toward harshness for crimes against religion and common law and one of some leniency with regard to political crimes. Islamic law abolished the death penalty in political matters long before our European law-makers. The fact that its prescriptions have been often violated does not indeed reduce its worthiness. It shows merely that it was ahead of its time in matters of morals.

INTRODUCTION A L'ETUDE DE DROIT MUSULMAN 763 (1953).

it can be readily imposed and thereby causes a minimal deprivation of liberty for the accused. He may thereafter attend to his business and serve the interests of his family. It is also in the interest of the community which thereby avoids having to take him under its responsibility as is necessary in the case of imprisonment. By the same token, the delinquent who thus escapes imprisonment is saved from being corrupted by the influence of incorrigible prisoners.

With regard to carrying out the penalty, flagellation is administered by means of striking the offender with a stick or an unknotted whip. Strokes are applied over the whole body after protecting the areas where they might be fatal. Each area of the body must receive its share; thus, blows should not be limited to a single area. Muslim jurists are not unanimous as to the number of lashes which the criminal must receive. The maximum number varies between thirty-nine and sixty-five with a minimum of three.

Al-Mawardi, for example, notes that there is a difference of opinion regarding the maximum number of lashes that can be imposed by *Ta'azir.*[12] The Shafi'i school[13] explicitly states that the maximum applied to a free man is to be thirty-nine while the slave receives only nineteen, thereby remaining below the minimum amount prescribed in fixed penalties, *e.g.*, forty lashes for drinking wine. Thus, the maximum *Ta'azir* punishment never reaches forty lashes for a free man, or twenty for a slave. According to Abu Youssef, the maximum number of lashes is seventy-five, but Malik[14] considered it unlimited and thus it may exceed that of fixed penalties. For Abu 'Abd Allah Zubayr,[15] *Ta'azir* is inferred from

---

[12] AL-MAWARDI, AL-AHKAM AL SULTANIYYA 505, 506, 507.

[13] This school is named for its founder, Imam Muhammad, b. Idis al-Shafe'i, born in Ghaza in 767 A.D. and died in Cairo in 819 A.D. He endeavored to determine the respective value of *Usul al -Fiqh* (sources of law) and to develop precise methods of logical reasoning, which were utilized by the *Hanfis*, in order to avoid misuse. Among his works are: AL-RISALA and KITAB AL-UMM. His doctrinal school centered in Egypt and attracted such jurists as al-Mawardi.

[14] Abu 'abd Allah Malik b. Anas was born in Medina in 715 A.D. and died in 793 A.D. He is the author of AL-MUWATTA' [THE SMOOTH PATH]. His system is based on the practices and customs of al-Medina which was taken from the Prophet after he left Mecca. This explains why he investigated extensively the manner of conduct and decisions which were unique to the Prophet. His influence spread to North Africa.

[15] Abu' Abd Allah al-Zubayr, b. Ahmad, a known *Sahfi'i* jurist (d. 939 A.D.) has stated:

> If it is a matter of acts which approximate the act of fornication, then one must take into consideration what has actually happened. If the man is taken by surprise at the very moment when he intended to commit the criminal act, then the maximum discretionary penalty to be inflicted on the two accomplices is seventy-five lashes. If they are caught wrapped in bed covers, with nothing separating them but only engaged in fondling short of committing the criminal act, then each gets sixty lashes. If they are not fondling each other, then only fifty lashes. If they are found in a room naked and in untidy appearance, but not fondling each other, then forty lashes are administered. If they are caught alone in a room but fully dressed, then thirty lashes each. If they are found talking to each other on a street corner, then twenty lashes each. If they are caught signaling each other but not talking, then ten lashes each. If he is caught in pursuit, with no other incriminating facts, then a few light slaps.

As to discretionary punishment incurred by acts of theft which do not require amputation, this jurist continues:

> The one who steals something worth at least the minimum legal value, but is not kept in custody in a properly secured place, receives the maximum discretionary punishment of seventy-five lashes. The thief of an object which was kept in

legal penalties which proscribe an analogous act. He considered seventy-five lashes as the maximum, that is, five lashes less than the legal penalty prescribed for slanderous accusation. Also, because of the difficulty in determining the number of lashes to be administered, the Malikis maintain that this decision should be left to the authorities sor the sovereign according to the circumstances.

Deprivation of Liberty

In matters of *Ta'azir*, Islamic law has also resorted to deprivation of liberty, whether in total, such as imprisonment, or in a less restrictive manner through local banishment, displacement, or expulsion.

Imprisonment This sanction is inflicted on first offenders and common criminals for crimes normally sanctioned by *Ta'azir*.Resorting to imprisonment becomes imperative only when flagellation is ineffective. Islamic law also has developed a time limit which varies from one day to six months or even a year. The maximum period is left to the judge or other competent authority.

Besides imprisonment for a fixed term, there is an indeterminate sentence. This penalty is usually reserved for incorrigible criminals and those who are deemed to be dangerous recidivists. The offender must submit to the penalty of imprisonment without interruption unless he actually repents[16] and truly reforms. In such a case, he is released because he no longer poses a danger to the community. This form of penal sanction is associated with security measures and is recognized by contemporary law as a means of repressing crime.[17]

Penalties Restrictive of Liberty These penalties include local banishment or exile. Among the offenses which require the infliction of these penalties, Islamic law has specified forgery, deceit,[18] and fundamental misinterpretation of the *Qu'ran*. Local banishment must be confined in space or duration and must be accompanied by supervision outside the delinquent's domicile. The movements of

---

custody, but whose value is below the required minimum legal, receives sixty lashes. If the object is worth less than the required minimum value and is also kept out of custody, then the thief receives fifty strokes. Forty lashes are administered to the criminal who begins collecting objects properly placed in a secured place but changes his mind prior to leaving the premises with the stolen property. For breaking into the place of security, entering without taking or carrying anything, thirty lashes. For breaking through or opening the door without completing the act, ten lashes. For breaking the wall (the place of security) without taking anything, twenty lashes. If the thief is caught carrying a pick or watching the place of custody, only a few light slaps are administered. Then, if other offenses are involved, we proceed in the same manner. However, one has to object that this scale, which seems to well deserve approval, nevertheless lacks all evidence on whose authority one might act.

[16] Repentance in Islamic law retains a religious character, according to which the criminal intends to return to the straight path as outlined by religious morality, and to regain favor in the eyes of the community.

[17] Contemporary authors suggest that: The term (duration) of security measures must be primarily unspecified. Neither the legislator nor the judge may fix the time period at the end of which the measure would deliver the desired results. Everything depends not only on the ascertained dangerous condition of the interested party, but also on the manner in which this state develops as the anticipated treatment unfolds. Also, the positivists have sanctioned the use of indeterminate "sentences" to react against the evil of individuals. It seems that Islamic law on this point has outstripped positive law by nearly thirteen centuries.

[18] G. LEVASSEUR & G. STEFANI, DROIT PENAL GENERAL ET PROCEDURE PENAL 296.

the offender must be restricted in such a case so that he will not become an example for others by his presence at the location where he has committed his crime.

Pecuniary Penalties

Muslim jurists have with reservations, accepted fines (compensation) as punishment in matters of *Ta'azir*. They believe that the availability of this penalty may lead judges to employ it to excess, thereby permitting them to plunder the people. Consequently, fines were cautiously introduced within the range of *Ta'azir* penalties. Some jurists consider fines as principal penalties while others see them as supplementary. In any event, Islamic law does not seem to require fines except for exceptional and supplementary reasons.

A fine is imposed by deducting or setting apart a segment of the criminal's wealth or possessions in lieu of corporal punishment. Where the criminal is genuinely contrite and his behavior improves, the deducted amount is returned to him. But under no circumstances is the amount withheld to be appropriated by the judge or added to the public treasury.

2. *Other Penalties Within the Scope of* Ta'azir

Ta'azir is the area of social control where the intervention of the judge is important and his discretionary authority is manifest. This is particularly clear in certain penalties which fall outside the scope of purely penal law and relate more to the moral and educational theories of penology.

There are several penalties designed to instill morality.

1. At the most basic level there is simply notice given to the interested party that he has committed a wrong. This notification is assured by the judge or his assistant by summoning the interested party in private. It is intended that such proceeding will have a psychological impact upon the criminal. Often, however, he is summoned to court in public. In both situations, the judge chooses these measures whenever he deems the crime not to be serious and if the accused is not a common criminal but a first offender whose misconduct is unintentional but culpable and deserving reproach.

2. Exhortation by the judge to do good and avoid evil deeds is utilized with those who have simply made a less than grave mistake. The judge's task in this context is to determine whether plain advice is sufficient for the offender to refrain from repeating his mistake in the future.

3. Blame (or Reproach). The accused is summoned to court before a judge who reproaches him, using harsh words without resorting to insults or polemics and without inflicting injury.

4. The judge also may ostracize the offender by excluding him from interaction with others until he recognizes and admits his error and expresses a willingness to return to the straight path.

5. The defendant may suffer dismissal from his employment if he shows lack of integrity and abuses the confidence of his superiors by bringing about injury to the public interest.

6. Finally, the judge may order the public exposure of the culprit's deeds.

Such penalty is inflicted upon the perpetrator of false witness, fraud or deceit.

THE GOALS SOUGHT BY A *TA'AZIR* PUNISHMENT

A just system of crime prevention necessarily must include a balance between deterrence and rehabilitation. The state must show its intolerance of wrongdoing but temper this stern attitude by a willingness to readmit reformed criminals. Recognizing those interests, Islamic societies rely upon *Ta'azir* to achieve two goals. First, the penalty must result in deterring the criminal and in repaying him in a manner proportionate to his deed, and secondly the penalty must lead to his rehabilitation and re-education. Islamic law insists upon deterrence instead of repression which often leads to torture and violation of human dignity.

CONDITIONS FOR INFLICTION OF *TA'AZIR*

Having defined the range of the infliction of *Ta'azir*, in comparison to punishment for *Hudud* crimes, it is convenient at this point to examine the modalities of inflicting *Ta'azir*.

Ta'azir is a system of punishment designed to suppress crime. It appears in diverse forms, using different methods geared toward precise goals. But its initiation is left to a large extent in the hands of the judge charged with the suppression and punishment of violations against God, society, and man. Some authors have even held that *Ta'azir* is a kind of delegation of power,[19] in contrast to penalties of *Hudud* or *Quesas* which are determined penalties and fall outside the discretion of the judge. It is useful, therefore, to determine how *Ta'azir* is applied and the significance of penalties applied through *Ta'azir*.

THE IMPLEMENTATION OF *TA'AZIR*

It has been emphasized that the key element of *Ta'azir* is the intervention by a judge to whom is delegated the authority to punish criminal conduct while bearing in mind the personality of the criminal and the gravity of the offense.

1. *The Role of the Judge*

The judge possesses a very broad, but limited, power of assessment. When the judge abuses his discretion he may incur liability.

<u>The Scope of the Judge's Power of Assessment</u>

Most Muslim authors hold that the judge receives his delegated authority within the framework of *Ta'azir*. Thus, he enjoys a power of assessment which bestows upon him the obligation to determine the punishment merited by the criminal. It is his duty to decide the appropriate penalty.

In determining the severity of punishment to be inflicted, the judge must

---

[19] It is reported that the second Muslim Caliph, Umar ibn al-Khattab, imposed punishment restrictive of liberty upon a certain individual after inflicting lashes and imprisonment on him. The offender had forged a seal similar to that of the public treasury and used it to embezzle some funds. A. 'AMIR, TA'ZIR IN ISLAMIC LAW 417 (1969).

take into consideration the status of the criminal, the circumstances under which the infraction was committed and the injury to the victim. On the other hand, after prescribing a penalty, the judge is not permitted to increase it. Islamic law does not recognize cumulative punishment. Thus, for example, the person who utters insults three times at the same place and time, may not be punished three times in the same manner. For this reason, most Islamic jurists, except some Maliki writers,[20] hold that the judge is obligated to choose the adequate punishment. If he chooses corporal punishment, for example, it is argued that he may not exceed a prescribed maximum. In essence, while the discretionary authority of the judge is considerable, it is merely a delegation of power by the sovereign for the purpose of administering justice. The sovereign may always limit that power by determining, for example, a list of crimes and penalties for the judge.

The Responsibility of the Judge

The authority granted to the judge also creates responsibility. If he imposes punishment outside of his delegated authority or in a manner inconsistent with it, he abuses his discretion and may himself be subject to certain sanctions. If he exceeds the maximum limit of punishment, the judge may be taken to task or sued.[21] Khalil declares that:

> Correctional punishment may surpass criminal penalties in rigor, without subjecting the magistrate to lawsuit if he has not caused intentional death or a grave infirmity to the condemned man.
>
> Nevertheless, the magistrate may be declared pecuniarly responsible, should he have entertained any doubts about the fatal result of the punishment which he decreed.[22]

2. The Measure of the Penal Sanction

In inflicting *Ta'azir*, the judge must examine two crucial elements: the personality of the criminal and the nature of the penalty to be inflicted.

3. Punishment as a Function of the Criminal Personality

The personality of the criminal is considered essentially from a moral point of view. Al-Mawardi says: "Correction inflicted upon respectable people of honorable background is less than that imposed on common or poor people, for the Prophet has said, 'Forgive the mistakes of people of good rank.' " The punishment of *Ta'azir*, therefore, varies according to the status of those who become liable. Thus, for example, it would be sufficient to ostracize an offender of high moral integrity. Turning away from him might prove sufficient to restore him to the straight path. By contrast, someone of a lower social rank might require a rebuke in a harsh tone of voice, or a humiliating reproach but one without cal-

---

[20] *Maliki* writers themselves adopt a broader position and hold that the judge's power of discretion applies to the nature of the penalty as well as to its severity.

[21] It is reported that after submitting to intimidation inflicted by the Caliph Umar ibn al-Khattab, a woman miscarried. Imam 'Ali, who was consulted on this matter by Umar himself, charged the latter with liability for the loss.

[22] KHALIL, ISLAMIC CODE art. 2034, 2035.

umny or abusive language.[23]

4. *Relation of Sentence to Offense*

This poses the problem of characterizing the infraction. Muslim jurists have concluded that the characterization of infractions must be determined while keeping in mind the maximum penalty in order not to make the system overly repressive.

5. *Prosecution*

Setting the Penal Sanction in Motion in *Ta'azir*

The right to prosecute belongs to the judge pursuant to his duty, or on the instructions of the sovereign, or upon the lodging of a complaint by any injured person. The Prophet has said: "He who witnessed a condemnable act must intervene in order to put an end to it . . . " However, once set in motion, the prosecution may not be stopped or suspended by the injured party because the *Ta'azir* penalty is imposed by reason of the social disturbance caused by the crime.

Criminal Procedure in Matters of *Ta'azir*

Similar to the investigation and prosecution of *Hudud* crimes, the procedure followed in matters of *Ta'azir* is comparatively simple and expeditious. For example, the judge has the authority to prosecute, examine witnesses and pass judgment. The infraction punished by *Ta'azir* may be established following different modes of evidence:

1. An admission or confession has no weight as evidence unless it aids in revealing the truth. The judge must examine and verify the criminal's assertions and should not take them into consideration unless all reasonable doubt of their sincerity is dispelled. Yet, in matters of *Ta'azir*, an admission stated once is sufficient to establish culpability.

2. As is generally true in Islamic law, testimony constitutes the primary mode of evidence. In fact, within the Muslim community, each believer must reveal to the judge all acts known to and witnessed by him. Testimony, which is an easy method of proof to ascertain, is governed by strict conditions in order to remain credible. The witness must be in possession of all his intellectual faculties, he must be an eyewitness to the alleged act and must not be related to nor harbor hostile feelings toward the accused. Finally he must be irreproachable and reputable. There also must be two witnesses in a lawsuit, and it must be noted that the testimony of a female witness carries only half the weight of that of a male.

MATTERS WHICH AFFECT *TA'AZIR* PUNISHMENT

These acts include those which affect the severity of the criminal sentence and those which bring about its complete abolition.

---

[23] It has been pointed out that the judge is obliged to respect the person of the criminal and his human dignity as he is a creature of God.

MATTERS WHICH AFFECT THE SEVERITY OF *TA'AZIR* PUNISHMENT

This is a question of grounds for immunity as distinct from aggravation and mitigation of the penalty.

1. *Grounds for Immunity from Punishment*

Muslim jurists have described situations where the penalty would not be inflicted although the crime was committed. This rule applies to all petty offenders, ordinarily virtuous people, who have committed a first offense. Also when the offender voluntarily mutilates himself as punishment, he should not also suffer *Ta'azir*. The husband's insults or indignities toward his spouse who has engaged in bad conduct also does not merit the additional sanction of *Ta'azir*. The same applies to affronts by parents to their children when the parents act within the limits of their parental authority and for the purpose of disciplining the child. These last two cases may be compared to situations in which contemporary penal law employs family immunity as grounds for avoiding punishment.

Generally, it seems that Islamic law, which has envisaged *Ta'azir* as a very flexible system to suppress crime, holds that the perpetrator of the crime avoids punishment only for reasons linked to a genuine penological policy and for social benefit. This policy is based essentially on the role of the judge who has extensive power at his disposal, which he employs more often in cases of aggravating or mitigating circumstance than in cases of immunity.

GROUNDS FOR MITIGATING PUNISHMENT

It was previously stated that the judge maintains power to appraise the degree of punishment which he may impose on the criminal through *Ta'azir* by taking into consideration the nature and gravity of the crime and the personality of the offender. The choice of punishment thus results from the judge's assessment of the acts themselves. Similarly, the grounds for mitigation are investigated thoroughly by the judge in each case.

Thus, for example, the judge considers the physical condition of the criminal which might involve hunger, disease or deterioration of the offender's mental faculties and cause him to break the law because of the necessities imposed on him by nature. He must also consider the moral state of the individual, which may result from physiological, pathological or psychological conditions, or from a physical or moral constraint or duress exercised over the party by another, or, finally, as a result of self-defense.

GROUNDS FOR AGGRAVATING PUNISHMENT

Certain grounds exist in Islamic penal law for the aggravation of punishment, similar to those found also in positive law. These grounds are the repetition of the same violation and general recidivism.

1. *Repetition of the Same Violation*

This may be illustrated by an example. If an individual, who is an apparently virtuous man, indulges himself in insults for the first time, then he incurs the sole punishment of remonstrance. If he repeats the offense, then he becomes liable to reprimand or remonstrance. If he repeats the offense, then he becomes liable to reprimand or censure. If he becomes a habitual offender, he receives lashes and will be imprisoned until he reforms. Thus, as this example shows, the aggravation of punishment is accomplished through successive degrees of severity.

2. *Recidivism*

Recidivism involves infliction of a harsher penalty against the perpetrator of repeated grave offenses, who has thereby placed himself in a state deemed dangerous to other individuals and society. According to Islamic law, choosing a life of crime aggravates the culpability of the criminal and consequently demands a harsher penalty including a life sentence or death.

THE ABOLITION OF PENAL SANCTIONS IN MATTERS OF *TA'AZIR*

There are three reasons leading to the abolition of penal sanctions in *Ta'azir*: death of the convict, pardon through the convict's repentance, and finally prescription.

1. *The Death of the Convict*

The question here is corporal punishment or deprivation of liberties which must be inflicted on the person of the criminal. These are abrogated with the demise of the convict.

As for pecuniary penalties, however, these are maintained. The fine is imposed and deducted from the convict's estate because it is considered a debt of the deceased.

2. *Grace or Pardon* ('afw)

Grace or pardon is defined as a waiver by the community of its rights to impose punishment which it acquired by virtue of the commission of offense. The community whose peace has been disturbed has the chance to exact reparation by punishing the criminal. It also has the right to revoke the penalty partially or totally. By comparison, *Hudud* penalties do not permit grace or pardon because they involve a question of curbing violations against divine right.

The Legal Justification of Grace Muslim jurists explain the significance of grace in Islamic law through the traditions and teachings of the Prophet. The Prophet has said, "Avoid punishing virtuous people," and, "Forgive honorable people their wrongdoings." Furthermore, the sovereign grants pardon whenever it is deemed expedient and within his province.

The Sphere of Grace According to al-Mawardi, *Ta'azir* as a discretionary punishment, is a purely governmental act whose purpose is the rehabilitation of the criminal. However, the sovereign must examine the crime involved before granting a pardon. Only if the violation does not infringe the rights of any individual is it lawful for the competent authority or the judge to grant a pardon, and then only after deciding that it is more expedient to pardon than to punish. It also is permissible to intervene on behalf of the offender who seeks leniency.

The Prophet said: "Intercede before me, and it is Allah who through the voice of this Prophet shall decide what He wants." If the right of an individual is found to be linked to discretionary punishment, as for example, in the case of injury or assault, the sovereign cannot set aside the rights of the plaintiff or victim by granting pardon to the offender. On the contrary, the sovereign is bound to guarantee the protection of the rights of individuals by punishing criminals. Only if the victim pardons the culprit beforehand may the sovereign then choose to do whatever he deems expedient, whether to punish the culprit in order to maintain law and order, or to pardon him. As to the consequences of offenses against individuals, the victim's rights, the right of society, and the reform of the offender are the primary considerations.

There is yet another situation which deserves mention. According to some jurists, if the interested parties (perpetrator and victim) have forgiven each other prior to bringing the matter before the sovereign or the judge, *Ta'azir* is not imposed and the state surrenders its right to punish the criminal act, even though it is considered as a social disturbance. Others argue that the sovereign has the right to chastise the offender whether or not the victim has forgiven him.

In summary, grace implies the revocation of punishment before it is imposed as well as the decision not to prosecute.

THE OFFENDER'S REPENTANCE

Repentance, which occurs when the accused returns to the straight path, avoids the penalty incurred by *Ta'azir*. In this situation, involving the abolition of the penalty, the offender's repentance may be effective even when the acts infringe upon the person or the rights of individuals. Moreover, if the crime constitutes a violation of divine right, or causes disturbance to the community, the repentance of the offender is admitted.

THE PRESCRIPTION OF THE PENALTY

According to most jurists, prescription applies also in matters of *Ta'azir*, whether it involves the prescription of the public action or the penalty itself. The sovereign has the authority to carry out the prescription to the extent that he perceives public benefit in it and when it does not infringe upon the rights of individuals. However, Islamic law is silent on the subject of the duration of the prescription on public action or punishment.

CONCLUSION

The study of *Ta'azir* suggests that certain penalties are imposed to compensate the punishment inflicted on the accused for the harm he has done, and to restore the order which he has impaired. Such is the case of expiation imposed upon the perpetrator of purely religious offenses repressed by *Hudud* and in the case of retaliation and *Diyya* which are prosecuted through *Quesas* penalties, the reparation for material and moral injuries caused to others. Most of the penalties arising out of these two categories, however, are based on the desire to divert the evildoer away from crime by making him fear exemplary punishment.

Besides these two forms of penal sanctions, there is a third encompassing the penalties of *Ta'azir*, which seeks in addition to reform the offender. If the suppression of religious crimes of blood offenses is excessively harsh, *Ta'azir* is a more nuanced mode of suppression, leaving much to the discretion of the sovereign or the judge. *Ta'azir* has consequently evolved as a coercive system of mixed character, intervening between private revenge and public or divine vengeance; it rests between retribution and intimidation, on the one hand, and reform and readjustment, on the other.

Ta'azir invokes the two penological principles of intimidation and social retribution which seeks to achieve social defense through fear of punishment. These principles indirectly inspire the advocates of modern social defense and the movement for the individualization of punishment by taking into consideration the personality of the criminal. They have also led to placing more power in the hands of criminal judges in assessing crimes and criminals than in the past. Since its inception at the dawn of Islam, the *Ta'azir* system has envisioned the ideal of balancing the interests of society with the rights of the individual and has long recognized that one objective promotes the other.

PUNISHMENT IN ISLAMIC CRIMINAL LAW

Ahmad Abd al-Aziz al-Alfi

CHARACTERISTICS OF PUNISHMENT IN THE *SHARI'A*

The *Shari'a* divides crime into three categories: *Hudud*, *Quesas* and *Ta'azir*. *Hudud* offenses are acts prohibited by God and punished by defined mandatory penalties because the acts violate a right protected by the *Qu'ran*. Jurists differ on the number of *Hudud* offenses. Some list seven such crimes: theft, highway robbery, adultery, defamation (false accusation of adultery), wine drinking, apostasy, and rebellion. Some jurists omit rebellion, while others restrict the list to the first four crimes only, classifying wine drinking and apostasy as crimes of *Ta'azir*, since neither the *Qu'ran* nor the *Sunna* prescribed specific penalties for them. A penalty imposed by virtue of being a divine right means that the proscription is necessary for the protection of a fundamental public interest.

Quesas crimes which include murder, maiming and battery, are crimes against the person. *Quesas* refers to a specified punishment in the *Qu'ran* and *Sunna*, and the decision to inflict it rests with the closest of kin as avenger of blood. It is his right to choose between inflicting the prescribed penalty, taking compensation (*Diyya*), or pardoning the offender. The ruler cannot pardon crimes incurring *Quesas* penalties, but if the nearest of kin grants a pardon, the ruler may in his discretion impose a *Ta'azir* punishment on the criminal.

Ta'azir crimes include all crimes for which there are no specified penalties in the *Qu'ran* or *Sunna*. Whether an act is punishable under *Ta'azir* is left to the ruler or judge to determine in accordance with the public interest and changing conditions and times.*

Furthermore, Islamic jurists agree that punishment cannot be imposed unless three requirements are satisfied. It must: (1) be consistent with the principle of legality;** (2) be individualized; and (3) apply equally to all persons.

Principle of legality Based on several *Qu'ranic* verses and *Hadiths*, it is

---

**Ed. Note:* For *Ta'azir* see Benmelha, *Ta'azir Crimes, supra*, at 211.

***Ed. Note:* For the principle of legality, see Kamel, *The Principle of Legality and Its Application in Islamic Criminal Justice, supra*, at 149. Al-Saleh, *The Right of the Individual to Personal Security in Islam, supra* at 55.

clear that the validity of punishment under Islamic *Shari'a* requires prior notice. Jurists have derived two fundamental principles from these texts. First, no criminal charge can be made unless the crime is defined by law. Secondly, there is a presumption of lawfulness, *i.e.*, all things are presumed permissible unless specifically prohibited by law.

The principle of the legality of punishment has been applied strictly to *Hudud* crimes. These crimes are specified and their penalties laid down precisely in the *Qu'ran*,* and the judge has no discretion as to the punishment imposed. This principle also applies to *Quesas* crimes, and as a consequence thereof the authority of the judge is similar to his authority with respect to crimes of *Hudud*. The penalty for *Quesas* crimes differs, however, in that the judge is required to refrain from inflicting the *Diyya* if the nearest of kin decides to pardon the offender, but the ruler has the authority to determine a *Ta'azir* penalty for these crimes if the nearest of kin opts for pardon.

As for *Ta'azir* crimes, there is great flexibility in applying the legality principle in order to adjust to changes in Islamic societies. *Ta'azir* might include an act forbidden by the *Qu'ran* for which a commensurate penalty is absent. Choosing the appropriate punishment is left to the discretion of the ruler or the judge.** Examples of such crimes are: bribery, bearing false witness, breach of trust, gambling, and tampering with weights and measures. It also applies to *Hudud* crimes which are not properly proven.*** Thus, for example, theft is punishable as a *Had* penalty only if the accused freely and voluntarily confesses twice in open court or if there is testimony by two competent witnesses.**** Furthermore, the infliction of *Had* punishment is prohibited if there is any doubt concerning the material elements of the crime or if the surrounding circumstances of the crime motivate its commission.***** The latter is an application of the principle of avoiding the execution of *Had* punishment if there is doubt. In these cases the criminal cannot be punished by a *Had* penalty, but if there is sufficient evidence, he can be punished by *Ta'azir*. For this type of crime, the aspect of the principle of legality which deals with criminalization is applied. As for the second aspect, which deals with punishment, it is characterized by great flexibility, for the ruler or the judge has the authority to choose the appropriate penalty among the penalties specified in the *Qu'ran*, the *Sunna*, or through the consensus of jurists (*Ijma'*).

Ta'azir punishment also might result from acts which, though not prohibited in themselves, are nevertheless forbidden because they harm the public interest. The bases for punishment in these cases are *Shari'a* principles which state that

---

**Ed. Note:* Also in the *Sunna* as in the case of adultery, its penalty of stoning to death is not prescribed in the *Qu'ran*.

***Ed. Note:* By "ruler" is also meant the legislative process. It must also be noted that the penalty for a *Ta'azir* crime must be of a type designed to rehabilitate or resocialize the offender. Thus, it too has limits which could be reviewed by the ruler or an appellate court.

****Ed. Note:* For evidentiary questions *see generally* Salama, *General Principles of Criminal Evidence in Islamic Jurisprudence*, *supra*, at 109.

*****Ed. Note: Id.*

******Ed. Note:* This is analogous to the defense of necessity or compulsion.

individual sacrifice is neccesary to protect the public welfare, and the greater evil is prevented by the lesser evil. Again, it is clear that the principle of legality, when applied to this type of crime, is characterized by great flexibility, in both aspects. Thus, under the *Ta'azir* system, determining the criminality of acts and prescribing their penalties is left to the ruler, who either decides them himself or delegates that authority to a judge. That practice was established in the earliest days of the Islamic state.

It is apparent that a system, in which the criminality of an act and its punishment is molded to fit each individual case and lacks a prior, general listing of criminal acts and their respective penalties, does not strictly accord with the principle of legality as undderstood in positive legal systems. Islamic jurists point out, however, that the ruler or judge is bound in the criminalization and punishment of such acts, to Islamic values and the public interest. However, it must be noted that such a general restriction is inconsistent with the principle of legality in its parent form, since the illegal act muct conform exactly to the prototype explicitly described by the law, which also prescribes the penalty.*

Ta'azir crimes were not codified at the inception of the Islamic state in order to give the ruler or the judge the flexibility to respond to subsequent changes of circumstances through the instrumentality of the criminal law. For that reason special emphasis was placed on the qualities and qualification of judges to whom so much discretion was given. The law assumed that the greater the confidence in the judge's knowledge and fairness, the less was the need to restrict him. Furthermore, the small number of judges and the simplicity of life and its related problems in the early days of Islam reduced the likelihood of unjust results. In any event appeal to the ruler could always redress any injustice.

In our times, however, the principles of the *Shari'a* mandate that the application of the principle of legality to crimes of *Ta'azir* be embodied in specific laws as necessities of contemporary life demand it. The degree to which Islamic jurists were sensitive to the importance of specifying crimes and penalties before their occurrence is evident from the rejection of *Qiyyas* (analogical reasoning) in *Hudud* and *Quesas* crimes. Thus, since *Hudud* crimes are prescribed by the *Qu'ran*, their foreordained character cannot be questioned, and since the essence of *Qiyyas* is reasoning from the cause to the principle, *Qiyyas* in *Hudud* is precluded. Also, *Qiyyas* allows for the possibility of error, but the possibility of error raises doubt, and *Hudud* are nullified by doubt.

Contemporary Islamic jurists call for the need to codify all crimes and penalties. For example, the Kingdom of Saudi Arabia, where Islamic *Shari'a* serves as public law, has specified some *Ta'azir* crimes and their penalties by statute. Egypt, which has a criminal code, also began a project to reform its penal law in accordance with Islamic legal principles including adherence to the principle of legality.

**Ed. Note:* Thus, *Ta'azir* resembles the doctrine of analogy which was relied upon at one time in Soviet and socialist law. *See* M. C. BASSIOUNI AND V. M. SAVITSKI, THE CRIMINAL JUSTICE SYSTEM OF THE USSR 139-40 (1979).

INDIVIDUALIZATION OF PUNISHMENT

A basic principle in Islamic law, as expressed in a number of *Qu'ranic* verses, is that responsibility for a crime is the criminal's alone and cannot be borne by anyone else.

Thus, the individualization of punishment under Islamic law is fundamental, whether as to *Had, Quesas* or *Ta'azir*. The *Diyya*, by contrast, is not strictly punishment, but is in the nature of compensation which must be paid to the victim as reparation for the injury. It is sometimes confused with punishment because the amount of compensation is specified in advance. That practice is evidence of the firm adherence to the principle of equality of all persons before the law, irrespective of social status. *Diyya* is paid to the nearest of kin in cases of murder and intentional injury if the victim or his family forego their rights of retribution under *Quesas*, choosing instead to accept the *Diyya*. It is also paid in cases of unintentional homicide, involuntary manslaughter and injury.

When the criminal is poor, his family or his tribe assumes collective responsibility for paying compensation (*Diyya*) in cases of homicide or assault. This rule is founded upon the policies of social solidarity and of alleviating further wardship by providing compensation to family. Some contemporary Islamic jurists believe that the present-day disintegration of family ties justifies relieving the criminal's family from paying the *Diyya*. Egypt requires, by contrast, that financial penalties are transferable to the convict's heirs should he die after conviction. This procedure has been criticized as a violation of the principle of the individualization of punishment, for the reason that the jurists of traditional schools agree that financial punishment ends with the death of the guilty.

EQUALITY OF PUNISHMENT

The equality of all people as a universal principle of Islamic *Shari'a* did not grant judges any discretionary power with respect to *Hudud* and *Quesas* penalties, since these are determined by the *Qu'ran*. As to *Ta'azir* crimes, the judge may take into account all the circumstances which may have influenced the offender in the commission of the crime. Consideration of such factors enables the judge to adjust the form and severity of punishment to the seriousness of the crime and degree of guilt.

Most jurists agree, in addition, that in accordance with the equality concept, the *Had* punishment can be imposed even on the *Imam* (Head of State). A few jurists hold, however, that if the *Imam* commits an act punishable by *Had*, punishment should not be carried out because the authority to punish is derived from him, and because the social strife which might ensue from punishing the Head of State is likely to outweigh the benefit of such execution.

THE OBJECTIVES OF PUNISHMENT UNDER *SHARI'A*

There is now such an increased emphasis on the reformation and rehabilitation of the offender in Islamic law that many people have mistakenly believed that those are the only objectives of the system. However, that view does not accurately reflect reality or represent the wishes of Muslim societies. For crime is not just an event which provides an occasion for rebuilding the character of the criminals, but an evil which the criminal intentionally and voluntarily inflicted on society. It is thus necessary for society to respond to such acts with punitive measures sufficiently painful to deter the criminal from walking in the criminal path again and to deter others. If reform were the only objective of punishment, it would frequently be unnecessary to punish. Also it would mean that those who could not be reformed could be punished.

It seems clear that punishment must nave the following three objectives: justice, general deterrence, and reformation or rehabilitation. Since crime is deemed to be a challenge to the prevailing values of society and a violation of the victim's rights, punishment must also seek justice for the victims of crimes. This is not to imply that punishment is nothing more than the thoughtless impulse of revenge. Rather, the search for justice entails a measured response which serves as an index of social values and progress. Satisfaction for the victim and his family is a necessary part of that search, which in turn plays an important role in the process of social control.

The deterrent function of punishment serves as a warning to the public not to commit crimes, to forbid them from imitating the criminal lest they suffer his fate, and to guarantee the safety of those who refrain from crime. Public deterrence is not achieved merely by defining the crime and prescribing its punishment. It depends essentially on the speed with which the accused is tried and punished.

The goals of justice and deterrence in no way diminish the goal of reformation, for its importance in Islamic law is not disputed, and its realization reflects the broadening of man's horizons and the nobility of his aspirations. The success of criminal and penal policy in any society is measured by the degree to which it harmonizes between these goals. Thus, the rehabilitation and reeducation of the criminal must be considered during the punishment stage to the degree it is compatible with the actual punishment imposed.

Islamic jurists consider punishment as a deterrent before the act and suppression after it. Thus, knowledge of punishment is intended to prevent the commission of the criminal act, and its execution thereafter should prevent the criminal from engaging in similar conduct in the future. This definition encompasses all three objectives of punishment, for achieving justice is basic to all the regulations and precepts of Islamic law.* Concern for reformation is evident from the view that the execution of punishment seeks to prevent the criminal from returning to crimes.

Achieving justice is a necessary goal of any system of punishment and for any form of penalty, whether it be *Had, Quesas* or *Ta'azir.* General and special deterrence takes precedence over rehabilitation in *Had* and *Quesas* punishment, as evidenced by the fact that the penalty must be carried out publicly. According to Muslim jurists the policy which underlies the public infliction of punishment is

**Ed. Note:* The author refers to the classic distinction between general and special deterrence. But there is substantial literature on the subject which questions many of these assumptions.

one of general prevention. *Had* penalties are best viewed as general deterrence against these specific grave crimes. These crimes, as noted above, are limited to seven even according to the most liberal count. Their applicability has been greatly narrowed by numerous exceptions and conditions and the principle that doubt nullifies *Had* penalties leading to their replacement by *Ta'azir* punishment in many cases is indicative of its general deterrence policy. It is also significant in this regard that repentence after commission of the crime nullifies the *Had* of rebellion, and some jurists hold that repentence also nullifies other *Hudud* offenses.*

As for *Ta'azir* penalties, the consensus is that their basic goal is discipline and correction. This form of punishment is designed to apply to the majority of crimes and to include any penalty that the ruler or judge finds appropriate, such as imprisonment, exile, flagellation, and verbal admonishment.

PROTECTION OF THE RIGHTS OF THE CONDEMNED IN THE ISLAMIC CRIMINAL JUSTICE SYSTEM

Protecting the rights of the condemned is particularly important if the penalty involves loss of liberty for an extended period, for then the likelihood that the convict's rights may be violated increases.

Islamic jurists have directed much attention to the development of *Quesas* and *Hudud* punishments, which are mostly corporal in nature. These include such penalties as lapidation, amputation, and whipping, all of which can be quickly executed. Nevertheless, these jurists sought to establish rules to insure that execution does not bring about more pain or injury than called for by the penalty. It is equally important that the protections afforded by these rules also apply to *Ta'azir* punishments.

It is universally recognized under Islamic law that the legal guardian (relative) of the victim has the right to demand retaliation for murder, on condition that such punishment is carried out under the supervision of the ruler or his representative. The purpose of this rule is to avoid torture of the convict as revenge. Execution of punishment by the guardian without official permission incurs *Ta'azir* upon him. The ruler should not allow the victim's guardian to inflict punishment, unless the latter possesses the appropriate qualifications. In addition to having expertise in inflicting *Quesas*, he must use a proper instrument, so as not to torture the convict. Failure to do so incurs *Ta'azir*, for the principles of retaliation stipulate that torture cannot be involved, and that execution should be swift.

The prevailing opinion among Islamic jurists is that the victim is not allowed to carry out *Quesas* penalties except in blood vengeance, even though he is an expert in applying *Quesas*. There is concern that he might punish the convict too severely. Instead, *Quesas* penalties for crimes of beating and wounding should be carried out by trained officials. Some jurists contend that blood vengeance is to

---

**Ed. Note:* This is a minority view since a *Had* contains a "Right of God," or divine right, which cannot be waived by men.

be carried out only by the sword, this being at one time the quickest means of inflicting death while causing a minimum of pain and avoiding torture. Contemporary jurists agree that if there is a quicker way than the sword, it should be used. Since such instruments exist in the possession of the state and since swordsmen are rare today, execution should always be carried out by the state.

THE RESPONSIBILITY FOR ERROR IN EXECUTION

The question of compensating the condemned for judicial errors remains a subject of intense discussion. Contemporary legal systems are far from agreement, and few compensate the accused or condemned who is found innocent for the time he spends in detention.

Islamic jurists since ancient times have struggled with this question. They agree, first of all, that the execution of *Had* punishments are mandatory and accordingly, those in charge of execution are not liable for the harm caused to the convict if punishment is carried out in a legally prescribed manner. Thus, if the executioner legally inflicts the *Had* penalty for adultery on a non-immune person (not a *mushan*), and the latter dies, the executioner is not liable. However, if he deliberately or mistakenly increases the number of lashes, he is legally liable for the consequences of the excess, even if it does not cause death. Furthermore, if the *Imam* or judge orders him to exceed the prescribed limit, without the executioner's knowing the limit but believing in obedience to the *Imam* or judge and acting thereon, then the *Imam* or judge and not the executioner is liable.*

Just as the *Imam* or judge is liable for his intentional acts, he is also liable for his errors.** However, jurists differ on the right of the victim of such error to receive compensation. Some hold that the *Imam* or judge and his family (*aela*) are responsible for compensation, since he is as responsible for his errors as anyone else. Others suggest that the public treasury should undertake that responsibility because the *Imam* or judge is a public servant and does not work for himself.***

Jurists apply the principle of judicial liability to *Ta'azir* penalties. Some believe that the *Imam* is liable to pay compensation for the death of a convict during the infliction of a *Ta'azir* penalty, since the purpose of *Ta'azir* is discipline and not death. Therefore, its application is subject to the safety of the convict. In summary, the principles of Islamic law provide for compensation of the convict for every unjust injury caused to him which results from error in the execution of punishment.

**Ed. Note:* There is a defense of "obedience to superior orders" which holds that if the actor did or did not have reasonable grounds to know that the act was criminal, otherwise the defense is not available.

***Ed. Note:* The *Imam* is not an insurer of the result. His intentional errors which give rise to responsibility are those committed unreasonably, in bad faith, or as a result of some other official misconduct.

****Ed Note:* These views also distinguish as to types of errors those committed with personal misconduct or malice are susceptible to personal liability, while those related to the public function are susceptible to public liability.

STAY OF EXECUTION

Islamic jurists agree on the necessity of delaying the execution of *Quesas* and *Had* penalties and analogous *Ta'azir* penalties, if the convict is sick, or the time is not proper for execution, or in cases of severe bad weather.* An exception to such reasons for delay is capital punishment, but other penalties must not be carried out in conditions that might lead to death. Some jurists also think that the execution of *Had* penalties should be delayed until a weak condemned becomes stronger, while others do not favor such delay. Still others insist that the penalty should be executed in such a way that the condemned does not suffer further harm due to his weakness.

Jurists also agree on the necessity of delaying punishment that might injure a pregnant woman and thereby compromise the viability of the fetus. Some maintain that punishment should wait until after delivery, while others insist that capital punishment should be delayed for two years after delivery to allow the mother to nurse her child.**

If the condemned becomes insane after conviction, some jurists maintain that such condition must not delay punishment, except in crimes of *Hudud* when confession was the only evidence on which the conviction was based. The rationale for this exception is that the person convicted of a *Had* crime has the right to retract this confession before and during the execution of punishment and if the condemned is insane, his ability to do so is impaired. Other jurists believe, however, that if there is other sufficiently incriminating evidence besides the confession, then subsequent insanity does not arrest the execution of punishment. The basis for this view is that the criminal is responsible for the crime when he commits it, and only his state of mind during the act is relevant for purposes of punishment. These jurists further argue that since punishment also aims at general deterrence, if the convict cannot appreciate the disciplinary aspect because of his insanity, the general deterrent function of punishment is still achieved because the public interest requires its execution in order to deter others.

The jurists who contend that insanity delays punishment until the condemned recovers apply it also to *Quesas* punishment, and some even argue that chronic insanity relieves the convict from punishment which in that event should be replaced by *Diyya*.

Finally, those who argue for a stay of execution due to insanity base their opinion on the view that execution of punishment is an extension of court proceedings. If one of the conditions of trial is that the convict be sane, then this condition must be extended to the punishment stage which is complementary to the trial.

**Ed. Note:* While the apparent reason is to insure presence at the execution, which is necessary for the general deterrence purposes of the punishment but also to guarantee the proper application of the penalty, the other reason is to give yet additional time to allow for withdrawal of a confession or discovering errors that could lead to the release of the condemned.

***Ed. Note:* This is based on the *Sunna*, as the Prophet delayed accepting a woman's confession until after she finished breast feeding.

THE PRINCIPLE OF CUMULATIVE PUNISHMENT*

Whenever a criminal is convicted of several crimes, the punishments imposed for such crimes are carried out concurrently or as one penalty. The execution of punishment rather than its adjudication thus becomes the criminal concern. Punishment for any crime committed prior to execution thereof becomes concurrent with other penalties which have not yet been carried out. In applying this principle, jurists agree that all the crimes committed be of equal severity. However, when the crimes are different in nature, the principle of concurrence is applied only if the penalties are designed to protect the same interest. Islamic jurists justify this principle on the grounds that the purpose of punishment includes correction and special deterrence. If, for example, the convict is a first-time offender, one sentence is sufficient to achieve this goal.

It is also agreed that the death penalty supersedes and encompasses other penalties. If a certain convict is sentenced to undergo penalties, one of which is the death penalty, then the latter is the only one imposed.

IMPRISONMENT

Imprisonment is a *Ta'azir* penalty whose main objectives are discipline and correction. Jurists have traditionally regarded it as the detention of the convict for a limited period, and it includes occasional visits to inspect the treatment given the prisoner. Ali ibn Abi Talib also paid surprise visits to jail to hear complaints from prisoners and to insure that they were not mistreated by the jailers. Also, the state is expected to provide food, clothing and medical care to the prisoners. The jurist Abu Youssef says that by jailing prisoners, the *Imam* deprives them of the means to earn a living and thus must provide them with the basic necessities of life, for depriving prisoners of such essentials might lead to their deaths.** Jurists also have established conditions against violating any of the rights of the prisoner, particularly the integrity of his beliefs, mind, body and dignity. The traditional Islamic view of imprisonment is expressed in terms of restricting the right of the convict to move freely about.

Finally, it is noteworthy that traditional Islamic jurists went beyond most modern penal systems in confronting the sexual problems of prison life. Some demanded that the wives of married prisoners be allowed to visit them occasionally for conjugal privileges. This practice is followed today in Saudi Arabia. The Prophet referred to a prisoner as *asir*, a designation indicating that the imprisoned convict is in the custody of the state, which in turn is responsible for him.***

**Ed. Note:* This principle gives weight to the theory of rehabilitation over that of deterrence and retribution.

***Ed. Note:* Abu Youssef also argues that the family of the imprisoned, which depends on him for their necessities, should also be supported by the state. An extension of that theory of Abu Youssef is that the victim or his family who could accept *Diyya* and insist on imprisonment should pay for the cost of imprisonment and support of the prisoner and his family. This is intended to reduce imprisonment and encourage compensation.

****Ed. Note:* This view of the Prophet emphasizes the theory of "incapacitation."

Ibn Qayyin al-Jawziyya expands the concept of the *asir* to include not only confinement to a place designed for this purpose, but also the restriction on his freedom which in any way guarantees that he will not resort to crime. He states: "It is not confining the person to a narrow place, but hindering and preventing him from inflicting harm on others." Thus, during the Caliphate of Umar ibn al-Khattab, a house was purchased in Medina to house convicts, a practice which was later followed by governors throughout the Islamic provinces.

Islamic jurists have long recognized the serious consequences of imprisonment. Some argue that it is as serious as *Hudud* penalties and should therefore be nullified in case of doubt. They would restrict its use to dangerous and incorrigible criminals who are held in prison until they show signs of repentance and only then are released.*

The *Sunna* contains examples of caring for prisoners and the Prophet's exhortations that the man to whom he had entrusted a prisoner care for him and treat him deferentially.

In one of the Prophet's deeds there is the instance where the Prophet confined an individual as a prisoner in the house of a follower and recommended to the guardian not only to take care of him, but to treat him with respect. Every other day the Prophet would stop by to ask about the conditions of the prisoner.

Under the Caliphate of Ali he would make unexpected visits to the prison to inspect its general conditions and hear any complaints that prisoners might have. The state provided food, clothing and medical care.

Abu Youssef (the famous judge who established a sub-school within the Hanafi school) held that since the ruler deprived the prisoner of his freedom, that it was the ruler's duty to provide all of the necessities of the prisoner who became his ward and responsibility.

All scholars agreed that a prisoner maintains certain rights such as freedom of opinion, integrity of his person, body and mind, preservation of his dignity and honor because imprisonment is only means of restricting a person's freedom.

In furtherance of the above many scholars have advocated (since the eighth century) the right to conjugal visitations on a periodic basis (for married persons). The government of Saudi-Arabia in application of such a principle permits conjugal visits to prisoners of both sexes.

The scholar ibn-Ferhon holds that the order of imprisonment must be issued by the judge who sentenced the prisoner and must contain the name of the prisoner, the crime for which he was found guilty, the period of imprisonment, the date at which imprisonment is to start, the date at which imprisonment is to terminate; all of this information is to be recorded in the records of the prison.

All of the above clearly indicates how Islamic law protects human rights, and how it is humane towards prisoners.

**Ed. Note:* Occuring until rehabilitation or resocialization.

Appendix A

SUMMARY OF THE FIRST INTERNATIONAL CONFERENCE ON THE PROTECTION OF HUMAN RIGHTS IN THE ISLAMIC CRIMINAL JUSTICE SYSTEM

INTRODUCTION

The First International Conference on the Protection of Human Rights in the Islamic criminal justice system was held in Siracusa, Italy, from May 28-31, 1979, at the invitation of the International Association of Penal Law and the International Institute for Higher Studies in Criminal Science and with the collaboration of the Arab Organization for Social Defense Against Crime. The Conference was attended by specialists from Arab and Muslim countries as well as from the West. Participants came from Egypt, Algeria, Syria, Jordan, the Sudan, Saudi Arabia, the United Arab Emirates, Lybia, Somalia and Mauritania, the United States, the United Kingdom, France, Italy, Belgium and Switzerland. Representatives of international governmental and non-governmental organizations also attended. These included U.N.S.D.R.I., the Arab Research and Study Institute, ALECSO, C.I.C.R., Amnesty International and the International League of Human Rights.

The Conference established a board consisting of the following members:

Prof. Pierre BOUZAT, Honorary Professor and Dean of the Faculty of Law in Rennes, President of A.I.D.P. and President of I.S.S.C.

Prof. M. Cherif BASSIOUNI, Professor of Law, DePaul University College of Law, Chicago, Secretary General of A.I.D.P. and Dean of I.S.I.S.C. Co-chairman of the Conference.

Prof. Giuliano VASSALLI, Professor of Penal Law at the University of Rome who also chaired the sessions of the Conference concerning the protection of human rights within the context of Islamic criminal law.

Prof. Georges ABI-SAAB, Professor of International Law at the University Institute for International Higher Studies in Geneva and also General Rapporteur of the Conference.

Prof. Gian Domenico PISAPIA, Professor of Penal Procedure at the University of Milan and Co-rapporteur of the Conference.

In addition to the opening session, six other working sessions were held on May 28, 29 and 31. Three sessions were devoted to the first theme of the Conference, *The Protection of Human Rights under Islamic Penal Law;* two sessions to the second theme, *The Protection of Human Rights under Islamic Criminal Procedure;* and the sixth session was devoted to the discussion and adoption of a resolution and a report. The report is intended to give a broad outline of the discussions and conclusions of the Conference.

I. GENERAL REMARKS

The two principal themes discussed at the Conference (the protection of human rights and Islamic penal law) arouse great interest. Recent trends and current events have brought the question of their compatibility to the forefront of debate in the legal community. It also is a topic of intense public interest.

Islam is the religion of more than 750 million people. Even where Muslim states have adopted legal systems along western lines (which is the case of the large majority), their societies remain profoundly imbued with the values of Islam. This fact cannot fail to affect their concept of law and their attitude toward it. Accordingly, an exchange of views between jurists from the western world and specialists in Muslim law will not fail to be mutually beneficial.

For western jurists, such an exchange is intended to allay misunderstandings which have long persisted, and by gaining insight into the approach of other legal systems to problems of criminal law, it was hoped that scholars would realize the relative nature of solutions thought to be absolute. In this way, they can envisage their own legal system within a broader context. For specialists in Muslim law, this exchange is designed to afford a new perspective on the subject, which necessitates inquiry beyond premises and purely religious data in order to explain the institutions, rules and regulations of Muslim law. Thus, the rationale, utility and social function underlying Islamic law will be manifest.

As a result, all participants will achieve mutual understanding and a more profound comprehension of their own institutions. This in turn will bring further advances in the protection of human rights.

II. THE PROTECTION OF HUMAN RIGHTS UNDER ISLAMIC PENAL LAW

The discussions of the Conference concerning this theme were based on the following three reports:

Cherif BASSIOUNI, "The Sources of Islamic Law, and the Protection of Human Rights in the Islamic Criminal Justice System;"

Taymour Mostafa KAMEL, "The Islamic Shariah and the Rule *nullum crimen nulla poena sine lege;*"

Ghaouti BENMELHA, "*Ta'azir* or Discretionary Punishment under Muslim Penal Law."

The Conference participants also read the following reports:

Ahmad Fathi BAHNASSI, "Criminal Responsibility in Muslim Doctrine and Jurisprudence;"

Mohamed Selim AL-'AWAA, "Basis of Islamic Penal Legislation;"

Abdel Ahad GAMAL EL DINE, "Legality in Islamic Law;"

Aly MANSOUR, "Principles of Penal Rules in Islamic Legislation;"

M. CHOUMET, "Legal Penalties (*Hudud*) in Islam."

After an initial period of development exemplyfying a remarkable degree of flexibility, Islamic legal thought was brought to a halt by the decision of Islamic jurists to "close the door of *Ijtihad*," in other words, no longer to allow interpretations. Thus the choice among existing interpretations was restricted. In this way, after having devised legal solutions that were far ahead of their time (especially in human rights), Islamic legal thought was untimely precluded from keeping step with the changes in society and ideas over the centuries. Since the nineteenth century, however, the doctrine of "closing the door to *Ijtihad*" has been questioned in an effort to revive and preserve the open and flexible spirit of the initial period. That goal might be achieved by engaging in a fundamental reinterpretation of the Koran and *Sunna* in the light of the conditions of contemporary Islamic societies, thereby supplanting the dominance of scholarly interpretations. This approach is valid since on those two sources are primary under Islamic law, while *Ijma'* and *Qiyyas* are merely interpretations.

Furthermore, with such an approach, it is possible to show that all the guarantees of human rights set forth in international conventions and reflecting the current international consensus on the minimum standards of any humane penal justice system, are by no means incompatible with the letter and spirit of Islamic law.

The Conference further revealed that for western jurists certain aspects of the Islamic system are difficult to reconcile with their concept of penal justice. Thus, for example, the religious basis of Islamic penal law is contrary to the fundamental trend of modern times to secularize penal law and base crimes and penalties uniquely on social necessity and utility. Secondly, the struggle against what is arbitrary and abusive can only be conducted at a lay level, since the assertion of a divine basis to Islamic law rules out all discussion on the implementation of solutions. Moreover, what is important is not so much the principles set out by the system, but rather the manner in which they are applied. However, the religious basis of these principles makes it extremely difficult to criticize their application. Finally, as far as *Ta'azir* is concerned, since the discretionary power of the judge may also cover indictment and penalty, it seems contrary to the fundamental principle of legality.

The discussions showed, however, that the gap between Islamic penal law and western penal law systems can be bridged.

It also was pointed out that the *Hudud, Talion* and *Diyya* (crimes of blood relations) account for a very limited number of crimes and penalties and that what is stated about them in the *Qu'ran* and *Sunna* is entirely in agreement with the modern principle of legality of crimes and penalties. Moreover, if certain penalties are regarded as too severe and if the sacred character of the *Qu'ran* prevents the texts concerning them to be changed, one should keep also in mind that the conditions for applying *Hudud* (especially the rules concerning evidence) are very restrictive so as to maximize the threat but minimize the possibility of their practical application. There is, in addition, sufficient scope for interpretation of special circumstances (related to the act and to the accused) as well as general circumstances (related to society) in order to avoid *Hudud*. This is so even when the conditions for their application are met so as to permit the application of *Ta'azir*.

The participants further concluded that despite its discretionary nature, *Ta'azir* is entirely in conformity with a penal legislative policy based on social necessity and utility. However, the nature of *Ta'azir* may seem to be contrary to the principle of legality, should such discretion be left to the judge. It should be noted, however, that certain discretionary powers of the judge to impose penalties does not radically differ from the principle of the individualization of penalties in modern penal law.

With respect to indictment, the contradiction between *Ta'azir* and the principle of legality is more apparent than real, since in a society with a relatively simple structure like that which existed at the beginning of Islam, a judge had manifold functions and notice requirements (which are the basis of the principle of legality) which stemmed from custom rather than from pre-established texts. This tribal-type society was not acquainted with the specialization of functions or the separation of powers, even though such concepts do not run contrary to the principles of Islam. In contemporary Islamic states, separation of powers exist in their government structures, and the discretionary power of *Ta'azir* is exercised by the legislator, rather than by the judge, in conformity with the principle of legality. In fact, the majority of modern penal codes adopted in the Arab world are justified on this basis.

III. THE PROTECTION OF HUMAN RIGHTS UNDER ISLAMIC PENAL PROCEDURE

The discussions of the Conference focused on this theme were based on the following two reports:

Mohammed ZEID, "Protection of Human Rights in Islamic Trials;"

Ahmed LOHEIB, "The Protection of Human Rights in the Islamic Criminal Justice System: Procedural Aspects."

The participants also read the following reports:

Ma'amoun SALAMA, "The General Principles of Evidence in Islamic Criminal Procedure;"

Mohammed AWAD, "The Rights of the Suspect in Muslim Law;"

Ahmad AL-ALFI, "The Guarantees of Human Rights in Muslim Law During the Carrying Out of a Penal Sentence."

The reports and the discussions contained the following highlights:

In Muslim law, criminal procedure is informal. Protection lies first and foremost in the choice of the judge and the limitations on his powers and responsibility through the guarantees that Muslim law provides the accused. Initially there was no clear-cut distinction between the preliminary investigation and the real trial. The judge acted as a magistrate whose functions encompassed investigation, incrimination and the imposition of penalties.

However, in Muslim law there is nothing to prevent these three stages from being separated and entrusted to different magistrates. Such, in fact, would be more in keeping with the flexible and evolving nature of Muslim law, since such a separation better achieves the common good as well as the aim of the principles and rules under present circumstances.

In Muslim law, the criminal procedural system is close to the accusatory rather than to the inquisitorial, thus providing the accused with broader and more comprehensive guarantees.

Certain fundamental guarantees provided by Muslim law in the penal procedure are as follows:

(1) the presumption of innocence;

(2) the protection of privacy and the inviolability of the home;

(3) the protection of physical integrity and the prohibition of torture;

(4) the duty of the judge to be neutral and fair;

(5) the equality of parties in penal procedure;

(6) consideration for the condition of the convict and assessment of the penalty and his rehabilitative potential of the penalty as reflected in the protection of the convict from slander.

During discussion of fundamental guarantees in Islamic criminal procedure, it is important to recall the famous letter of Calife Omar Ibn El Khattab in which he appointed Abu Moussa El Ashiari magistrate in Yemen. The instructions set out in that letter constitute a Declaration of Human Rights in the field of justice, and emphasize the Islamic concept of the role of the judge in his twofold pursuit of truth and justice.

Dr. Georges ABI-SAAB

Professor of International Law
Institut des Hautes Etudes Internationales,
The University of Geneva

General Rapporteur of the Conference

Appendix B

PARTICIPANTS

FIRST INTERNATIONAL CONFERENCE ON THE PROTECTION OF HUMAN RIGHTS IN THE ISLAMIC CRIMINAL JUSTICE SYSTEM

MAY 1979

Mr. Abdul Wahab Mir Ahmad ABDOOL
Deputy-Prosecutor
Ministry of Justice
Abu Dhaby (U.A.E.)

Prof. Georges ABI-SAAB
Professor of International Law
Institut des Hautes Etudes Internationales
Geneva (Switzerland)

Mr. Mohammed AICHONBA
Graduate School of Specialization in Criminal Law
Rome (Algeria)

Prof. Salvatore ARDIZZONE
Professor of Criminal Law
The University of Palermo
(Italy)

Mr. Ahmad ATAIGHA
Graduate School of Specialization in Criminal Law
Rome (Lybia)

Mr. Mohammed El-Ghali BA
Judge, Councillor to the Supreme Court
Naouakchott (Mauritania)

Dr. Ahmad Fathi Fathy BAHNASSI
Institute of Arab Research and Studies
Cairo (Egypt)

Prof. M. Cherif BASSIOUNI
Professor of Law, DePaul University
Secretary General, International Association of Penal Law
Dean, International Institute of Higher Studies in Criminal Sciences
Chicago, Illinois (U.S.A.)

Dr. Ghaouti BENMELHA
Attorney at Law before the Supreme Court and Adjunct Professor of Law,
The University of Algiers
Algiers (Algeria)

Ms. Maureen BERMAN
Executive Director
International League of Human Rights
New York (U.S.A.)

Mr. Mohamed BOURBIA
Ministry of Interior
Algiers (Algeria)

Prof. Pierre BOUZAT
Professor, Honorary Dean, Faculty of Law of Rennes
President, International Association of Penal Law
President, International Institute of Higher Studies in Criminal Sciences
Rennes (France)

Mr. Mohamed CHENA
Graduate School of Specialization in Criminal Law
Rome (Algeria)

Prof. Anthony D'AMATO
Professor of International Law
Northwestern University
Chicago, Illinois (U.S.A.)

The Hon. Vitaliano ESPOSITO
Judge, Supreme Court of Italy
Rome (Italy)

Mr. John EVRARD
Research Assistant to Professor Bassiouni
DePaul University, College of Law
Chicago, Illinois (U.S.A.)

Dr. Abdel-Ahad GAMAL EL DINE
Professor of Criminal Law
The University of Ein Shams;
Cultural Councillor, Embassy of Egypt in Paris
(Egypt)

The Hon. Giuseppe DI GENNARO
Director General
Ministry of Justice
Rome (Italy)

Dr. Ali Ahmed HASSAN
Judge, Supreme Court
Khartoum (Sudan)

Prof. Anita K. HEAD
Associate Professor of Law
University of Kansas
Lawrence, Kansas (U.S.A.)

Mr. Zaghez HEFNAWI
Editor-in Chief, Police Review
Ministry of Interior
Algiers (Algeria)

Prof. Zeljiko HORVATIC
Professor of Criminal Law and Associate Dean
University of Rijeka
Faculty of Law
Zagreb (Yugoslavia)

Mr. Mohamed HOUNI
Graduate School of Specialization in Criminal Law
Rome (Lybia)

Mr. Yasin HUSSEIN
Legal Advisor, Ministry of Justice
Mogadisho (Somalia)

Mr. Taymour KAMEL
Judge, Council of State
(Egypt)

Prof. Riad KHANI
Professor of Criminal Law
University of Damascus
Damascus (Syria)

Dr. Ahmed LEHEB
Ministry of Interior,
Riyadh (Saudi Arabia)

Dr. Ugo LEONE
Acting Director
U.N.S.D.R.I.
Rome (U.N.)

Prof. Alessasndro MALINVERNI
Professor of Criminal Law
The University of Turin
Turin (Italy)

Ms. Katrina MORTIMER
Middle East Research Department
Amnesty International
London (U.K.)

Prof. Mahmud MOSTAFA
Professor of Criminal Law, Former Dean,
The University of Cairo
Cairo (Egypt)

Prof. John F. MURPHY
Professor of Law
The University of Kansas
Lawrence, Kansas (U.S.A.)

Prof. Bruce OTTLEY
Assistant Professor of Law, DePaul University;
Former District Court Judge, Papua, N.G.
Chicago, Illinois (U.S.A.)

Prof. Piero PARADISO
Professor of Criminology
The University of Catania
Catania (Italy)

Prof. Gian Domenico PISAPIA
Professor of Criminal Procedure
The University of Milan
Milan (Italy)

Mr. Nigel RODLEY
Legal Advisor
Amnesty International
London, (U.K.)

Mr. M. El Said SAID ZAYED
Director of Law Program, Radio Cairo
Cairo (Egypt)

Dr. Yves SANDOZ
Deputy Director
Division of Legal Affairs
International Committee of the Red Cross
Geneva (Switzerland)

Prof. Mahmoud AL-SARTAWI
Professor of Islamic Law
The University of Jordan
Amman (Jordan)

Dr. Harry SCOBLE
Co-Director
Human Rights Internet
Washington, D.C. (U.S.A.)

Prof. Ahmed Fathi SOROUR
Professsor of Criminal Law and
Chairman of the Department of Criminal Law
The University of Cairo
Cairo (Egypt)

Prof. Alfonso STILE
Professor of Criminal Law
The University of Urbino
Urbino (Italy)

Prof. Giuliano VASSALLI
Professor of Criminal Law, The University of Rome
Rome (Italy)

Dr. Christine VAN DEN WIJNGAERT
Instructor in Criminal Law
The Free University of Brussels
Brussels (Belgium)

Dr. Charles VAN DOREN
Vice President, Encyclopedia Britannica
Associate Director, Institute for Philosophical Research
Chicago, Illinois (U.S.A.)

Prof. Mohammad ZEID
Professor of Criminal Law and Dean
Cairo University in Khartoum
Khartoum, (Sudan)

APPENDIX C

RESOLUTION*

WHEREAS the First International Conference on the Protection of Human Rights in the Islamic Criminal Justice System has been held in Siracusa, Italy, at the International Institute of Higher Studies in Criminal Sciences, May 28 - 31, 1979;

WHEREAS it has been established to the satisfaction of all participants from both Islamic and non-Islamic nations that the letter and spirit of Islamic Law on the subject of the protection of the rights of the criminally accused are in complete harmony with the fundamental principles of human rights under international law as well as in complete harmony with the respect accorded to the equality and dignity of all persons under the constitutions and laws of Muslim and non-Muslim nations of the world;

WHEREAS the basic human rights embodied in the principles of Islamic Law include the following rights of the criminally accused, inter alia:

(1) the right of freedom from arbitrary arrest, detention, torture, or physical annihilation;

(2) the right to be presumed innocent until proven guilty by a fair and impartial tribunal in accordance with the Rule of Law;

(3) the application of the Principle of Legality which calls for the right of the accused to be tried for crimes specified in the Qu'ran or other crimes whose clear and well-established meaning and content are determined by Shariah Law (Islamic Law) or by a criminal code in conformity therewith;

(4) the right to appear before an appropriate tribunal previously established by law;

---

*The First International Conference on "The Protection of Human Rights in Islamic Criminal Justice" took place at the International Institute of Advanced Criminal Sciences in Siracusa, Italy, May 28-31, 1979 under the chairmanship of Professors M. Cherif Bassiouni and Ahmad Fathi Sorour. In attendance were 55 jurists, mostly penalists, from 18 countries. (Among them were officials from Egypt, Syria, Libya, Saudi-Arabia, U.A.E., Algeria, Somalia, Mauritania, Jordan, Sudan as well as scholars from the U.S., France, Italy, Belgium, Yugoslavia, the U.K., and Switzerland.) The four-day conference heard and discussed reports on substantive crimes in Islamic law, the development of criminal codification, criminal procedure, the rights of accused in the criminal justice system, and penalties. At the conclusion of the conference the participants voted unanimously (with one abstention) this resolution which embodies those standards of criminal justice which are in harmony, if not in conformity, with guarantees embodied in internationally protected human rights.

(5) the right to a public trial;
(6) the right not to be compelled to testify against oneself;
(7) the right to present evidence and to call witnesses in one's defense;
(8) the right to counsel of one's own choosing;
(9) the right to a decision on the merits based upon legally admissible evidence;
(10) the right to have the decision in the case rendered in public;
(11) the right to benefit from the spirit of Mercy and the goals of rehabilitation and resocialization in the consideration of the penalty to be imposed; and
(12) the right of appeal;

WHEREAS the aforementioned rights of due process of law contained in Islamic Law are in complete harmony with the prescriptions of the International Covenant on Civil and Political Rights which has been signed or ratified by many nations including a significant number of Muslim and Islamic nations and which reflects generally accepted principles of international law contained in the Universal Declaration of Human rights of 1948, and the U.N. Declaration on the Standard Minimum Rules for the Treatment of Offenders;

NOW THEREFORE the participants of the Conference in their individual capacities, desirous of upholding the aforementioned principles and the values they embody, and desirous of ensuring that the practices and procedures of Islamic and Muslim nations conform thereto, solemnly delcare that:

Any departure from the aforementioned principles would constitute a serious and grave violation of Shariah Law, international human rights law, and the generally accepted principles of international law reflected in the constitutions and laws of most nations of the world.

Siracusa
May 31, 1979

Glossary of Terms

Ahkam Plural of *Hukm*, means judgments or rulings.

Allah God, the Creator.

Al-Tashri'i al-Jina'i Criminal legislation.

Ayat Verse of the *Qu'ran*.

Dhimmi Also *Zhimmi*—a person who is one of the people of the book, *i.e.* a Christian or a Jew.

Diwan Refers to tribunal, usually *Diwan al-Mazalim*.

Diyya Compensation (damages) for *Quesas* crimes.

Fiqh Jurisprudence.

Had A crime against the law of God (7 crimes specified in the *Qu'ran*, for which prosecution and punishment in case of guilt is mandatory).

Hadith Sayings of the Prophet; see also *Sunna*.

Hanafi One of the four *Sunni* schools of jurisprudence; named after its founder.

Hanbali One of the four *Sunni* schools of jurisprudence; named after its founder.

Hudud Plural of *Had*.

Ijma' Literally means consensus. A source of law and a method of interpreting the principles and norms of the *Shari'a*.

Ijtihad Independent reasoning. A source of law and a secondary source of interpretation in the absence of other primary sources.

Ilm Usul al-Fiqh The science of the principles of jurisprudence.

Imam Literally means the leader; applies to the leader (founder) of a school of jurisprudence; the leader of the Muslims who is the Caliph is also the Imam; the leader of the prayer. In this book the word is used in connection with the names of founders of schools of jurisprudence and other religious scholars whose works are considered authoritative.

Khalifa Also *Caliph*—literally means the descendant or successor—applied to the elected ruler of the Islamic nation (who is the successor to the Prophet Muhammad).

Malki One of the four *Sunni* schools of jurisprudence named after its founder.

Mazalim Complaints or grievances; applies to a judge (*Qadi al-Mazalim*) and tribunal (*Diwan al-Mazalim*) specialized to hear such cases.

Qadi Also *Kadi*, judge.

Qiyyas Also *Queyas*—literally means measuring—reasoning by analogy. A source of law and a method of interpreting the principles and norms of the *Shari'a*.

Quesas Crimes against the person (murder, homicide, maiming, serious bodily harm) for which retaliation or compensation (*Diyya*) is due

Qu'ran Holy book, the principal source of law.

Shari'a Islamic law. Body of norms, principles and rules deriving from the *Qu'ran*.

Siyassat al-Shari'a The policy (and philosophy) of the *Shari'a*.

Sunna Deeds and sayings of the Prophet; follows the *Qu'ran* as a source of law.

Sunni Those who follow the *Sunna*, the tradition of the Prophet (approximately 90% of the world's Muslim population). It implies the orthodox tradition of Islam in contraposition to the *Shi'a* which has by *Sunni* standards differed from it.

Surat Chapter of the *Qu'ran*.

Ta'azir Literally means to admonish or punish (with a view to correcting). Refers to offenses against the public welfare, safety and morals, or harmful acts against persons or private interests which are neither *Hudud* nor *Quesas* and for which prosecution and punishment is discretionary.

Urf Also *ourf;* custom and usage. A source of law.

Usul Principles.

Bibliography

By Ahmad Fathi Bahnassi

I. BASIC SOURCES

AL-SHAFI'I, MUHAMMAD IBN IDRIS. AHKAM AL-QUR'AN [QU'RANIC RULES]. Cairo: Maktab Nashr al-Thaqafah al-Islamiyah, 1951-52.

AL-JASSAS, AHMAD IBN 'ALI. AHKAM AL-QUR'AN [QU'RANIC RULES]. Egypt: al-Matba'ah al-Bahiyah al Misriyah, 1928.

IBN AL-'ARABI, MUHAMMAD IBN 'ABD ALLAH. AHKAM AL-QUR'AN [QU'RANIC RULES]. Egypt: Matba'at al-Sa'adah, 1912.

AL-QURTUBI, MUHAMMAD IBN AHMAD. AL-JAMI' LI-AHKAM AL-QUR'AN [QU'RANIC RULES]. Cairo: Matba'at Dar al-Kutub al-Misriyah, 1945?-50.

AL-SHA'RANI,'ABD AL-WAHHAB IBN AHMAD. AL-MIZAN. Cairo: al-Matba'ah al-'Amirah, 1856.

AL-SUYUTI, JALAL AL-DIN. AL-ASHBAH WA-AL-NAZA'IR FIQAWA'ID WA-FURU' FIQH AL-SHAFI'IYAH. Cairo: Dar Ihya' al-Kutub al-'Arabiyah, n.d.

ABU YOUSSEF, YA'QUB IBN IBRAHIM. AL-RADD 'ALA SIYAR AL-AWZA'I. Hyderbad: Lajnat Ihya' al-Ma'arif al-Nu'maniyah, 1938.

IBN AL-ATHIR, MAJD AL-DIN AL-JAZARI. JAMI' AL-USUL FI AHADITH AL-RASUL. Egypt: Maktabat al-Halwani, 1969.

NASIF, MANSUR 'ALI. AL-TAJ AL-JAMI' LIL-USUL FI AHADITH AL-RASUL. 4th ed. Cairo: Dar Ihya' al-Kutub al-'Arabiyah, 1968.

AL-BUKHARI, MUHAMMAD IBN ISMA'IL. ZAD AL-MUSLIM. Cairo: Matba'at Misr, 1956.

AL-DAHHAK AL-SHAYBANI, ABU BAKR AHMAD. KITAB AL-DIYYAT. Cairo: Matba'at al-Taqaddum, 1903.

II. ISLAMIC JURISPRUDENCE

Hanafi Works:

AL-KASANI, ABU BAKR IBN MAS'UD. BADA'I AL-SANA'I FI TARTIB AL-SHARA'I. Egypt: Sharikat al-Matbu'at al-Ilmiyah, 1909-10.

AL-ZAYLA'I, 'UTHMAN IBN 'ALI. TABYIN AL-HAQA'IQ, SHARH KANZ AL-DAQA'IQ. Cairo: al-Matba'ah al-Kubra al-Amiriyah, 1893.

IBN 'ABIDIN, MUHAMMAD AMIN IBN 'UMAR. RADD AL-MUHTAR 'ALA AL-DURR AL'MUKHTAR. Cairo: Dar al-Tiba'ah al-Misriyah, 1851. *Also known as:* HASHIYAT IBN 'ABIDIN.

IBN AL-HUMAM, KAMAL AL-DIN. SHARH FATH AL-QADIR. (With a supplement including: Qadizade, *Nata'ij al-afkar fi kashf al-rumuz wa-al-asrar;* al-Marghinani, *al-Hidayah;* al-Babarti, *Sharh al-'inayah 'ala al-hidayah;* and Sa'di Jalabi, *Hashiyah 'ala al-'inayah.*) Cairo: Matba'at Bulaq, 1895-98.

Al-Sarakhsi, Muhammad ibn Ahmad. Al-Mabsut. Cairo: Matba'at Sami, 1906.

Mawla Khusraw. Durar al-hukkam fi sharh ghurar al-ahkam. (With *Hashiyat at Shurunbalali* known as *Ghunyat dhawi al-Ahkam.*) Cairo: al-Matba'ah al-Wahbiyah, 1875.

Abu Youssef, Ya'qub ibn Ibrahim. Kitab al-kharaj. (Includes *al-Jami' al-saghir* by al-Shaybani.) Cairo: al-Matba'ah al-Amiriyah, 1883.

Maliki Works:

Ibn Rushd al-Hafid, Abu al-Walid al-Qurtubi. Bidayat al-mujtahid wa-nihayat al-muqtasid. Cairo: Dar al-Kutub al-'Arabiyah al-Kubra, 1907.

Al-Hattab, Muhammad ibn 'Abd al-Rahman. Mawahib al-jalil li-sharh mukhtasar Khalil. Cairo: Matba'at al-Sa'adah, 1909.

Malik ibn Anas. Al-Mudawwanah al-Kubra. (Ibn Sahnun's version.) Baghdad: Maktabat al-Muthanna, n.d.

Al-Qarafi, Shihab al-Din Ahmad ibn Idris. Al-Dhakhirah. Cairo: Matba'at Kulliyat al-Shari'ah, 1961.

Al-Zurqani, Muhammad ibn 'Abd al-Baqi. Sharh 'ala mukhtasar Khalil. Cairo: Matba'at Bulaq, 1873.

Ibn Farhun al-Ya'muri Ibrahim ibn Muhammad. Tabsirat al-hukkam fi usul al-aqdiyah wa-manahij al-ahkam. Cairo: al-Matba'ah al-Bahiyah, 1882.

Al-Khirshi, Muhammad ibn 'Abd Allah. (Commentary on *Mukhtasar Khalil.*) Cairo: al-Matba'ah al-Amiriyah, 1897.

Al-Qarafi, Shihab al-Din Ahmad ibn Idris. Al-Furuq. With commentaries by ibn al-Shat and Muhammad 'Ali. Cairo: Dar Ihya' al-Kutub al-'Arabiyah, 1924.

Al-Baji, Abu al-Walid. Al-Muntaqa: (A Commentary on *al-Muwatta'*.) 1912.

Hanbali Works:

Ibn Taymiyah, Ahmad ibn 'Abd al-Halim. Majmu'at Fatawa Ibn Taymiyah. (Includes his *Iqamat al-dalil 'ala ibtal al-tahlil* and *al-Ikhtiyarat al-'ilmiyah.*) Cairo: Matba'at Kurdistan al-'Ilmiyah, 1909.

Ibn Qayyim al-Jawziyah. I'lam al-muwaqqi'in 'an rabb al-'alamin. Cairo: Dar al-Kutub al-Hadithah, 1961.

Ibn Qudamah, Muwaffaq al-Din. Al-Mughni. Egypt: Matba'at al-Imam, 1974.

Ibn Taymiyah, Ahmad ibn 'Abd al-Halim. Al-Siyasah al-shar'iyah fi islah al-ra'i wa-al-ra'iyah. Cairo: al-Matba'ah al-Khayriyah, 1904.

Abu Ya'la al-Farra'. Al-Ahkam al-sultaniyah. Cairo: Mustafa al-Babi al-Halabi, 1938.

Ibn Qayyim al-Jawziyah. Al-Turuq al-hukmiyah fi al-siyasah al-shar'iyah. Cairo: Sharikat Tab' al-Kutub al-'Arabiyah, 1898.

Al-Muttaqi, 'Ali ibn 'Abd al-Malik. Kanz al-'ummal fi sunan al-aqwal wa-al-af'al. Hyderabad: Da'irat al-Ma'arif al-Nizamiyah, 1894-97.

Shafi'i Works:

Al-Shafi'i, Muhammad ibn Idris. Al-Umm. (Related by Abu Muhammad al-Rabi' al-Muradi.) Cairo: al-Matba'ah al-Amiriyah, 1901.

Al-Shirazi, Ibrahim 'Ali ibn Yusuf. Al-Muhadhdhab fi fiqh al-Imam al-Shafi'i. Cairo: Dar al-Kutub al-'Arabiyah, 1913.

Al-Mawardi, 'Ali ibn Muhammad. Al-Ahkam al-sultaniyah. Egypt: Matba'at al-Watan, 1880-81.

Al-Bajuri, Ibrahim ibn Muhammad. Commentary on Fath al-qarib (of Ibn Qasim al-Ghazzi). Cairo: Matba'at Nabhan,1924.

AL-RAMLI, SHAMS AL-DIN. NIHAYAT AL-MUHTAJ ILA SHARH AL-MINHAJ. (With commentaries by al-Shabramallisi and al-Rashidi.) Cairo: al-Maktabah al-Islamiyah, 1939.

AL-SHIRBINI, MUHAMMAD IBN AHMAD. MUGHNI AL-MUHTAJ ILA MA'RIFAT ALFAZ AL-MINHAJ. A commentary on *al-Minhaj* by al-Nawawi. Cairo: al-Maktabah al-Tijariyah al-Kubra, 1955.

AL-SHAFI'I, MUHAMMAD IBN IDRIS. AL-RISALAH. Cairo: Mustafa al-Babi al-Halabi, 1940.

Shi'i Works:

AL-MURTADI, AHMAD IBN YAHYA. AL-BAHR AL-ZAKHKHAR. Beirut: Mu'assasat al-Risalah, 1975.

AL-HILLI, JA'FAR IBN AL-HASAN. AL-MUKHTASAR AL-NAFI'. Egypt: Wizarat al-Awqaf, n.d.

Zahiri Works:

IBN HAZM, 'ALI IBN AHMAD. AL-MUHALLA. Cairo: Idarat al-Tiba'ah al-Muniriyah, 1927-32.